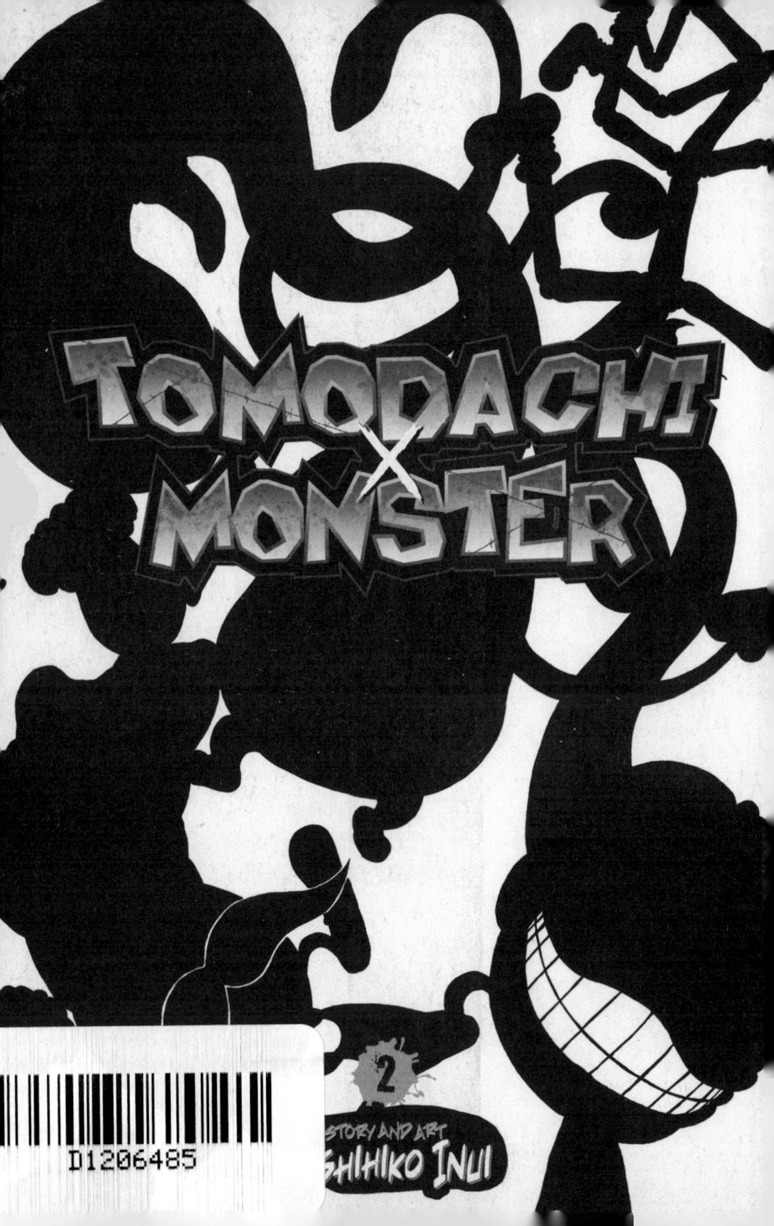
TOMODACHI
X
MONSTER
2
STORY AND ART
SHIHIKO INUI

Wataru, an introverted elementary school student, was drawn to the mountains one day by a mysterious voice. Once there, he met a creepy but somewhat cute monster called a Friend. Wataru named his Friend "Peke." He was soon attacked by another elementary school student who also had a Friend, which led to Wataru being captured and imprisoned in the basement of an abandoned building.

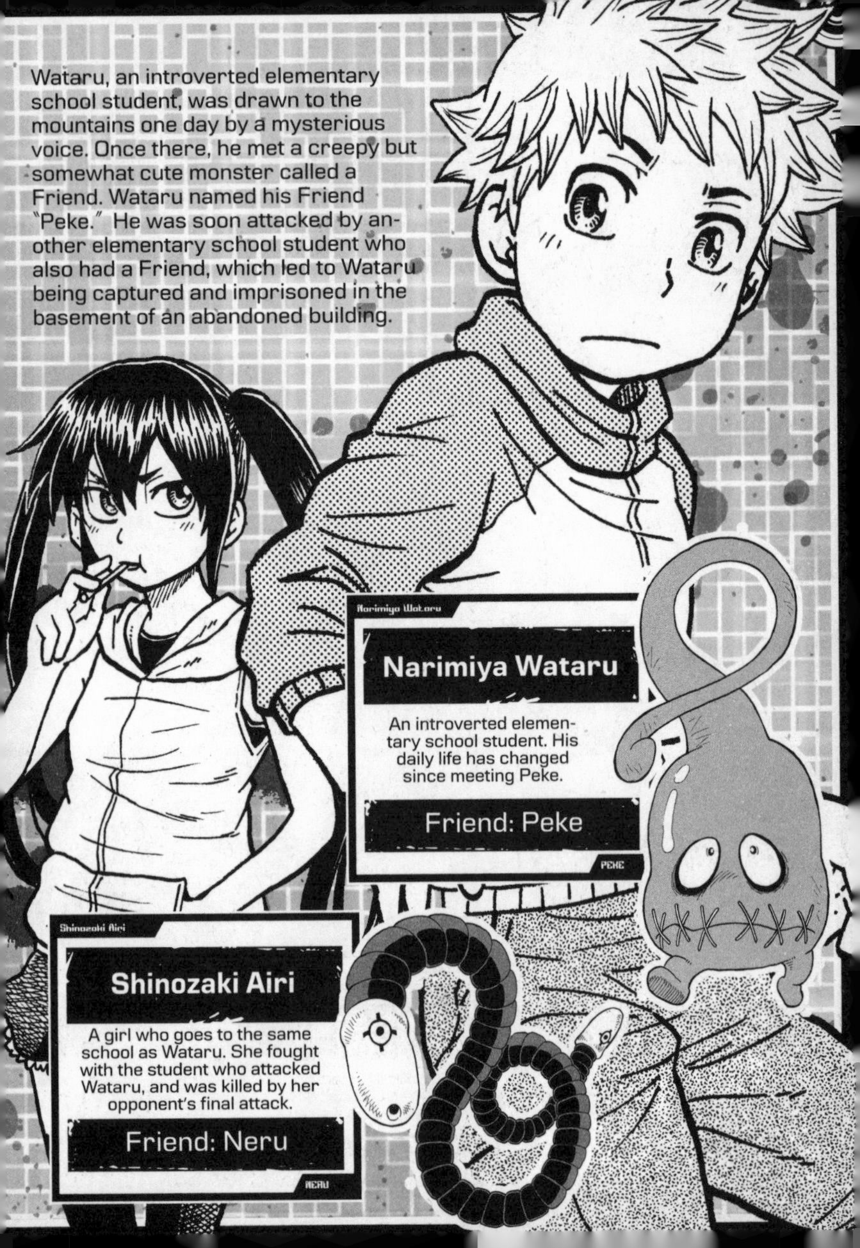

Narimiya Wataru
Narimiya Wataru
An introverted elementary school student. His daily life has changed since meeting Peke.
Friend: Peke
PEKE
Shinozaki Airi
Shinozaki Airi
A girl who goes to the same school as Wataru. She fought with the student who attacked Wataru, and was killed by her opponent's final attack.
Friend: Neru
NERU

MONSTER

Tsukasa, the leader of the group who attacked and captured Wataru, invited Wataru to join his group of children with Friends, called "Carnival." Wataru, however, loudly declared that he would never join a group that had problems with killing people. Along with Peke, Wataru made a stand against Tsukasa. Initially, the pair was overwhelmed by their opponent's powerful Friend, but at a critical moment, Peke evolved and they were able to escape the situation.

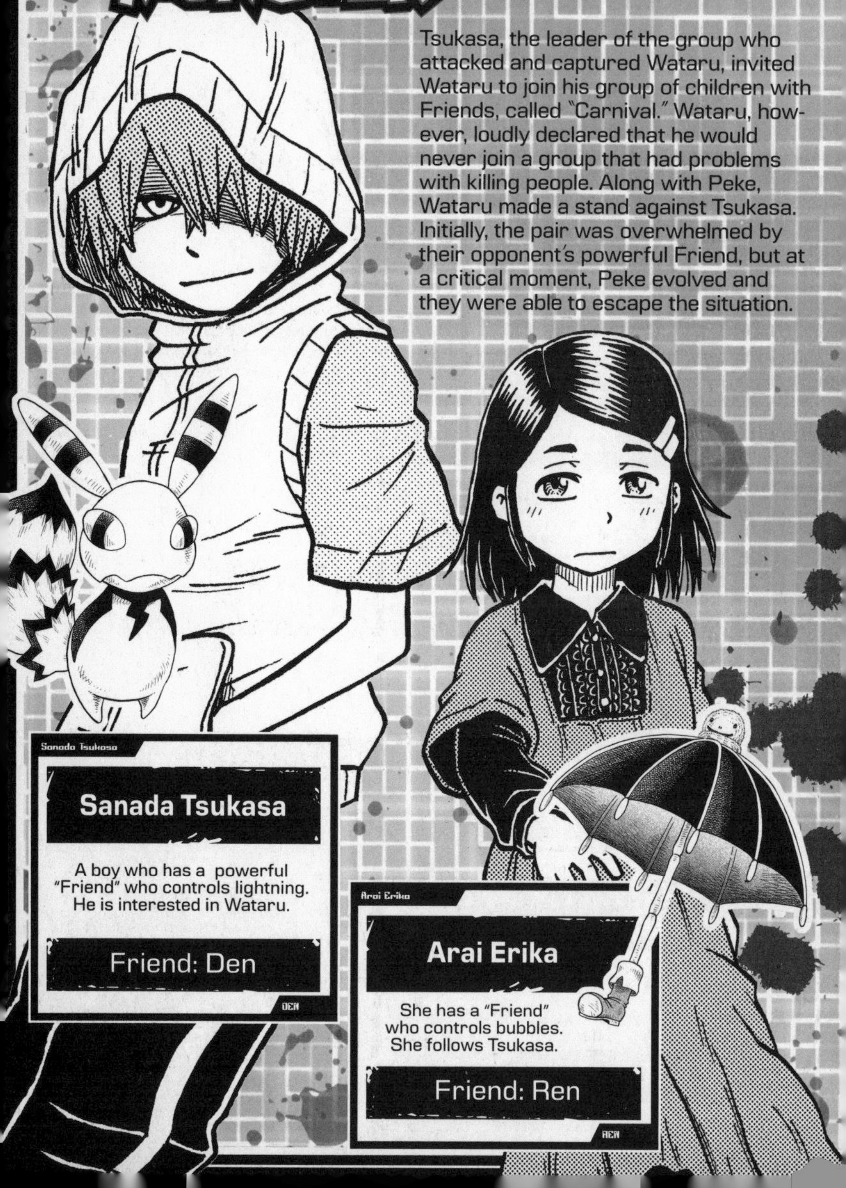

Sanada Tsukasa
Sanada Tsukasa
A boy who has a powerful "Friend" who controls lightning. He is interested in Wataru.
Friend: Den
DEN
Arai Erika
Arai Erika
She has a "Friend" who controls bubbles. She follows Tsukasa.
Friend: Ren
REN

SEVEN SEAS ENTERTAINMENT PRESENTS

TOMODACHI × MONSTER

story and art by **Yoshihiko Inui**   VOLUME 2

TRANSLATION
Lu Huan

ADAPTATION
Janet Houck

LETTERING AND RETOUCH
James Adams

LOGO DESIGN
Karis Page

COVER DESIGN
Nicky Lim

PROOFREADER
Danielle King

PRODUCTION MANAGER
Lissa Pattillo

EDITOR-IN-CHIEF
Adam Arnold

PUBLISHER
Jason DeAngelis

TOMODACHI × MONSTER VOLUME 2
© Yoshihiko Inui 2014
All rights reserved.
First published in Japan in 2014 by Futabasha Publishers Ltd., Tokyo.
English version published by Seven Seas Entertainment, LLC.
Under licence from Futabasha Publishers Ltd.

Seven Seas books may be purchased in bulk for educational, business, or promotional use. For information on bulk purchases, please contact Macmillan Corporate & Premium Sales Department at 1-800-221-7945 (ext 5442) or write specialmarkets@macmillan.com.

Seven Seas and the Seven Seas logo are trademarks of Seven Seas Entertainment, LLC. All rights reserved.

ISBN: 978-1-626922-96-9

Printed in Canada

First Printing: May 2016

10 9 8 7 6 5 4 3 2 1

FOLLOW US ONLINE: *www.gomanga.com*

READING DIRECTIONS

This book reads from *right to left*, Japanese style. If this is your first time reading manga, you start reading from the top right panel on each page and take it from there. If you get lost, just follow the numbered diagram here. It may seem backwards at first, but you'll get the hang of it! Have fun!!

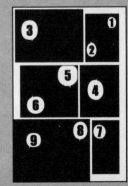

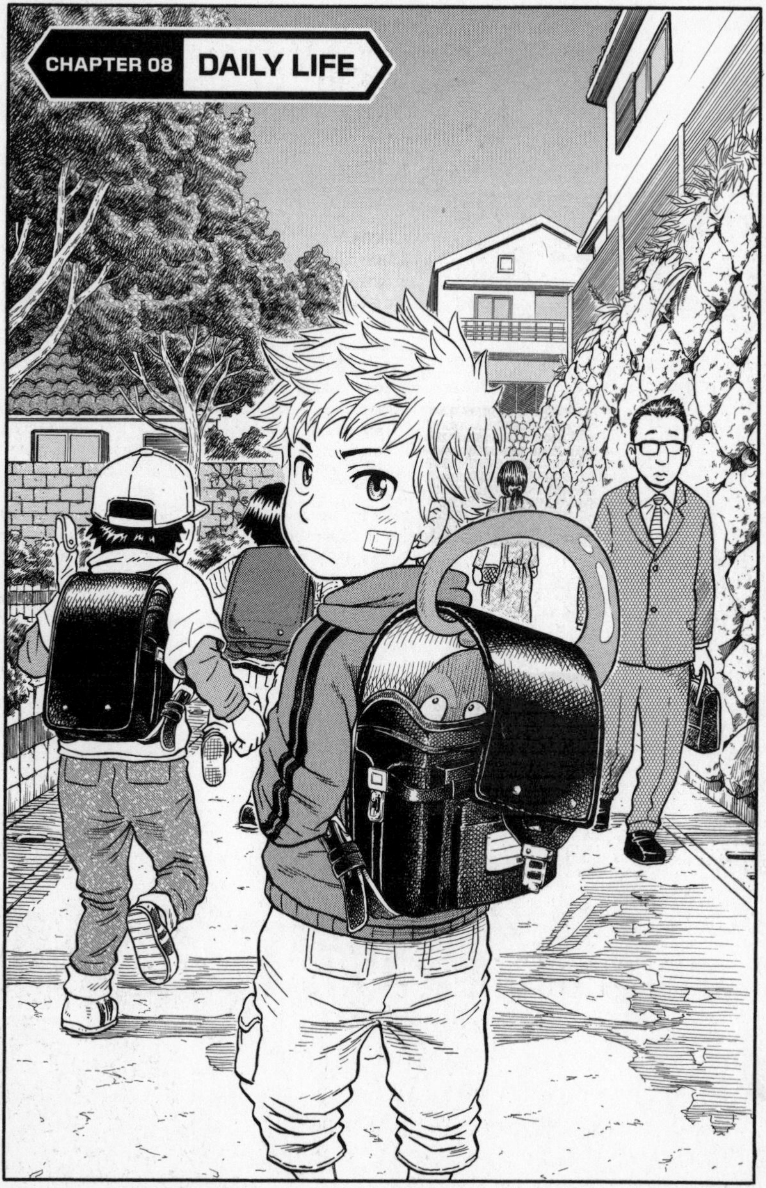
CHAPTER 08
DAILY LIFE

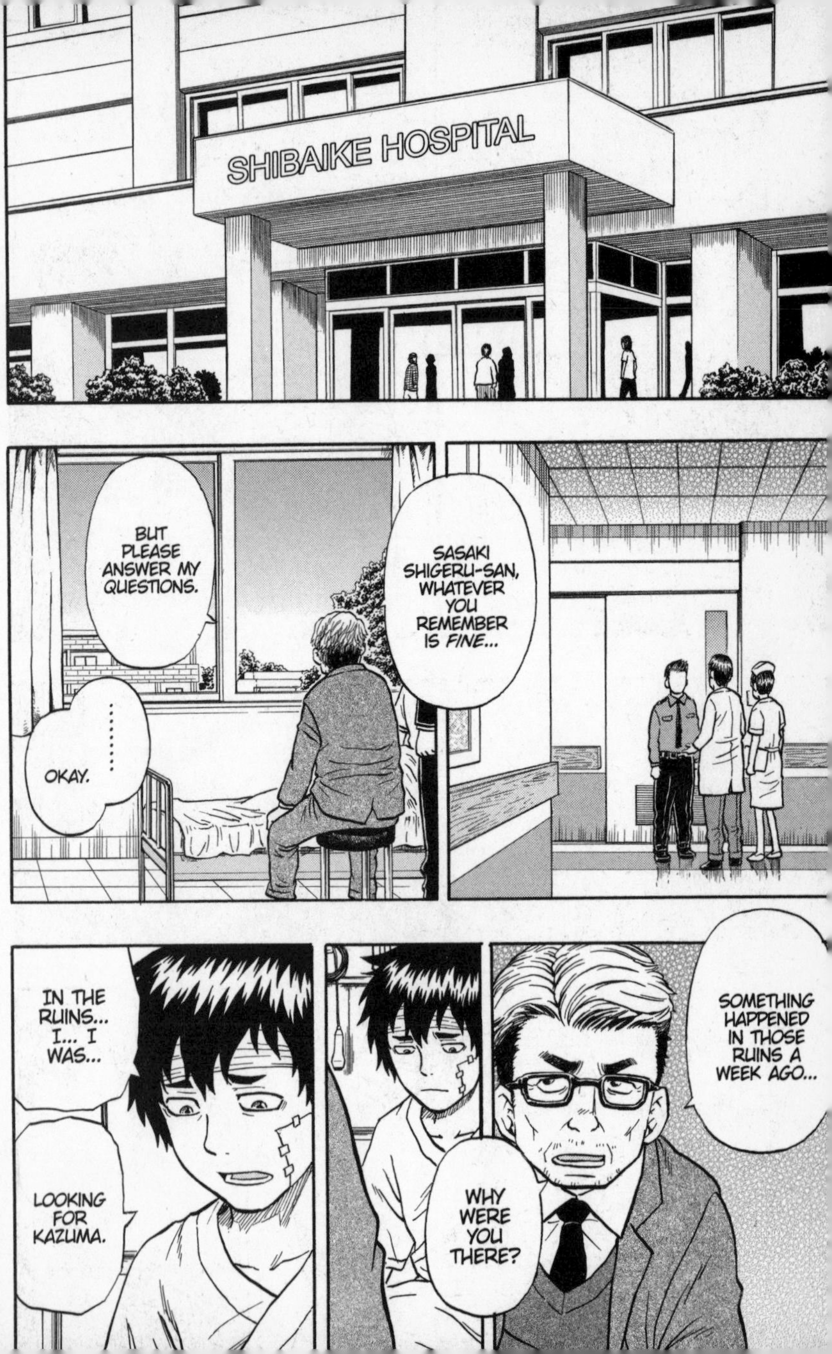
SHIBAIKE HOSPITAL
SASAKI SHIGERU-SAN, WHATEVER YOU REMEMBER IS *FINE*...
BUT PLEASE ANSWER MY QUESTIONS.
...... OKAY.
SOMETHING HAPPENED IN THOSE RUINS A WEEK AGO...
WHY WERE YOU THERE?
IN THE RUINS... I... I WAS...
LOOKING FOR KAZUMA.

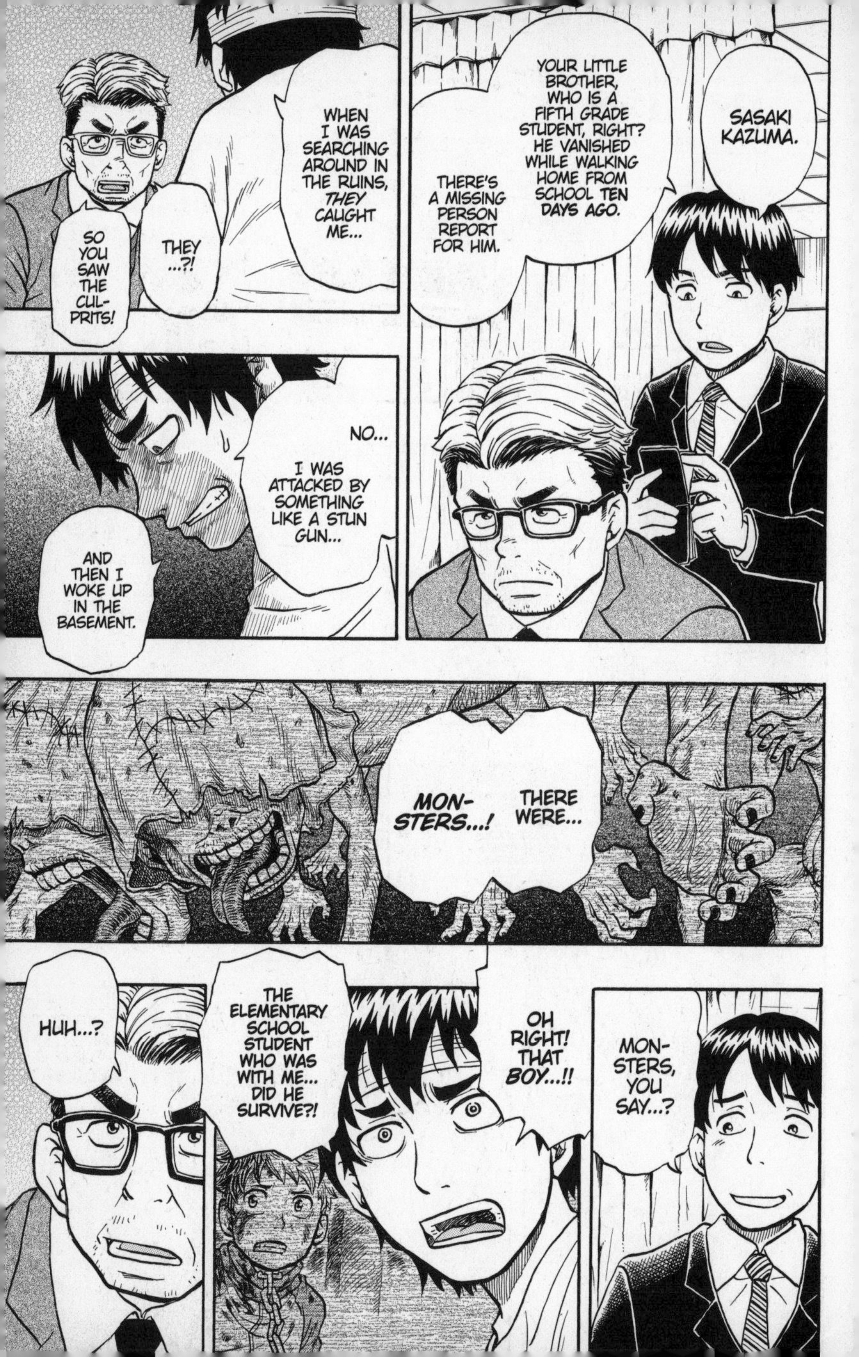
SASAKI KAZUMA.
YOUR LITTLE BROTHER, WHO IS A FIFTH GRADE STUDENT, RIGHT? HE VANISHED WHILE WALKING HOME FROM SCHOOL TEN DAYS AGO.
THERE'S A MISSING PERSON REPORT FOR HIM.
WHEN I WAS SEARCHING AROUND IN THE RUINS, *THEY* CAUGHT ME...
THEY ...?!
SO YOU SAW THE CUL-PRITS!
NO...
I WAS ATTACKED BY SOMETHING LIKE A STUN GUN...
AND THEN I WOKE UP IN THE BASEMENT.
THERE WERE...
MON-STERS...!
MON-STERS, YOU SAY...?
OH RIGHT! THAT *BOY*...!!
THE ELEMENTARY SCHOOL STUDENT WHO WAS WITH ME... DID HE SURVIVE?!
HUH...?

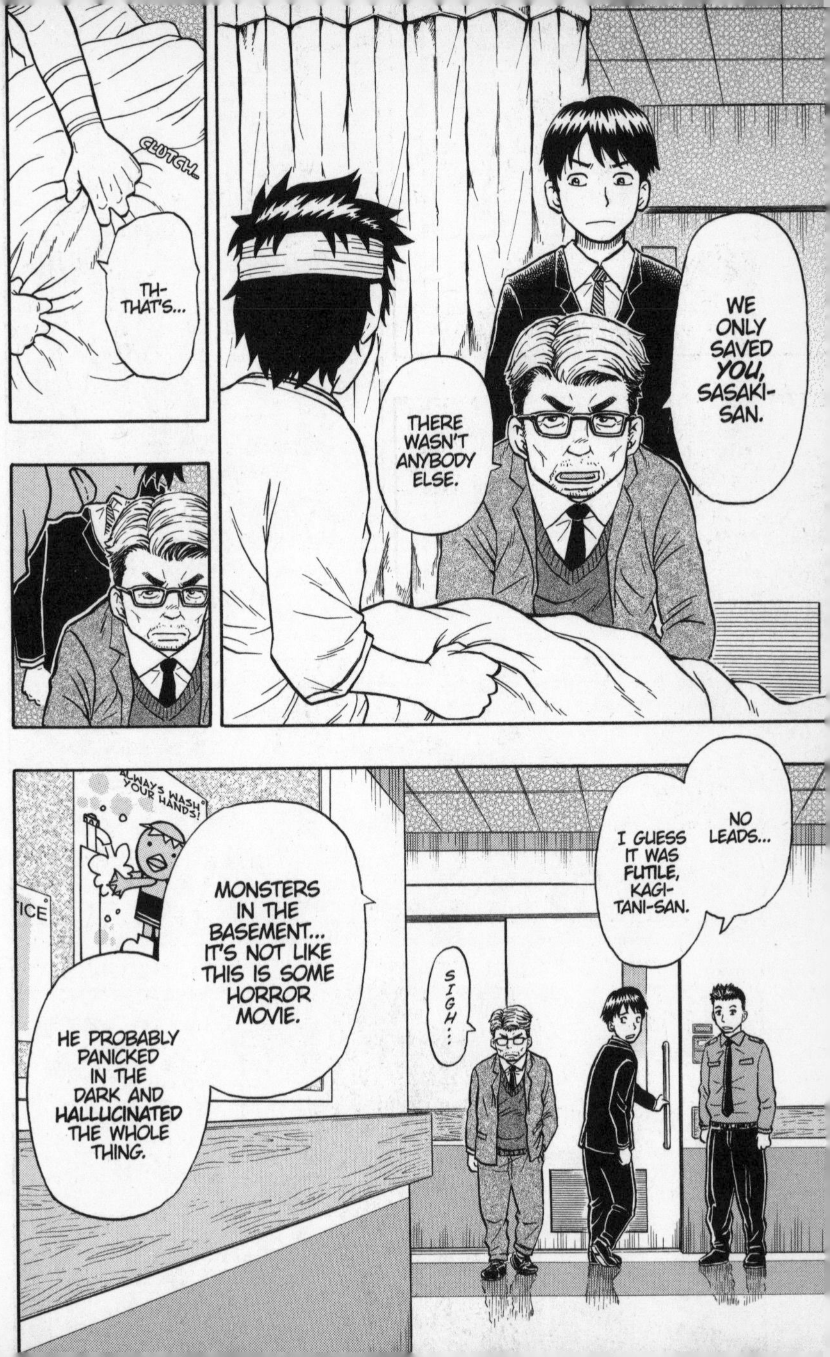
WE ONLY SAVED YOU, SASAKI-SAN.
THERE WASN'T ANYBODY ELSE.
CLUTCH...
TH-THAT'S...
NO LEADS...
I GUESS IT WAS FUTILE, KAGI-TANI-SAN.
SIGH...
ALWAYS WASH YOUR HANDS!
ICE
MONSTERS IN THE BASEMENT... IT'S NOT LIKE THIS IS SOME HORROR MOVIE.
HE PROBABLY PANICKED IN THE DARK AND HALLUCINATED THE WHOLE THING.

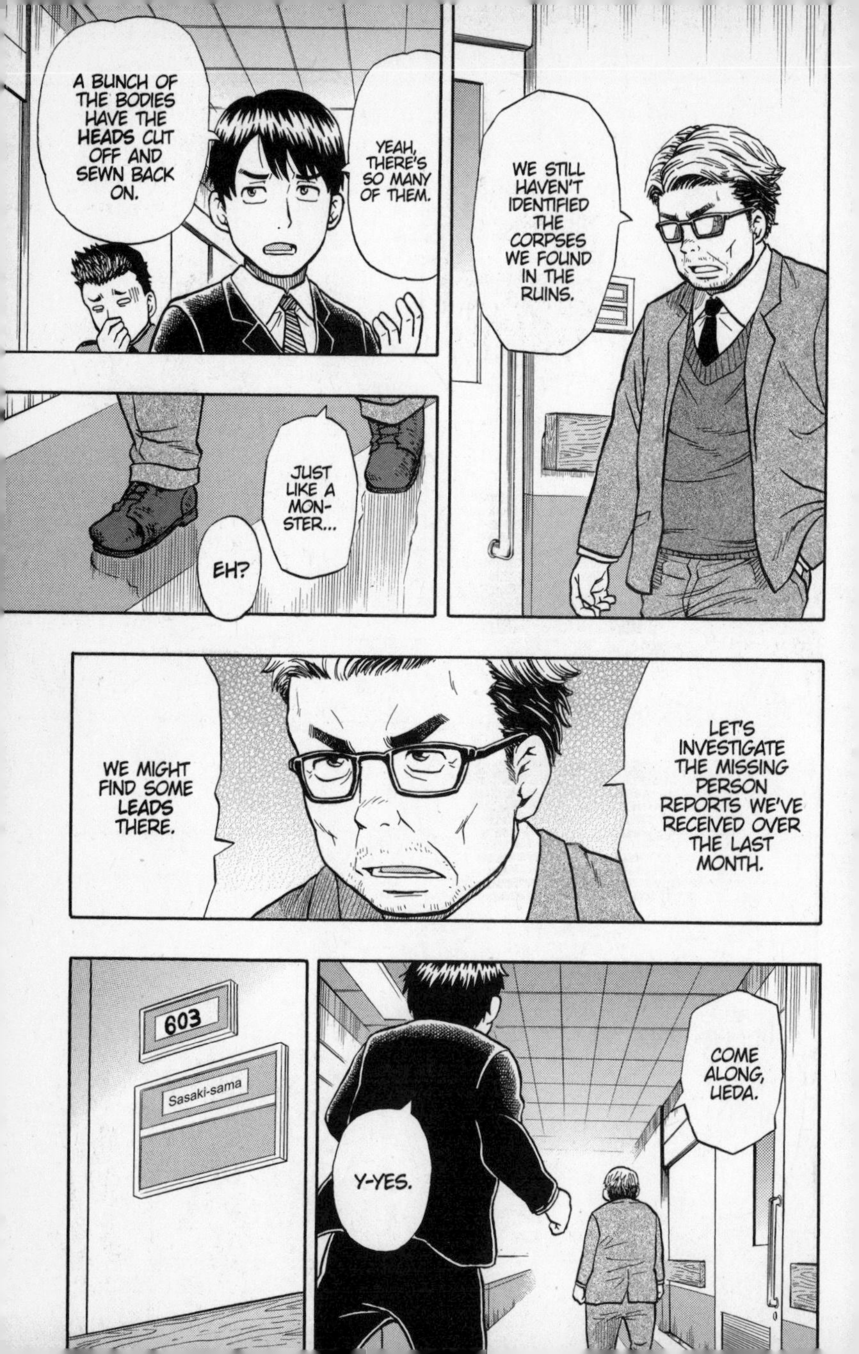
WE STILL HAVEN'T IDENTIFIED THE CORPSES WE FOUND IN THE RUINS.
YEAH, THERE'S SO MANY OF THEM.
A BUNCH OF THE BODIES HAVE THE HEADS CUT OFF AND SEWN BACK ON.
JUST LIKE A MON-STER...
EH?
LET'S INVESTIGATE THE MISSING PERSON REPORTS WE'VE RECEIVED OVER THE LAST MONTH.
WE MIGHT FIND SOME LEADS THERE.
COME ALONG, UEDA.
Y-YES.
603
Sasaki-sama

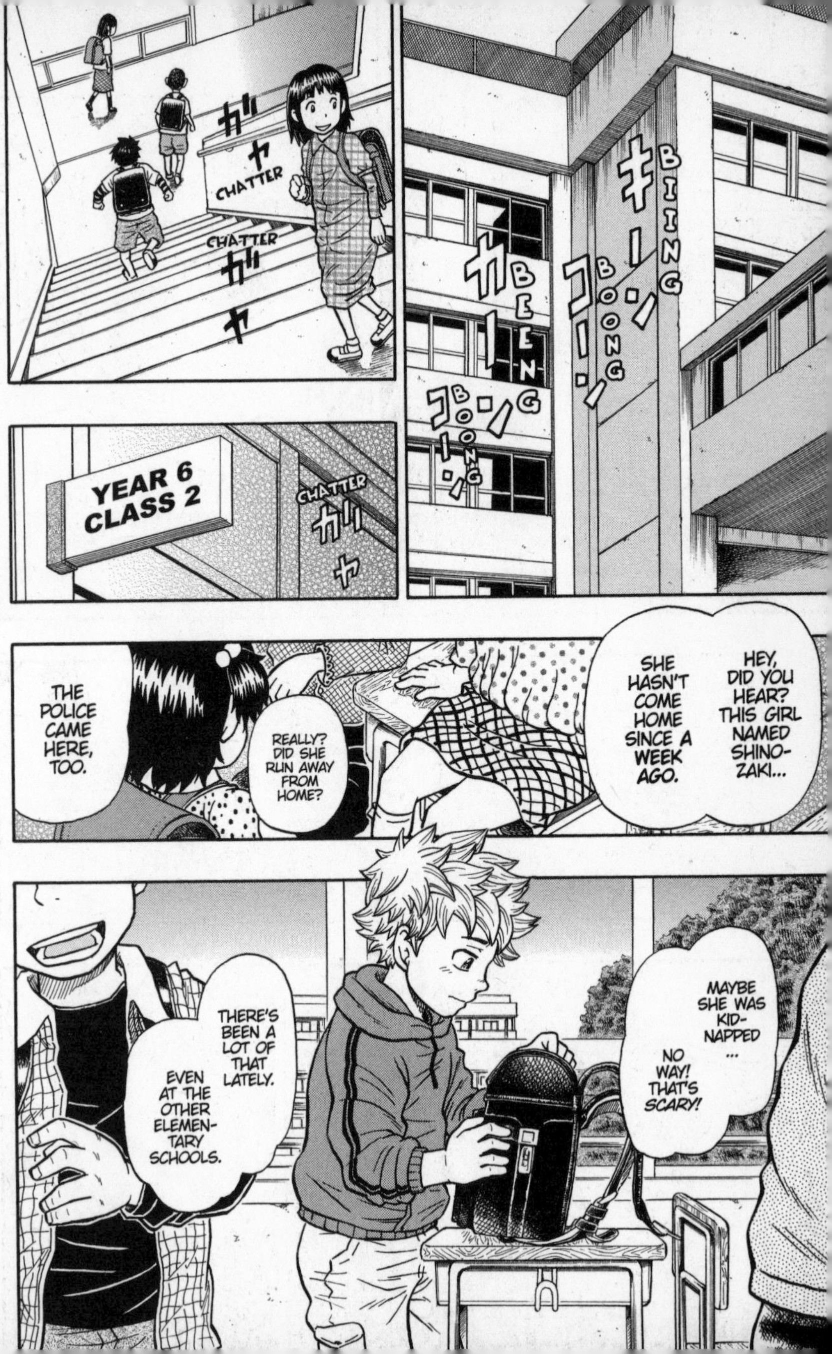
キーン
BIING
コーン
BOONG
カーン
BEENG
コーン
BOONG
ガヤ
CHATTER
CHATTER
ガヤ
YEAR 6 CLASS 2
CHATTER
ガヤ
HEY, DID YOU HEAR? THIS GIRL NAMED SHINO-ZAKI...
SHE HASN'T COME HOME SINCE A WEEK AGO.
REALLY? DID SHE RUN AWAY FROM HOME?
THE POLICE CAME HERE, TOO.
MAYBE SHE WAS KID-NAPPED...
NO WAY! THAT'S *SCARY!*
THERE'S BEEN A LOT OF THAT LATELY.
EVEN AT THE OTHER ELEMEN-TARY SCHOOLS.

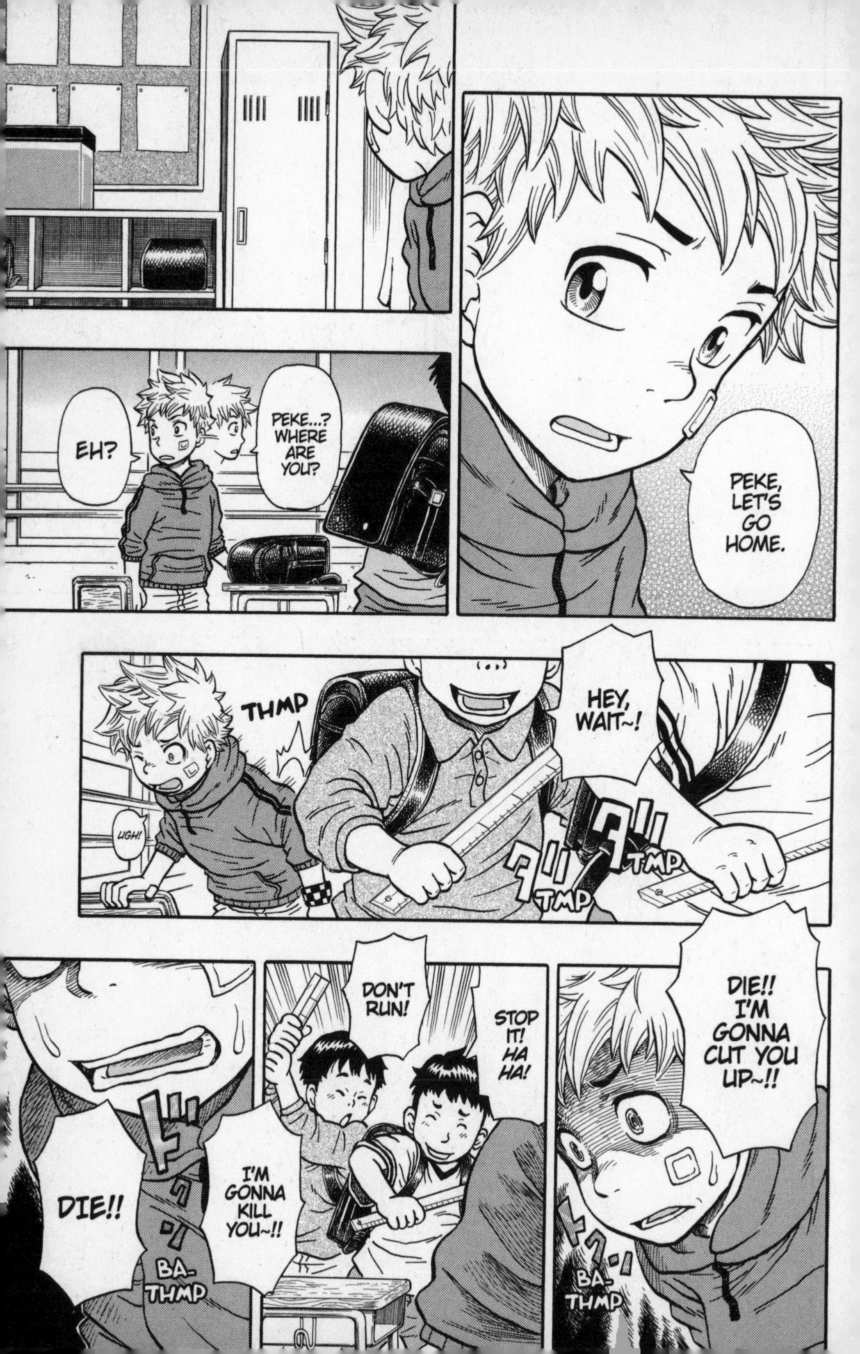
PEKE, LET'S GO HOME.
PEKE...? WHERE ARE YOU?
EH?
HEY, WAIT~!
TMP
TMP
THMP
UGH!
DIE!! I'M GONNA CUT YOU UP~!!
BA-THMP
STOP IT! HA HA!
DON'T RUN!
I'M GONNA KILL YOU~!!
DIE!!
BA-THMP

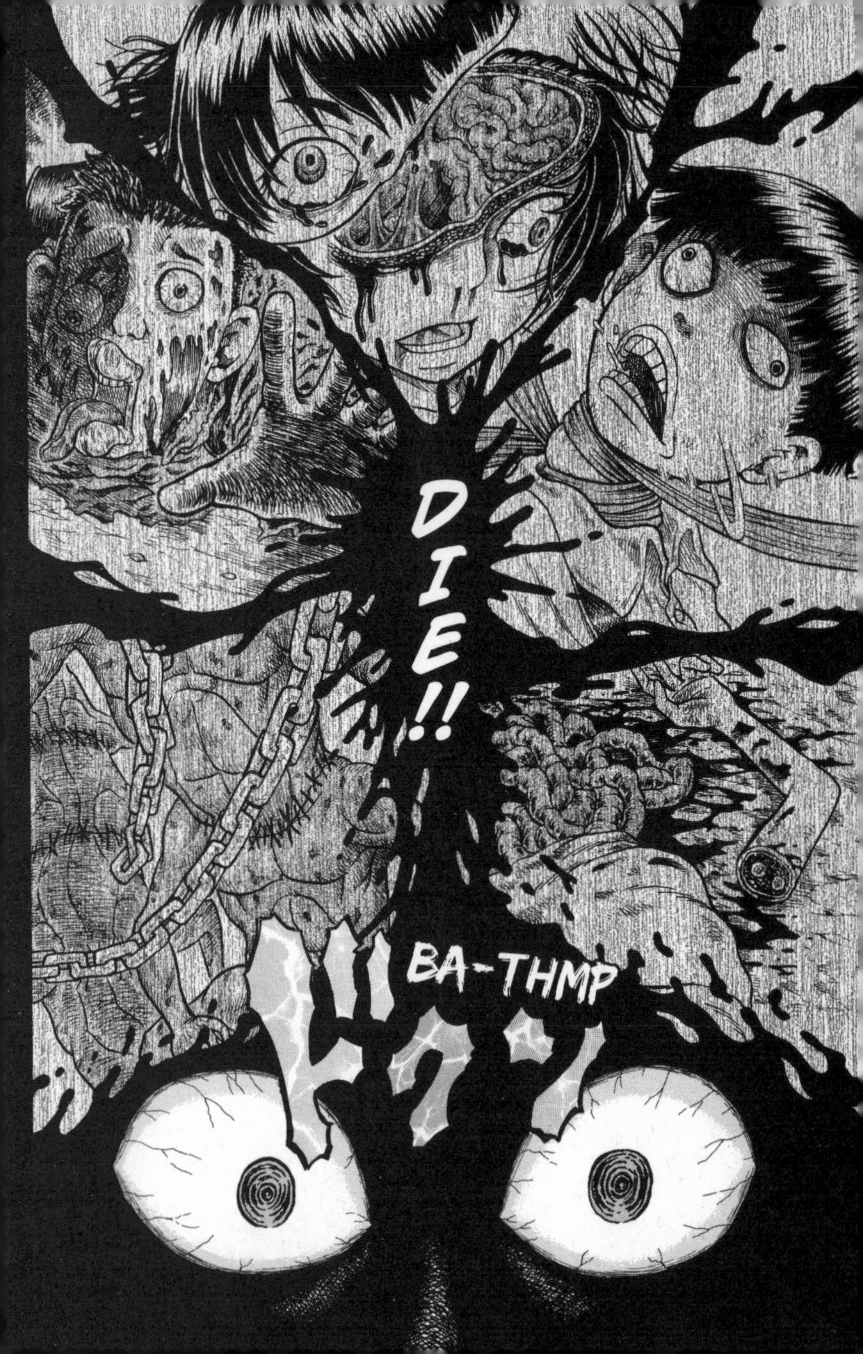
DIE!!
BA-THMP

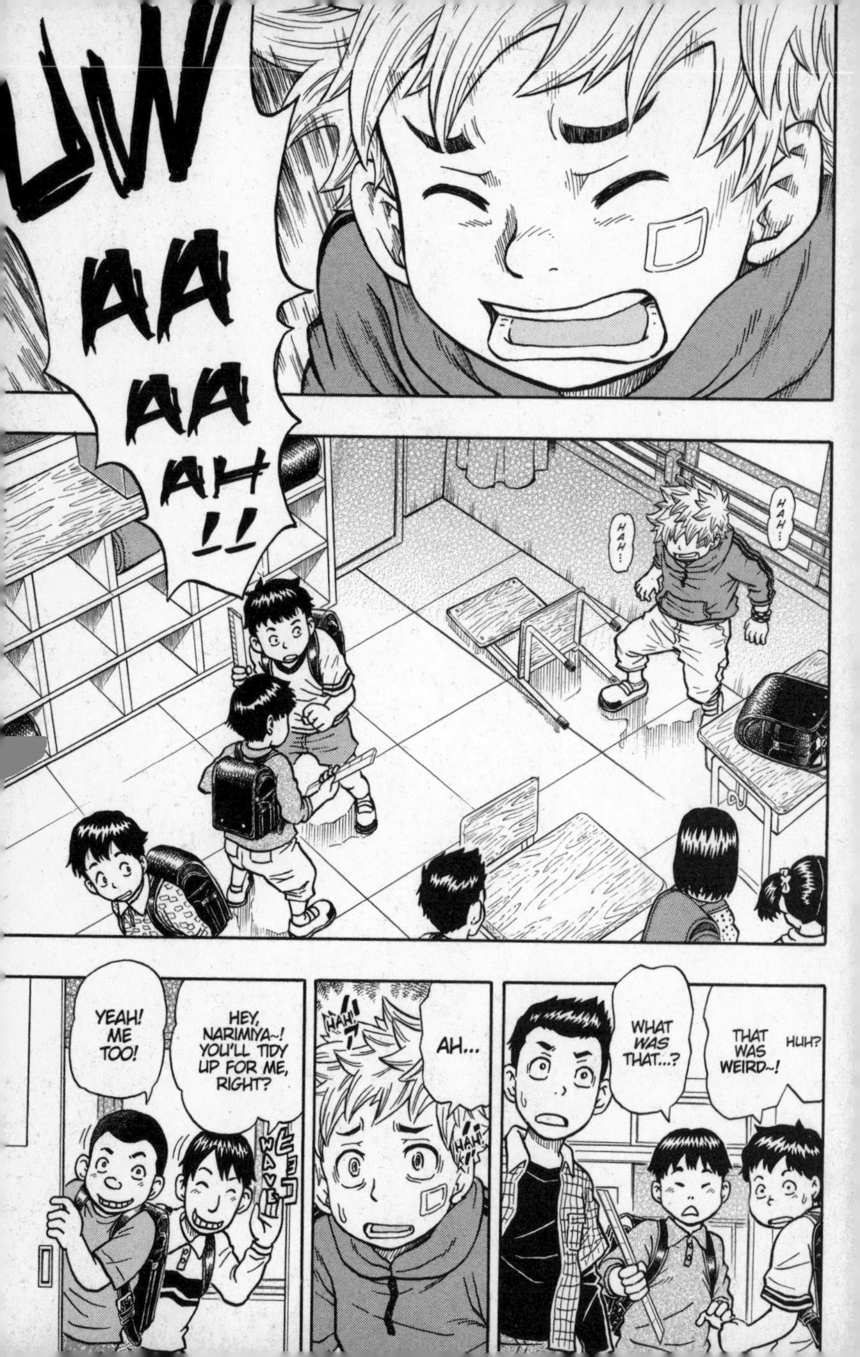
UWAAAAAAAH!!
HAH...
HAH...
HUH?
THAT WAS WEIRD~!
WHAT WAS THAT...?
AH...
HAH! HAH!
HAH! HAH!
HEY, NARIMIYA~! YOU'LL TIDY UP FOR ME, RIGHT?
WAVE WAVE
YEAH! ME TOO!

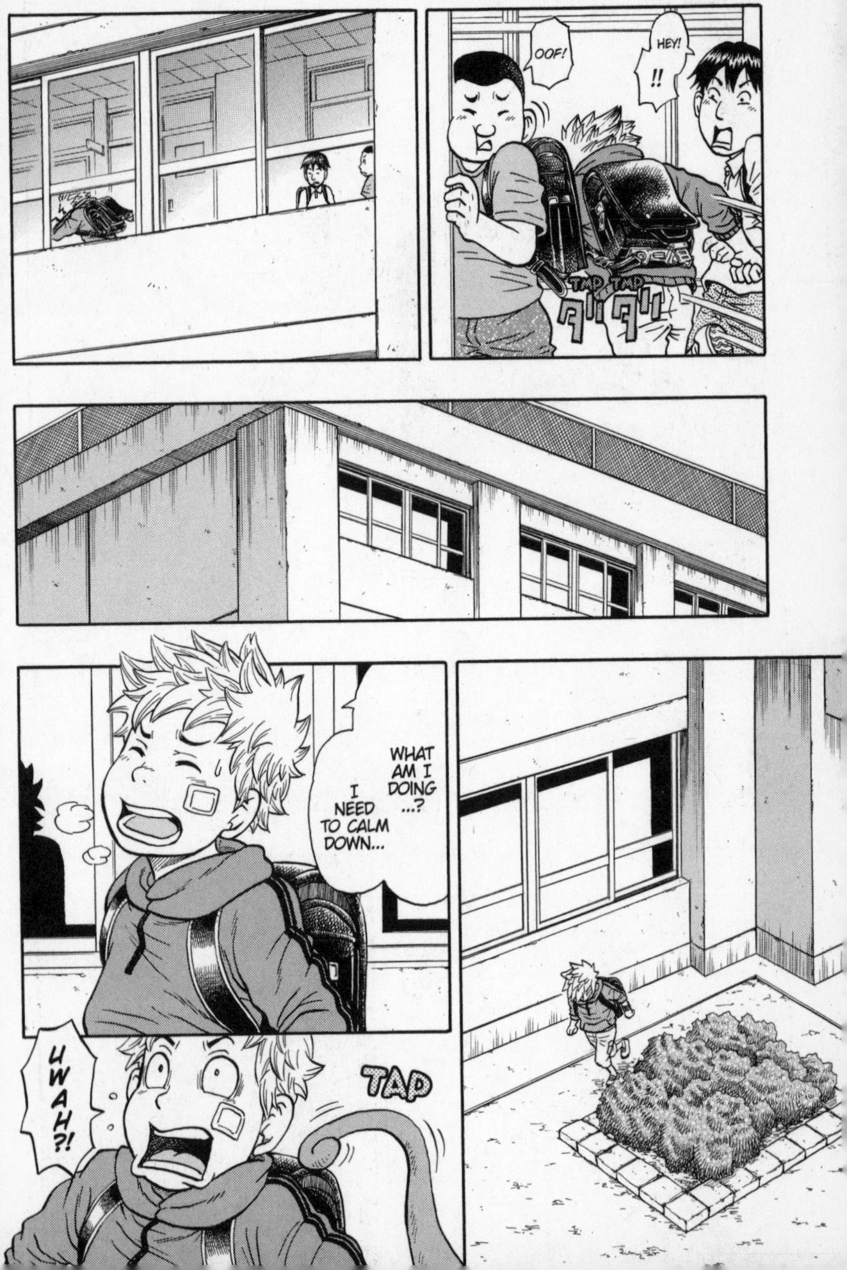
HEY! !!
OOF!
TAP TAP
WHAT AM I DOING ...?
I NEED TO CALM DOWN...
TAP
UWAH?!

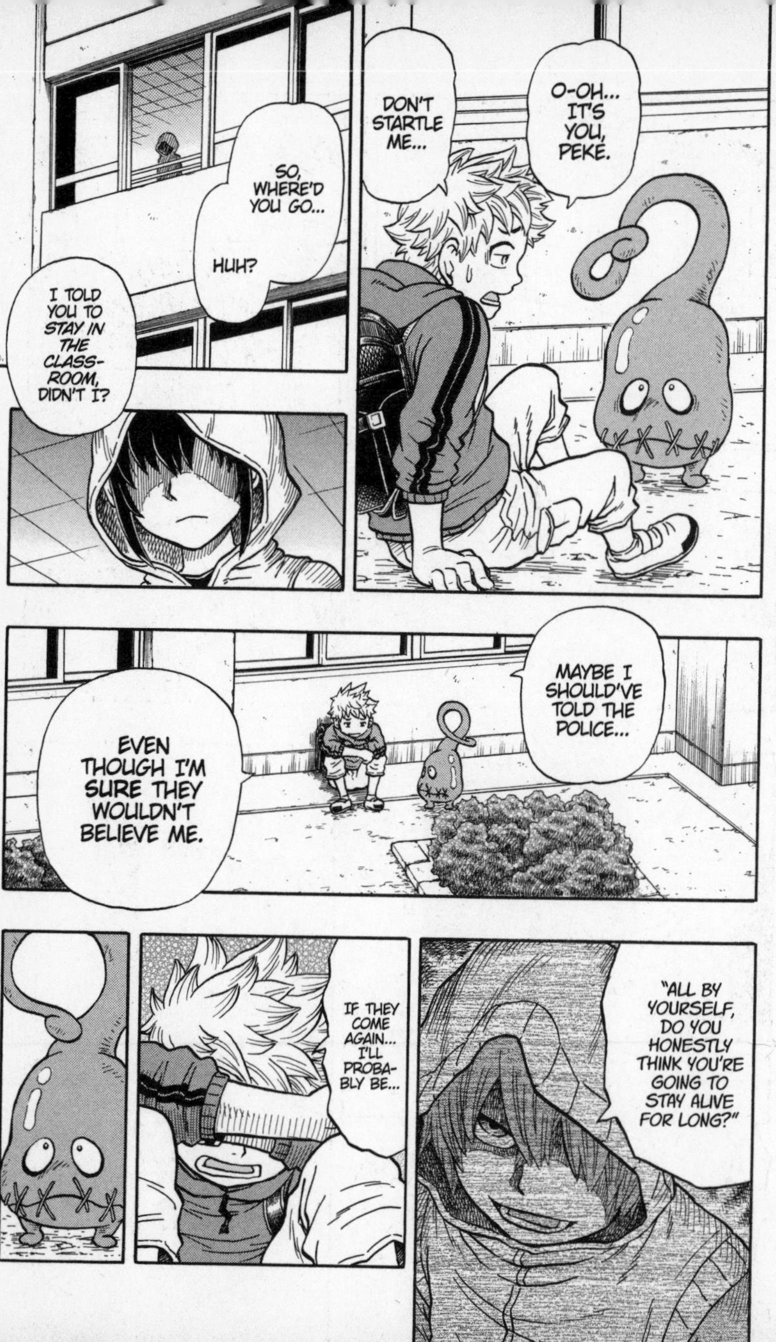
O-OH... IT'S YOU, PEKE.
DON'T STARTLE ME...
SO, WHERE'D YOU GO...
HUH?
I TOLD YOU TO STAY IN THE CLASS-ROOM, DIDN'T I?
MAYBE I SHOULD'VE TOLD THE POLICE...
EVEN THOUGH I'M SURE THEY WOULDN'T BELIEVE ME.
"ALL BY YOURSELF, DO YOU HONESTLY THINK YOU'RE GOING TO STAY ALIVE FOR LONG?"
IF THEY COME AGAIN... I'LL PROBA-BLY BE...

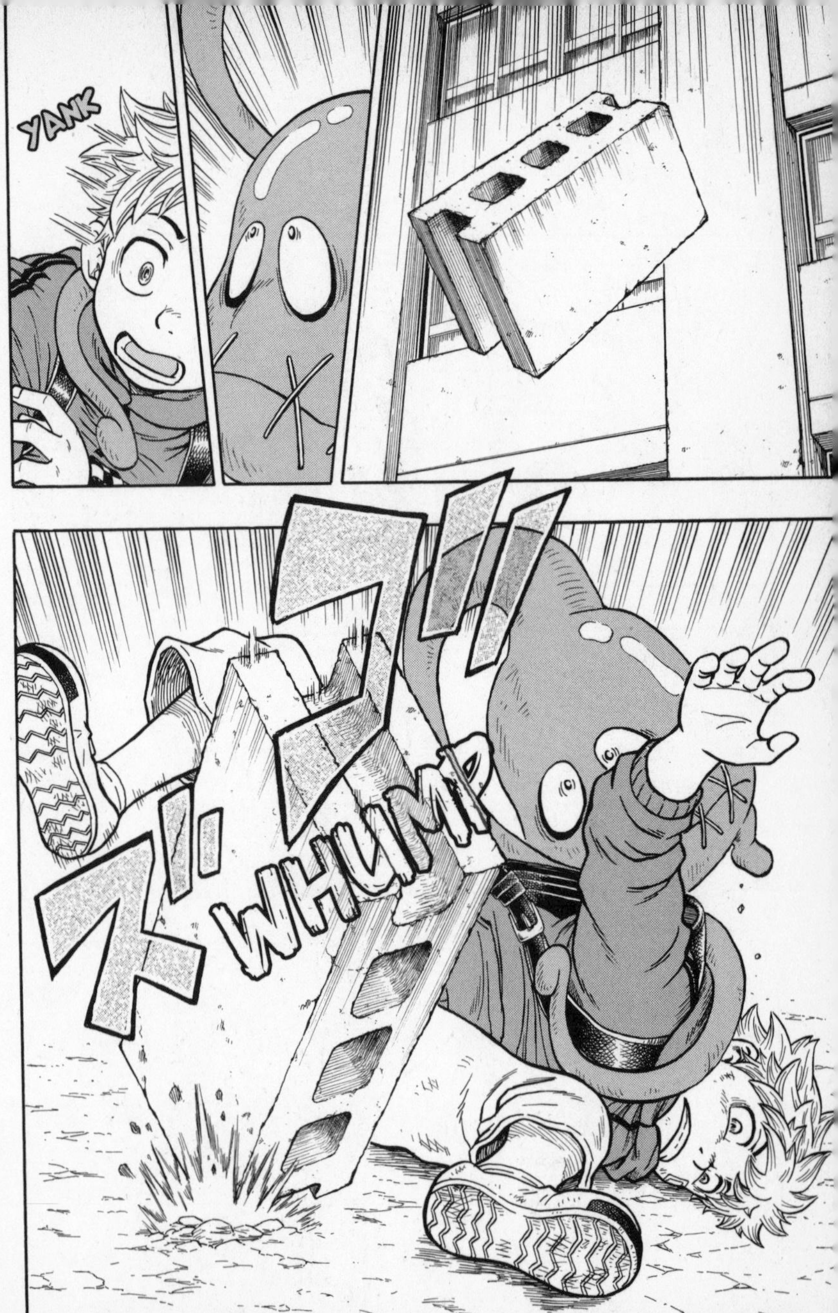
YANK
WHUM

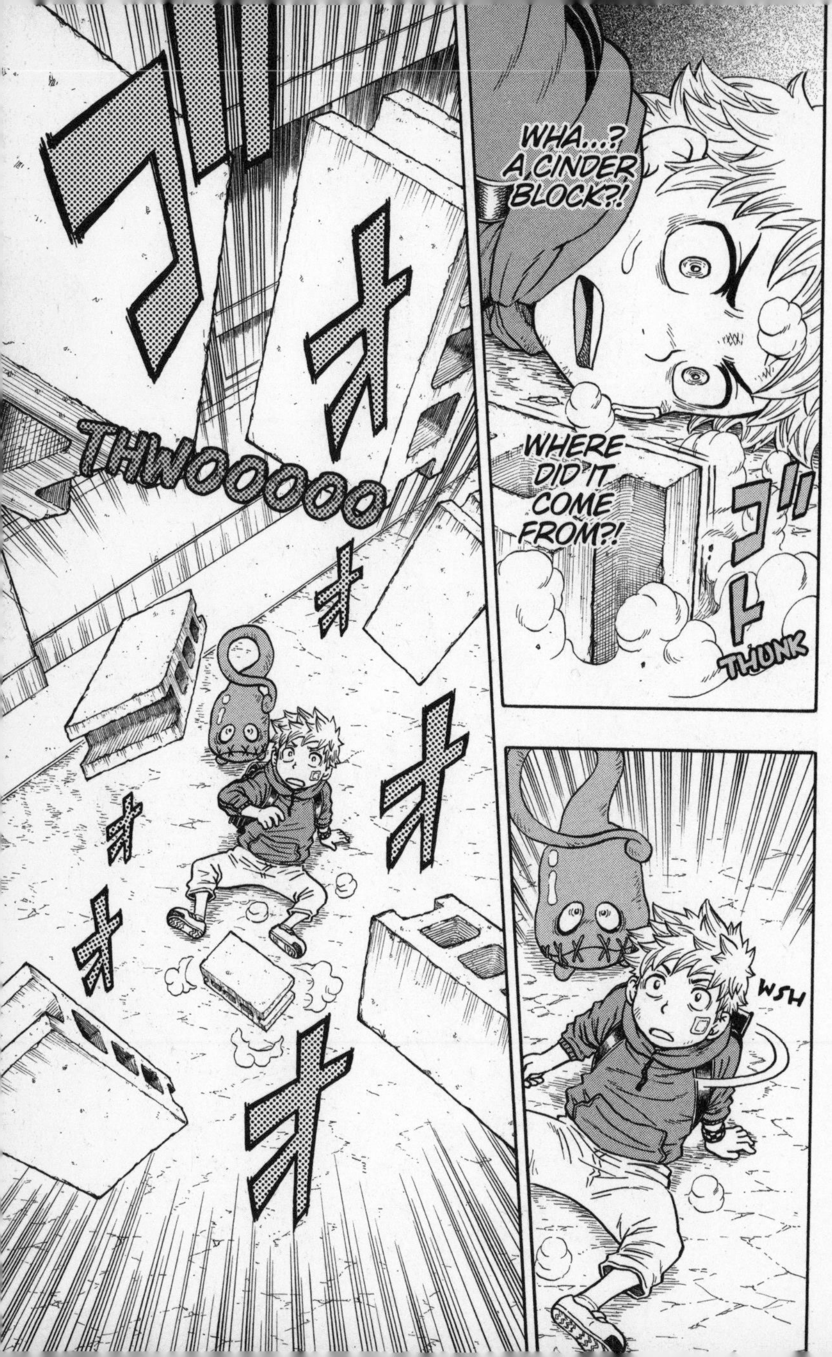
WHA...? A CINDER BLOCK?!
WHERE DID IT COME FROM?!
THUNK
WSH
THWOOOOOO

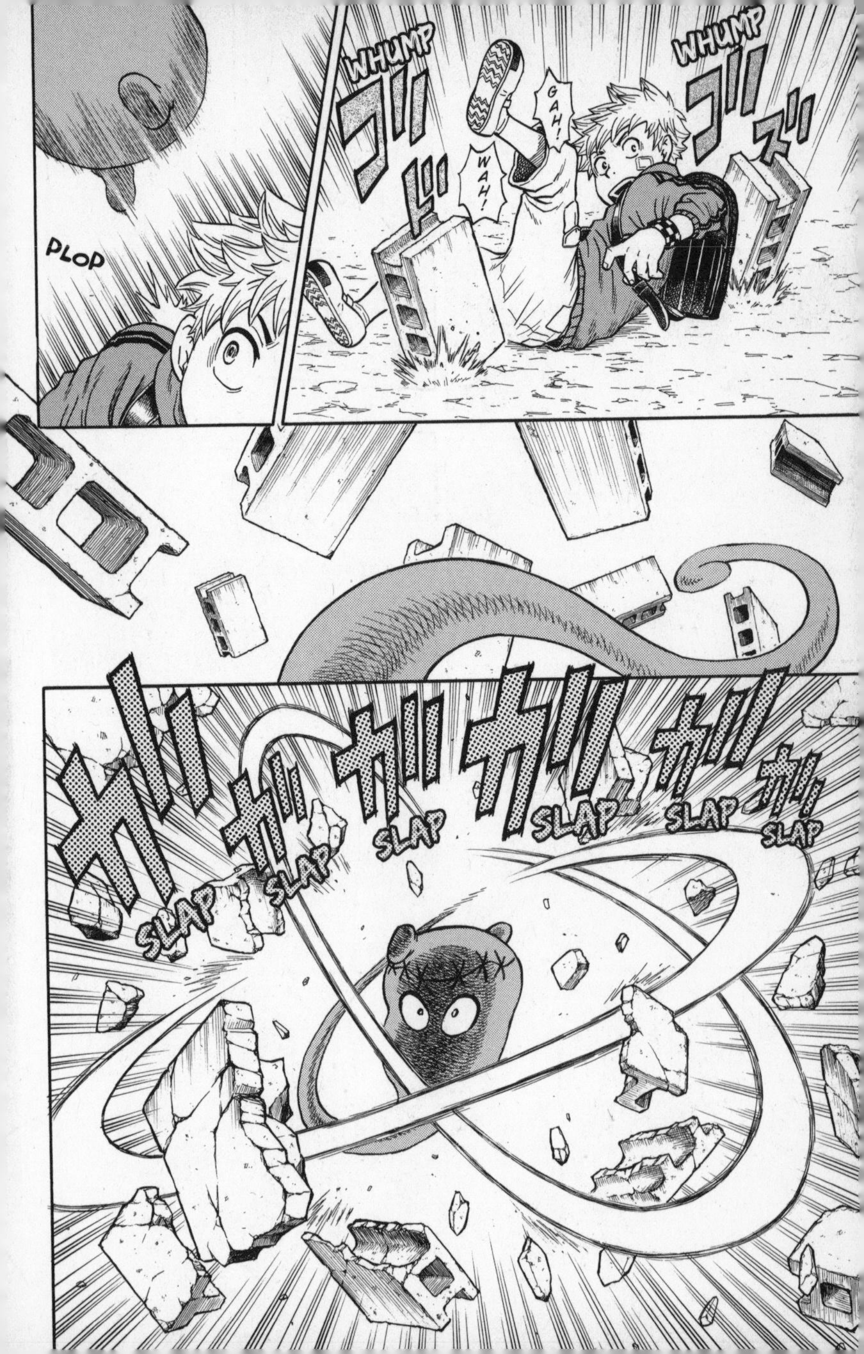
WHUMP
GAH!
WAH!
WHUMP
PLOP
SLAP
SLAP
SLAP
SLAP
SLAP
SLAP

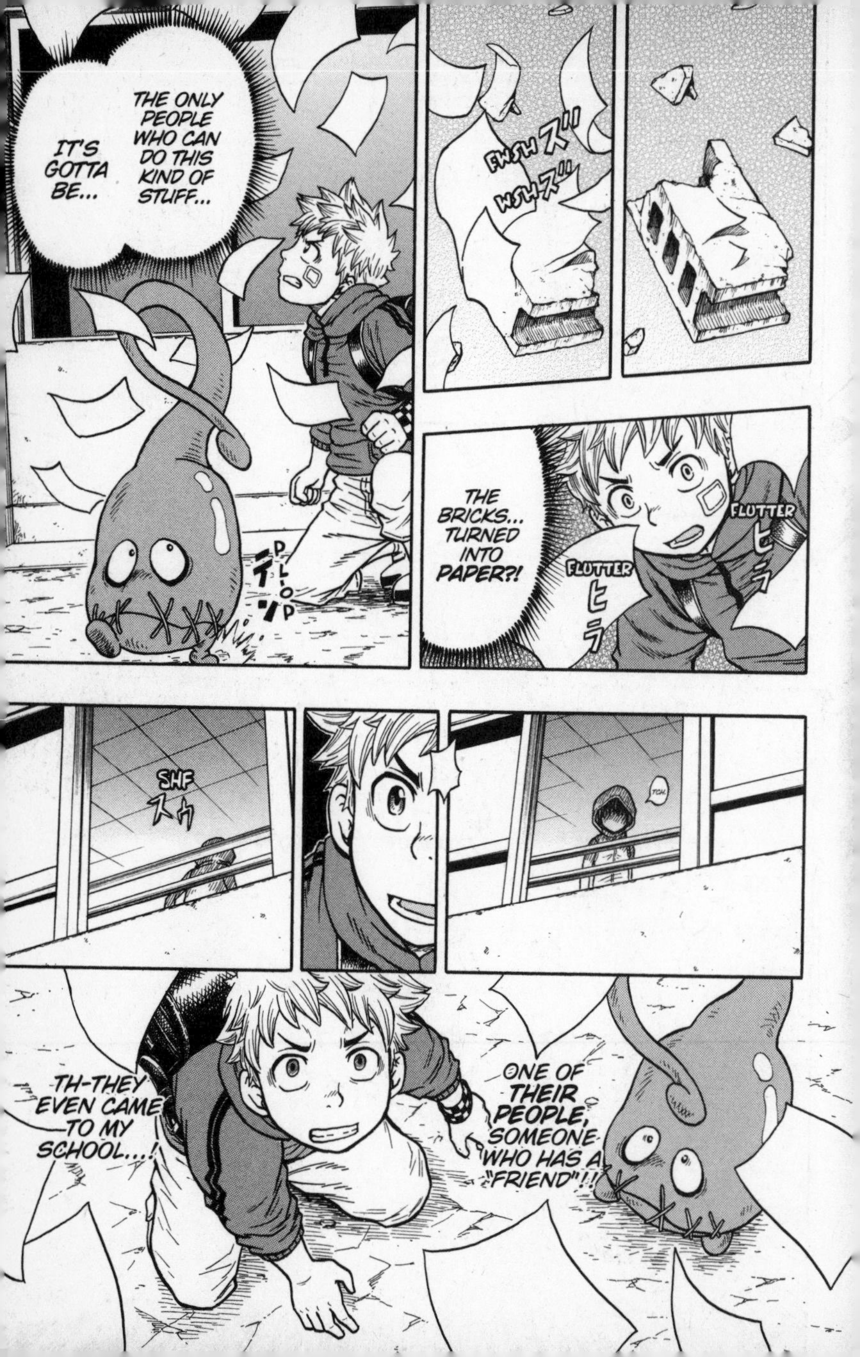
FWSH ズ
WSH ズ
THE BRICKS... TURNED INTO PAPER?!
FLUTTER ヒラ
FLUTTER ヒラ
THE ONLY PEOPLE WHO CAN DO THIS KIND OF STUFF...
IT'S GOTTA BE...
PLOP ティッ
TCH
SHF スゥ
ONE OF THEIR PEOPLE, SOMEONE WHO HAS A "FRIEND"!!
TH-THEY EVEN CAME TO MY SCHOOL...!

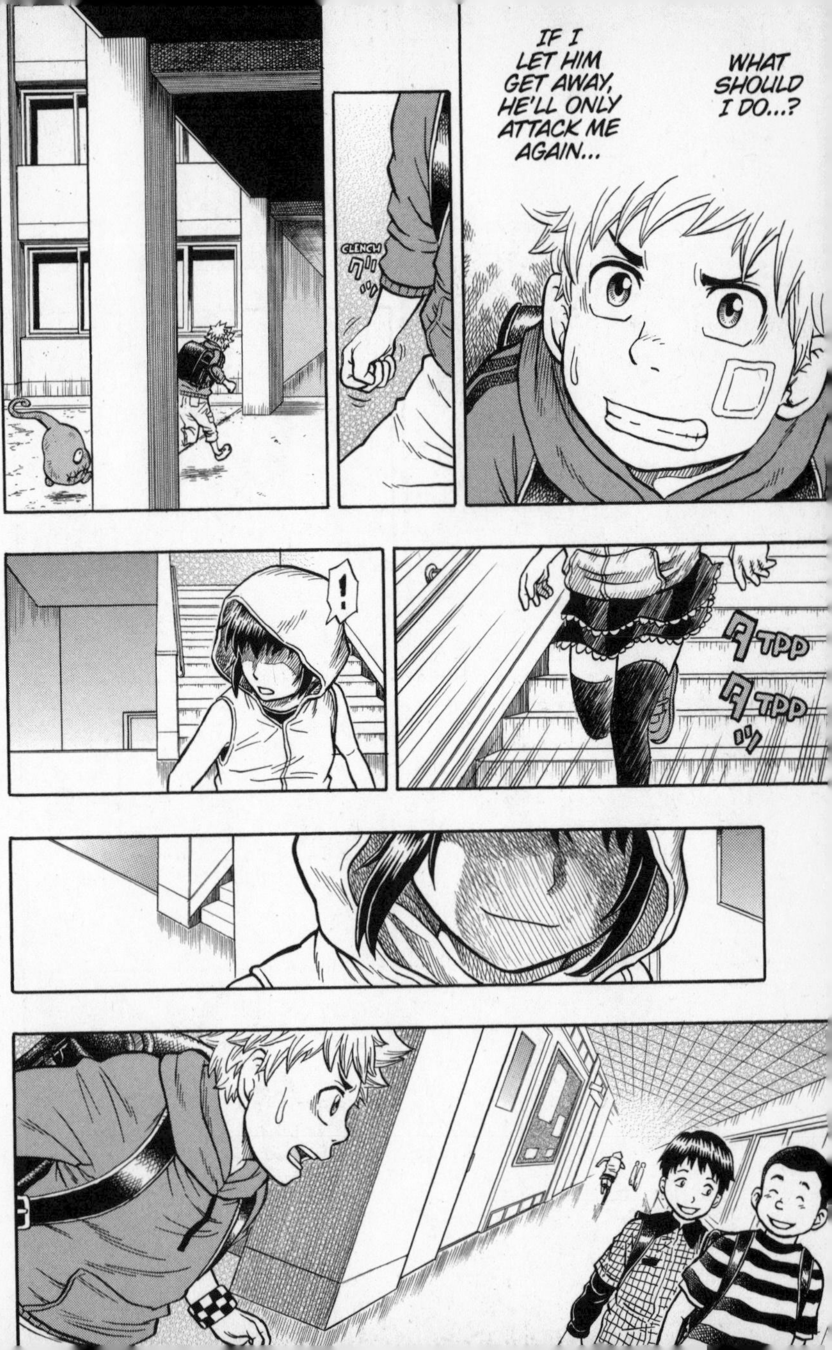
WHAT SHOULD I DO...?
IF I LET HIM GET AWAY, HE'LL ONLY ATTACK ME AGAIN...
CLENCH
グッ
!
TPP
TPP

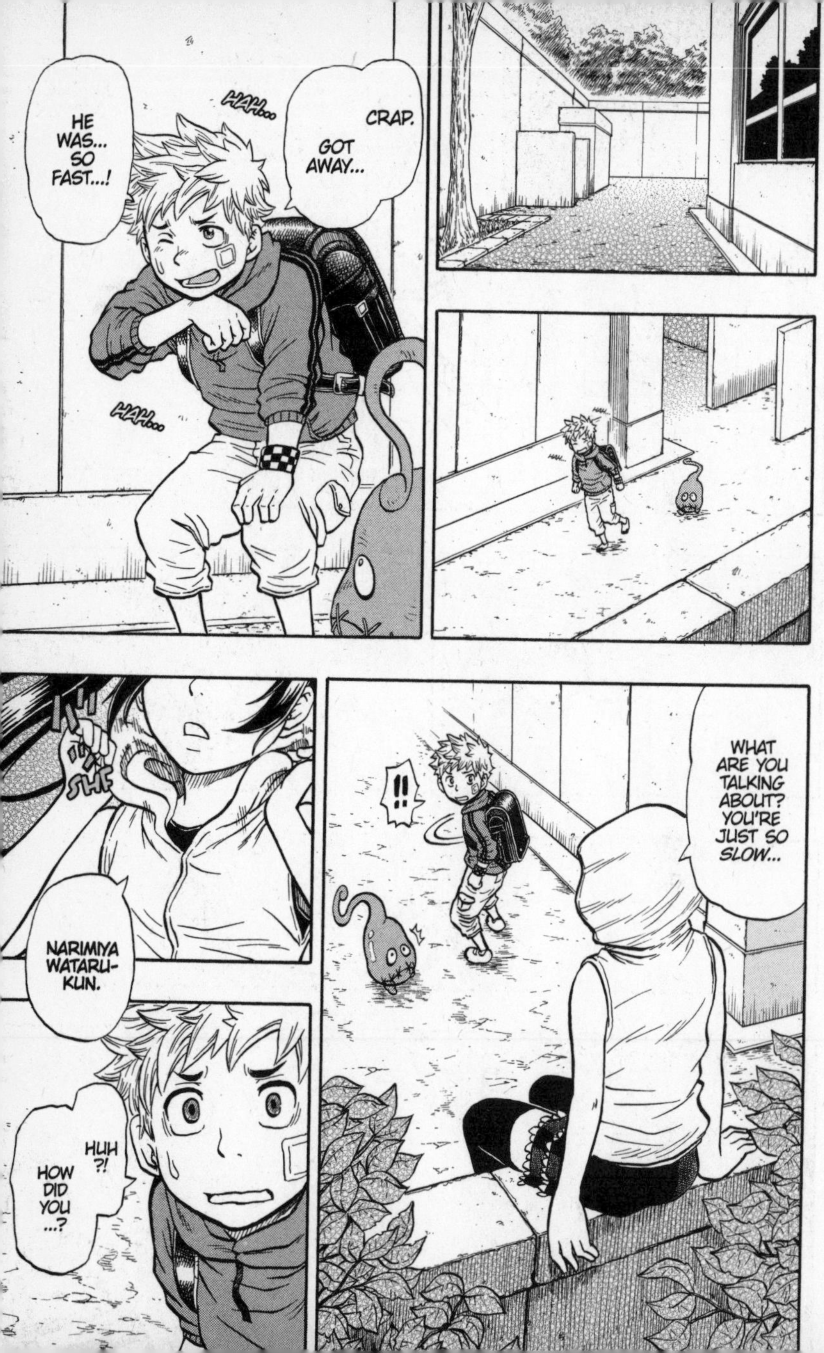
CRAP.
GOT AWAY...
HAH...
HE WAS... SO FAST...!
HAH...
WHAT ARE YOU TALKING ABOUT? YOU'RE JUST SO SLOW...
!!
SHF
NARIMIYA WATARU-KUN.
HUH?!
HOW DID YOU ...?

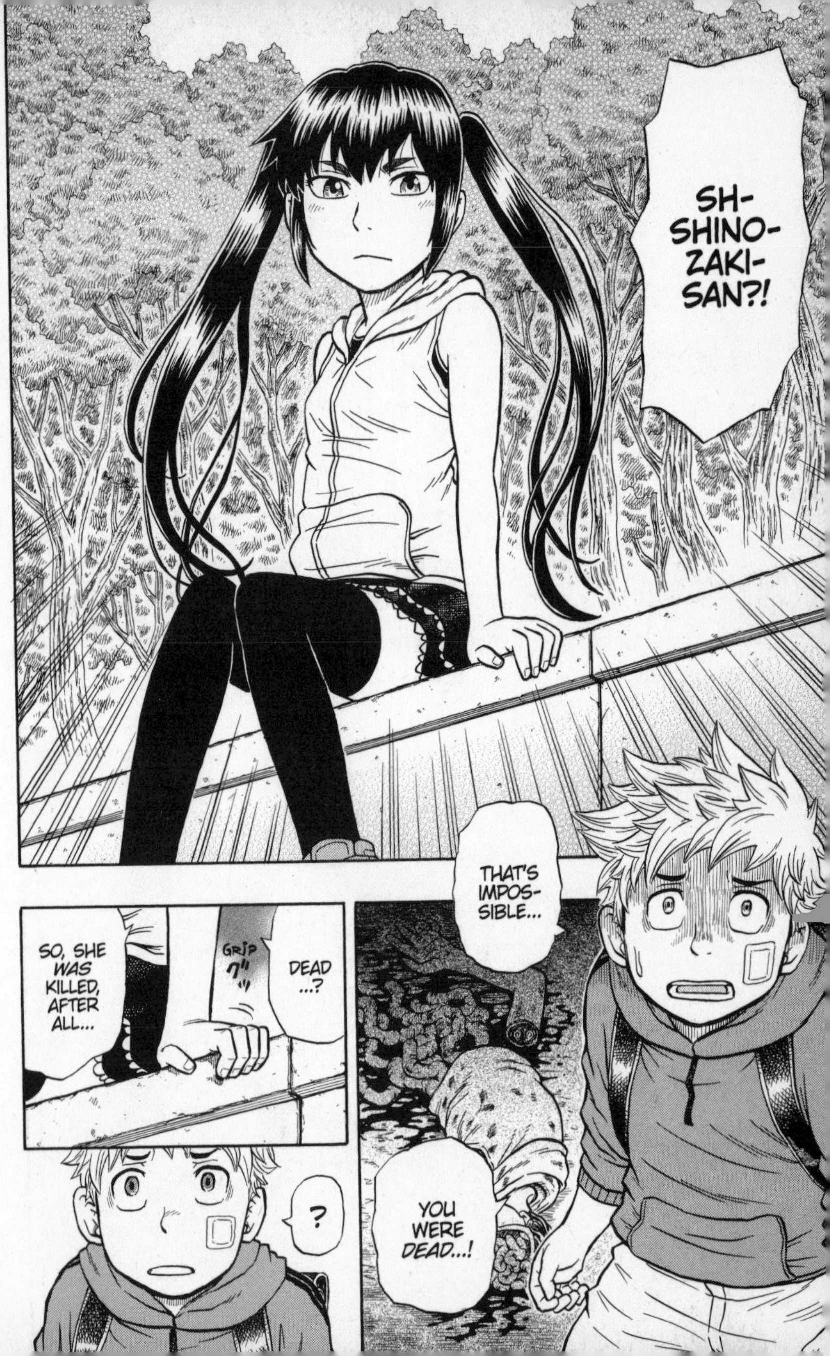
SH-SHINO-ZAKI-SAN?!
THAT'S IMPOSSIBLE...
YOU WERE DEAD...!
DEAD ...?
GRIP グッ
SO, SHE WAS KILLED, AFTER ALL...
?

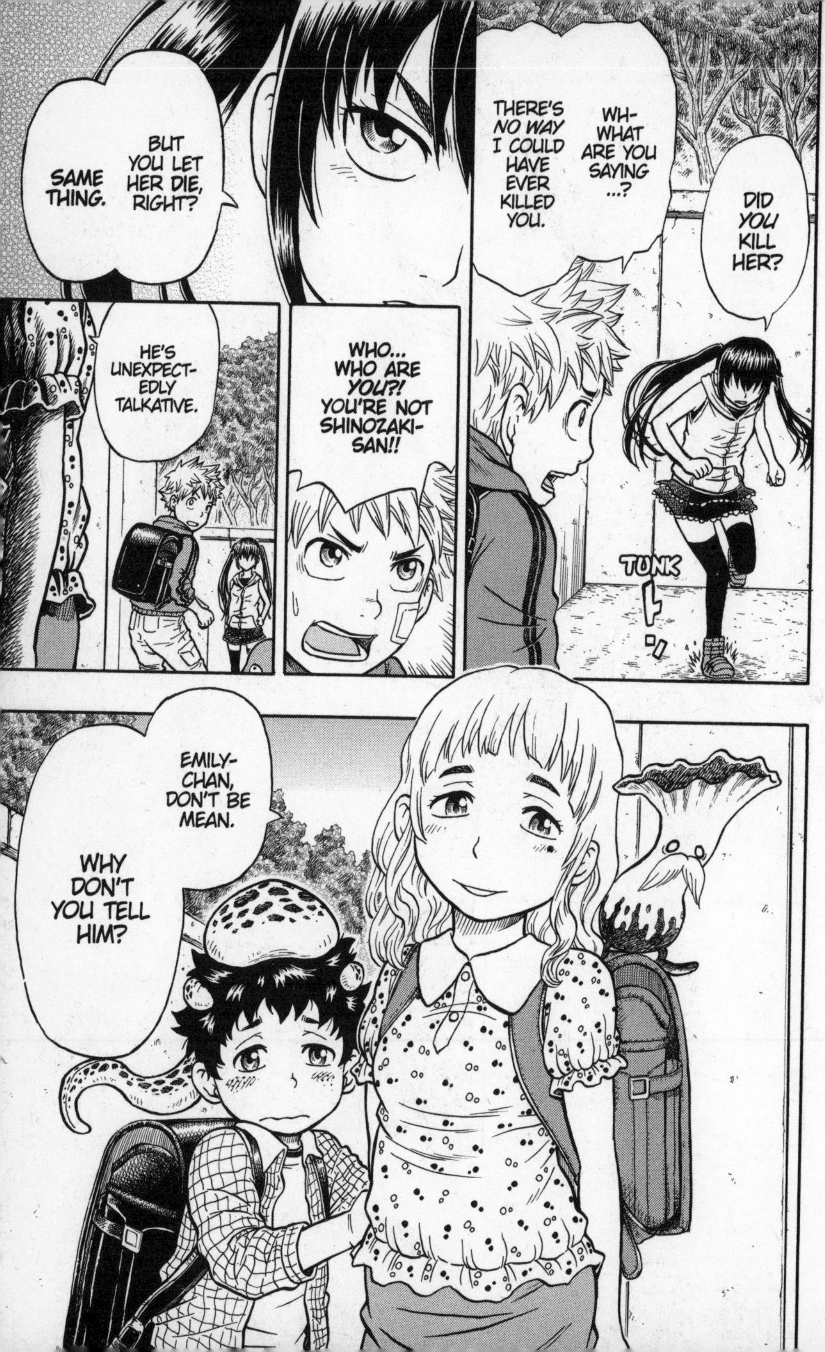
DID YOU KILL HER?
TUNK
WH- WHAT ARE YOU SAYING ...?
THERE'S NO WAY I COULD HAVE EVER KILLED YOU.
BUT YOU LET HER DIE, RIGHT?
SAME THING.
WHO... WHO ARE YOU?! YOU'RE NOT SHINOZAKI-SAN!!
HE'S UNEXPECTEDLY TALKATIVE.
EMILY-CHAN, DON'T BE MEAN.
WHY DON'T YOU TELL HIM?

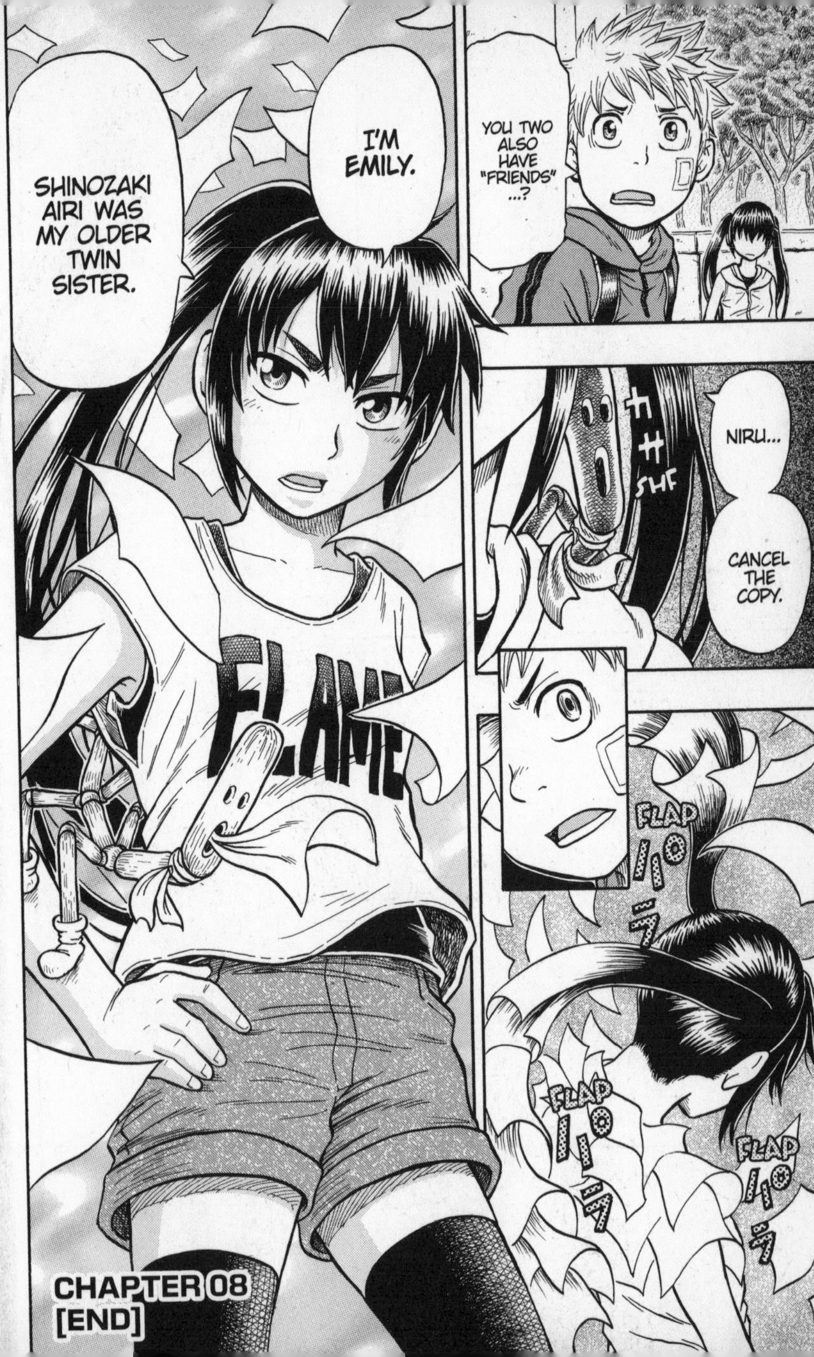
YOU TWO ALSO HAVE "FRIENDS" ...?
SHF
NIRU...
CANCEL THE COPY.
FLAP
FLAP
FLAP
I'M EMILY.
SHINOZAKI AIRI WAS MY OLDER TWIN SISTER.
CHAPTER 08 [END]

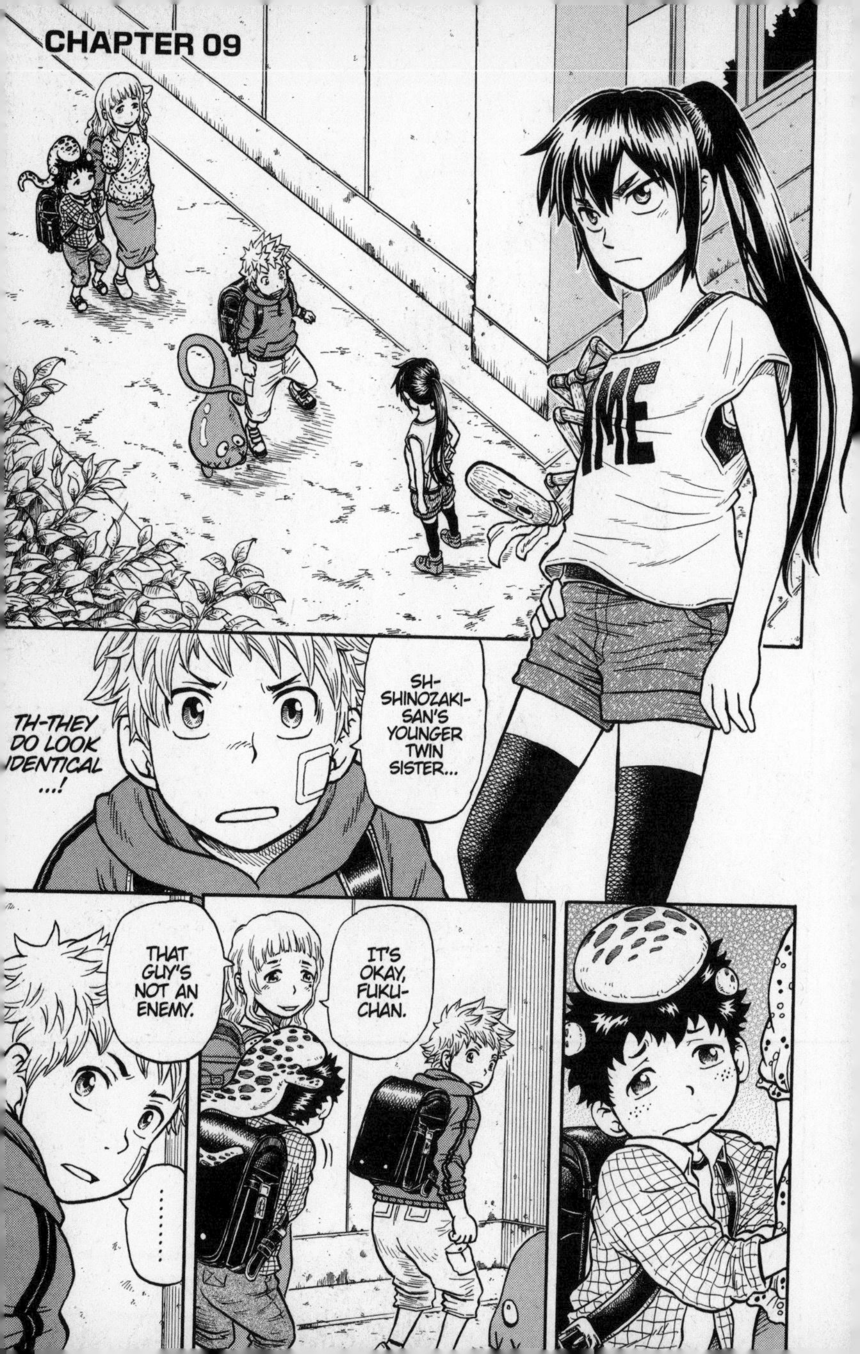
CHAPTER 09
SH-SHINOZAKI-SAN'S YOUNGER TWIN SISTER...
TH-THEY DO LOOK IDENTICAL ...!
IT'S OKAY, FUKU-CHAN.
THAT GUY'S NOT AN ENEMY.
......

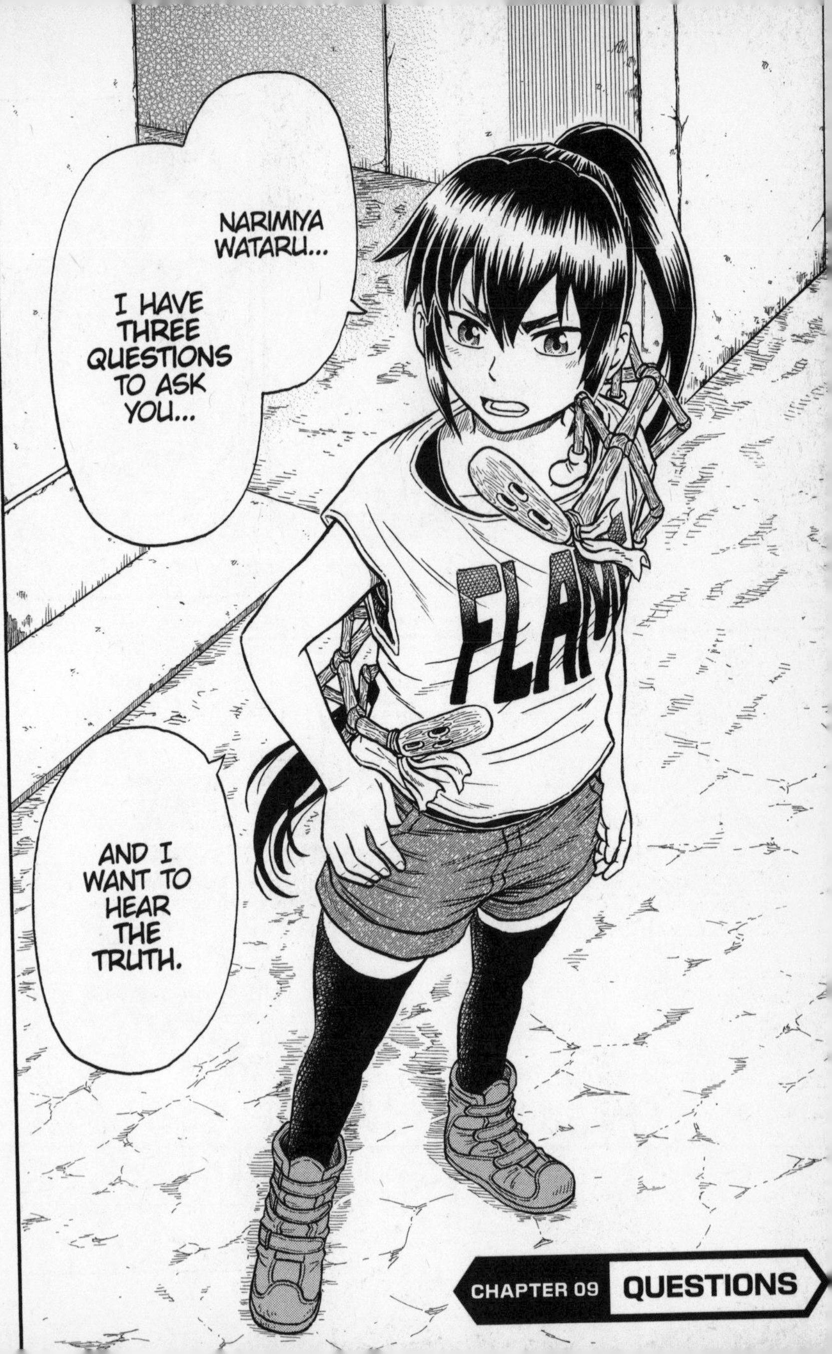
NARIMIYA WATARU... I HAVE THREE QUESTIONS TO ASK YOU...
AND I WANT TO HEAR THE TRUTH.

CHAPTER 09 QUESTIONS

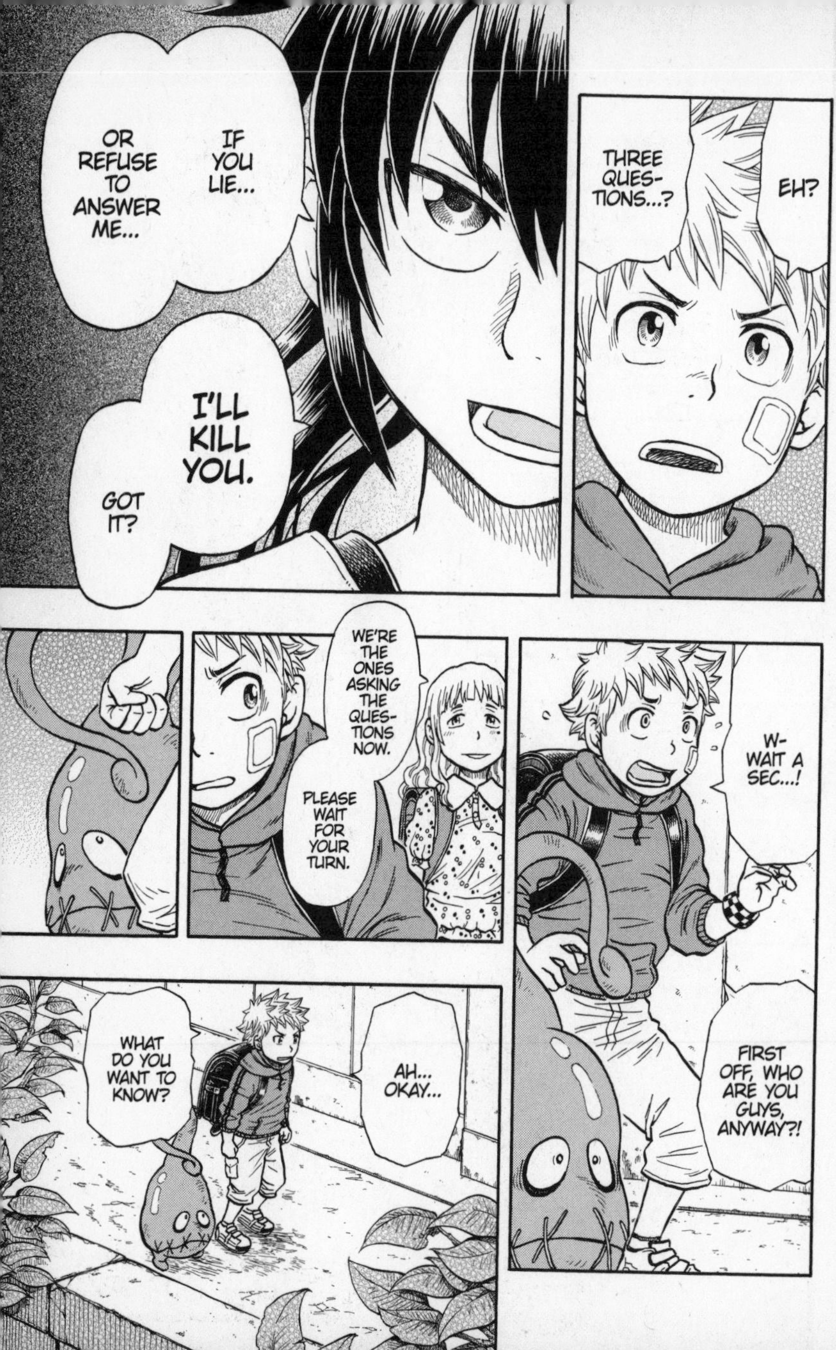
EH?
THREE QUES-TIONS...?
IF YOU LIE...
OR REFUSE TO ANSWER ME...
I'LL KILL YOU.
GOT IT?
W-WAIT A SEC...!
FIRST OFF, WHO ARE YOU GUYS, ANYWAY?!
WE'RE THE ONES ASKING THE QUES-TIONS NOW.
PLEASE WAIT FOR YOUR TURN.
AH... OKAY...
WHAT DO YOU WANT TO KNOW?

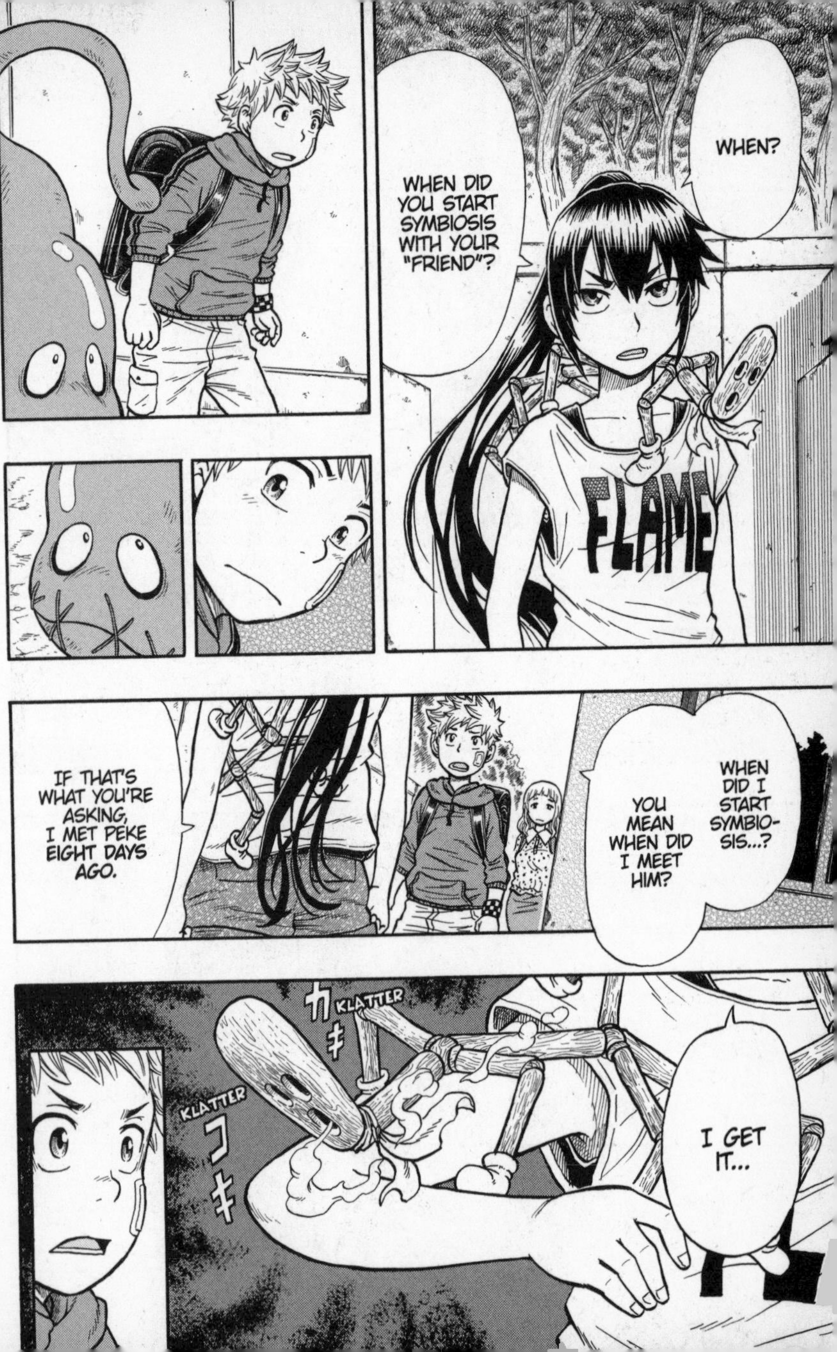
WHEN?
WHEN DID YOU START SYMBIOSIS WITH YOUR "FRIEND"?
WHEN DID I START SYMBIO-SIS...?
YOU MEAN WHEN DID I MEET HIM?
IF THAT'S WHAT YOU'RE ASKING, I MET PEKE EIGHT DAYS AGO.
I GET IT...
カキ KLATTER
コキ KLATTER

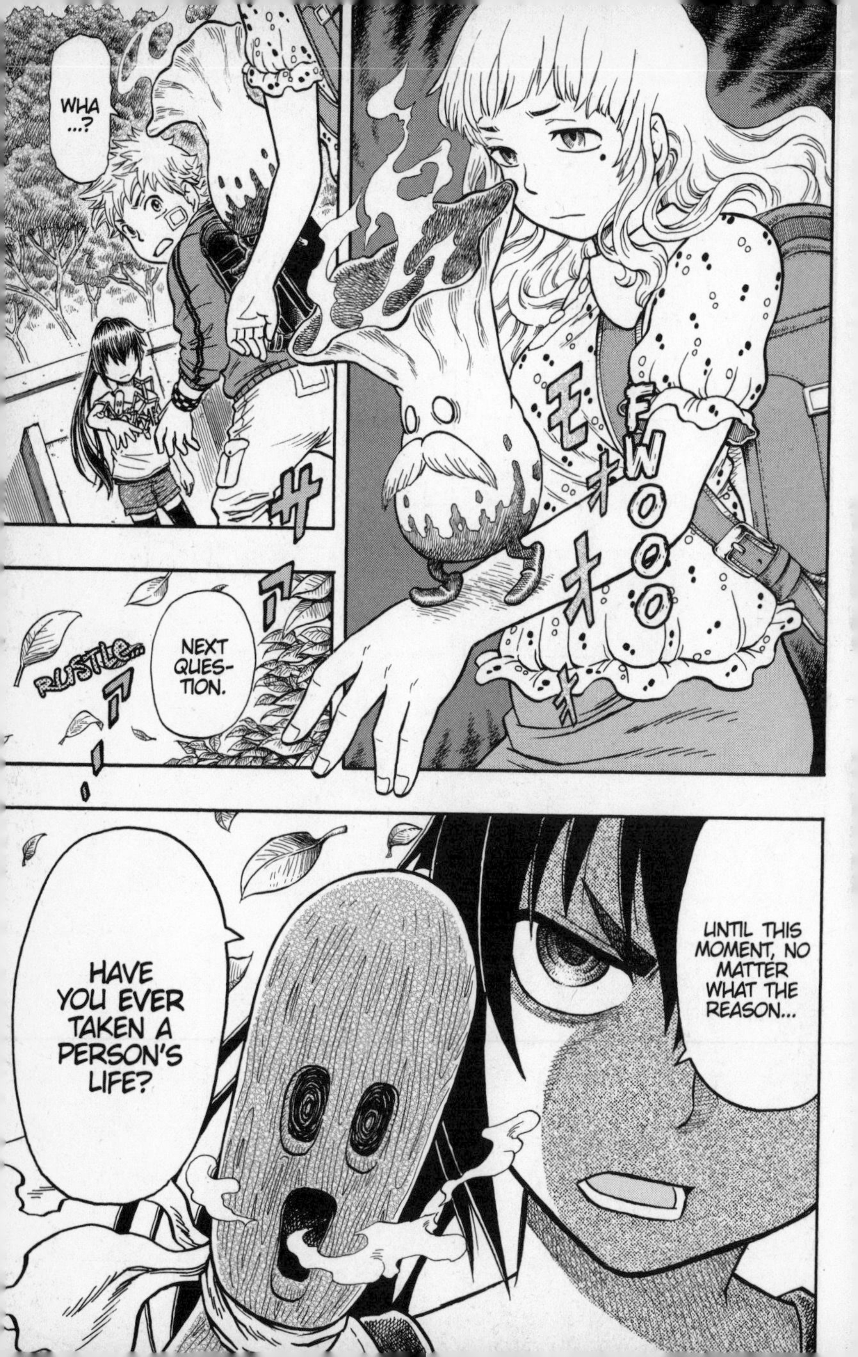
FWOOO
WHA ...?
RUSTLE...
NEXT QUES-TION.
UNTIL THIS MOMENT, NO MATTER WHAT THE REASON...
HAVE YOU EVER TAKEN A PERSON'S LIFE?

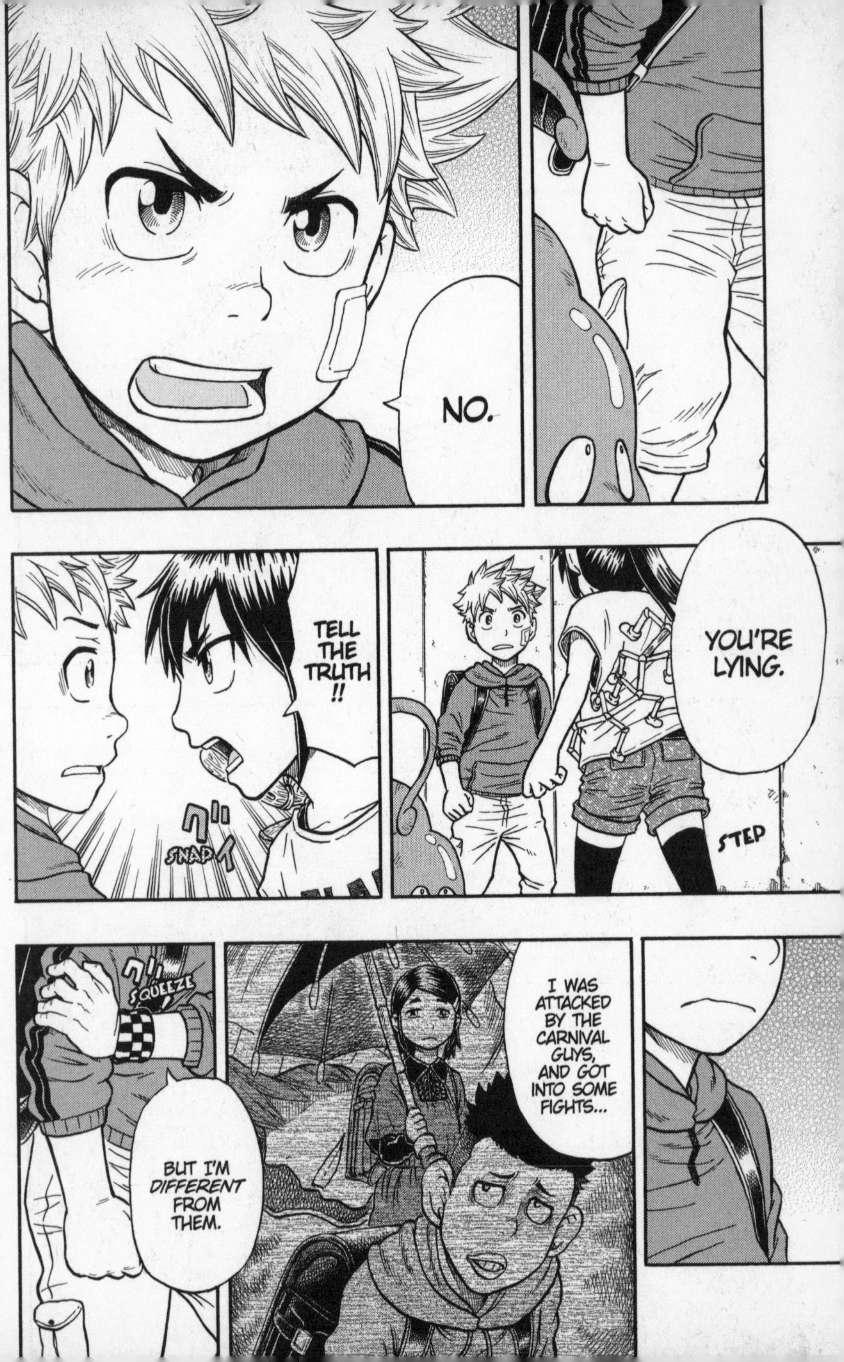
NO.
YOU'RE LYING.
STEP
TELL THE TRUTH!!
SNAP
I WAS ATTACKED BY THE CARNIVAL GUYS, AND GOT INTO SOME FIGHTS...
SQUEEZE
BUT I'M DIFFERENT FROM THEM.

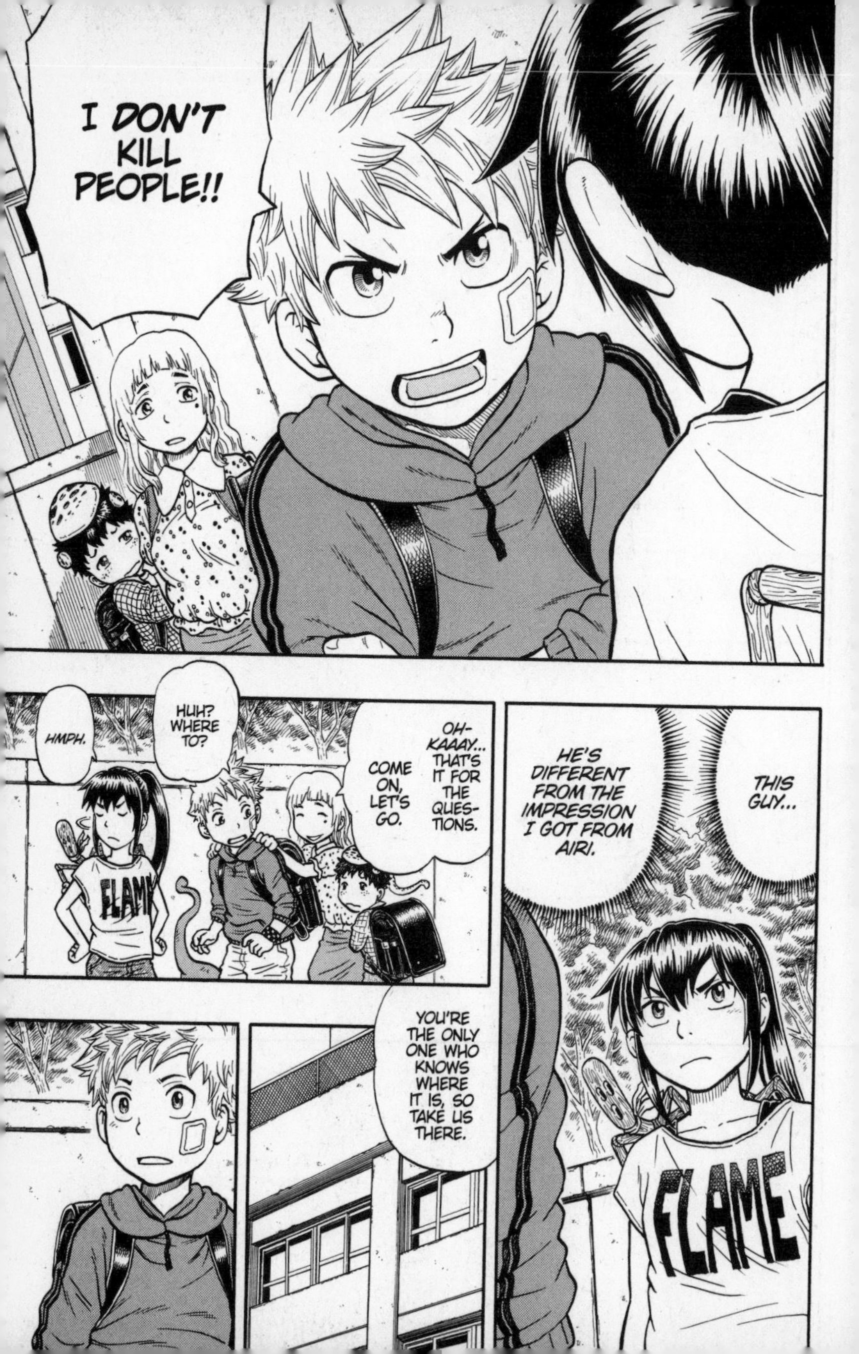
I DON'T KILL PEOPLE!!
THIS GUY...
HE'S DIFFERENT FROM THE IMPRESSION I GOT FROM AIRI.
OH-KAAAY... THAT'S IT FOR THE QUES-TIONS.
COME ON, LET'S GO.
HUH? WHERE TO?
HMPH.
YOU'RE THE ONLY ONE WHO KNOWS WHERE IT IS, SO TAKE US THERE.
FLAME

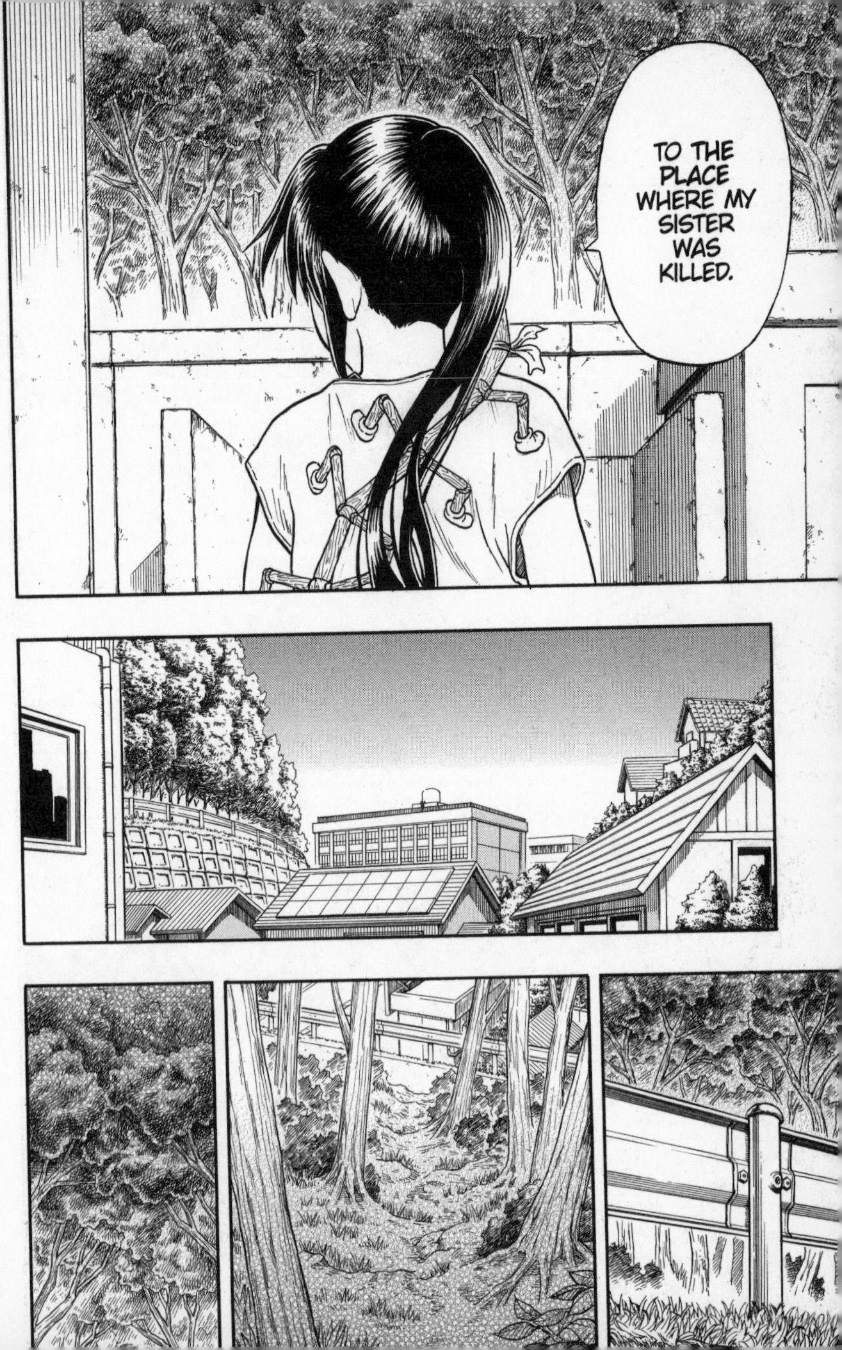
TO THE PLACE WHERE MY SISTER WAS KILLED.

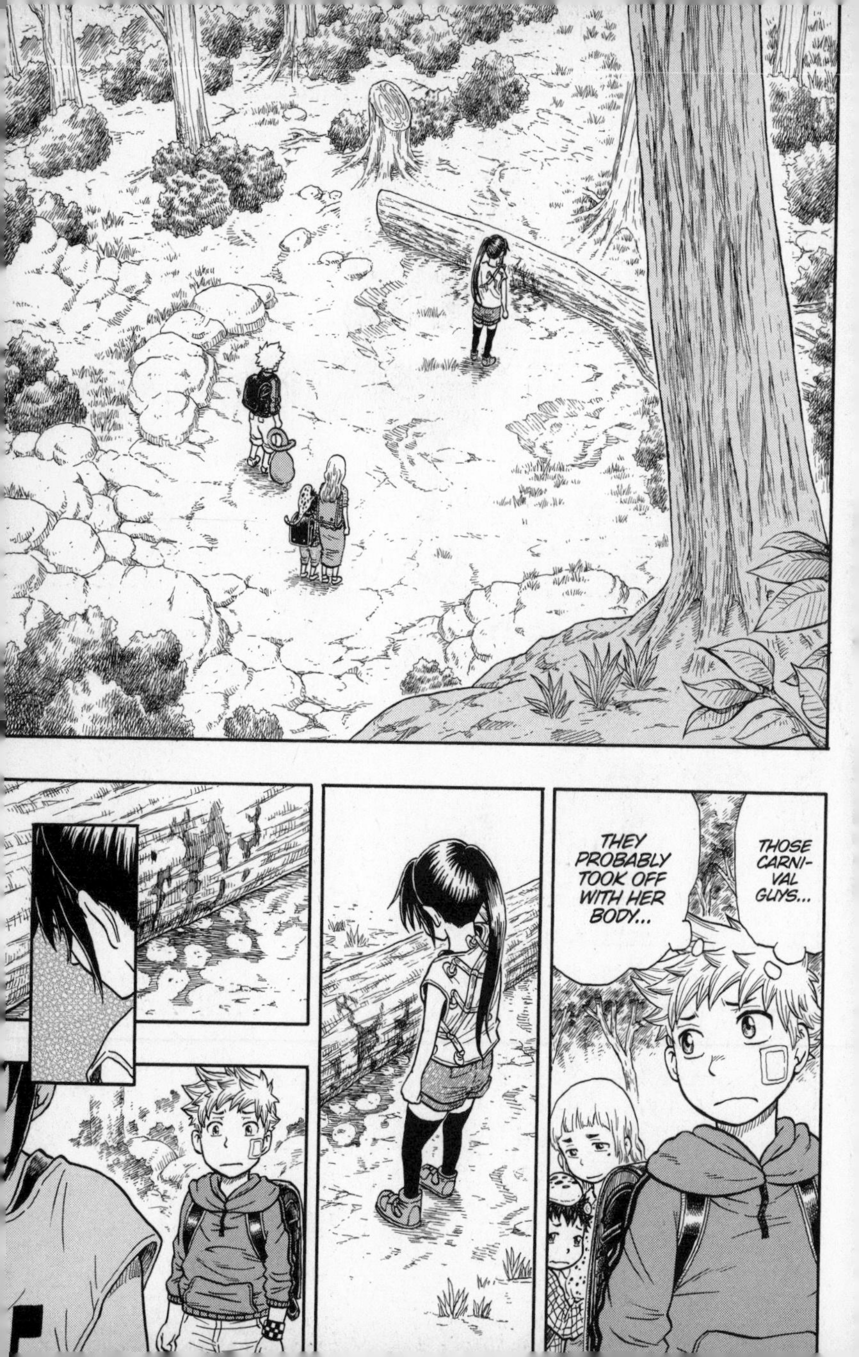
THOSE CARNI-VAL GUYS...
THEY PROBABLY TOOK OFF WITH HER BODY...

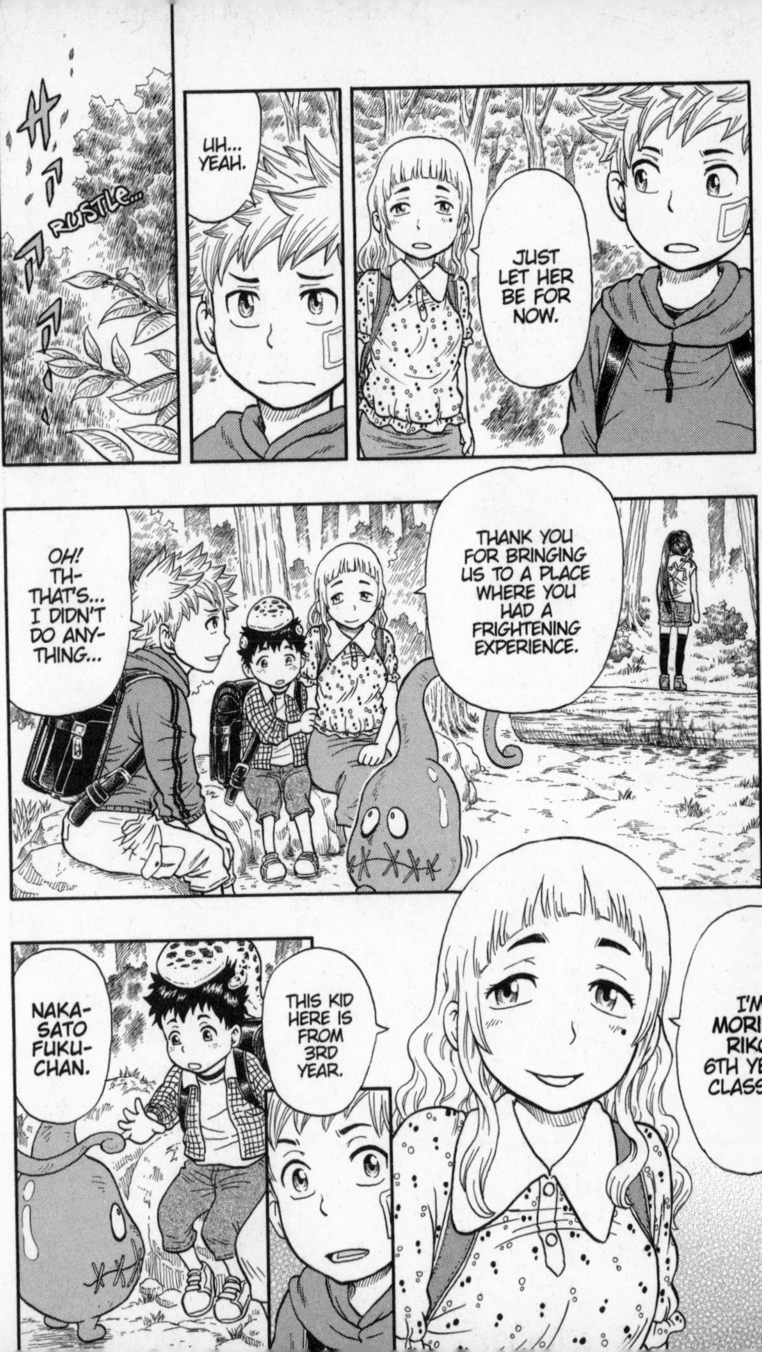
JUST LET HER BE FOR NOW.
UH... YEAH.
RUSTLE...
THANK YOU FOR BRINGING US TO A PLACE WHERE YOU HAD A FRIGHTENING EXPERIENCE.
OH! TH-THAT'S... I DIDN'T DO ANY-THING...
I'M MORINO RIKO, 6TH YEAR, CLASS 4.
THIS KID HERE IS FROM 3RD YEAR.
NAKA-SATO FUKU-CHAN.

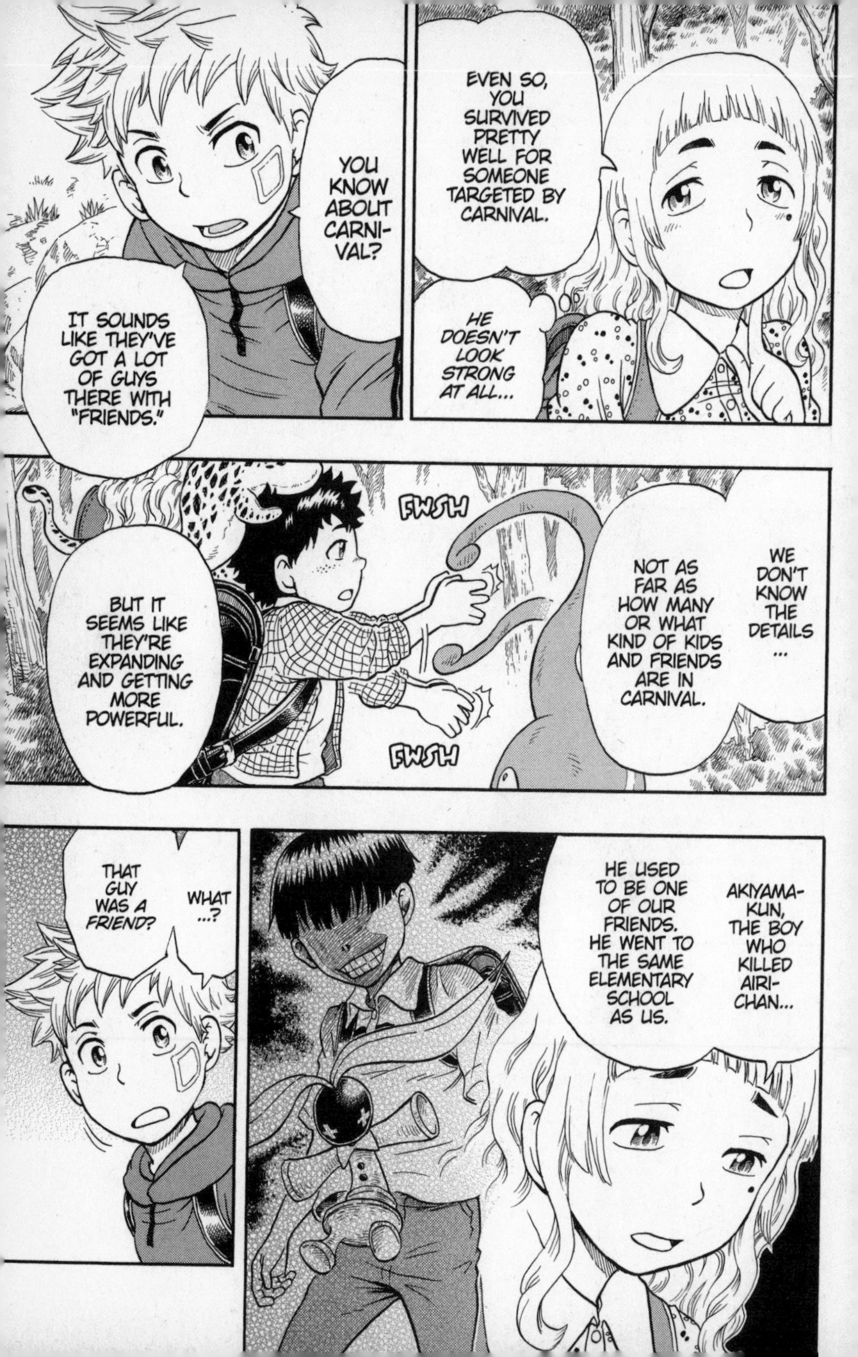
EVEN SO, YOU SURVIVED PRETTY WELL FOR SOMEONE TARGETED BY CARNIVAL.
HE DOESN'T LOOK STRONG AT ALL...
YOU KNOW ABOUT CARNI-VAL?
IT SOUNDS LIKE THEY'VE GOT A LOT OF GUYS THERE WITH "FRIENDS."
WE DON'T KNOW THE DETAILS...
NOT AS FAR AS HOW MANY OR WHAT KIND OF KIDS AND FRIENDS ARE IN CARNIVAL.
FWSH
FWSH
BUT IT SEEMS LIKE THEY'RE EXPANDING AND GETTING MORE POWERFUL.
AKIYAMA-KUN, THE BOY WHO KILLED AIRI-CHAN...
HE USED TO BE ONE OF OUR FRIENDS. HE WENT TO THE SAME ELEMENTARY SCHOOL AS US.
WHAT ...?
THAT GUY WAS A FRIEND?

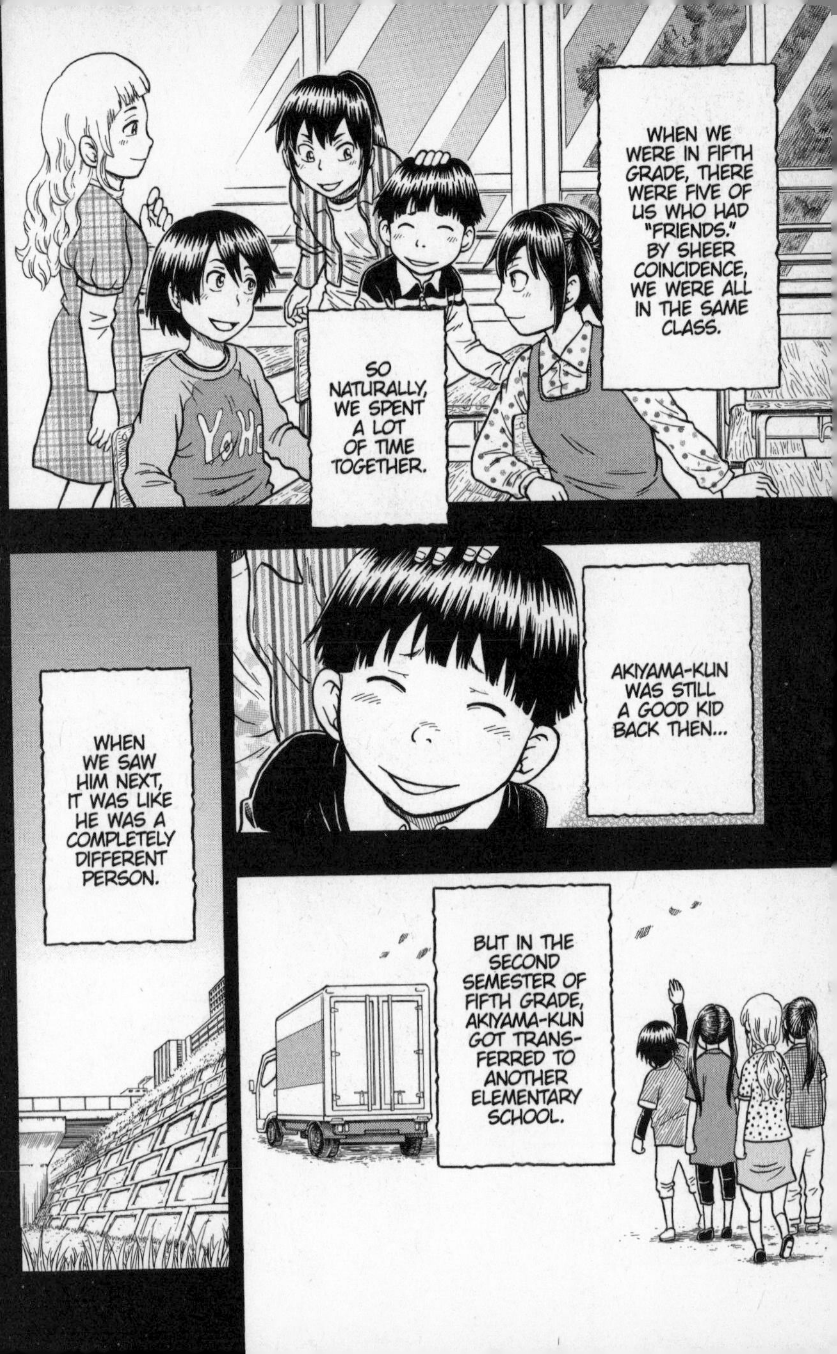
WHEN WE WERE IN FIFTH GRADE, THERE WERE FIVE OF US WHO HAD "FRIENDS." BY SHEER COINCIDENCE, WE WERE ALL IN THE SAME CLASS.
SO NATURALLY, WE SPENT A LOT OF TIME TOGETHER.
AKIYAMA-KUN WAS STILL A GOOD KID BACK THEN...
BUT IN THE SECOND SEMESTER OF FIFTH GRADE, AKIYAMA-KUN GOT TRANS-FERRED TO ANOTHER ELEMENTARY SCHOOL.
WHEN WE SAW HIM NEXT, IT WAS LIKE HE WAS A COMPLETELY DIFFERENT PERSON.

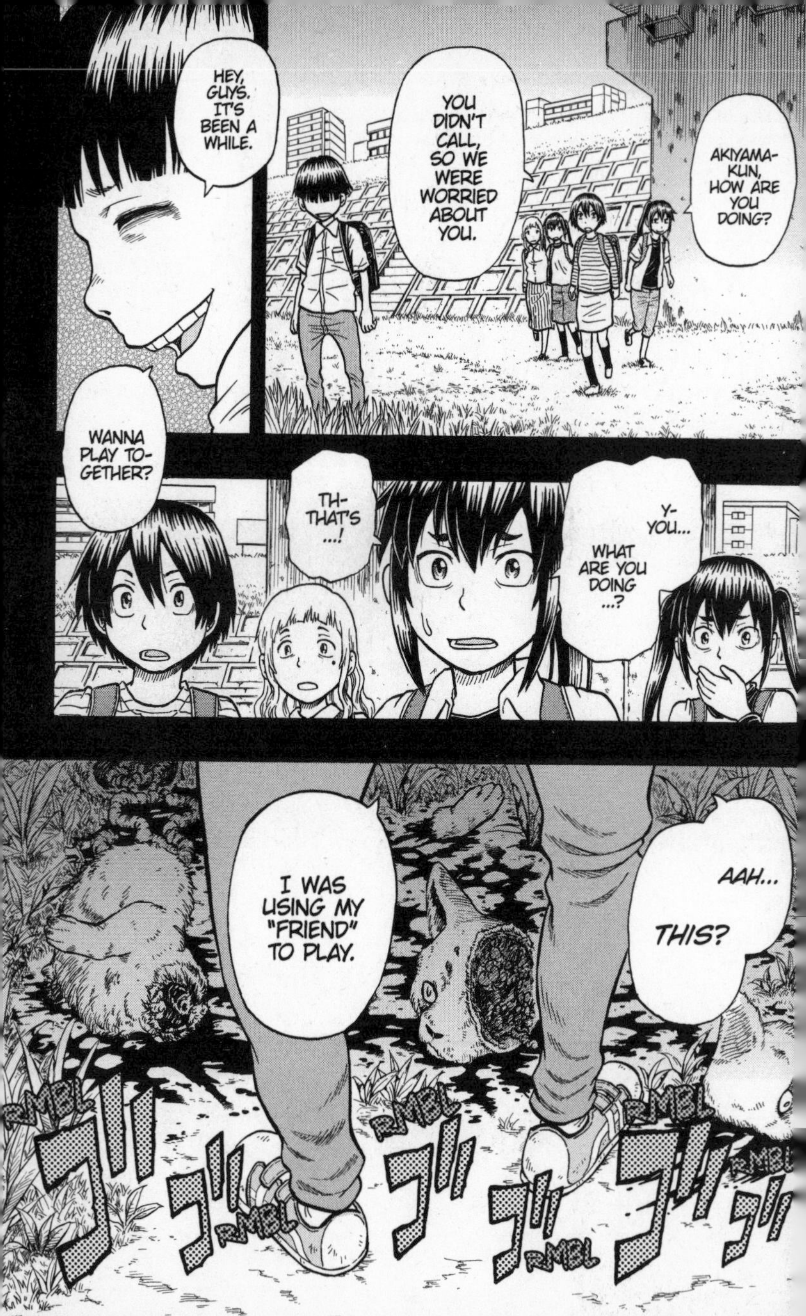
AKIYAMA-KUN, HOW ARE YOU DOING?
YOU DIDN'T CALL, SO WE WERE WORRIED ABOUT YOU.
HEY, GUYS. IT'S BEEN A WHILE.
WANNA PLAY TO-GETHER?
Y-YOU...
WHAT ARE YOU DOING ...?
TH-THAT'S ...!
AAH...
THIS?
I WAS USING MY "FRIEND" TO PLAY.
RMBL
RMBL
RMBL
RMBL
RMBL
RMBL

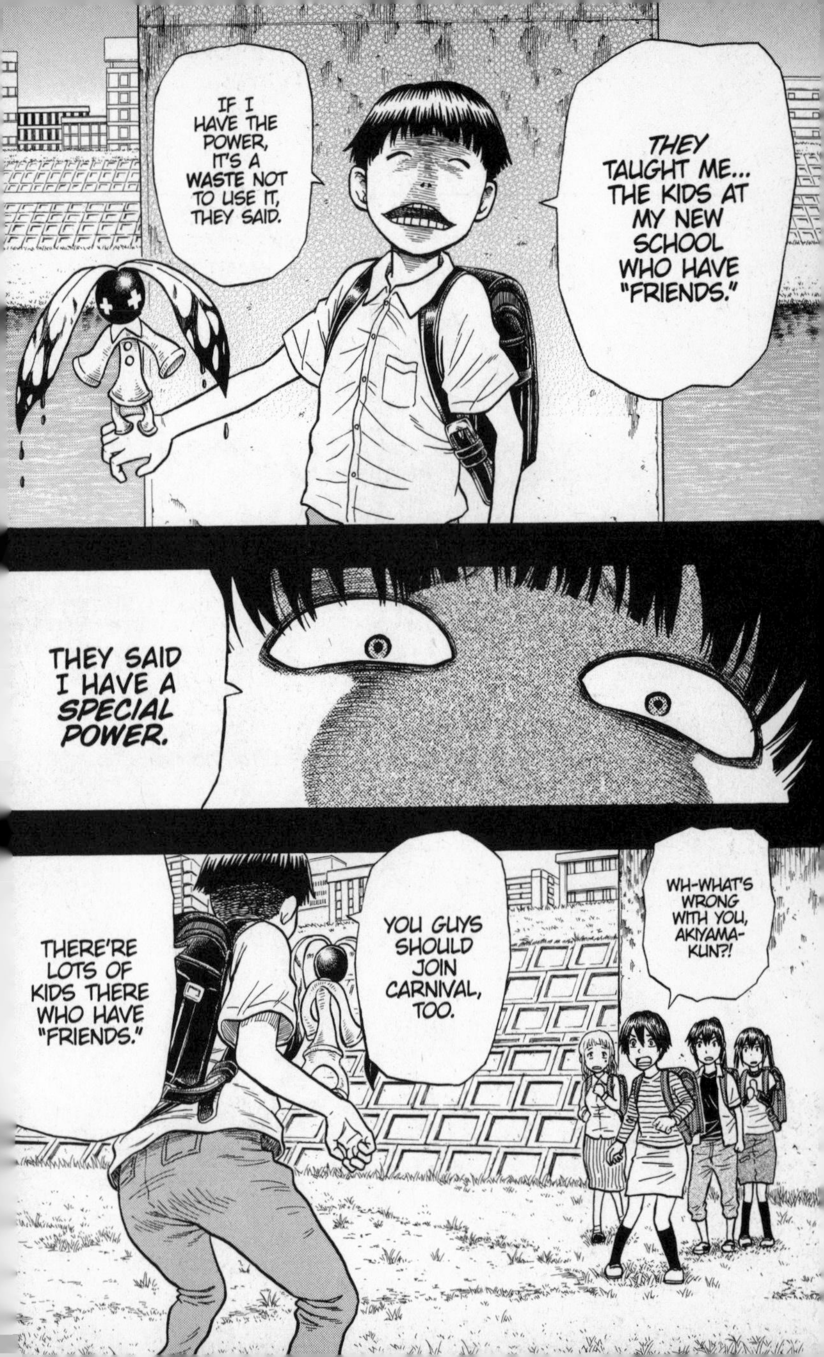
THEY TAUGHT ME... THE KIDS AT MY NEW SCHOOL WHO HAVE "FRIENDS."
IF I HAVE THE POWER, IT'S A WASTE NOT TO USE IT, THEY SAID.
THEY SAID I HAVE A *SPECIAL POWER.*
WH-WHAT'S WRONG WITH YOU, AKIYAMA-KUN?!
YOU GUYS SHOULD JOIN CARNIVAL, TOO.
THERE'RE LOTS OF KIDS THERE WHO HAVE "FRIENDS."

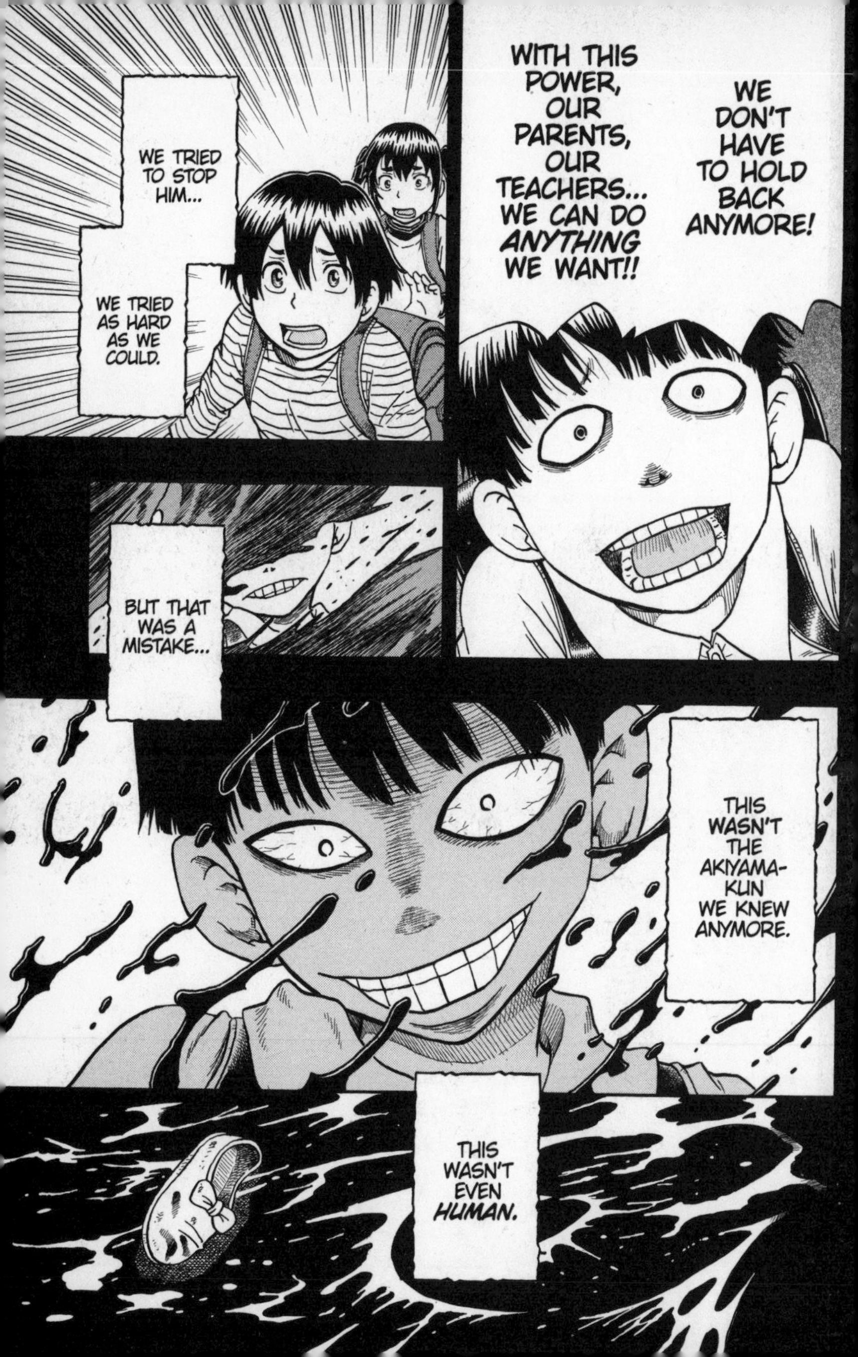
WE DON'T HAVE TO HOLD BACK ANYMORE!
WITH THIS POWER, OUR PARENTS, OUR TEACHERS... WE CAN DO *ANYTHING* WE WANT!!
WE TRIED TO STOP HIM...
WE TRIED AS HARD AS WE COULD.
BUT THAT WAS A MISTAKE...
THIS WASN'T THE AKIYAMA-KUN WE KNEW ANYMORE.
THIS WASN'T EVEN *HUMAN*.

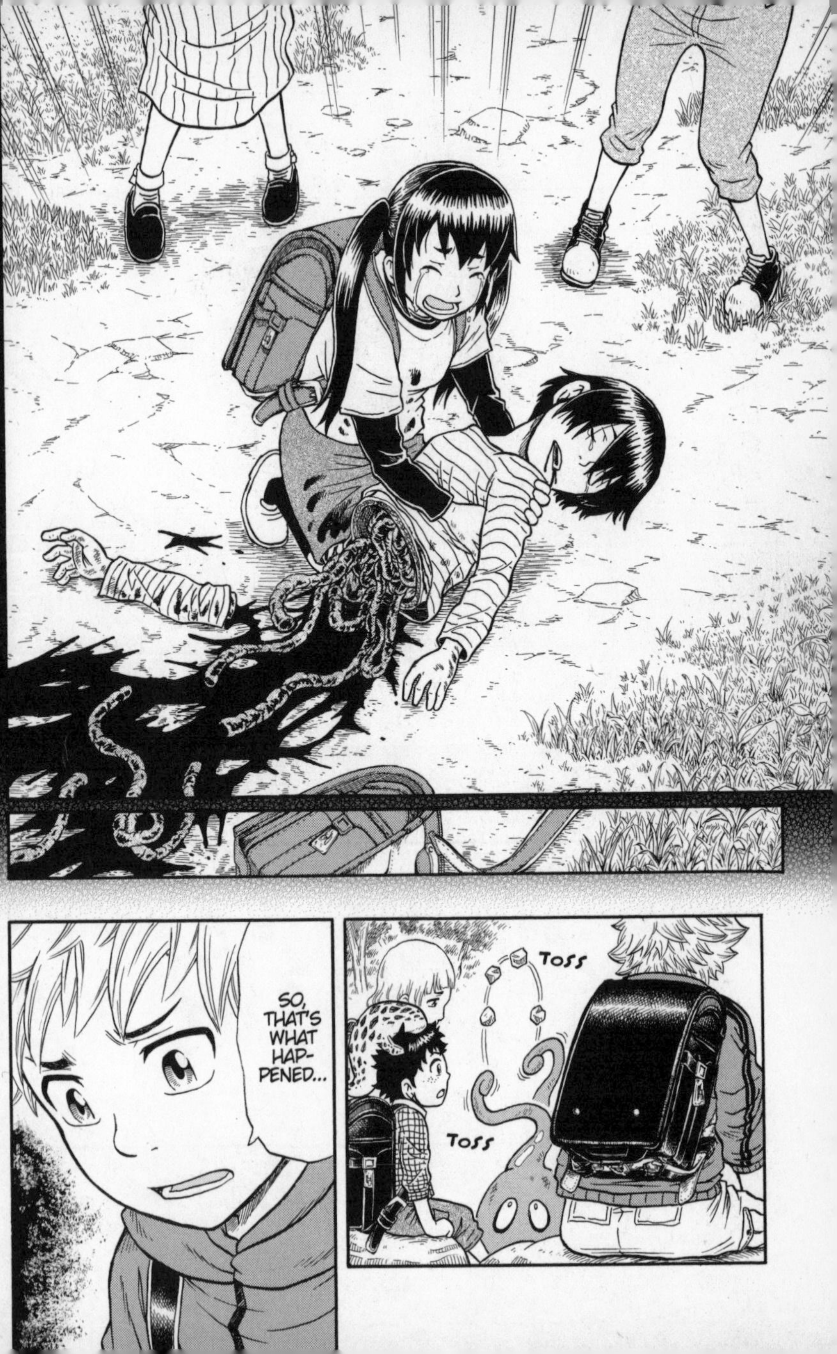
TOSS
TOSS
SO, THAT'S WHAT HAP-PENED...

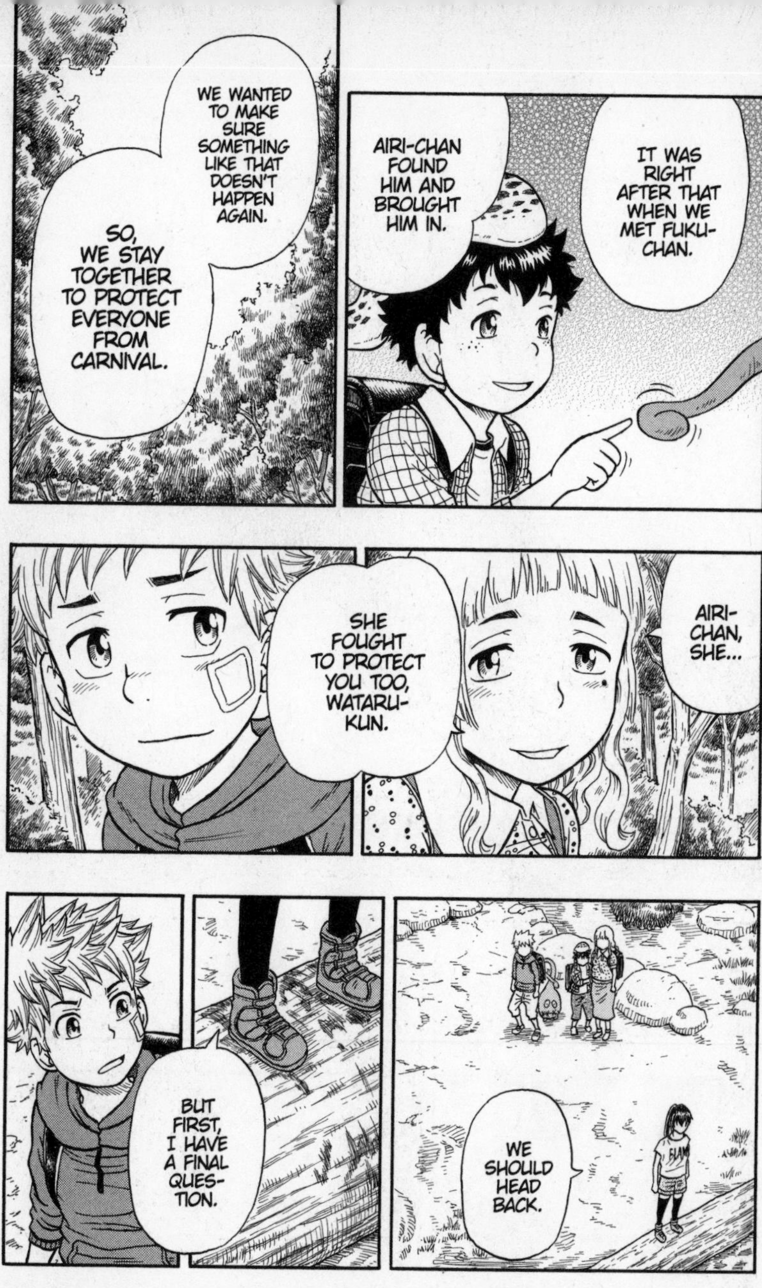
IT WAS RIGHT AFTER THAT WHEN WE MET FUKU-CHAN.
AIRI-CHAN FOUND HIM AND BROUGHT HIM IN.
WE WANTED TO MAKE SURE SOMETHING LIKE THAT DOESN'T HAPPEN AGAIN.
SO, WE STAY TOGETHER TO PROTECT EVERYONE FROM CARNIVAL.
AIRI-CHAN, SHE...
SHE FOUGHT TO PROTECT YOU TOO, WATARU-KUN.
WE SHOULD HEAD BACK.
BUT FIRST, I HAVE A FINAL QUES-TION.

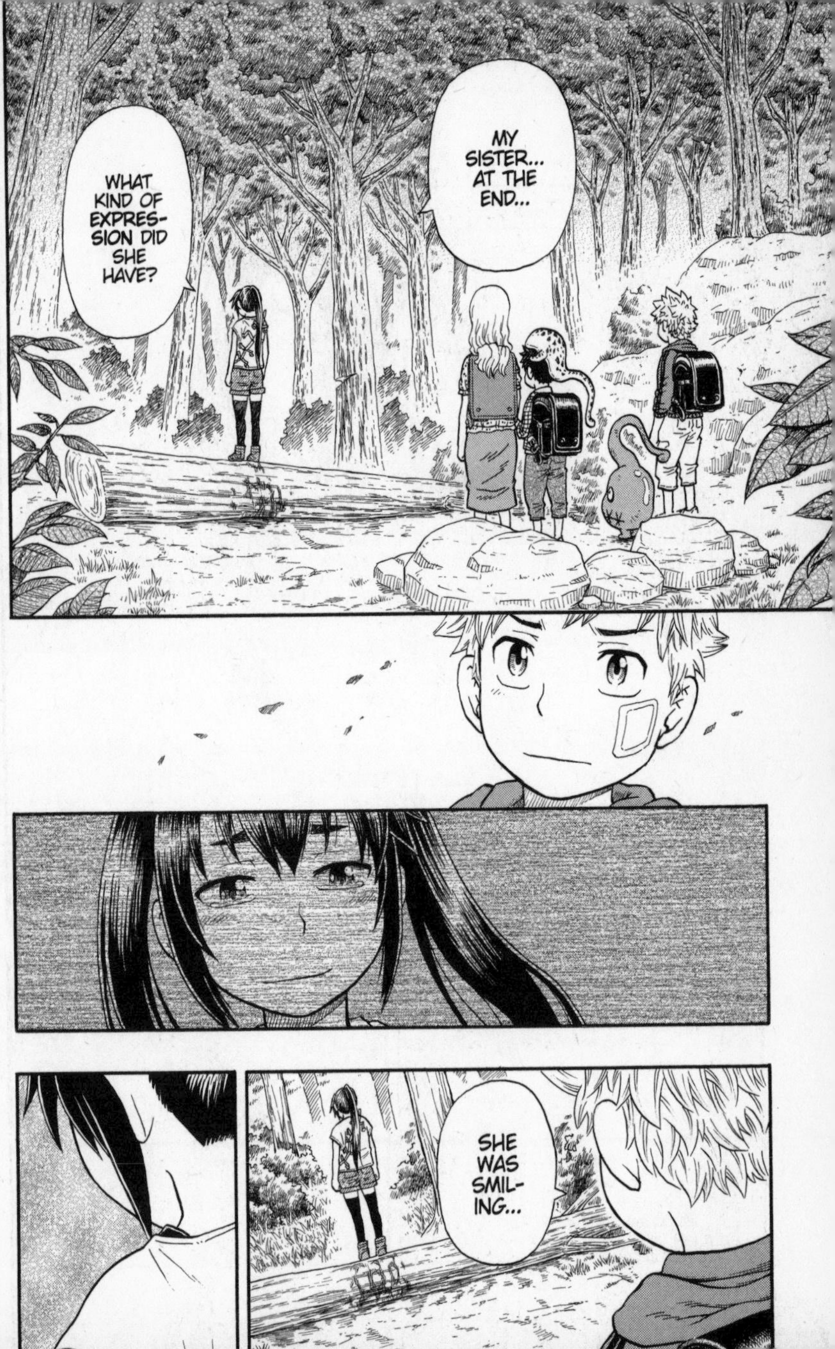
MY SISTER... AT THE END...
WHAT KIND OF EXPRESSION DID SHE HAVE?
SHE WAS SMILING...

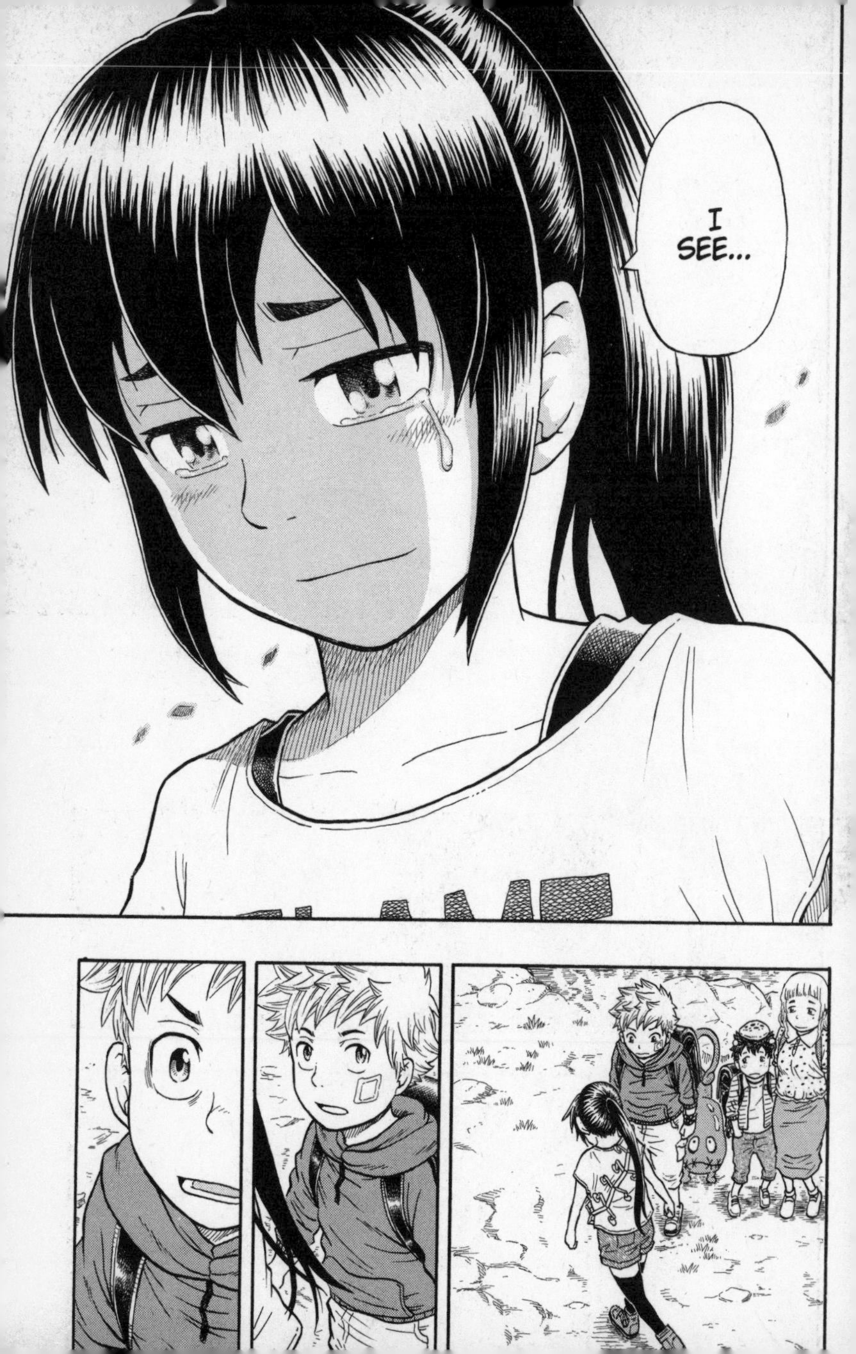
I SEE...

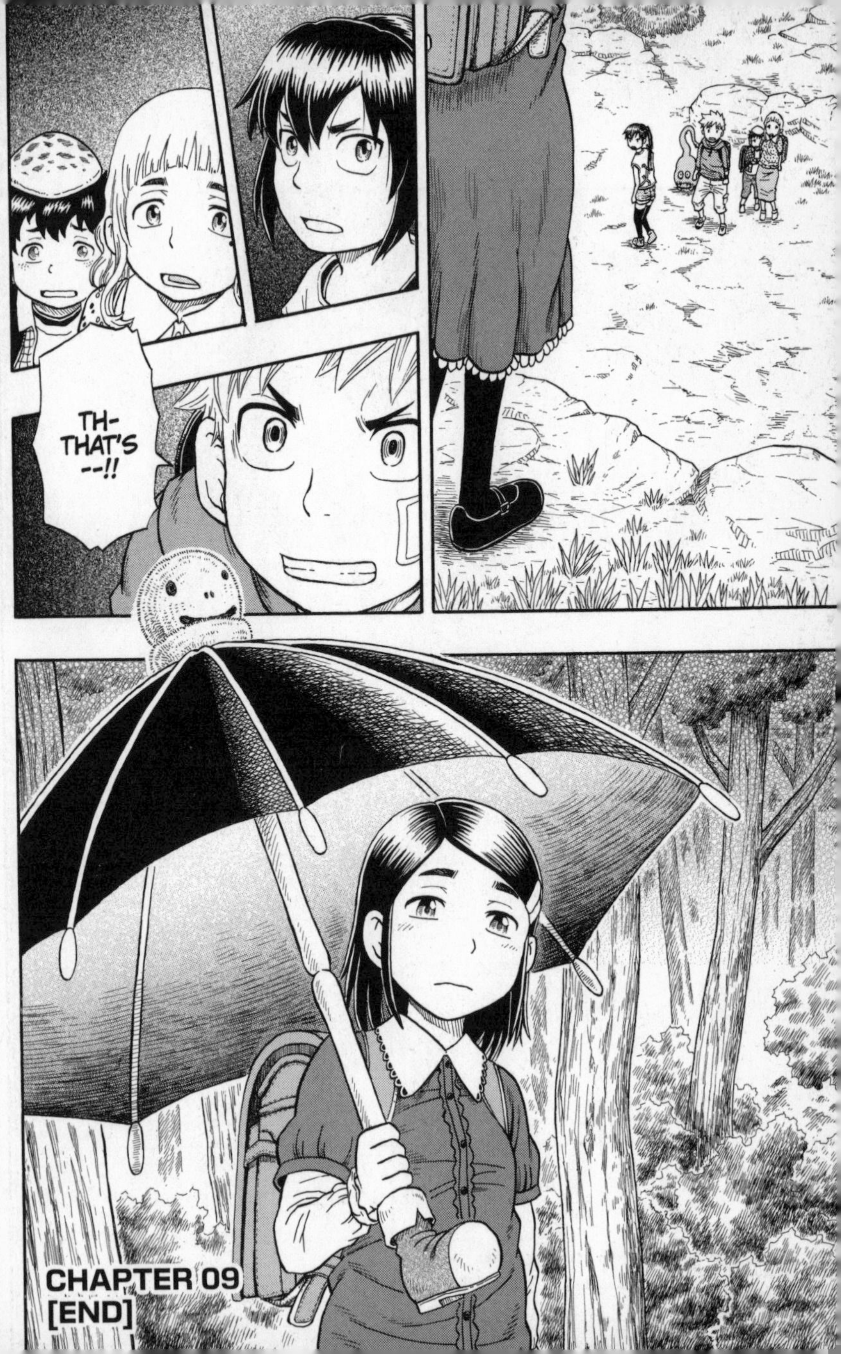
TH-
THAT'S
--!!
CHAPTER 09
[END]

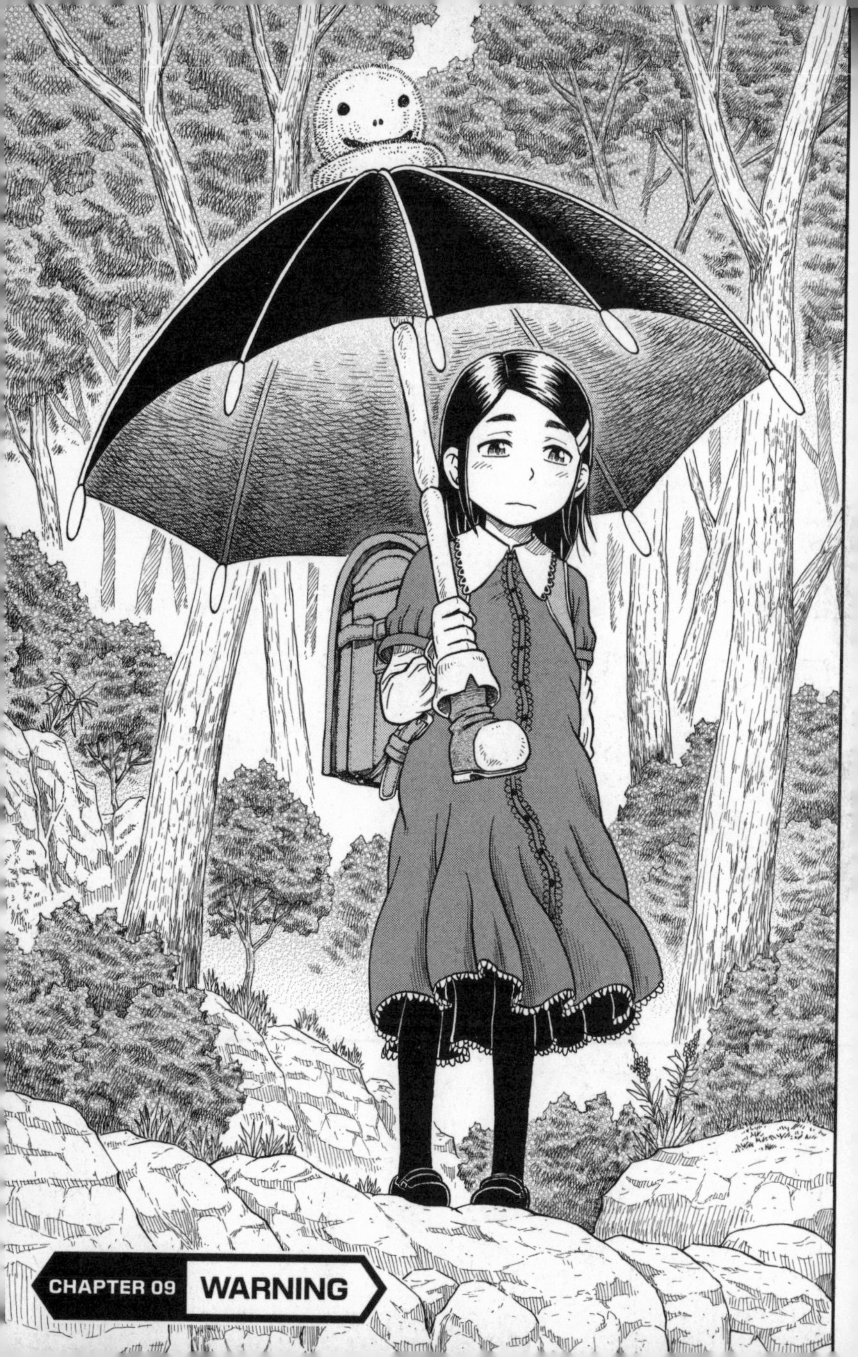
CHAPTER 09
WARNING

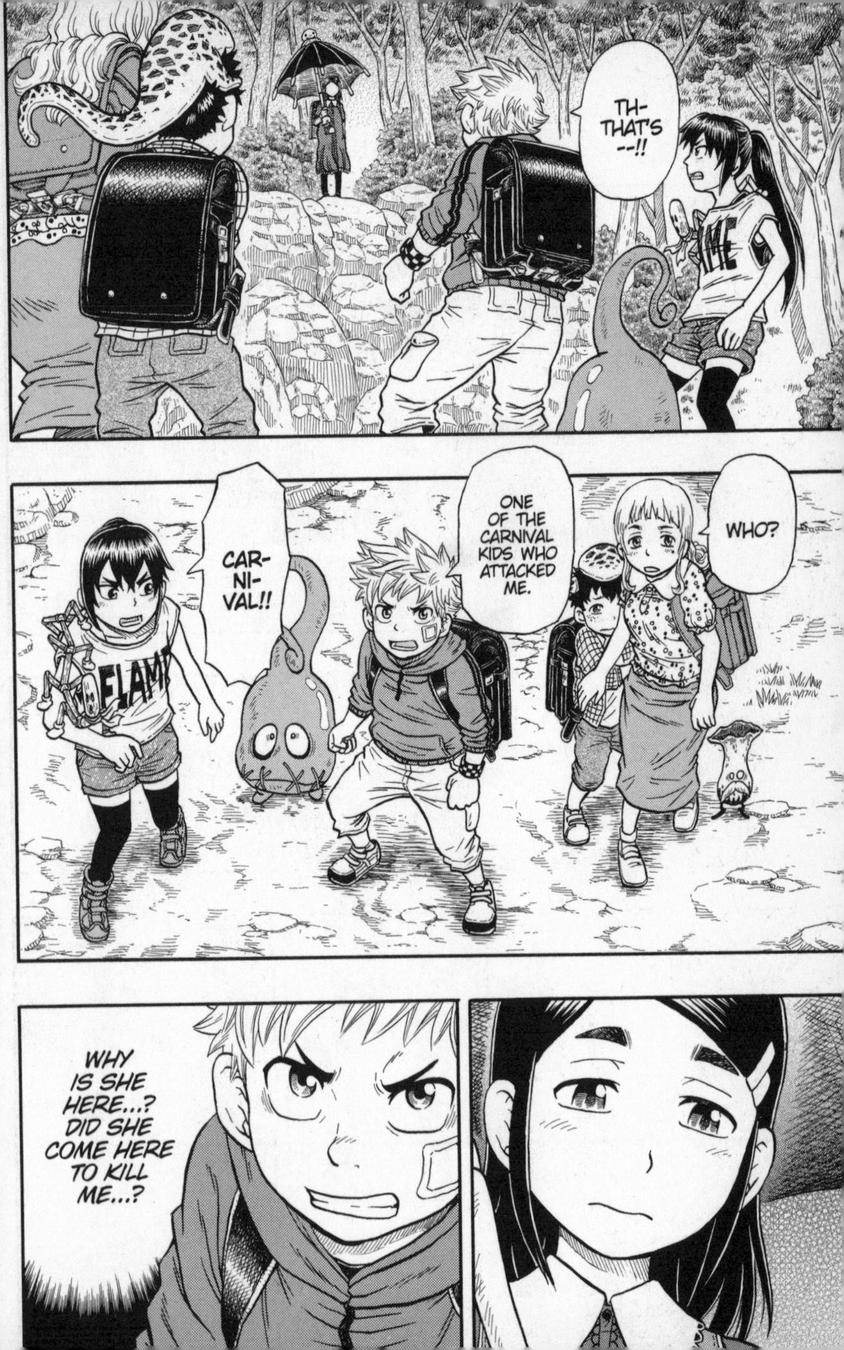
TH- THAT'S --!!
WHO?
ONE OF THE CARNIVAL KIDS WHO ATTACKED ME.
CAR- NI- VAL!!
WHY IS SHE HERE...? DID SHE COME HERE TO KILL ME...?

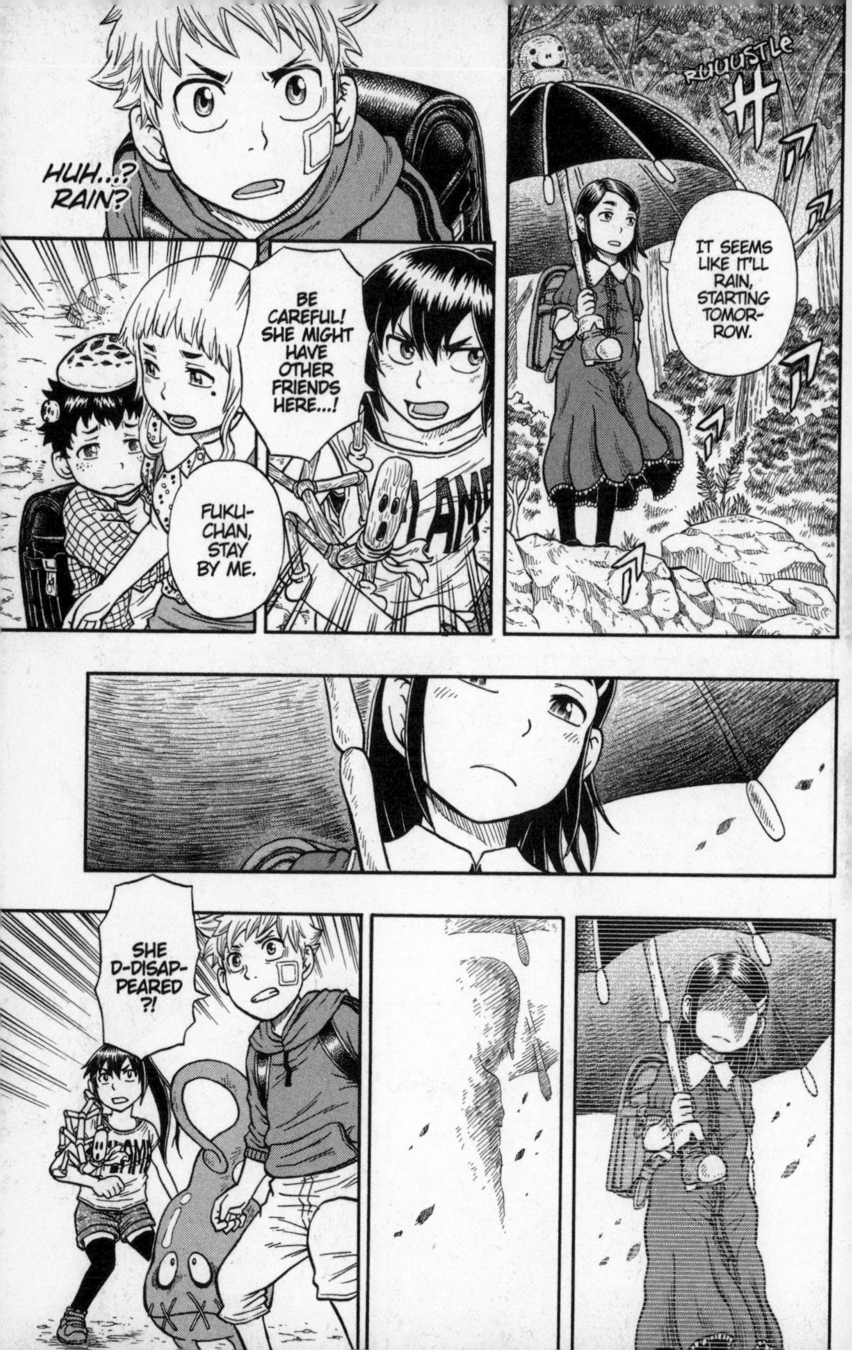
RUUUSTLE
IT SEEMS LIKE IT'LL RAIN, STARTING TOMOR-ROW.
HUH...? RAIN?
BE CAREFUL! SHE MIGHT HAVE OTHER FRIENDS HERE...!
FUKU-CHAN, STAY BY ME.
SHE D-DISAP-PEARED ?!

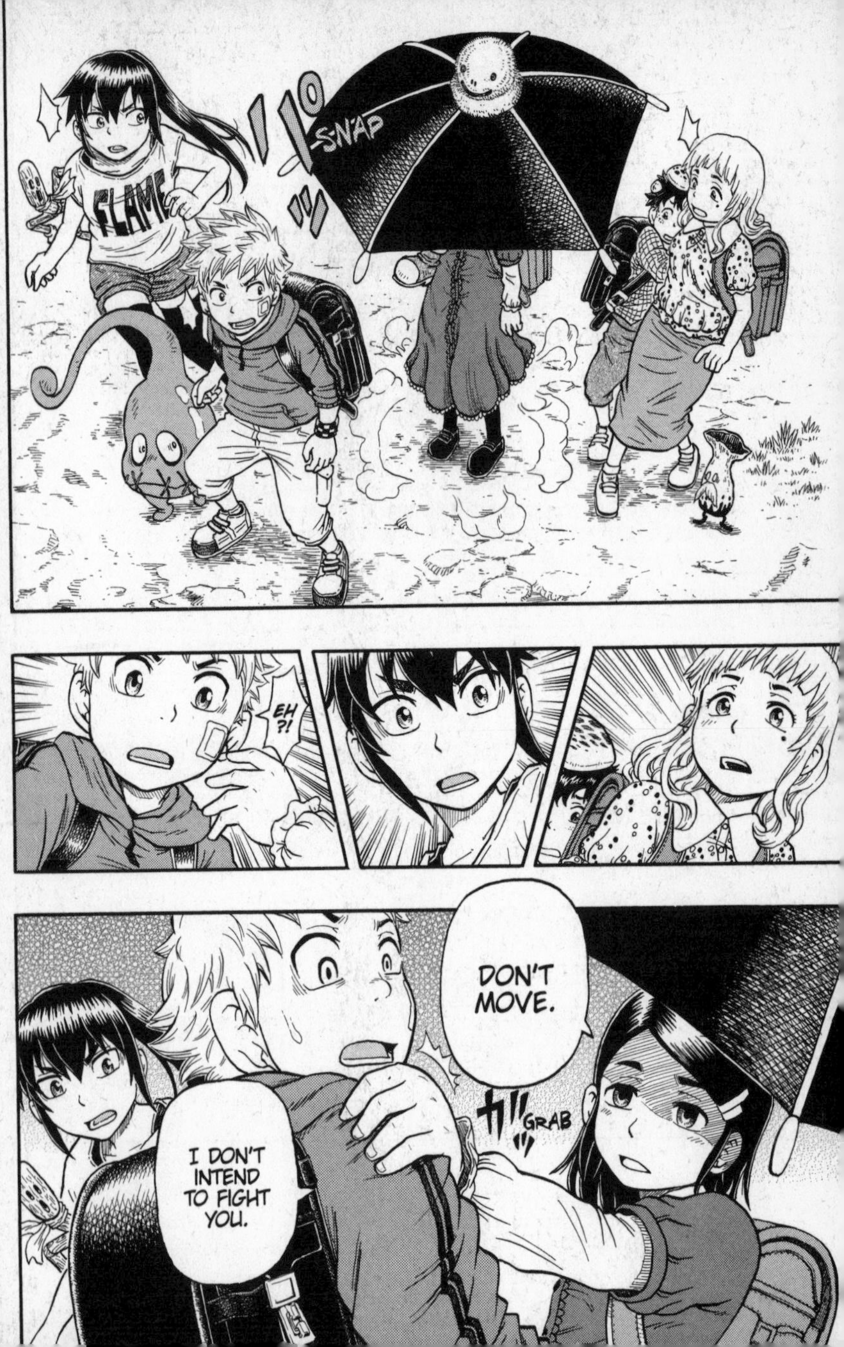
SNAP
EH ?!
DON'T MOVE.
GRAB
I DON'T INTEND TO FIGHT YOU.

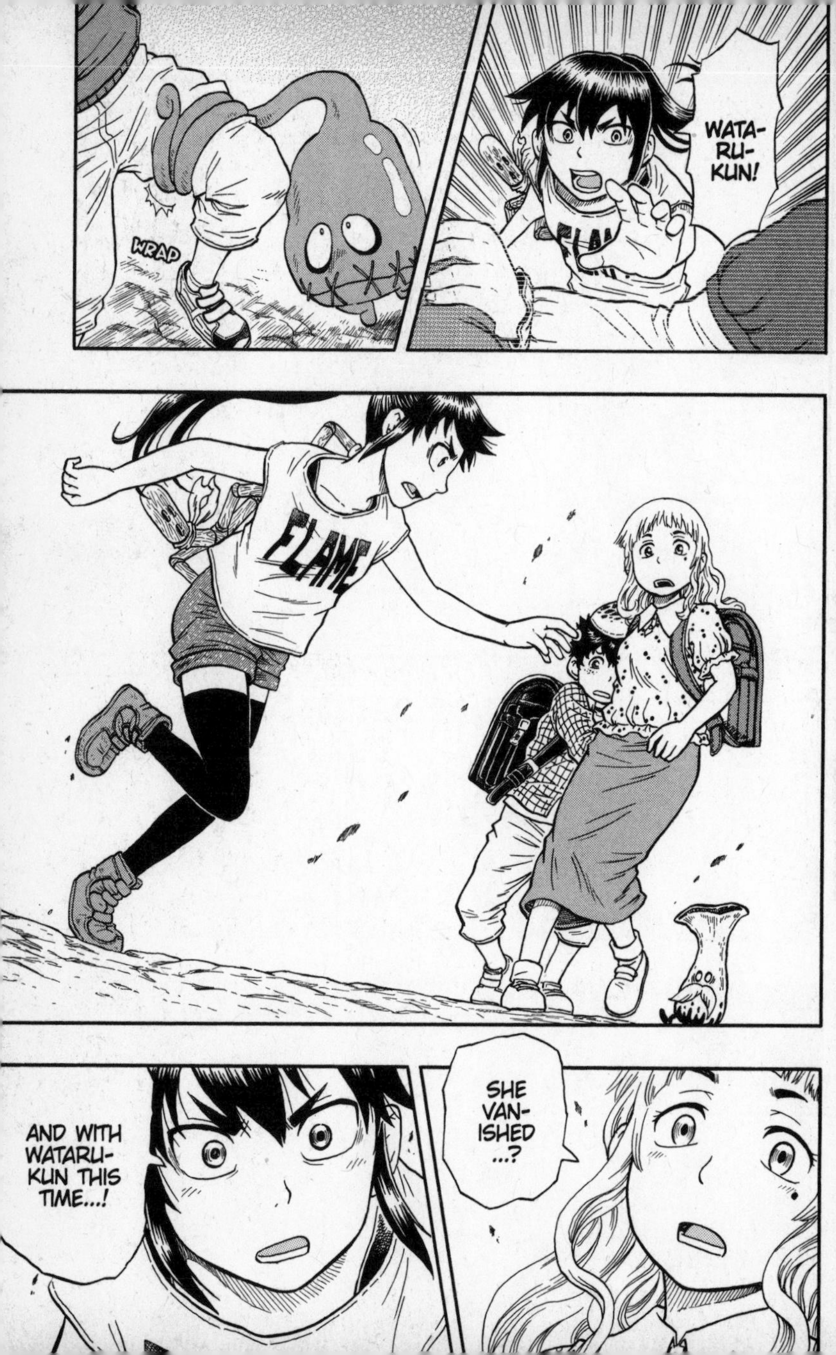
WATA-
RU-
KUN!
WRAP
SHE
VAN-
ISHED
...?
AND WITH
WATARU-
KUN THIS
TIME...!

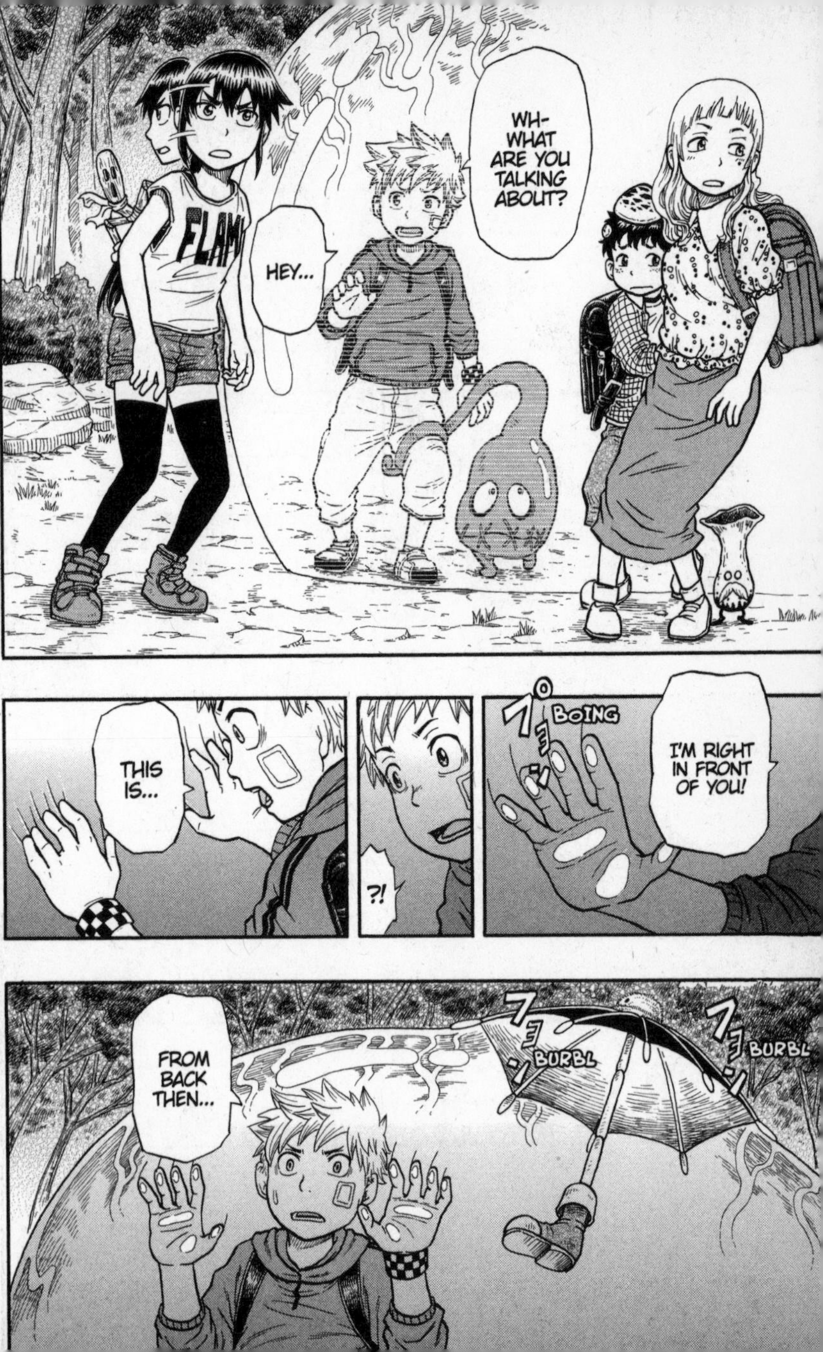
WH- WHAT ARE YOU TALKING ABOUT?
HEY...
BOING
I'M RIGHT IN FRONT OF YOU!
?!
THIS IS...
BURBL
BURBL
FROM BACK THEN...

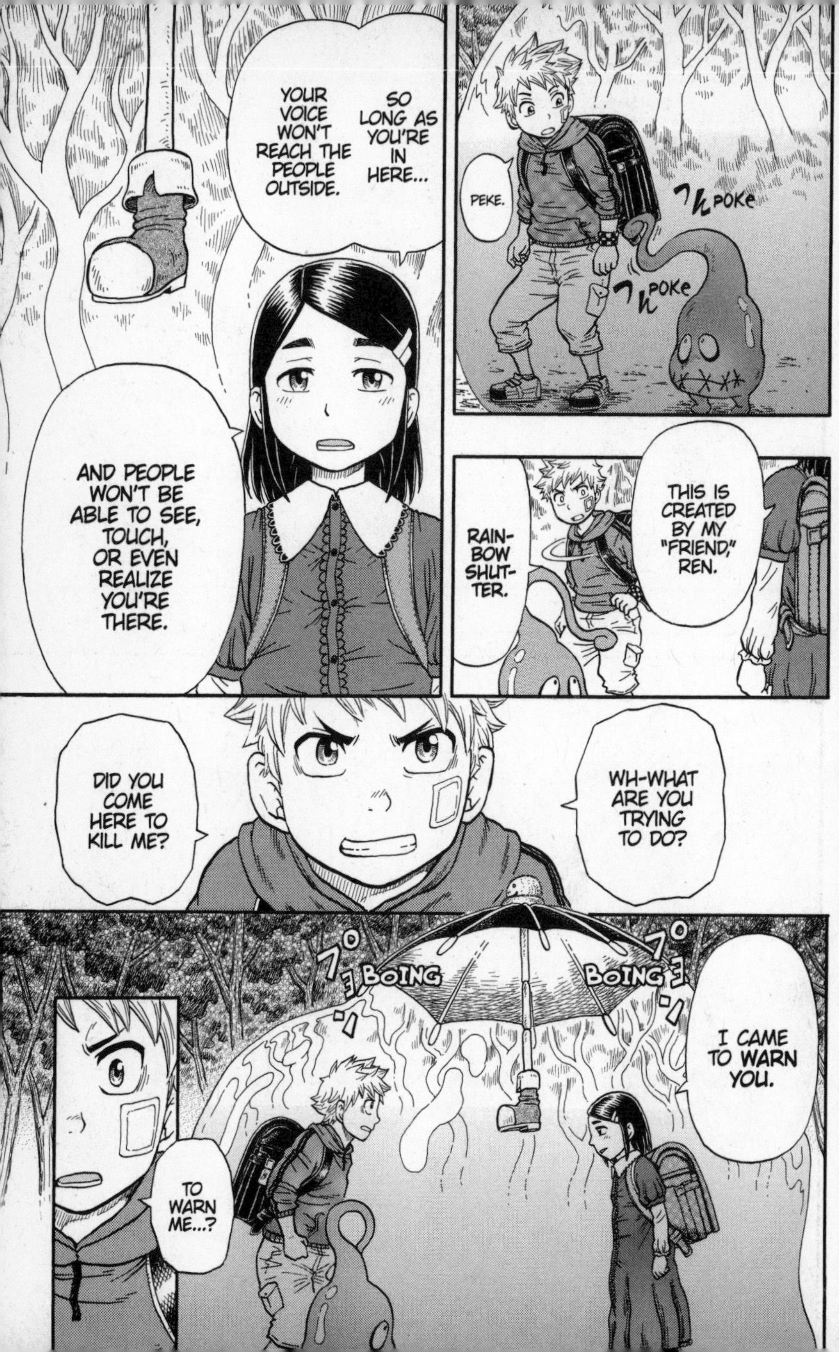

POKE
POKE
PEKE.
THIS IS CREATED BY MY "FRIEND," REN.
RAIN-BOW SHUT-TER.
SO LONG AS YOU'RE IN HERE...
YOUR VOICE WON'T REACH THE PEOPLE OUTSIDE.
AND PEOPLE WON'T BE ABLE TO SEE, TOUCH, OR EVEN REALIZE YOU'RE THERE.
WH-WHAT ARE YOU TRYING TO DO?
DID YOU COME HERE TO KILL ME?
BOING
BOING
I CAME TO WARN YOU.
TO WARN ME...?

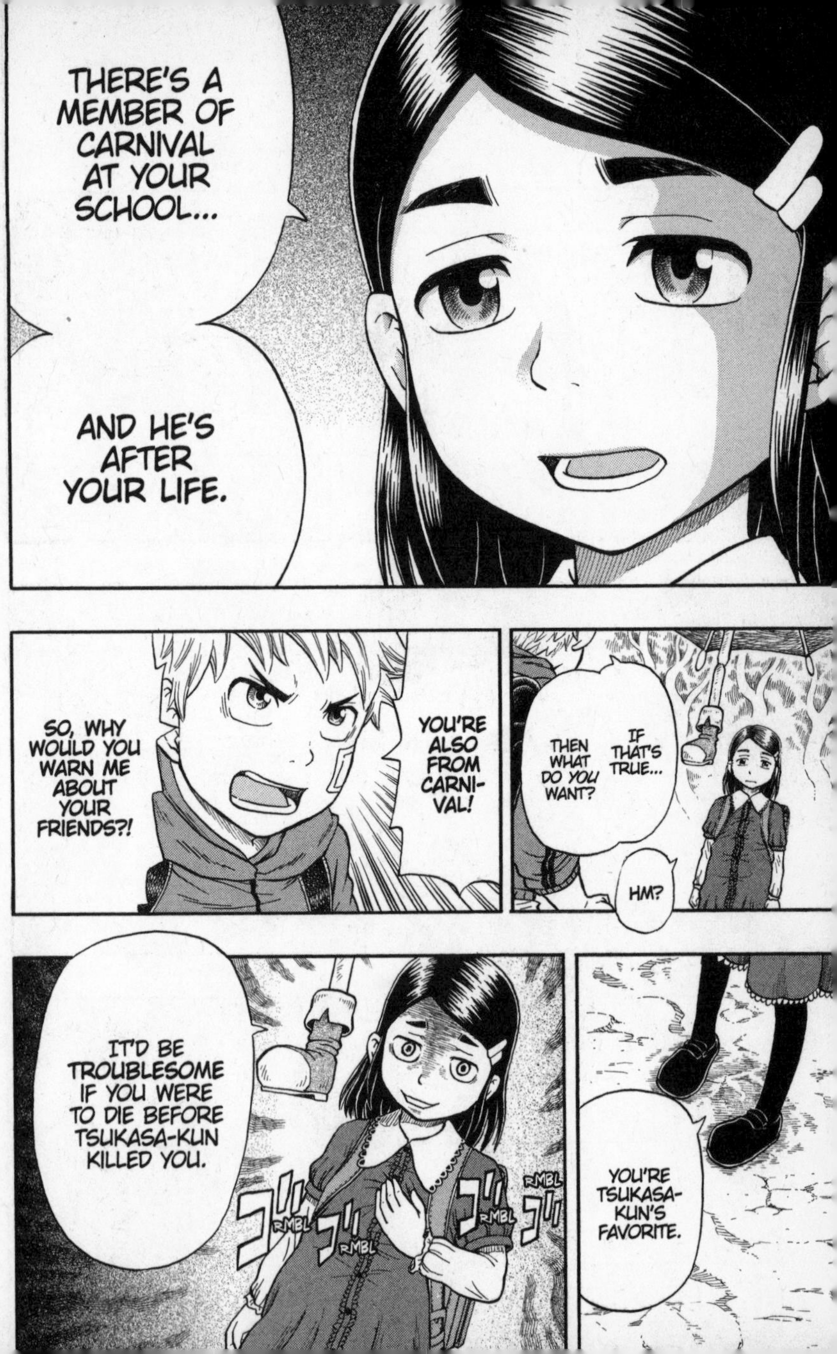
THERE'S A MEMBER OF CARNIVAL AT YOUR SCHOOL...
AND HE'S AFTER YOUR LIFE.
IF THAT'S TRUE...
THEN WHAT DO YOU WANT?
HM?
YOU'RE ALSO FROM CARNIVAL!
SO, WHY WOULD YOU WARN ME ABOUT YOUR FRIENDS?!
YOU'RE TSUKASA-KUN'S FAVORITE.
IT'D BE TROUBLESOME IF YOU WERE TO DIE BEFORE TSUKASA-KUN KILLED YOU.
RMBL
RMBL
RMBL
RMBL

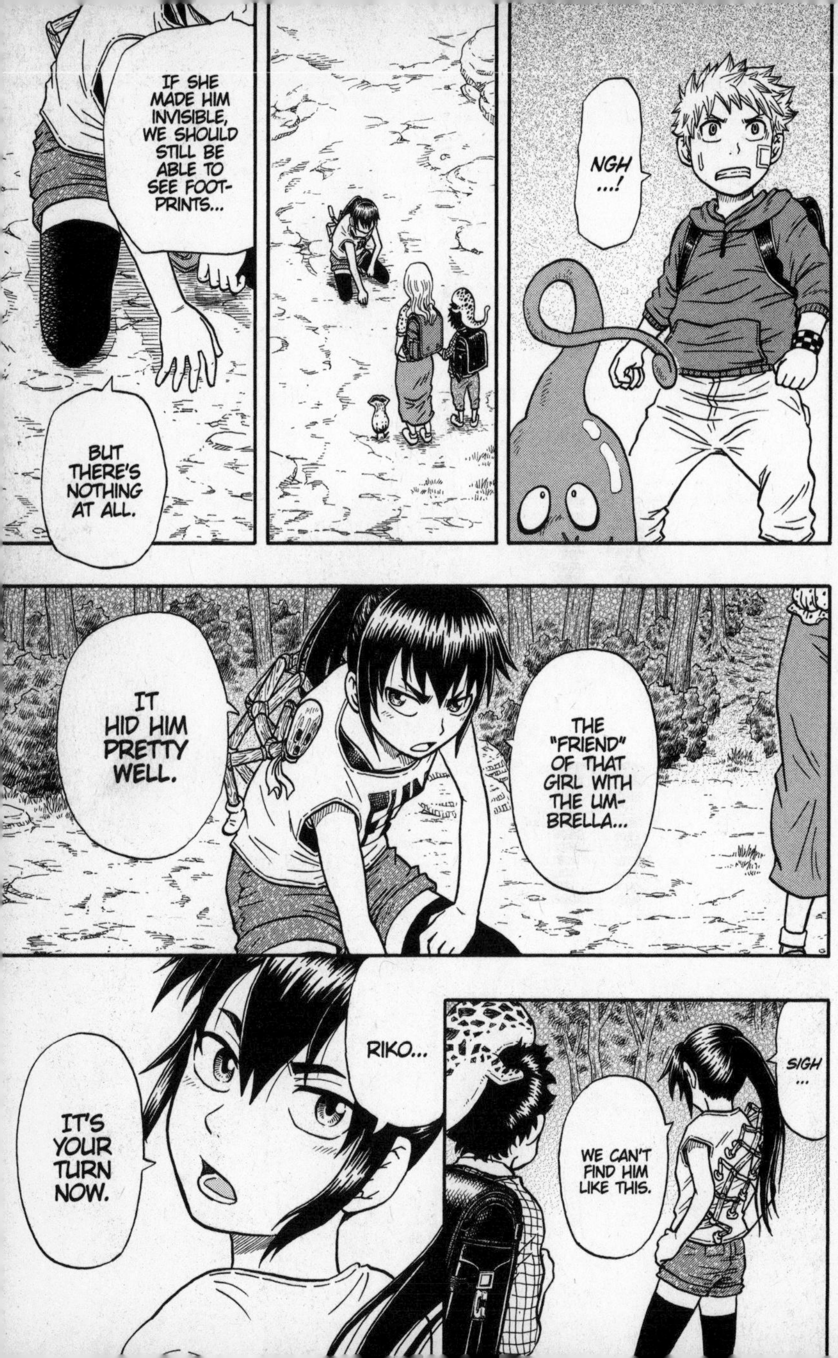
NGH ...!
IF SHE MADE HIM INVISIBLE, WE SHOULD STILL BE ABLE TO SEE FOOT-PRINTS...
BUT THERE'S NOTHING AT ALL.
THE "FRIEND" OF THAT GIRL WITH THE UM-BRELLA...
IT HID HIM PRETTY WELL.
SIGH ...
WE CAN'T FIND HIM LIKE THIS.
RIKO...
IT'S YOUR TURN NOW.

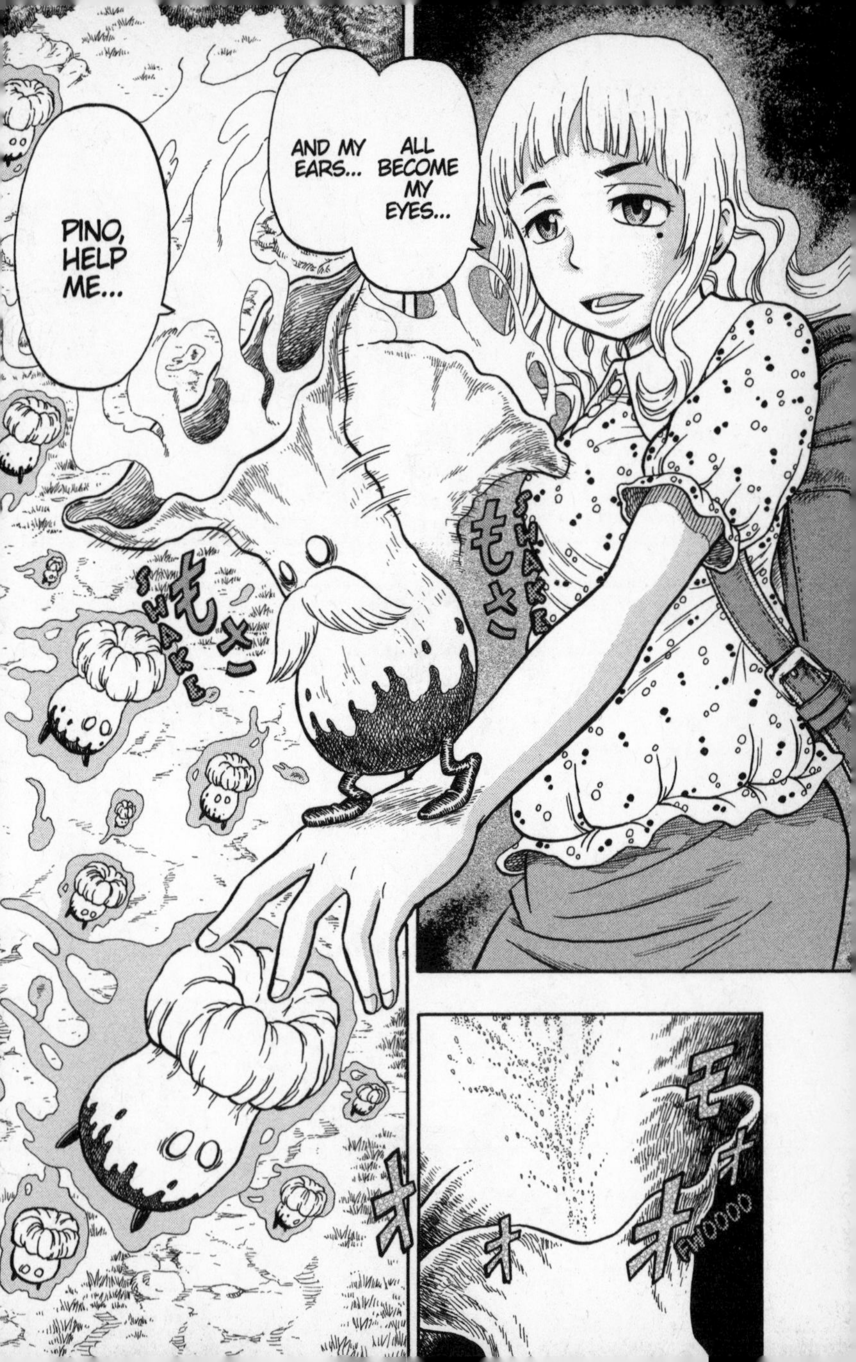

AND MY EARS... ALL BECOME MY EYES...
PINO, HELP ME...
もさ
SHAKE
もさ
SHAKE
モォォォ
FWOOOO

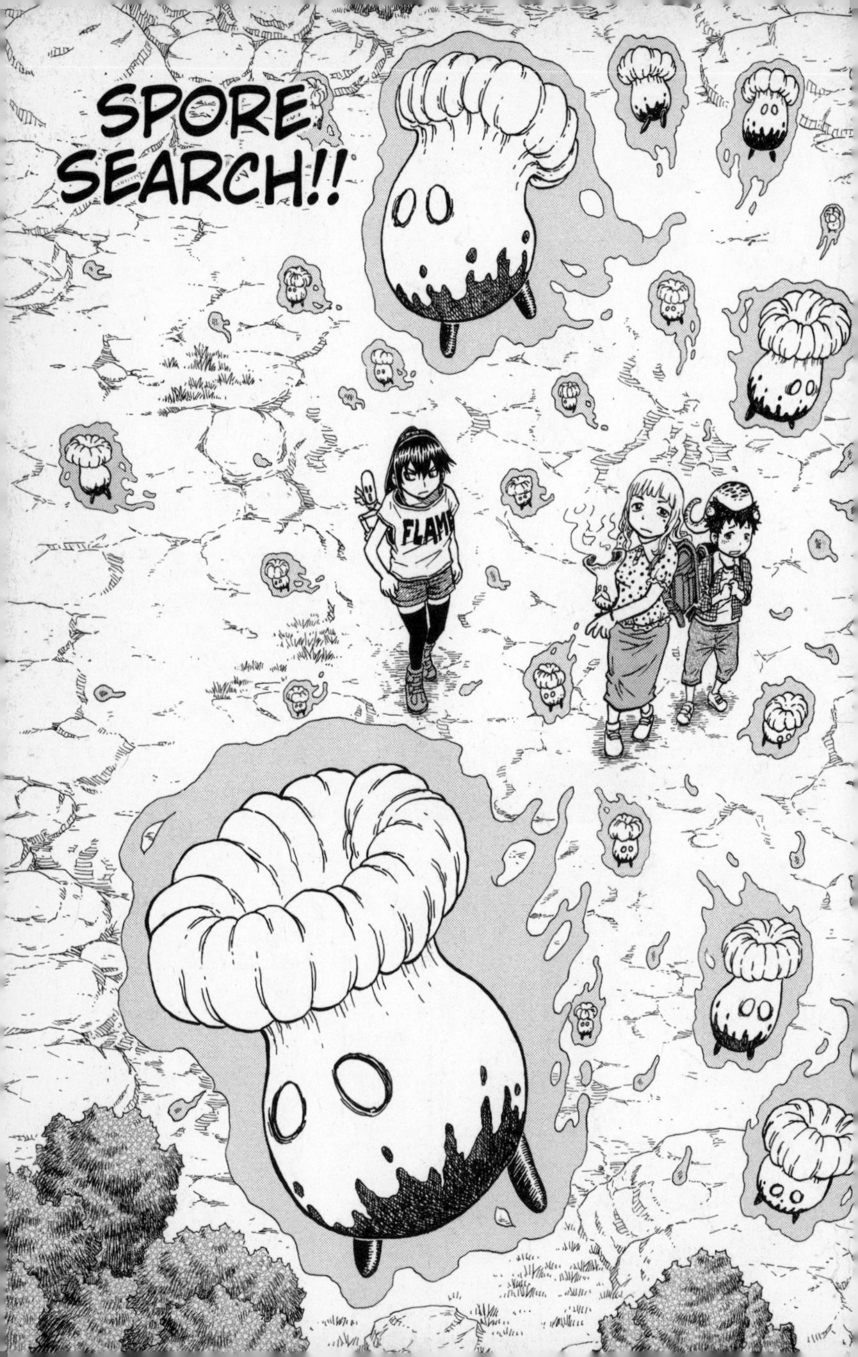
SPORE SEARCH!!

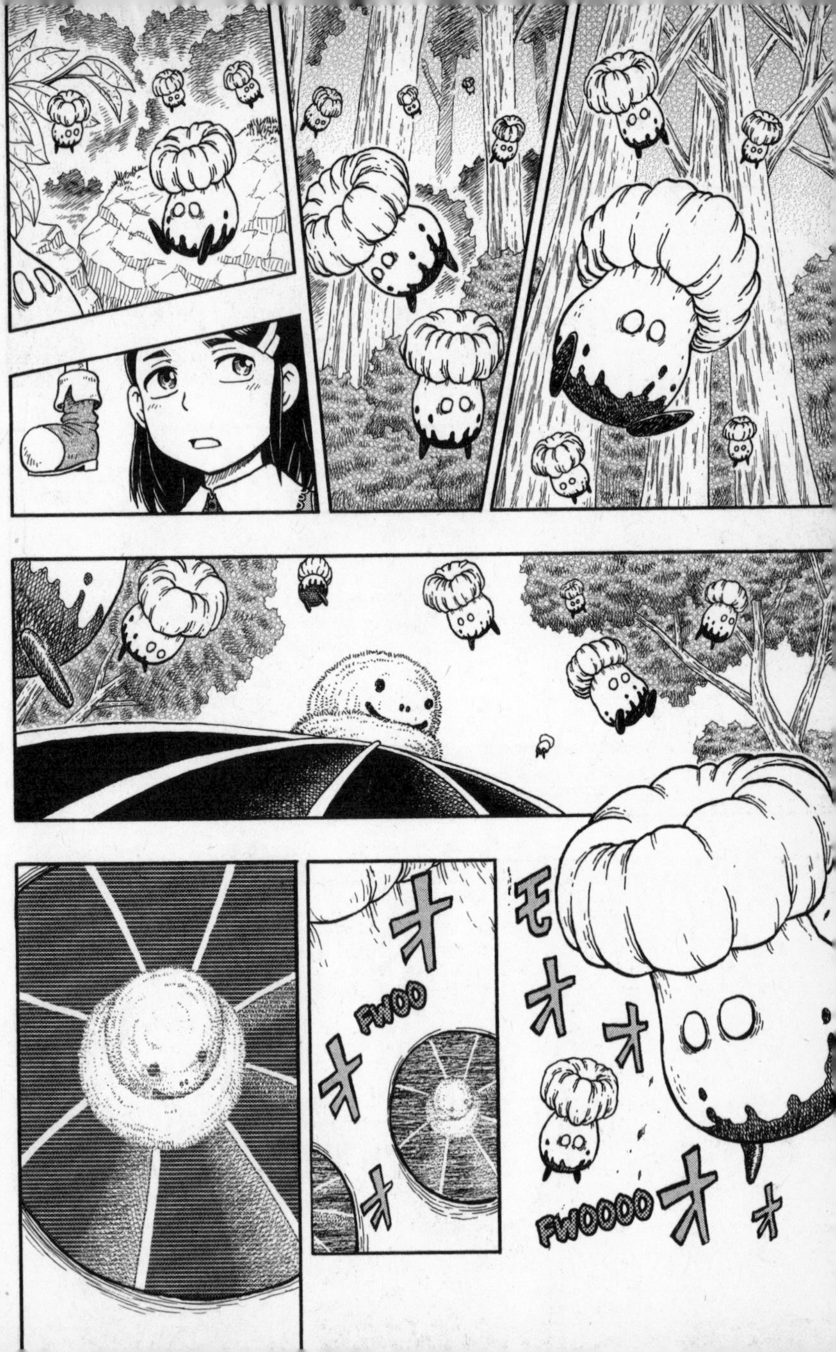
モオオオオオ
FWOOOO
オオオ
FWOO

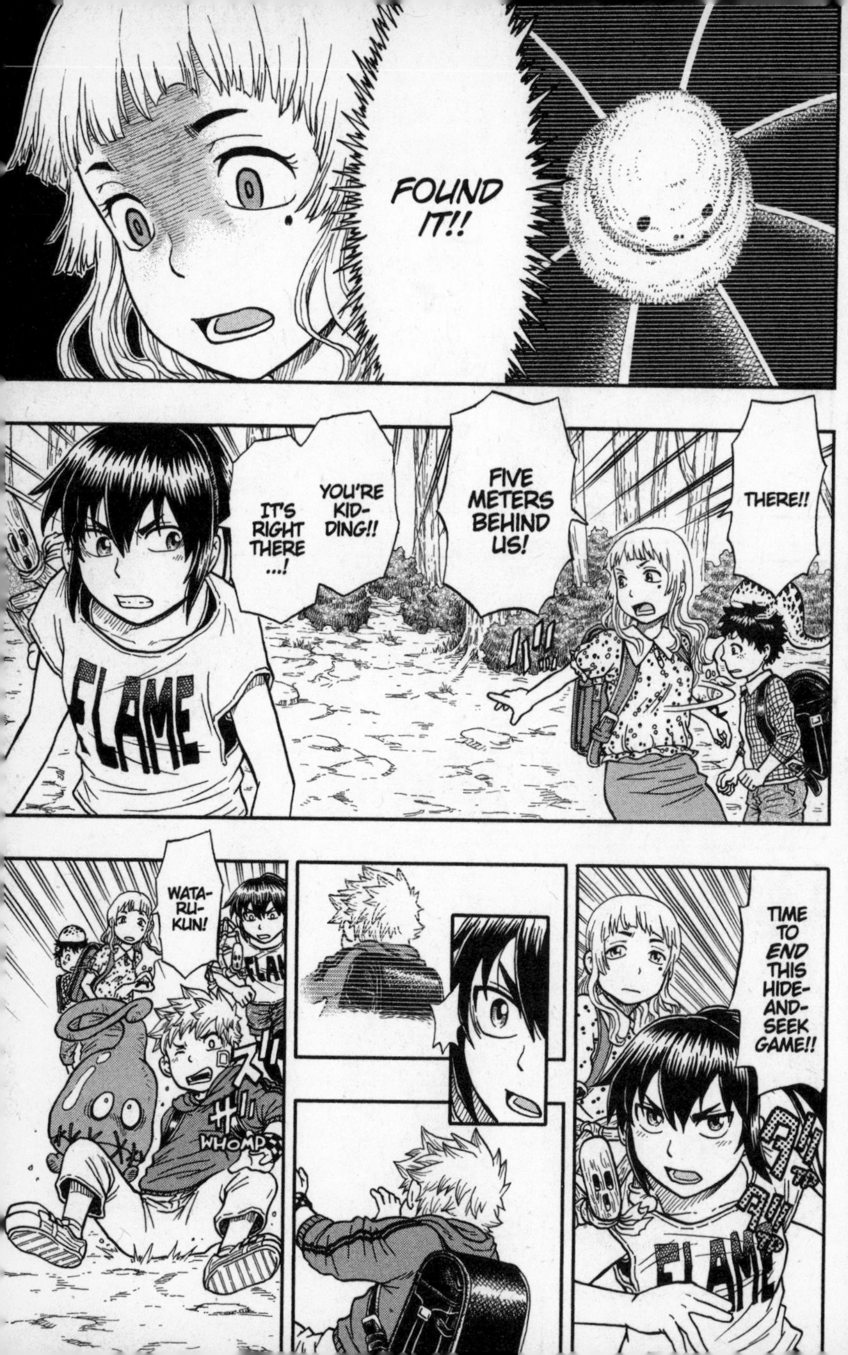
FOUND IT!!
THERE!!
FIVE METERS BEHIND US!
YOU'RE KID-DING!!
IT'S RIGHT THERE ...!
TIME TO END THIS HIDE-AND-SEEK GAME!!
WATA-RU-KUN!
WHOMP

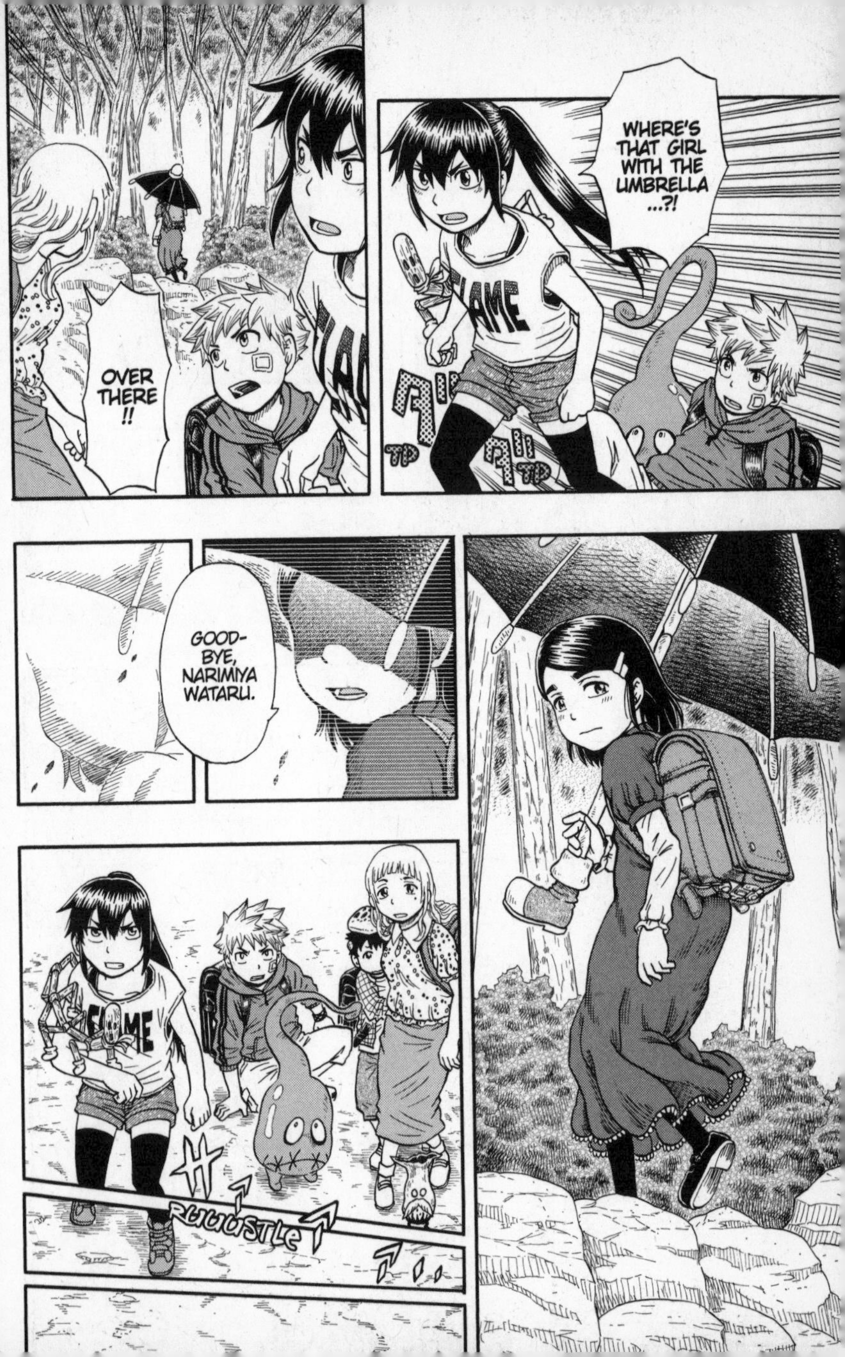
WHERE'S THAT GIRL WITH THE UMBRELLA ...?!
TP
TP
OVER THERE !!
GOOD-BYE, NARIMIYA WATARU.
RUUUSTLE

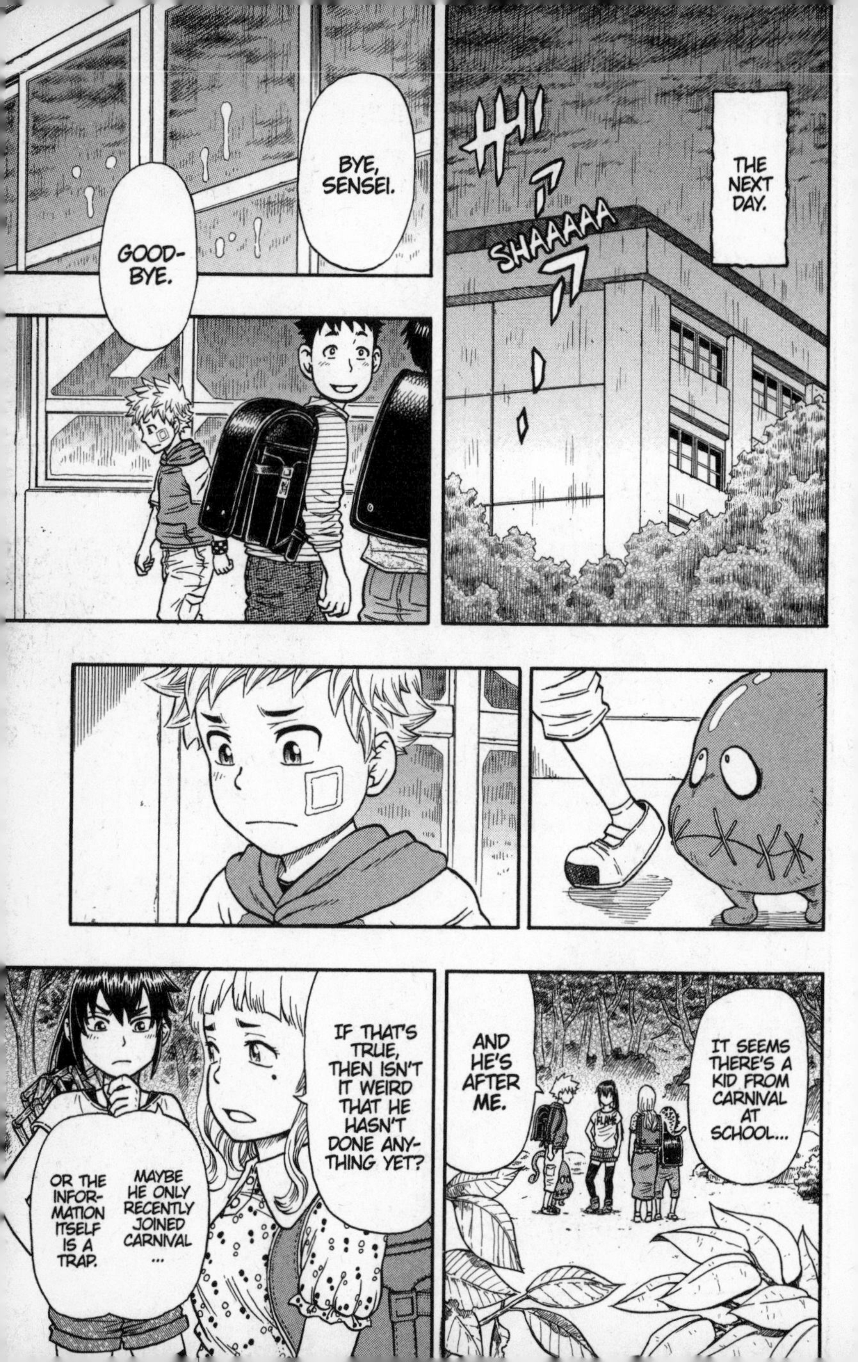
THE NEXT DAY.
HI
SHAAAAA
BYE, SENSEI.
GOOD-BYE.
IT SEEMS THERE'S A KID FROM CARNIVAL AT SCHOOL...
AND HE'S AFTER ME.
IF THAT'S TRUE, THEN ISN'T IT WEIRD THAT HE HASN'T DONE ANYTHING YET?
MAYBE HE ONLY RECENTLY JOINED CARNIVAL ...
OR THE INFORMATION ITSELF IS A TRAP.

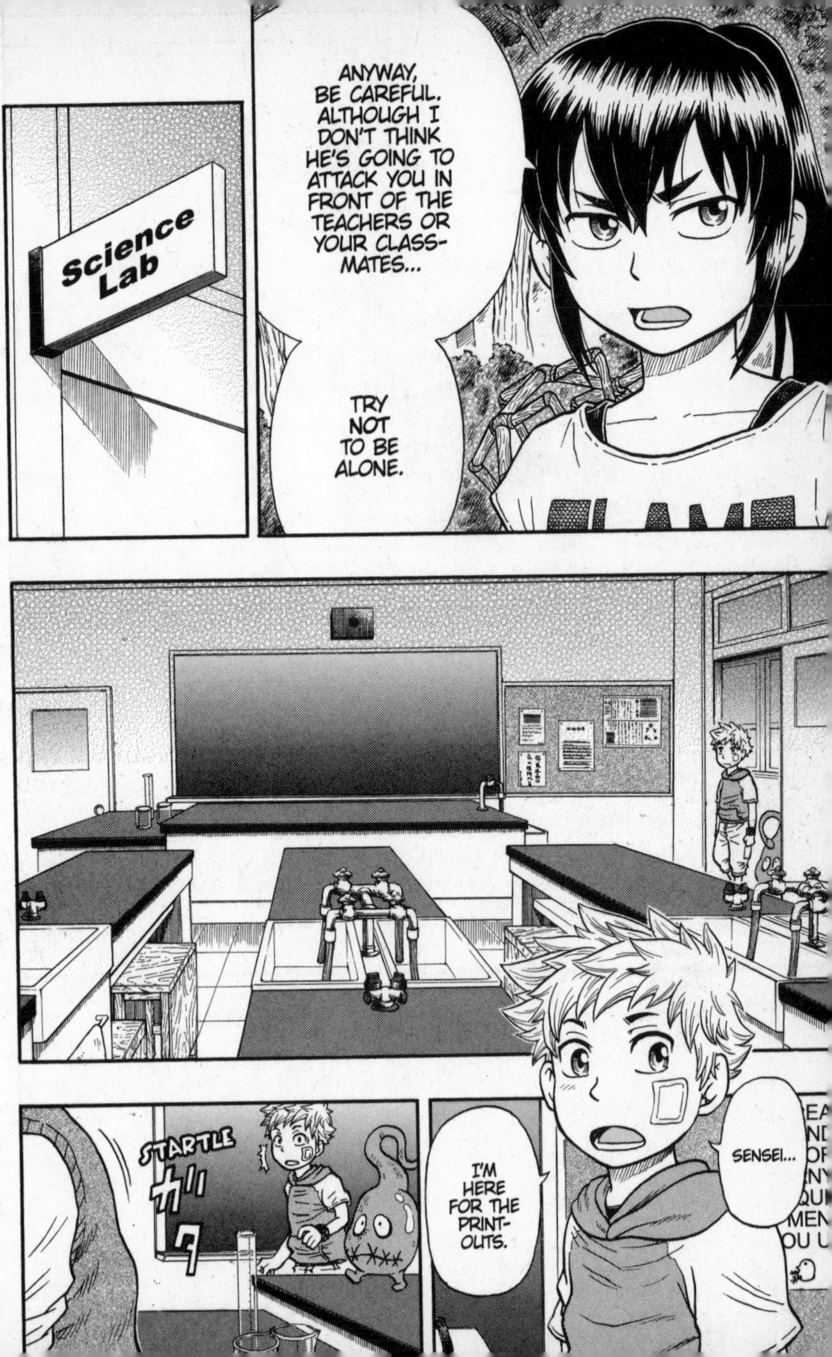
ANYWAY, BE CAREFUL. ALTHOUGH I DON'T THINK HE'S GOING TO ATTACK YOU IN FRONT OF THE TEACHERS OR YOUR CLASS-MATES...
TRY NOT TO BE ALONE.
Science Lab
SENSEI...
I'M HERE FOR THE PRINT-OUTS.
STARTLE

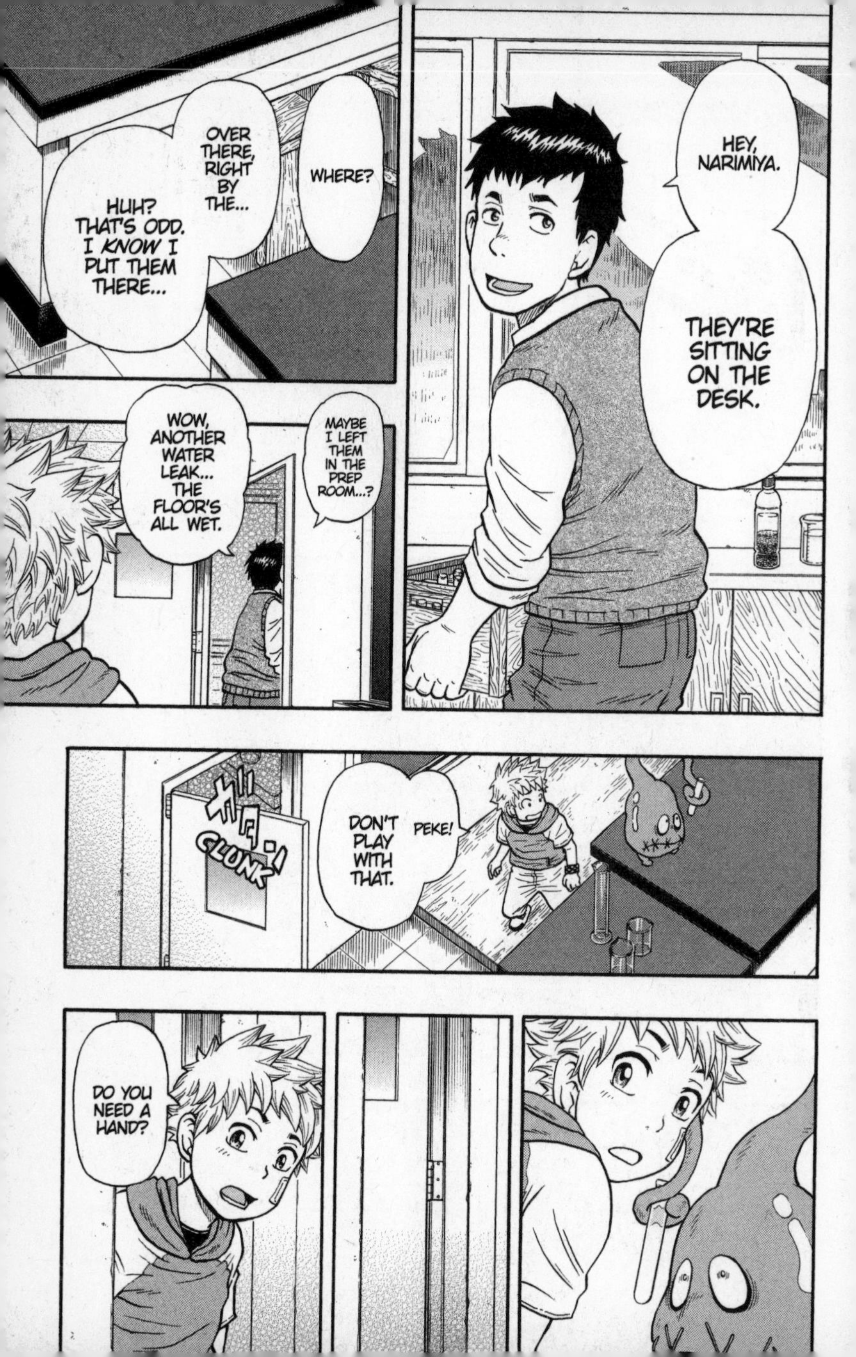
HEY, NARIMIYA.
THEY'RE SITTING ON THE DESK.
WHERE?
OVER THERE, RIGHT BY THE...
HUH? THAT'S ODD. I *KNOW* I PUT THEM THERE...
MAYBE I LEFT THEM IN THE PREP ROOM...?
WOW, ANOTHER WATER LEAK... THE FLOOR'S ALL WET.
PEKE!
DON'T PLAY WITH THAT.
CLUNK
DO YOU NEED A HAND?

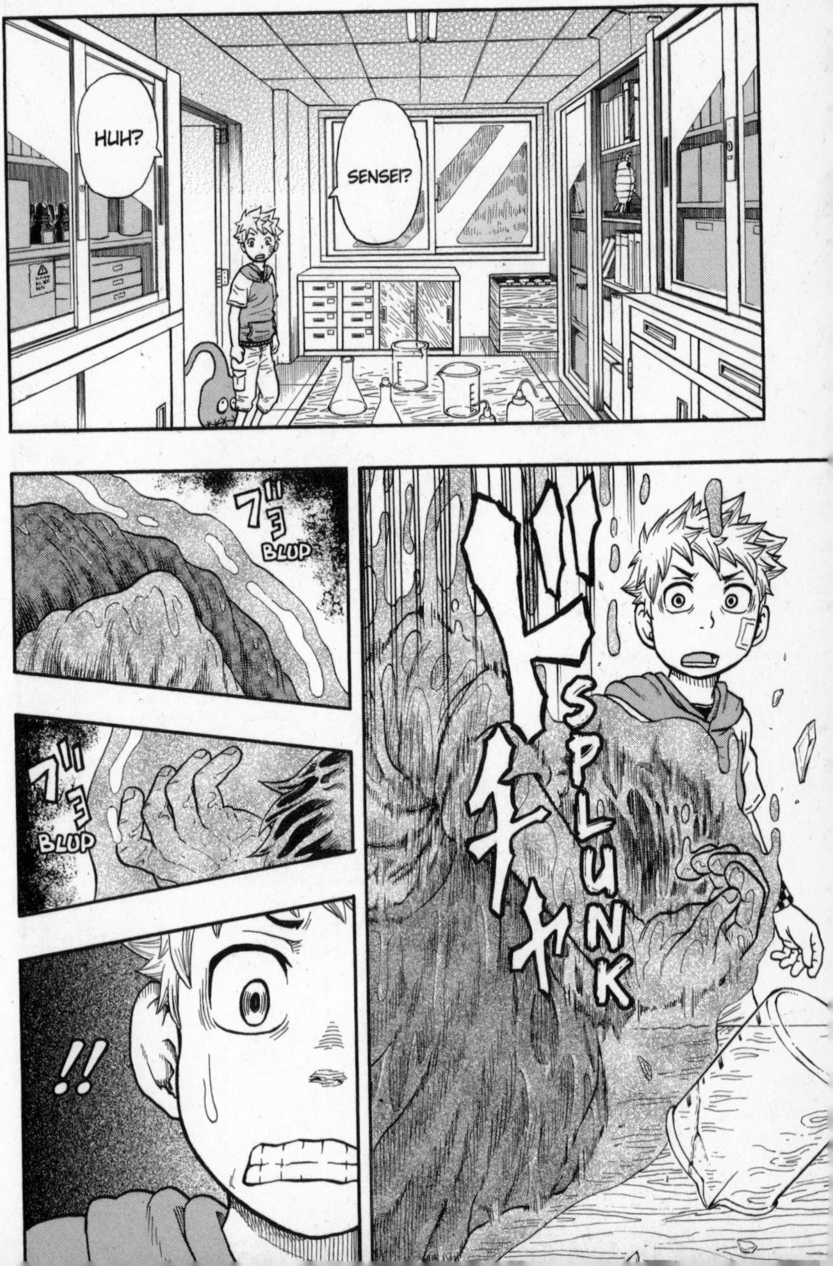
HUH?
SENSEI?
SPLUNK
BLUP
BLUP
!!

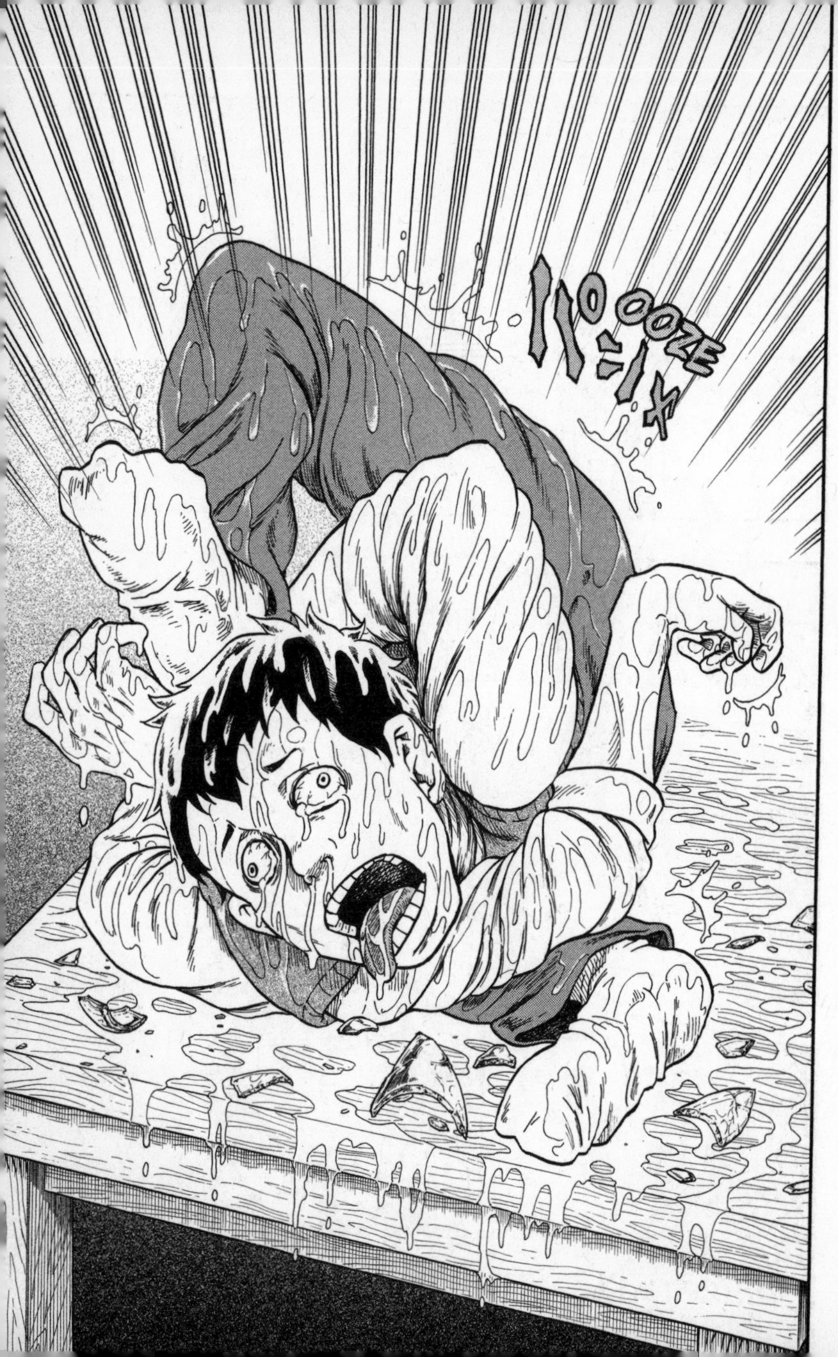
OOZE

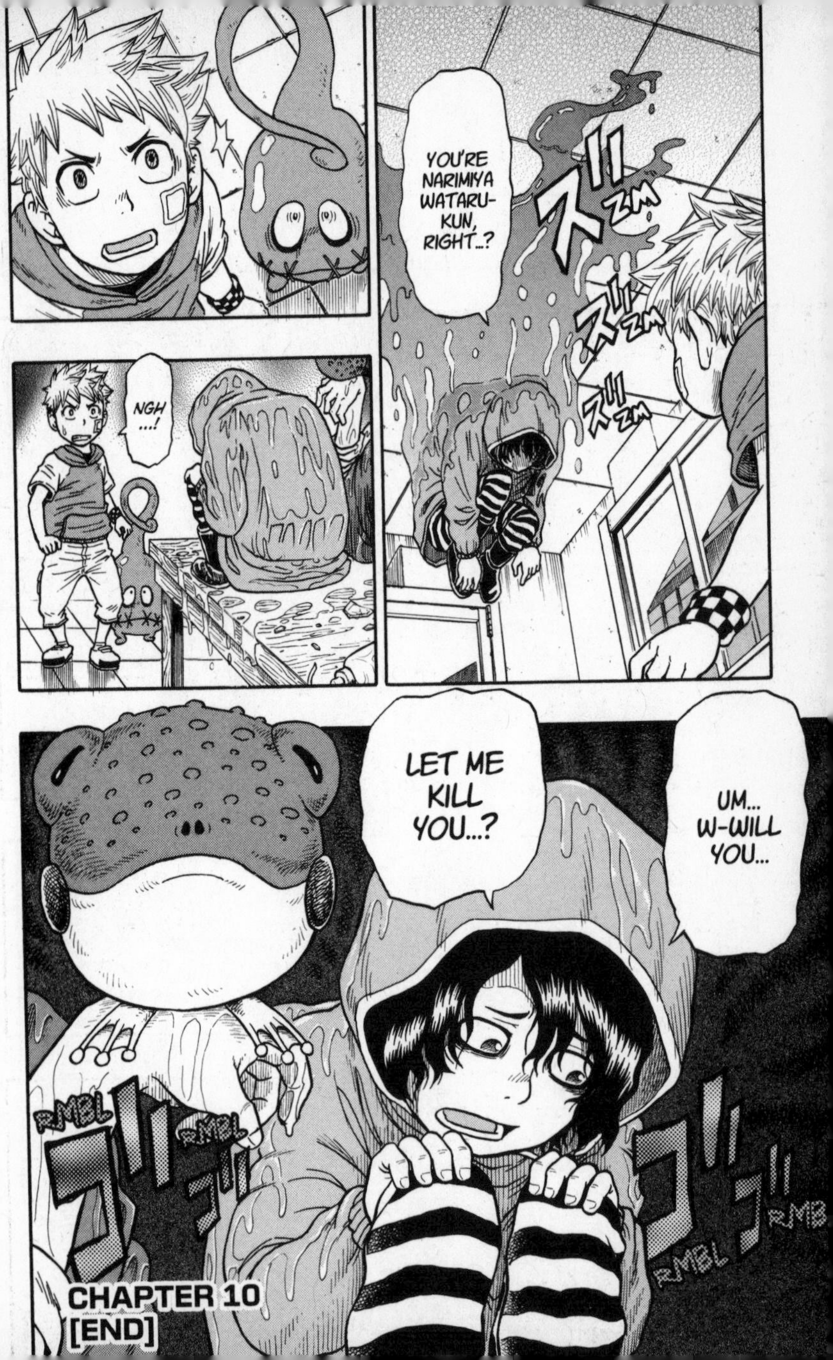

YOU'RE NARIMIYA WATARU-KUN, RIGHT...?
ZM
ZM
ZM
NGH ...!
UM... W-WILL YOU...
LET ME KILL YOU...?
RMBL RMBL
RMBL RMB
CHAPTER 10 [END]

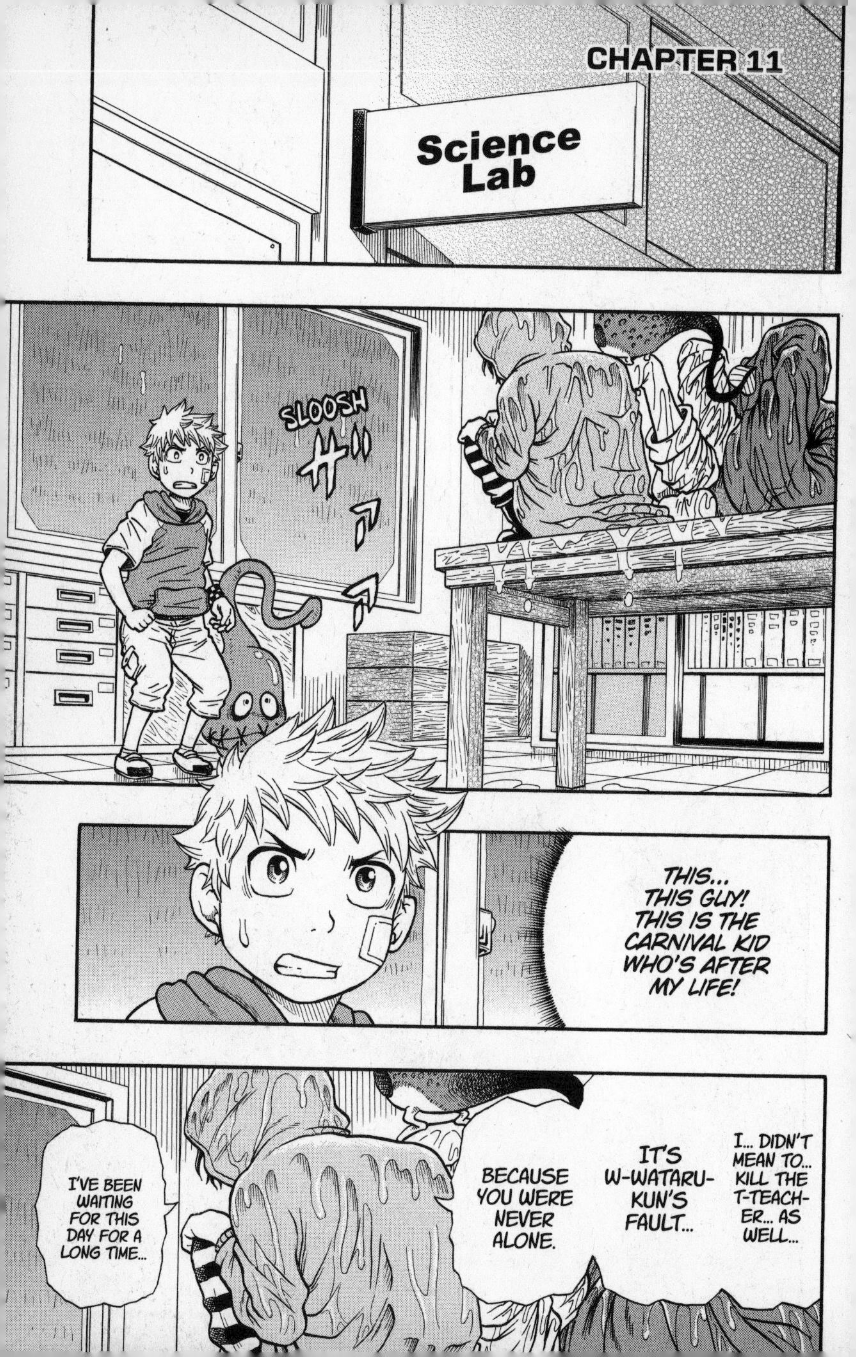
CHAPTER 11
Science Lab
SLOOSH
THIS... THIS GUY! THIS IS THE CARNIVAL KID WHO'S AFTER MY LIFE!
I... DIDN'T MEAN TO... KILL THE T-TEACHER... AS WELL...
IT'S W-WATARU-KUN'S FAULT...
BECAUSE YOU WERE NEVER ALONE.
I'VE BEEN WAITING FOR THIS DAY FOR A LONG TIME...

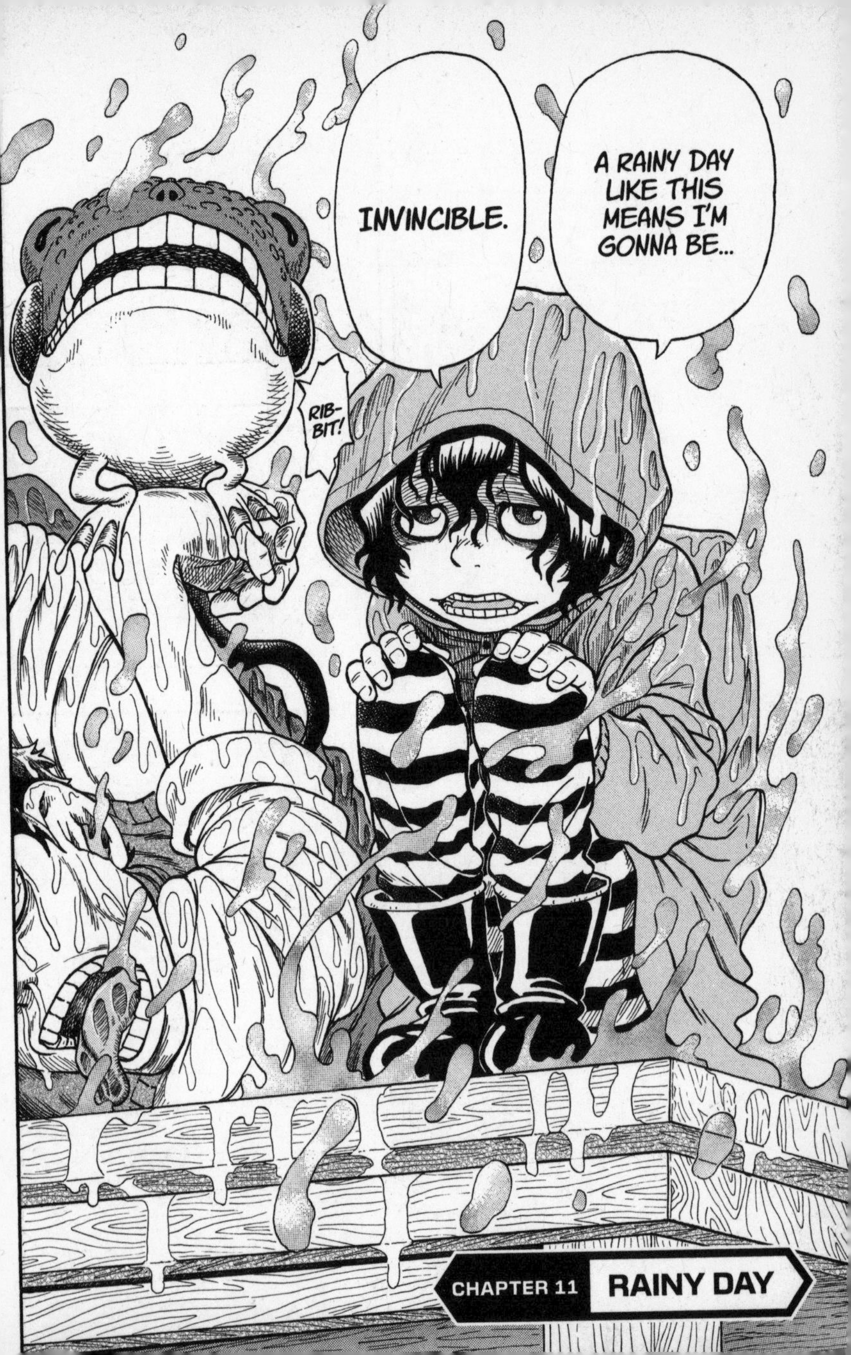
A RAINY DAY LIKE THIS MEANS I'M GONNA BE...
INVINCIBLE.
RIB-BIT!
CHAPTER 11
RAINY DAY

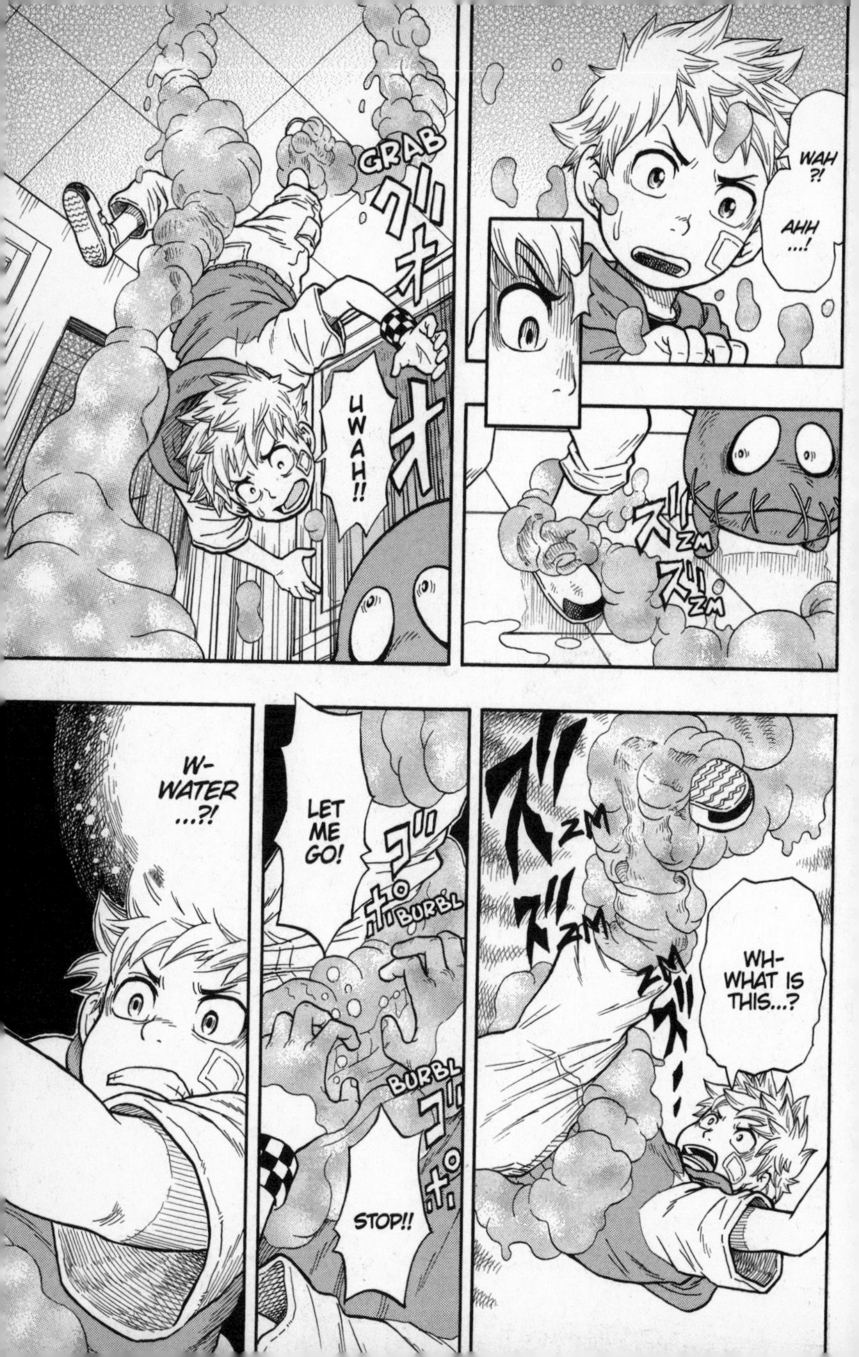
WAH ?!
AHH ...!
ZM
ZM
GRAB
UWAH!!
ZM
ZM
ZM
WH- WHAT IS THIS...?
LET ME GO!
BURBL
BURBL
STOP!!
W- WATER ...?!

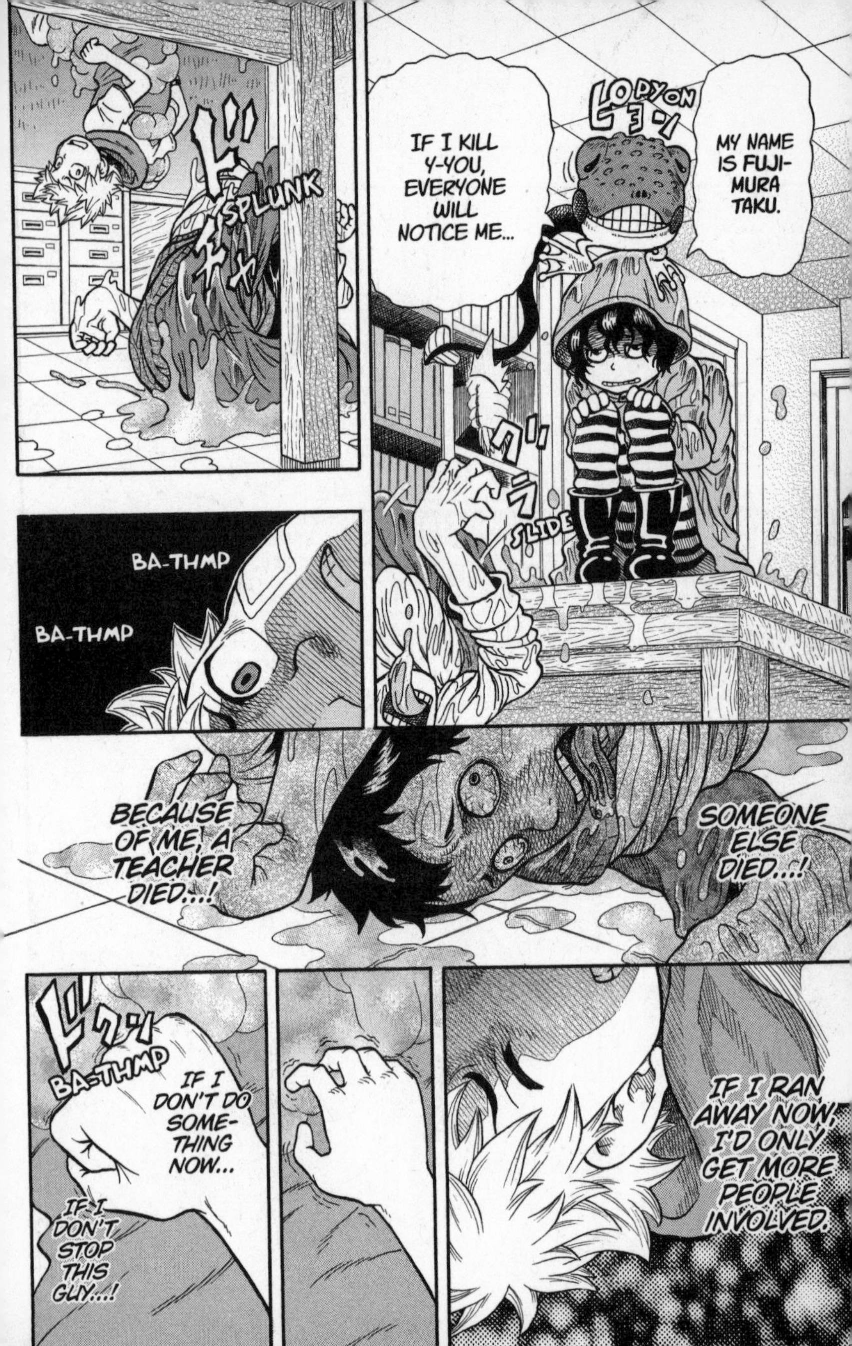
PYON
MY NAME IS FUJI-MURA TAKU.
IF I KILL Y-YOU, EVERYONE WILL NOTICE ME...
SLIDE
SPLUNK
BA-THMP
BA-THMP
SOMEONE ELSE DIED...!
BECAUSE OF ME, A TEACHER DIED...!
IF I RAN AWAY NOW, I'D ONLY GET MORE PEOPLE INVOLVED.
BA-THMP
IF I DON'T DO SOME-THING NOW...
IF I DON'T STOP THIS GUY...!

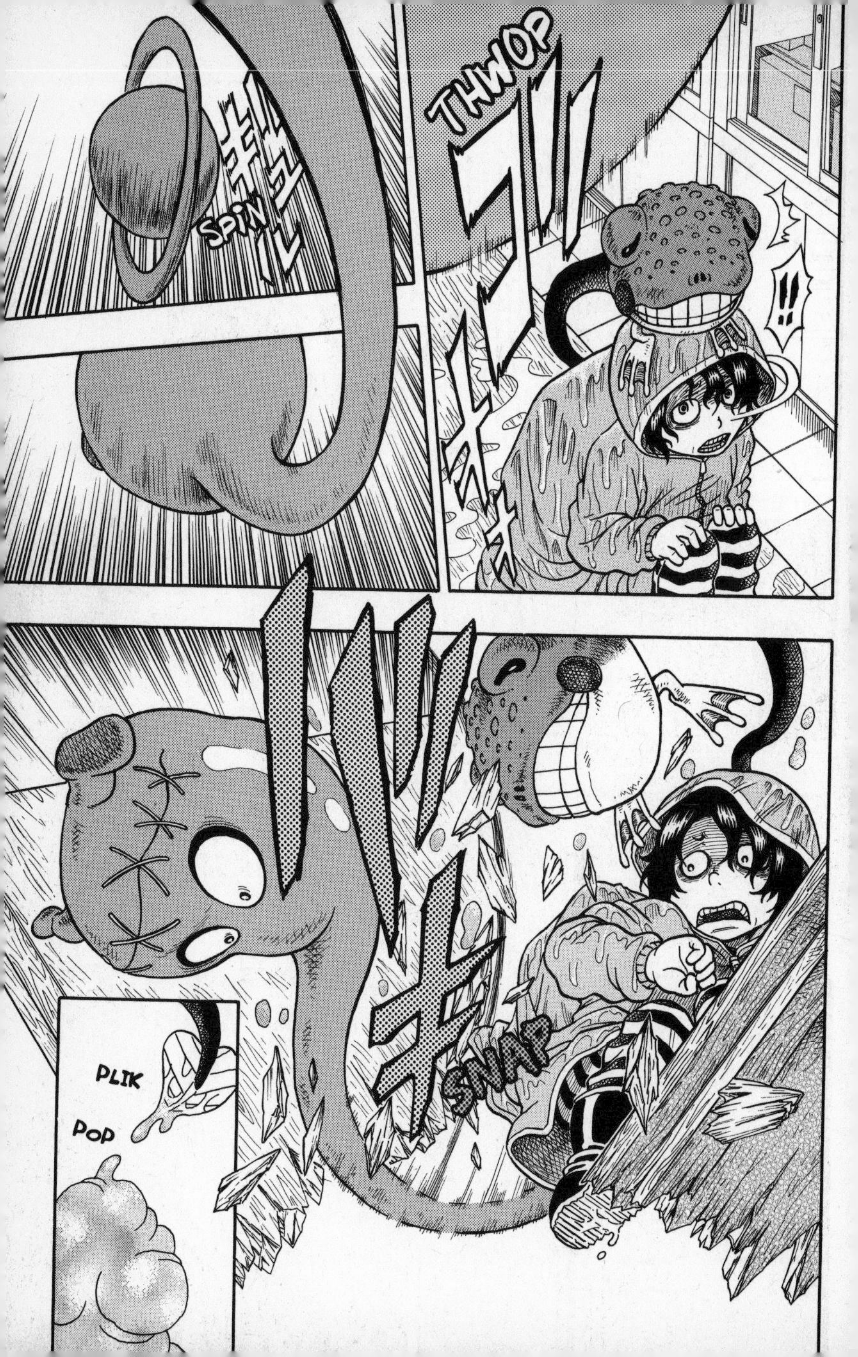
THWOP
!!
SPIN
SNAP
PLIK
POP

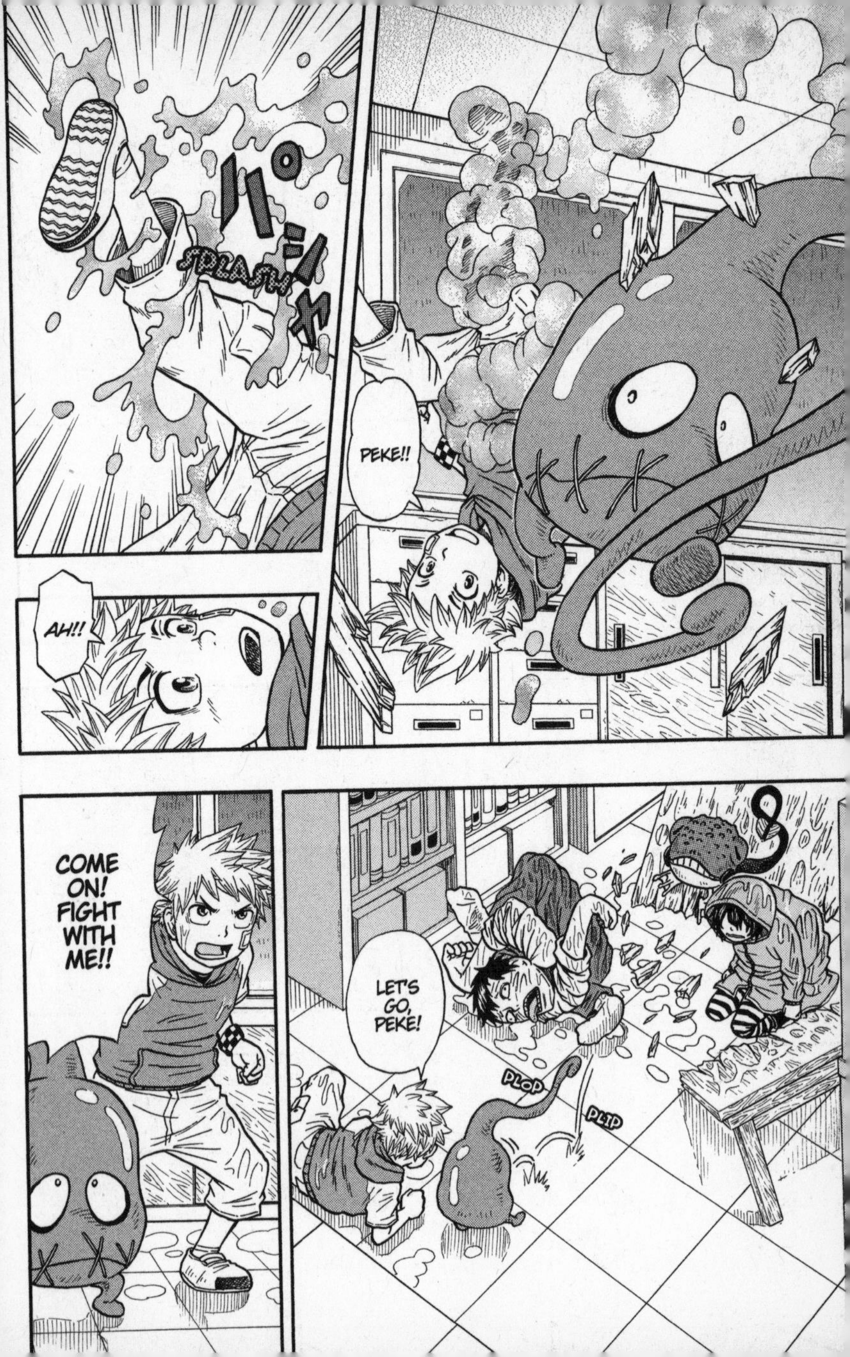
PEKE!!
SPLASH
AH!!
LET'S GO, PEKE!
PLOP
PLIP
COME ON! FIGHT WITH ME!!

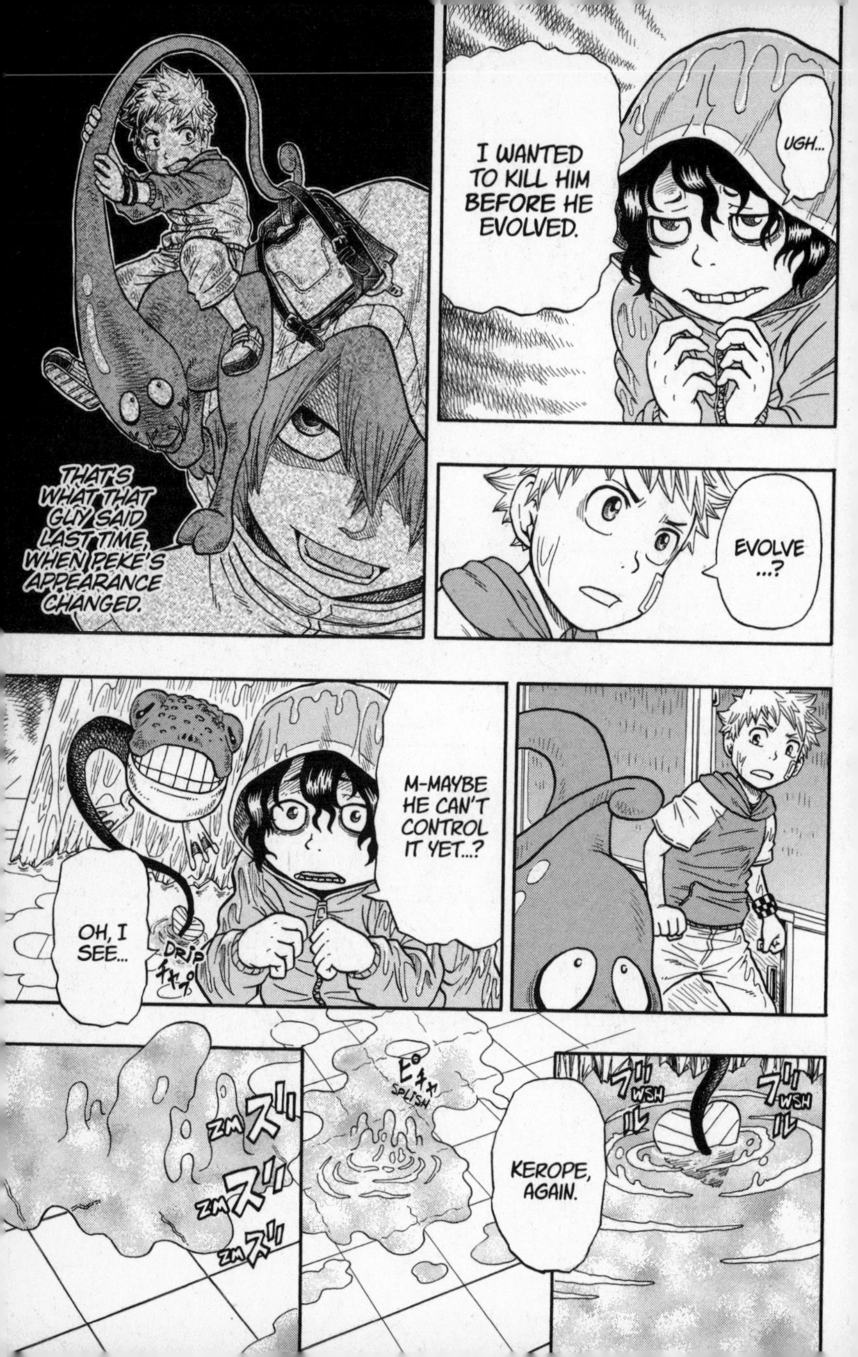
UGH...
I WANTED TO KILL HIM BEFORE HE EVOLVED.
EVOLVE ...?
THAT'S WHAT THAT GUY SAID LAST TIME, WHEN PEKE'S APPEARANCE CHANGED.
M-MAYBE HE CAN'T CONTROL IT YET...?
OH, I SEE...
DRIP
チャプ
ブル
WSH
ブル
WSH
KEROPE, AGAIN.
ピチャ
SPLISH
ZM
ズ
ZM
ズ
ZM
ズ

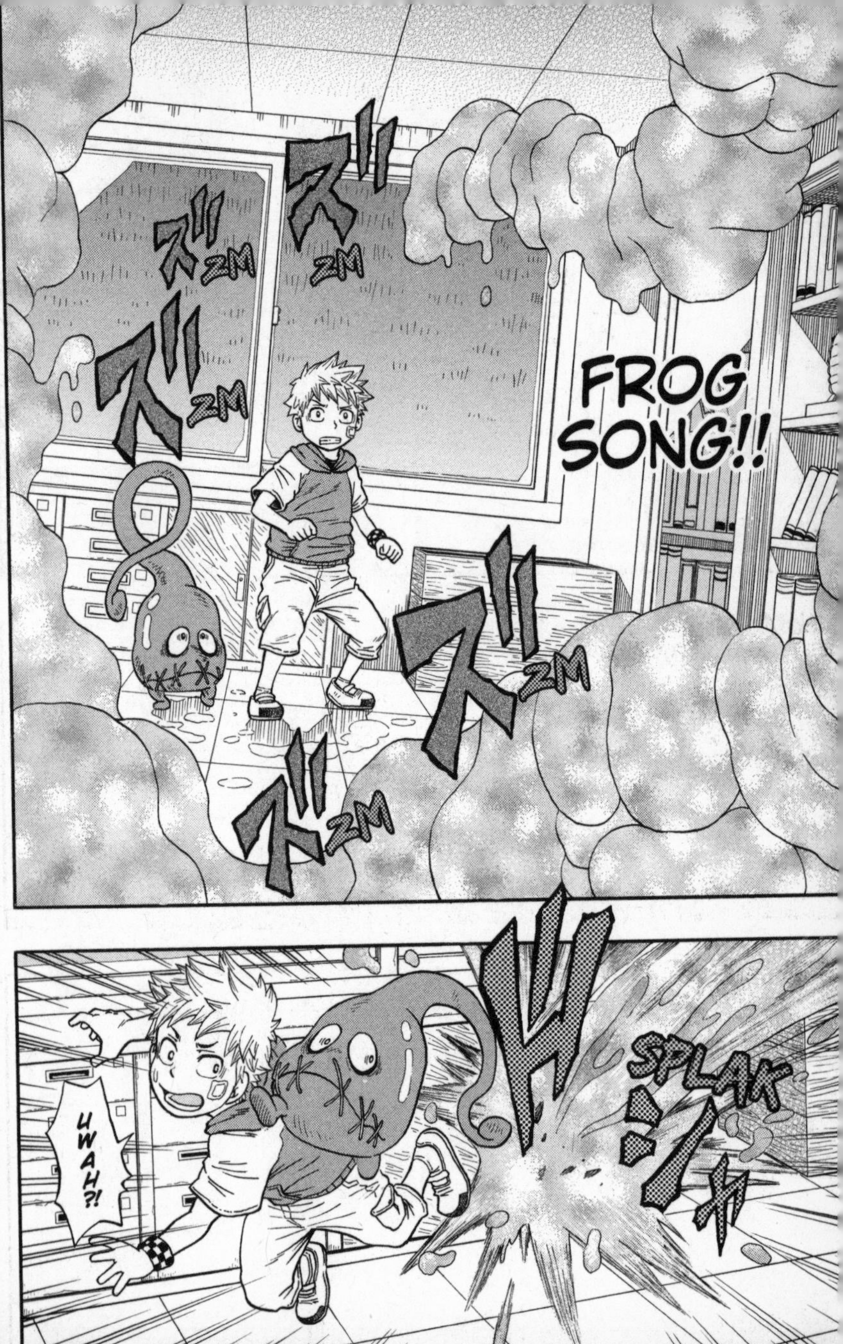
FROG SONG!!
ZM
ZM
ZM
ZM
ZM
ZM
SPLAK
UWAH?!

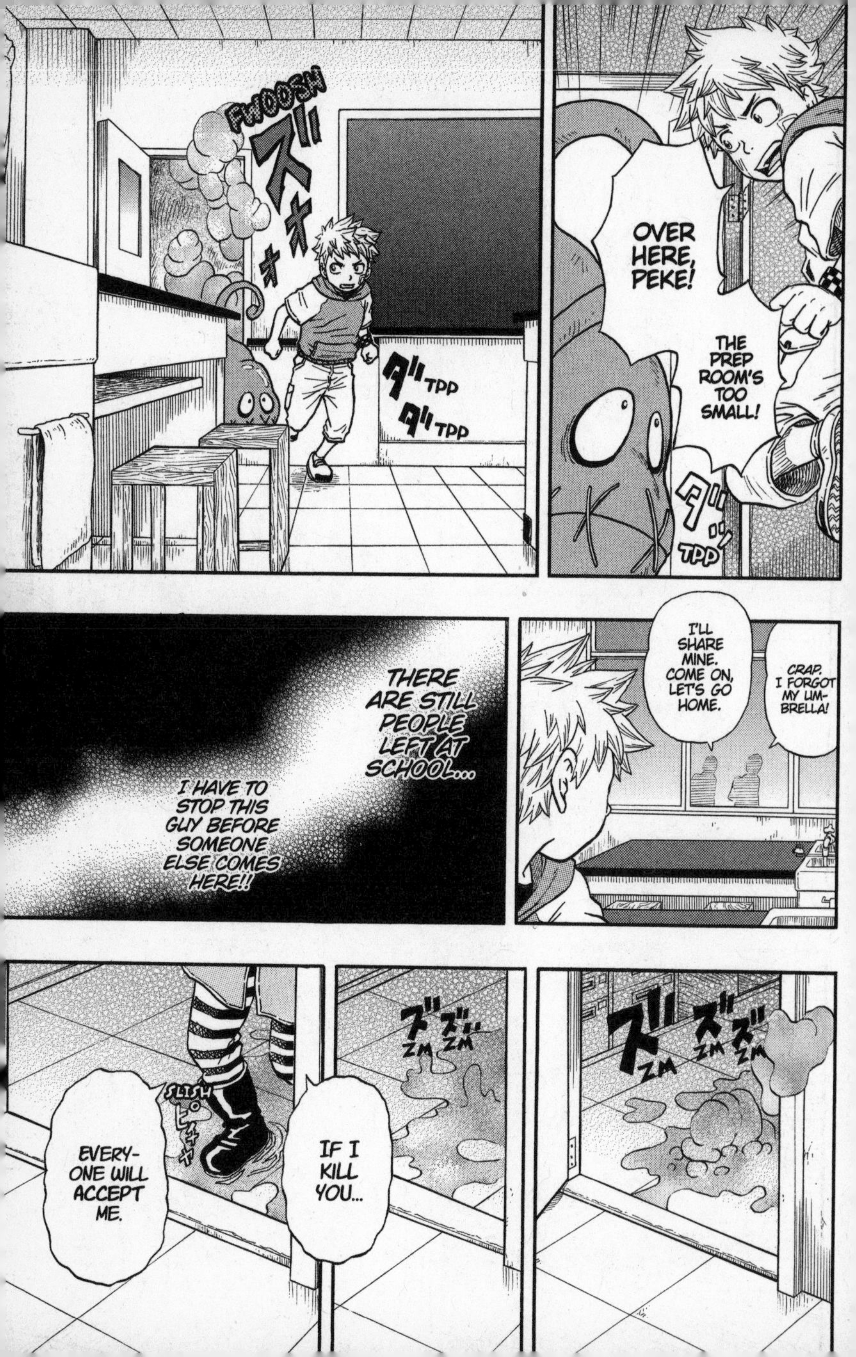
OVER HERE, PEKE!
THE PREP ROOM'S TOO SMALL!
TPP
FWOOSH
TPP
TPP
CRAP. I FORGOT MY UM-BRELLA!
I'LL SHARE MINE. COME ON, LET'S GO HOME.
THERE ARE STILL PEOPLE LEFT AT SCHOOL...
I HAVE TO STOP THIS GUY BEFORE SOMEONE ELSE COMES HERE!!
ZM ZM ZM
ZM ZM
IF I KILL YOU...
SLISH
EVERY-ONE WILL ACCEPT ME.

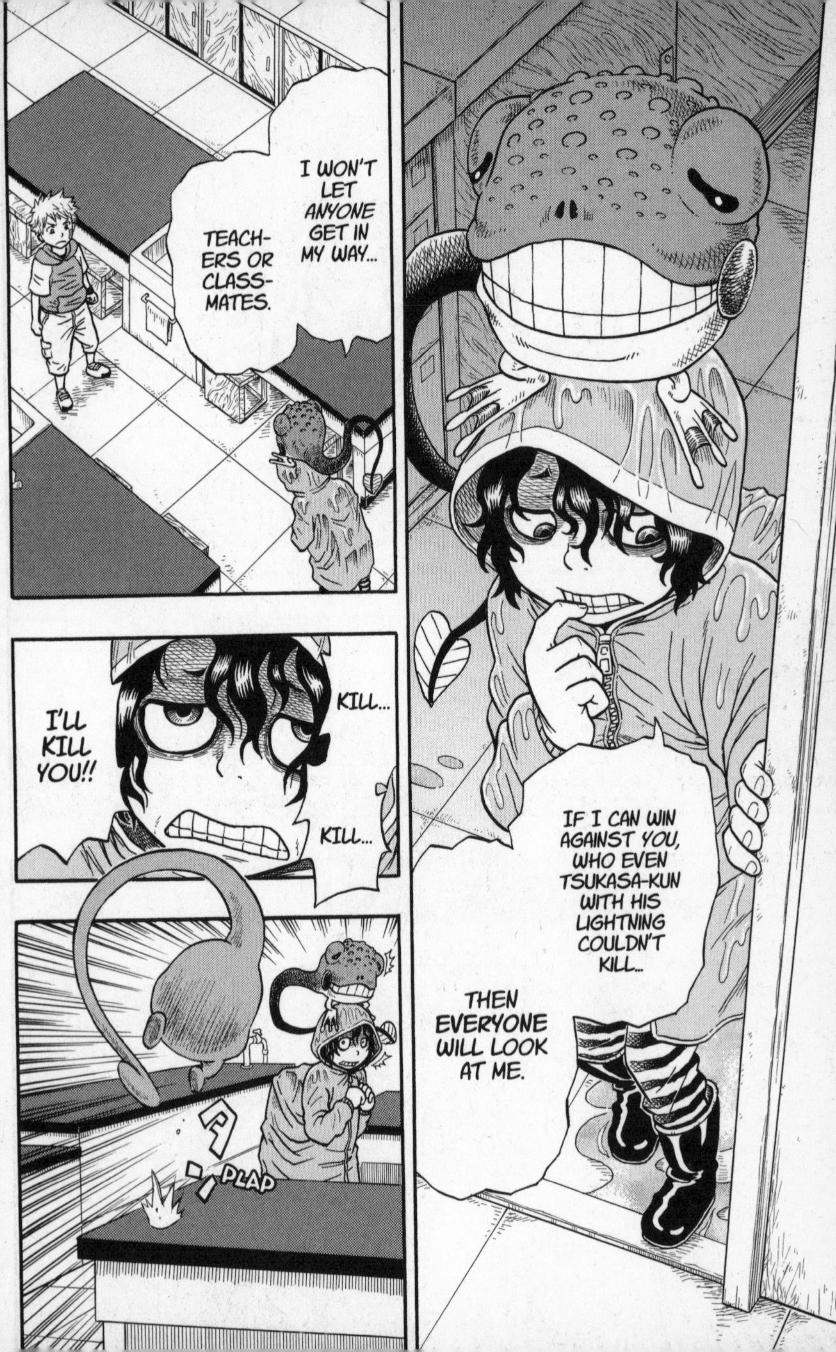
IF I CAN WIN AGAINST YOU, WHO EVEN TSUKASA-KUN WITH HIS LIGHTNING COULDN'T KILL...
THEN EVERYONE WILL LOOK AT ME.
I WON'T LET ANYONE GET IN MY WAY...
TEACHERS OR CLASSMATES.
KILL...
KILL...
I'LL KILL YOU!!
PLAP

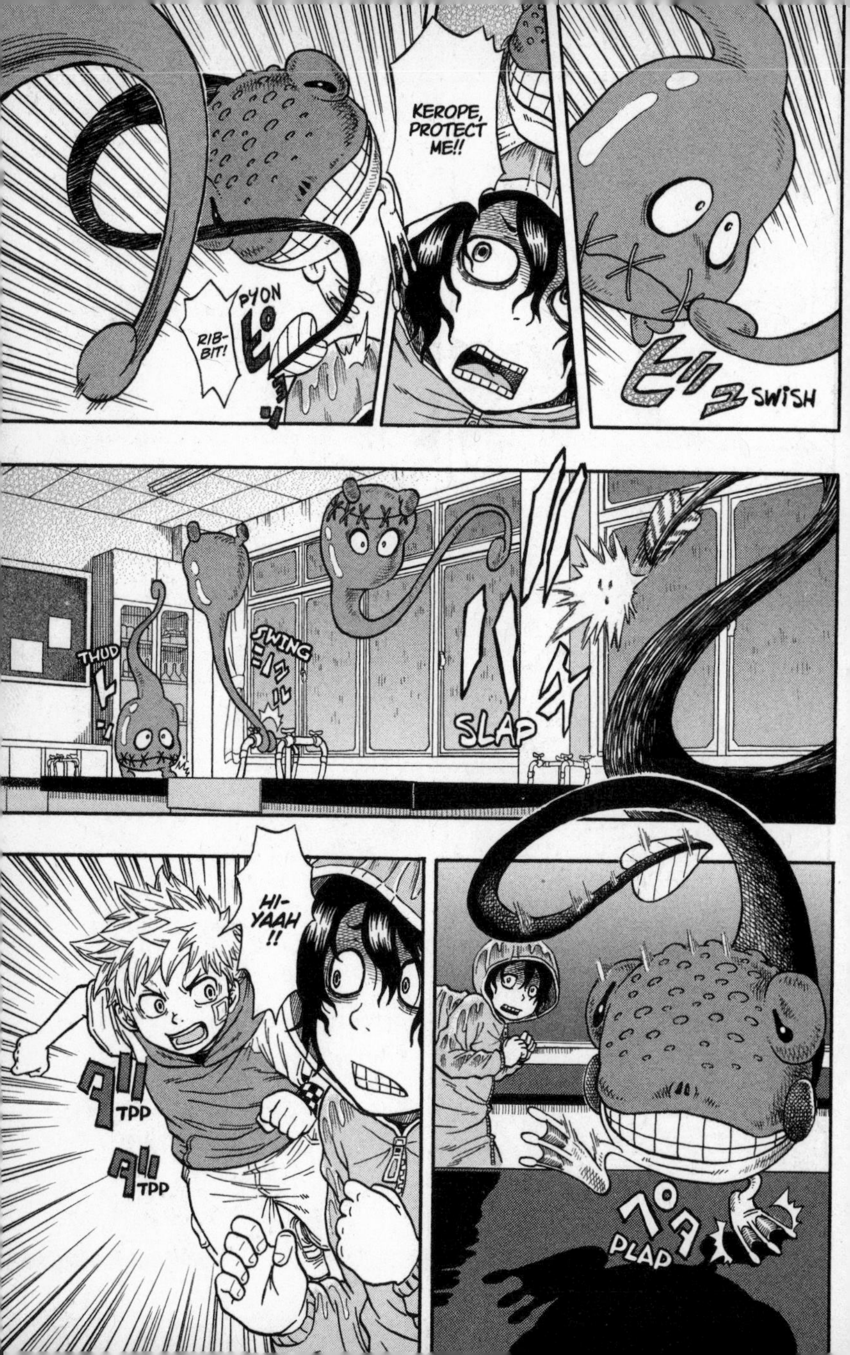
SWISH
KEROPE, PROTECT ME!!
PYON
RIB-BIT!
SLAP
SWING
THUD
PLAP
HI-YAAH!!
TPP
TPP

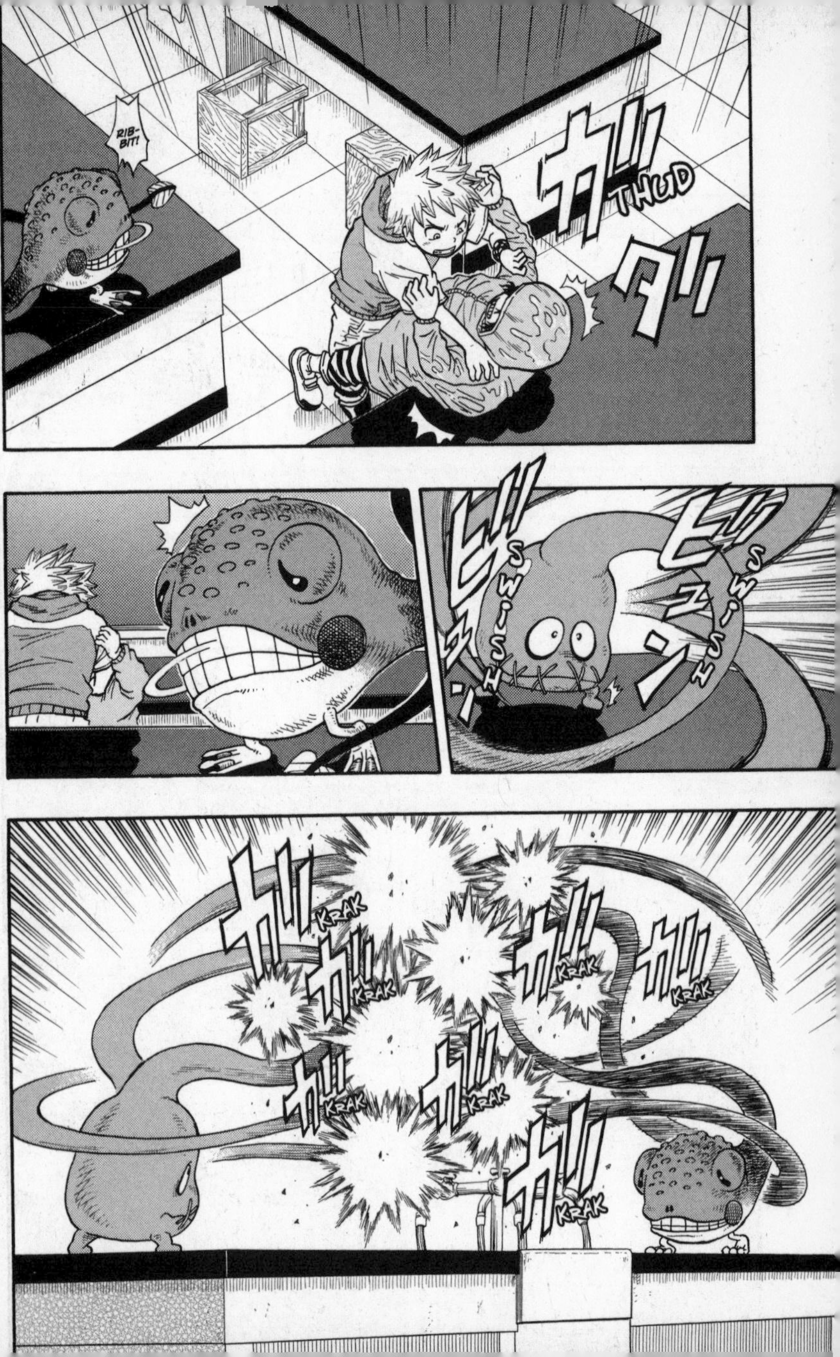
THUD
RIB-BIT!
SWISH
SWISH
KRAK
KRAK
KRAK
KRAK
KRAK
KRAK
KRAK

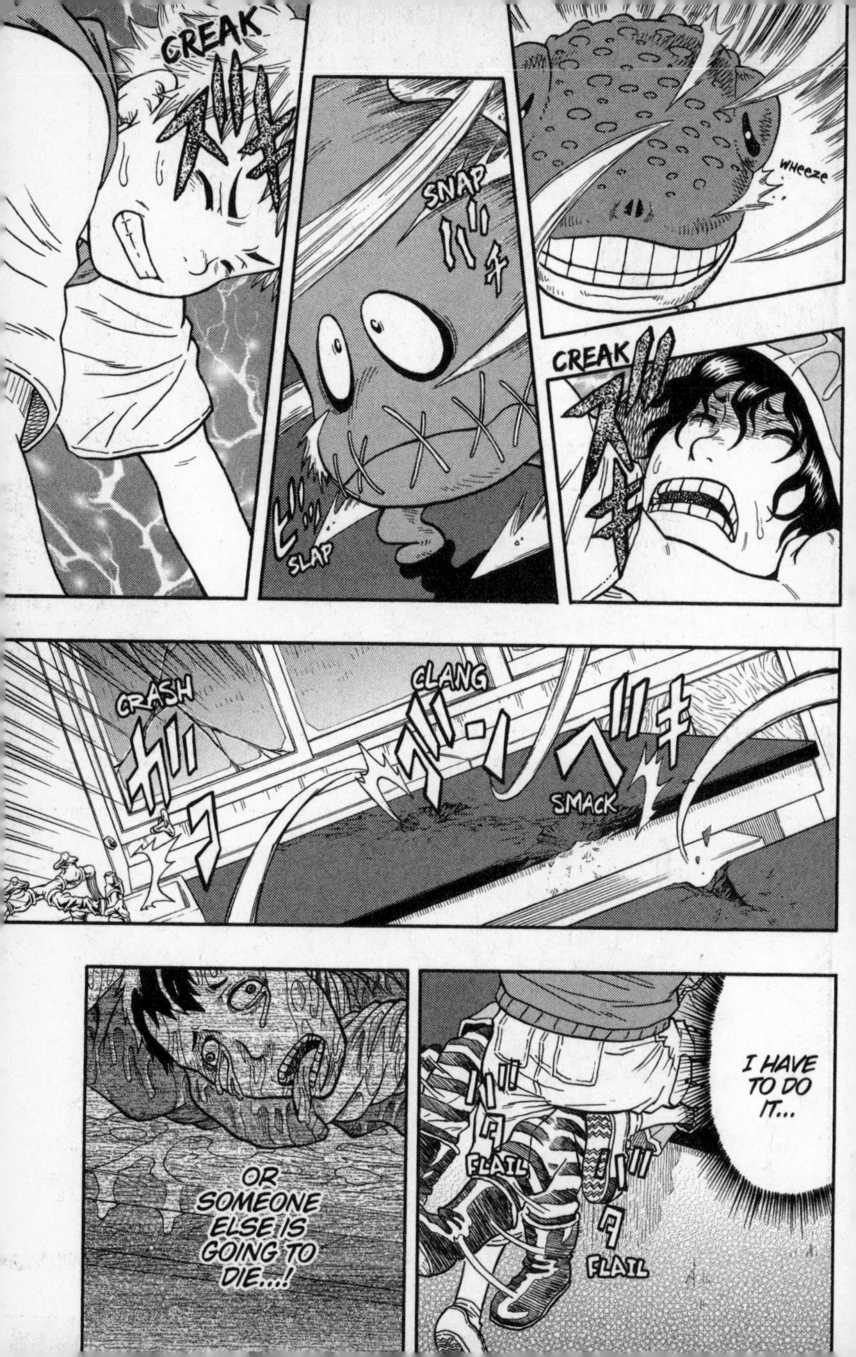
WHEEZE
CREAK
SNAP
SLAP
CREAK
CLANG
CRASH
SMACK
I HAVE TO DO IT...
FLAIL
FLAIL
OR SOMEONE ELSE IS GOING TO DIE...!

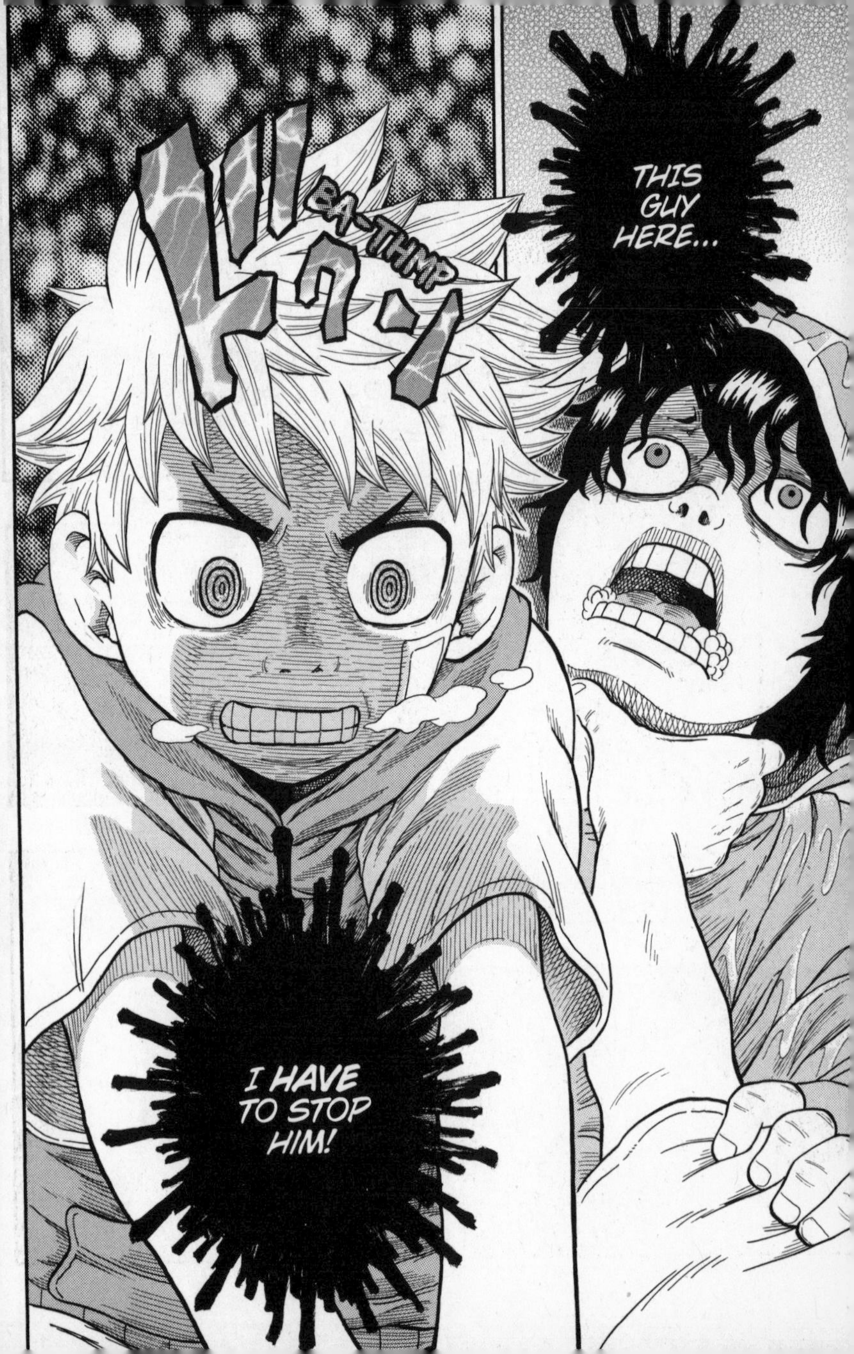
THIS GUY HERE...
BA-THUMP
I HAVE TO STOP HIM!

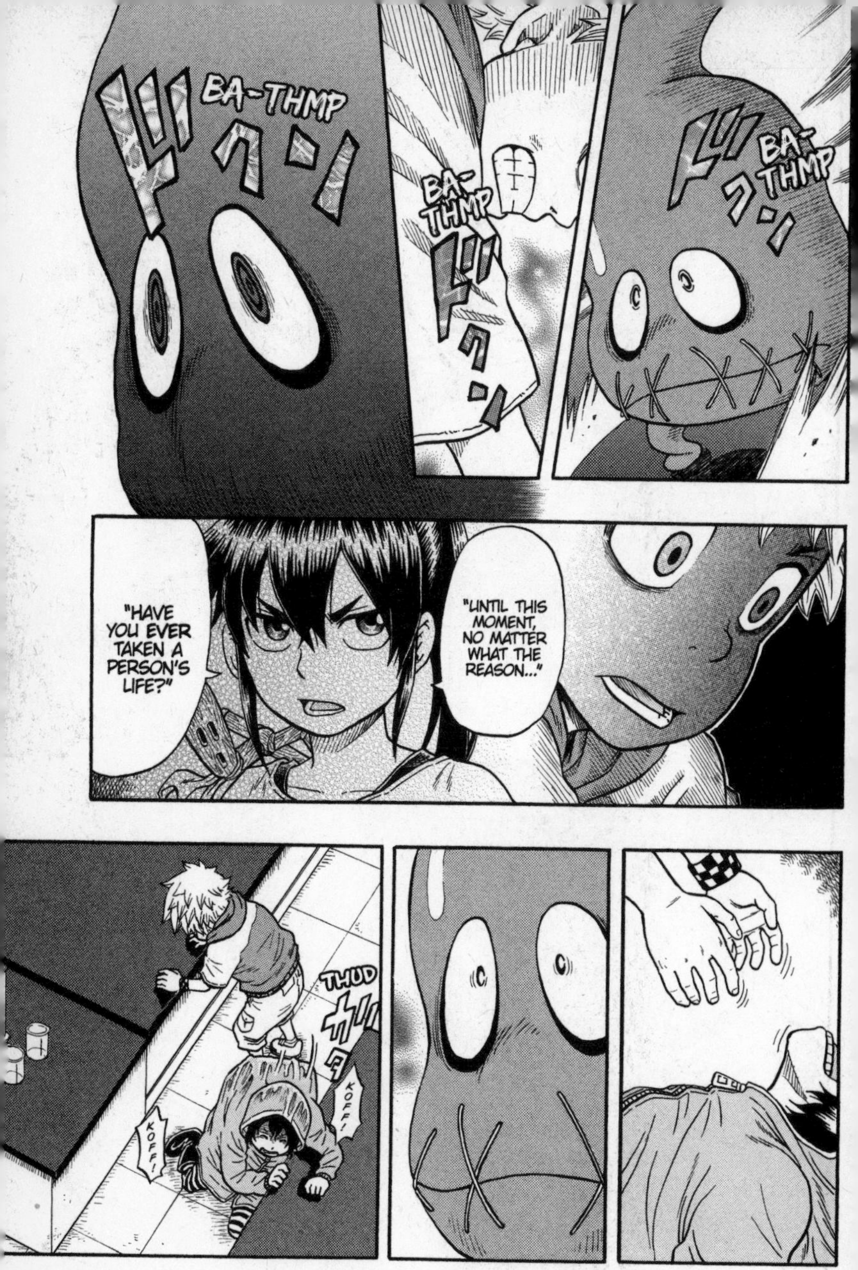
BA-THMP
BA-THMP
BA-THMP
"UNTIL THIS MOMENT, NO MATTER WHAT THE REASON..."
"HAVE YOU EVER TAKEN A PERSON'S LIFE?"
THUD
KOFF!
KOFF!

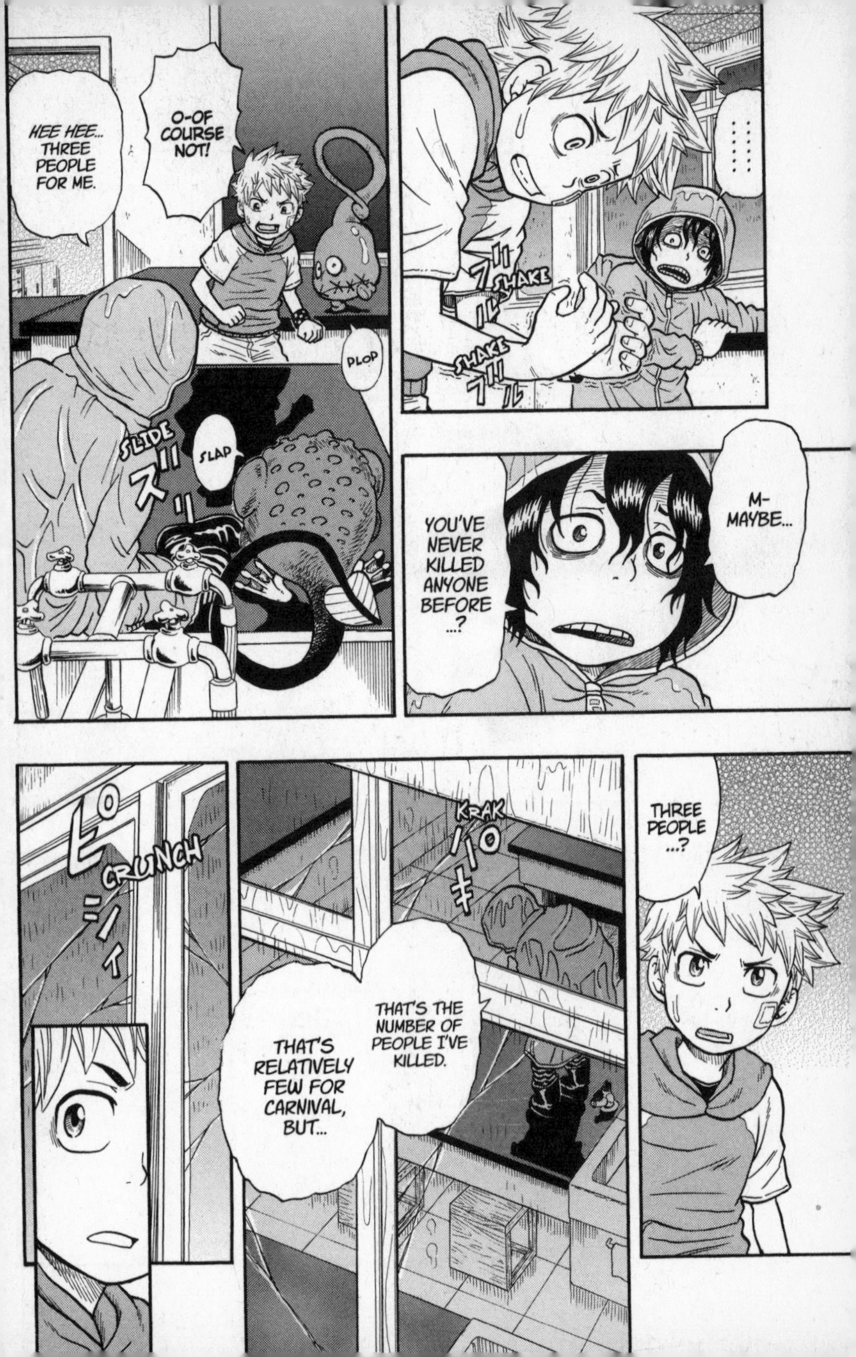
...
SHAKE
SHAKE
M-MAYBE...
YOU'VE NEVER KILLED ANYONE BEFORE ...?
O-OF COURSE NOT!
HEE HEE... THREE PEOPLE FOR ME.
PLOP
SLAP
SLIDE
THREE PEOPLE ...?
KRAK
THAT'S THE NUMBER OF PEOPLE I'VE KILLED.
THAT'S RELATIVELY FEW FOR CARNIVAL, BUT...
CRUNCH

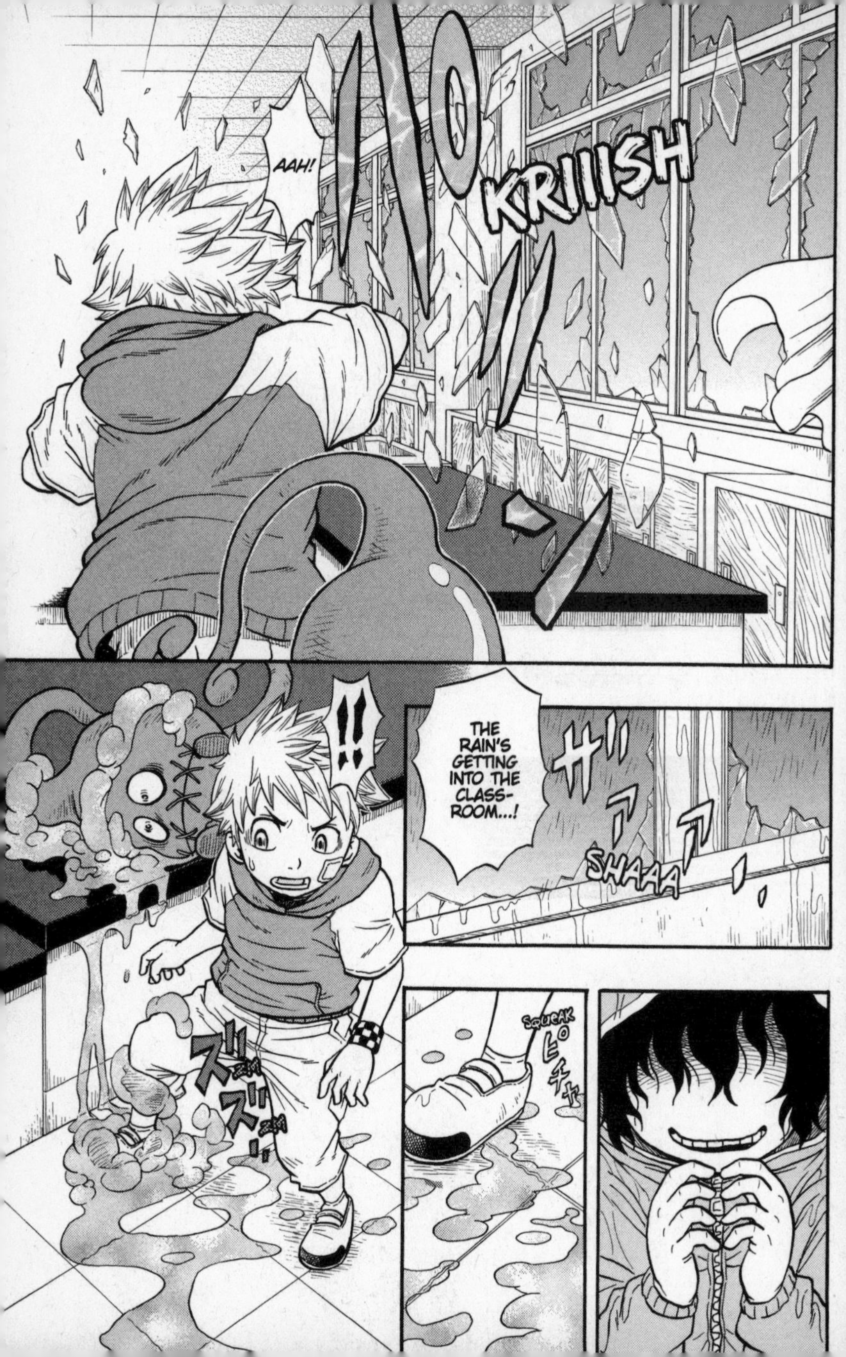
KRIIISH
AAH!
THE RAIN'S GETTING INTO THE CLASSROOM...!
SHAAA
!!
ZM
ZM
SQUEAK

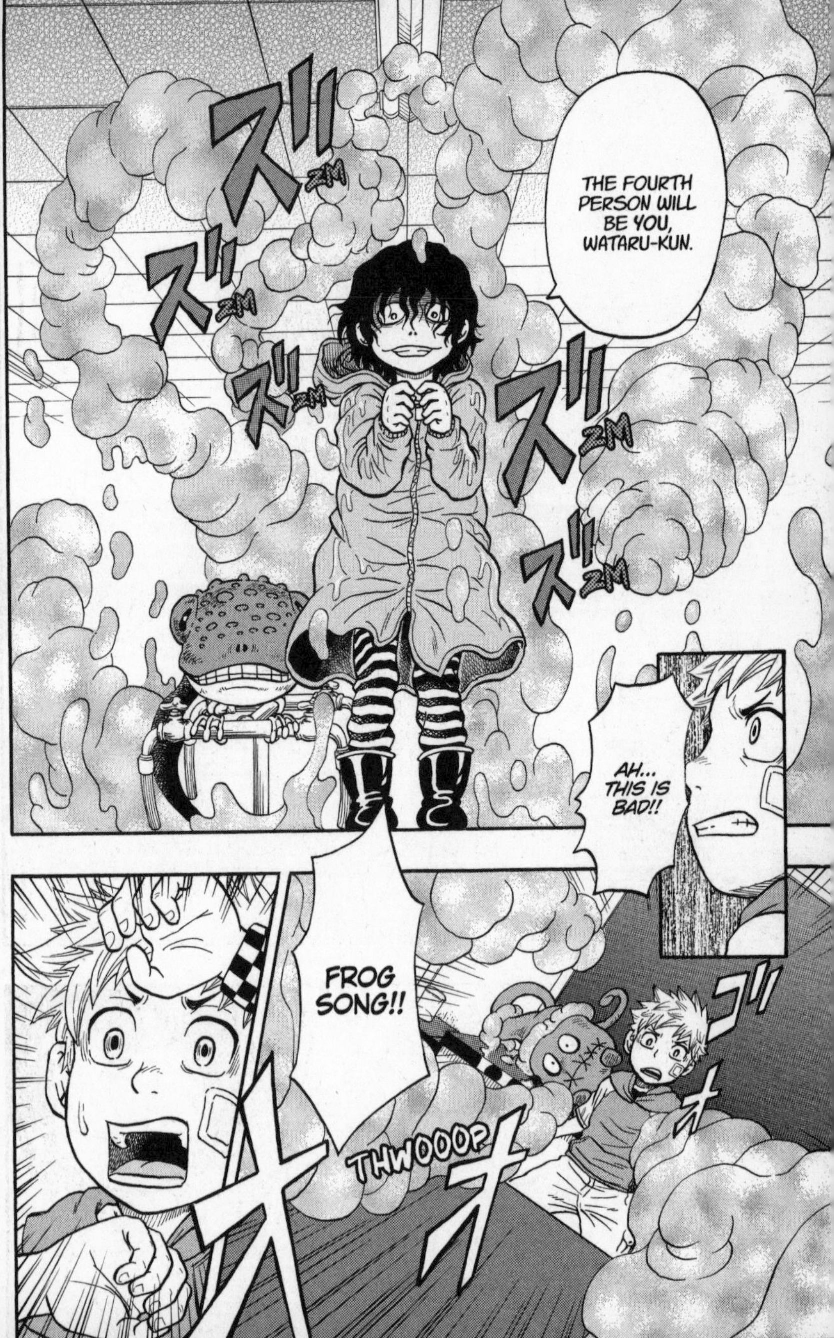
ZM
ZM
ZM
THE FOURTH PERSON WILL BE YOU, WATARU-KUN.
ZM
ZM
AH... THIS IS BAD!!
FROG SONG!!
THWOOOP

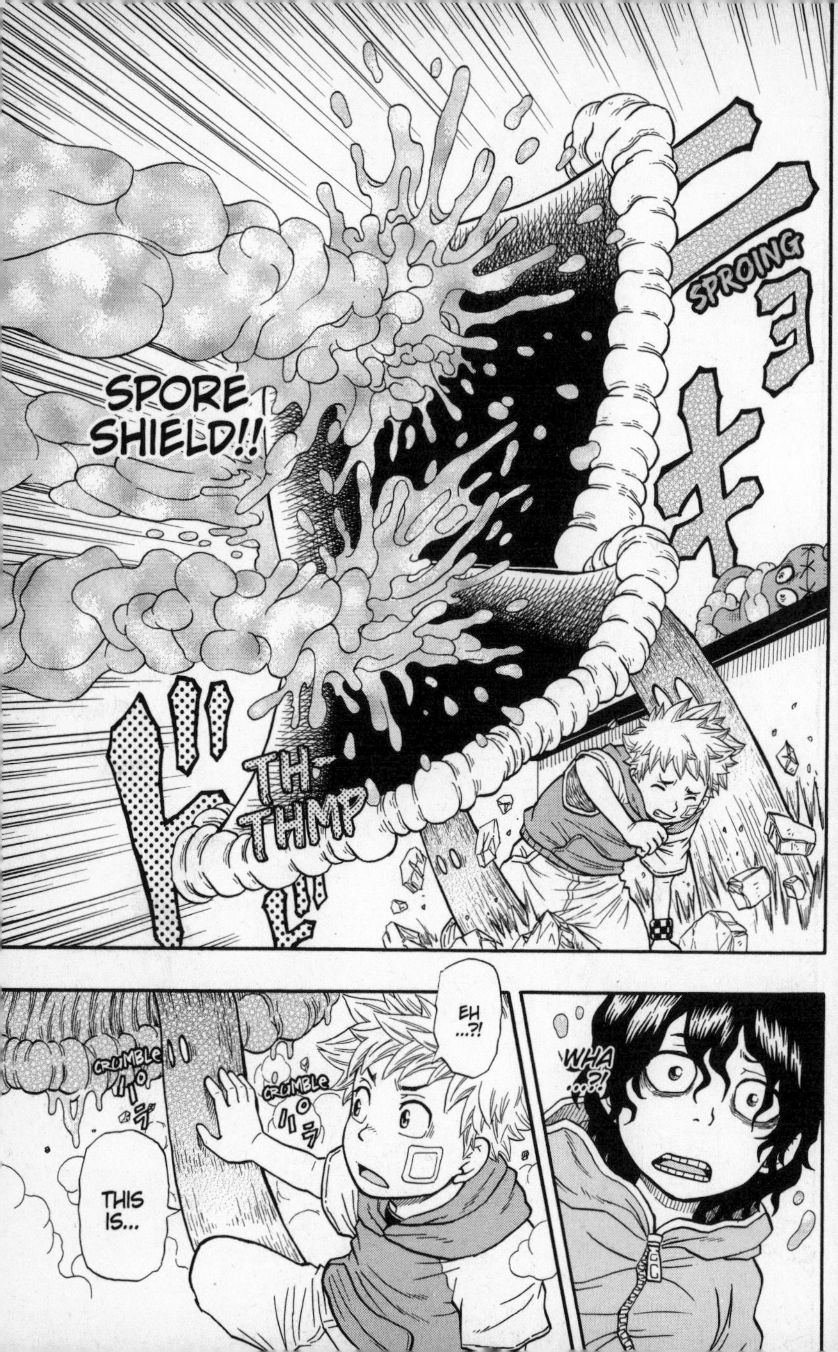
SPROING
SPORE SHIELD!!
TH-THMP
WHA...?!
EH ...?!
CRUMBLE
CRUMBLE
THIS IS...

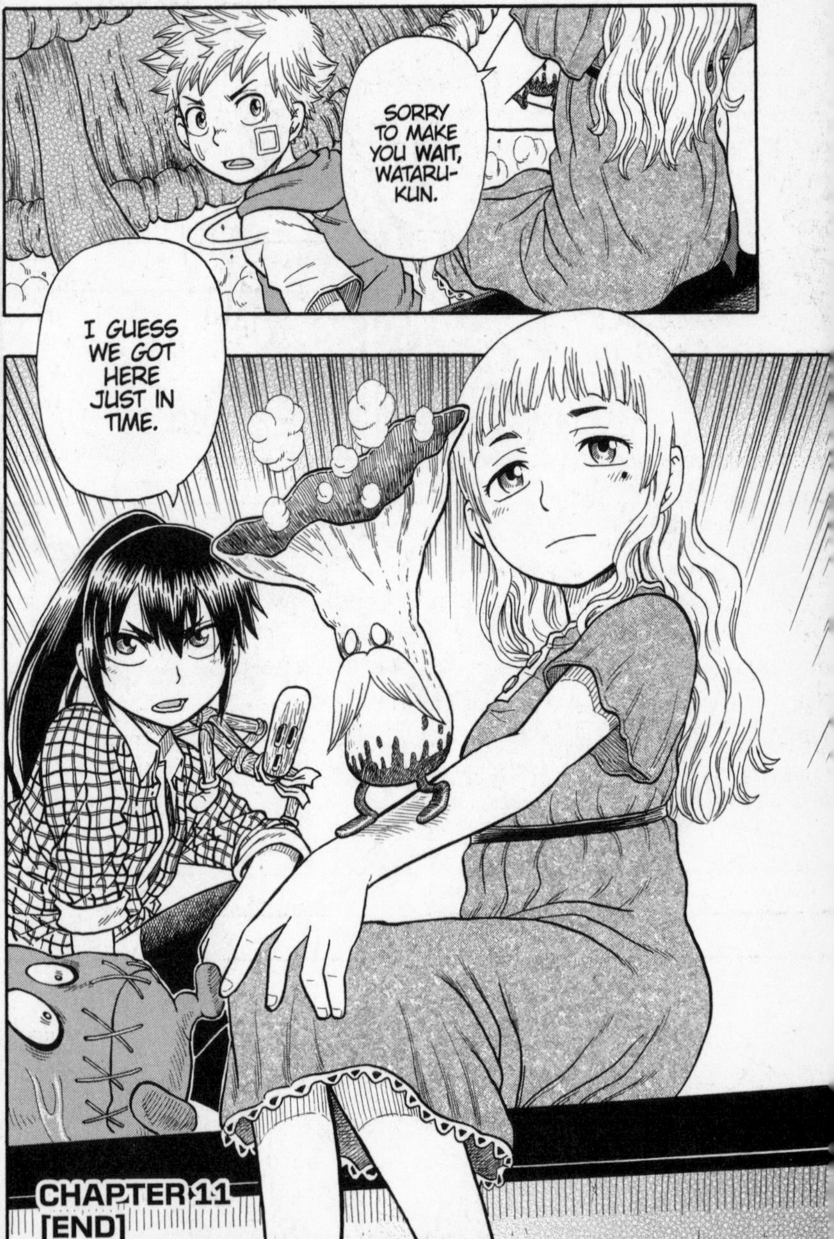
SORRY TO MAKE YOU WAIT, WATARU-KUN.
I GUESS WE GOT HERE JUST IN TIME.
CHAPTER 11 [END]

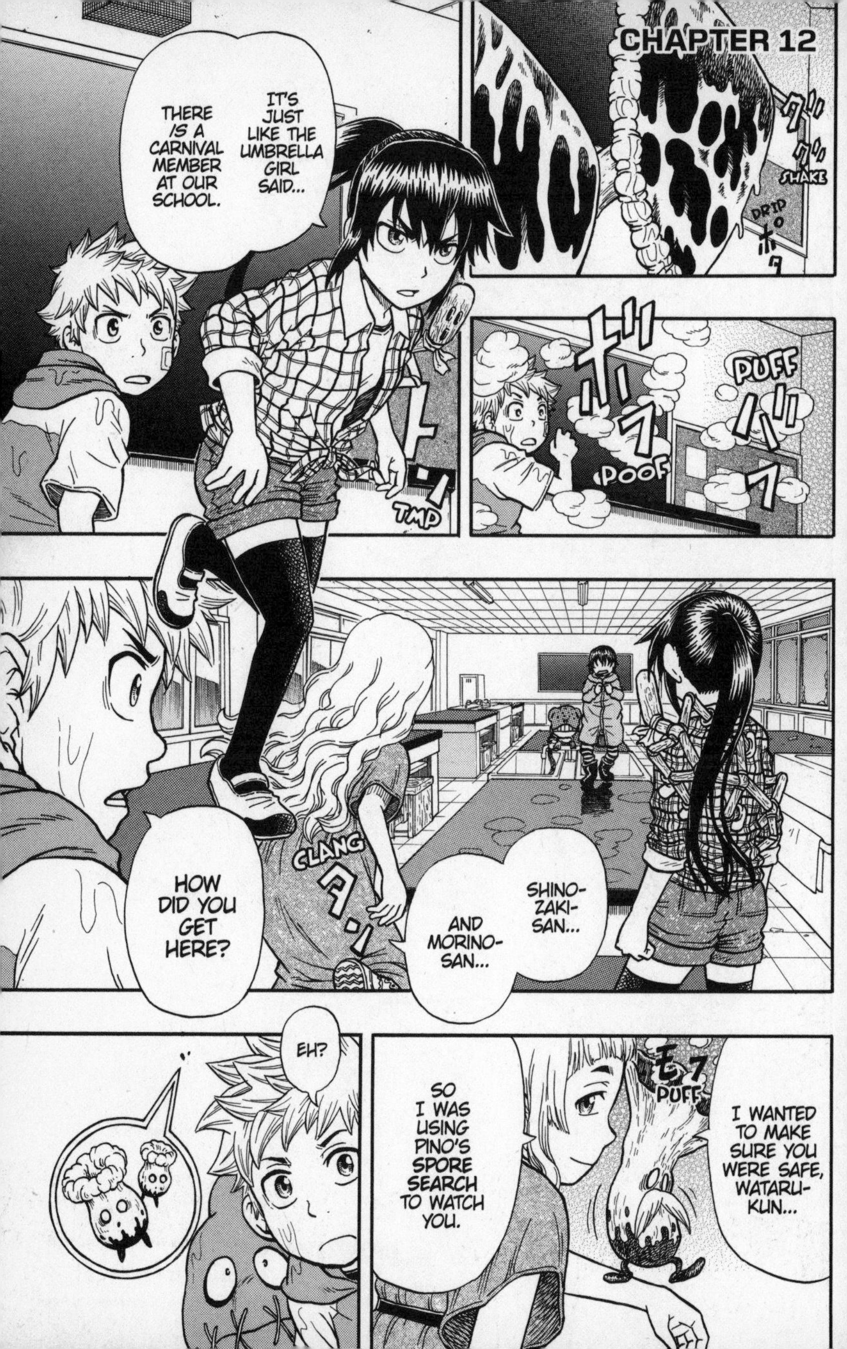
CHAPTER 12
SHAKE
DRIP
PUFF
POOF
IT'S JUST LIKE THE UMBRELLA GIRL SAID...
THERE IS A CARNIVAL MEMBER AT OUR SCHOOL.
TMP
SHINO-ZAKI-SAN...
AND MORINO-SAN...
HOW DID YOU GET HERE?
CLANG
I WANTED TO MAKE SURE YOU WERE SAFE, WATARU-KUN...
PUFF
SO I WAS USING PINO'S SPORE SEARCH TO WATCH YOU.
EH?

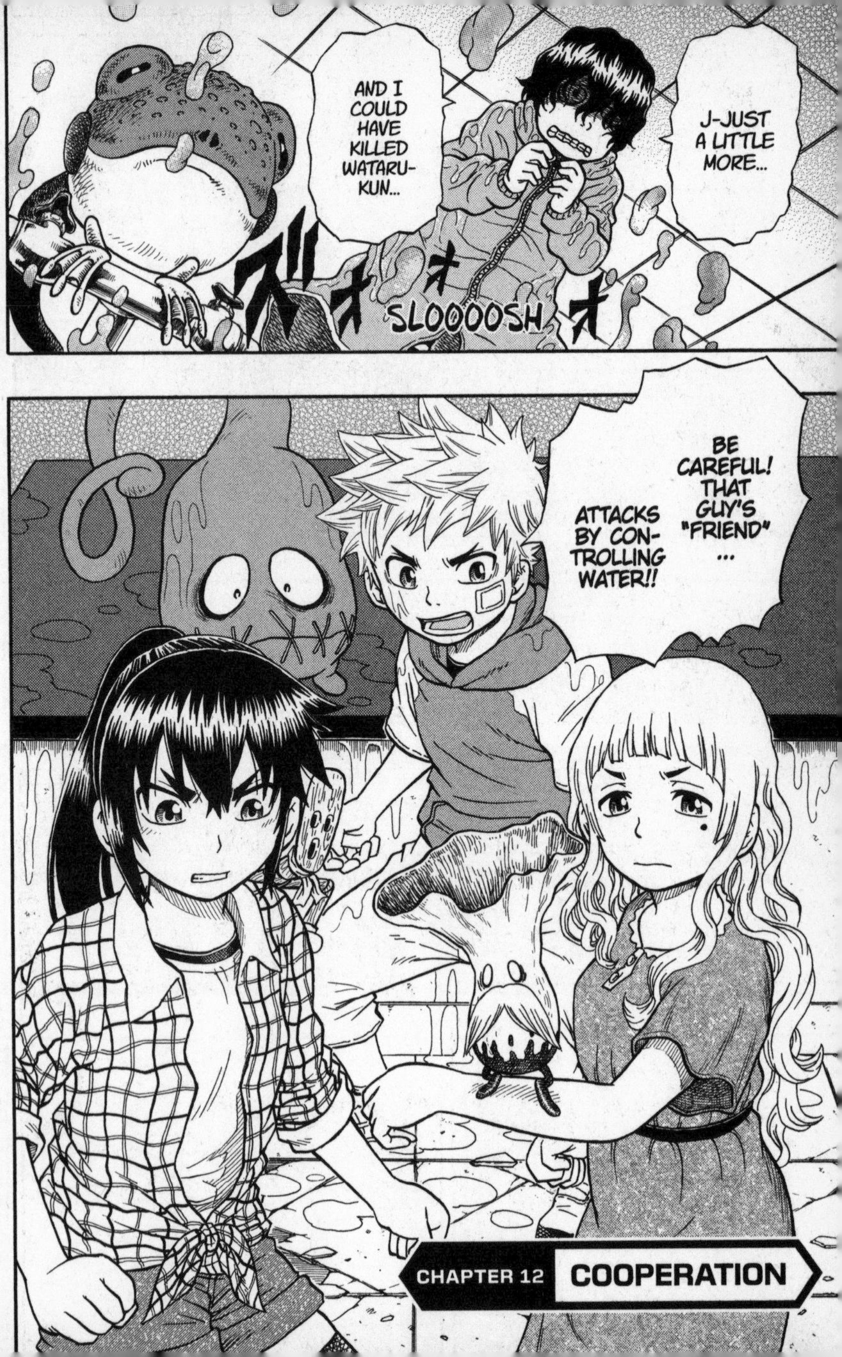
J-JUST A LITTLE MORE...
AND I COULD HAVE KILLED WATARU-KUN...
SLOOOOSH
BE CAREFUL! THAT GUY'S "FRIEND" ...
ATTACKS BY CON-TROLLING WATER!!
CHAPTER 12 COOPERATION

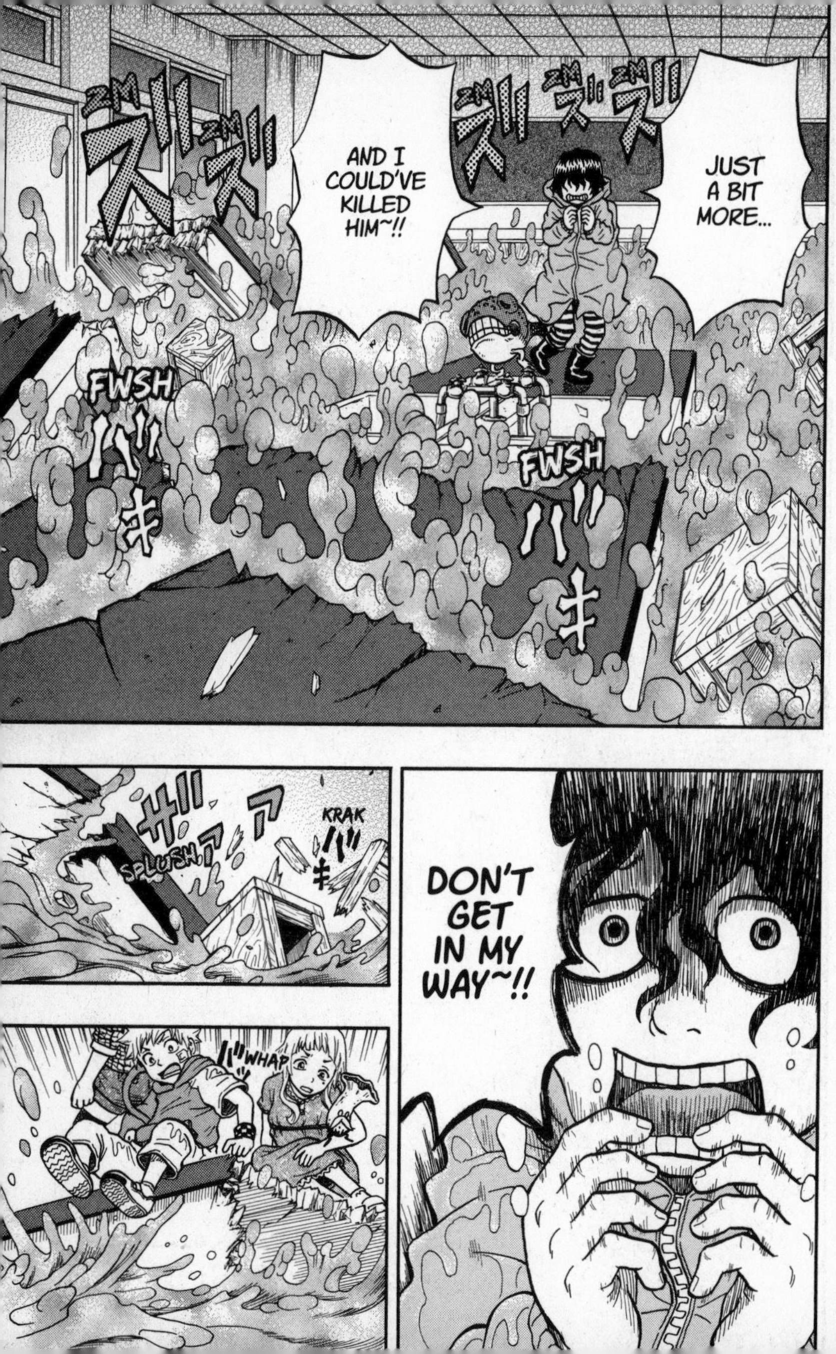
ZM
ZM
ZM
JUST A BIT MORE...
ZM
ZM
AND I COULD'VE KILLED HIM~!!
FWSH
FWSH
DON'T GET IN MY WAY~!!
KRAK
SPLUSH
WHAP

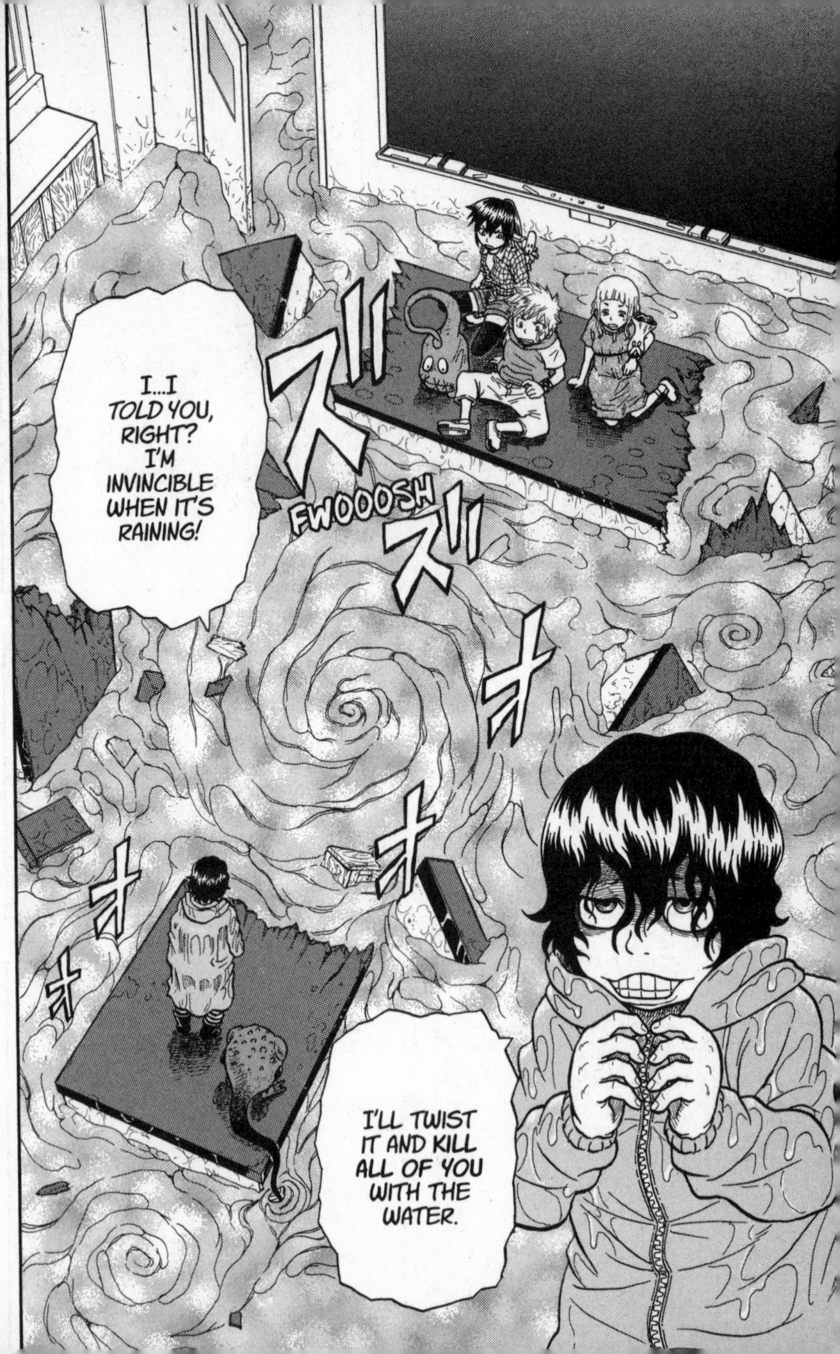
I...I TOLD YOU, RIGHT? I'M INVINCIBLE WHEN IT'S RAINING!
ズズオオオオ
FWOOOSH
I'LL TWIST IT AND KILL ALL OF YOU WITH THE WATER.

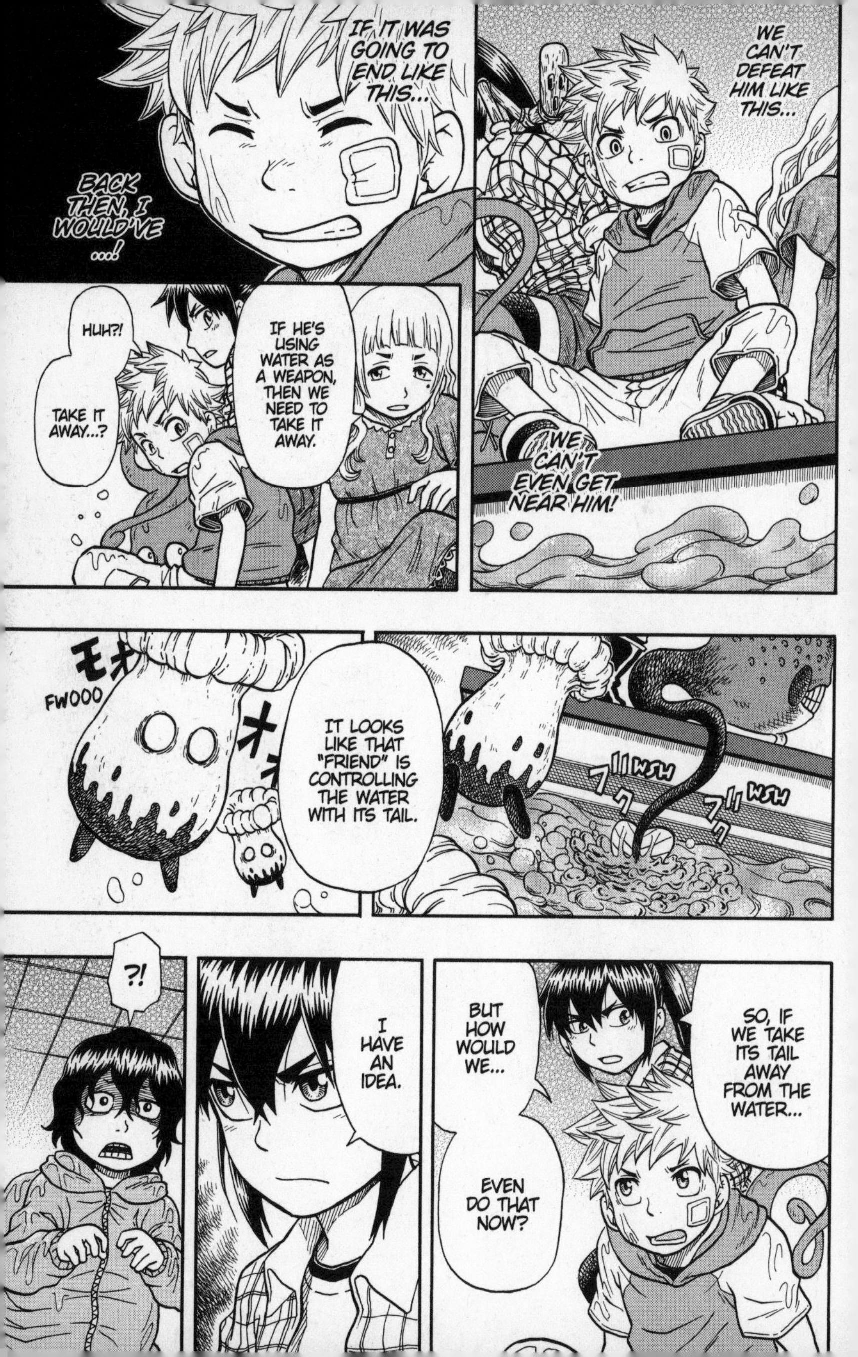
WE CAN'T DEFEAT HIM LIKE THIS...
WE CAN'T EVEN GET NEAR HIM!
IF IT WAS GOING TO END LIKE THIS...
BACK THEN, I WOULD'VE ...!
IF HE'S USING WATER AS A WEAPON, THEN WE NEED TO TAKE IT AWAY.
HUH?!
TAKE IT AWAY...?
WSH
WSH
IT LOOKS LIKE THAT "FRIEND" IS CONTROLLING THE WATER WITH ITS TAIL.
FWOOO
SO, IF WE TAKE ITS TAIL AWAY FROM THE WATER...
BUT HOW WOULD WE... EVEN DO THAT NOW?
I HAVE AN IDEA.
?!

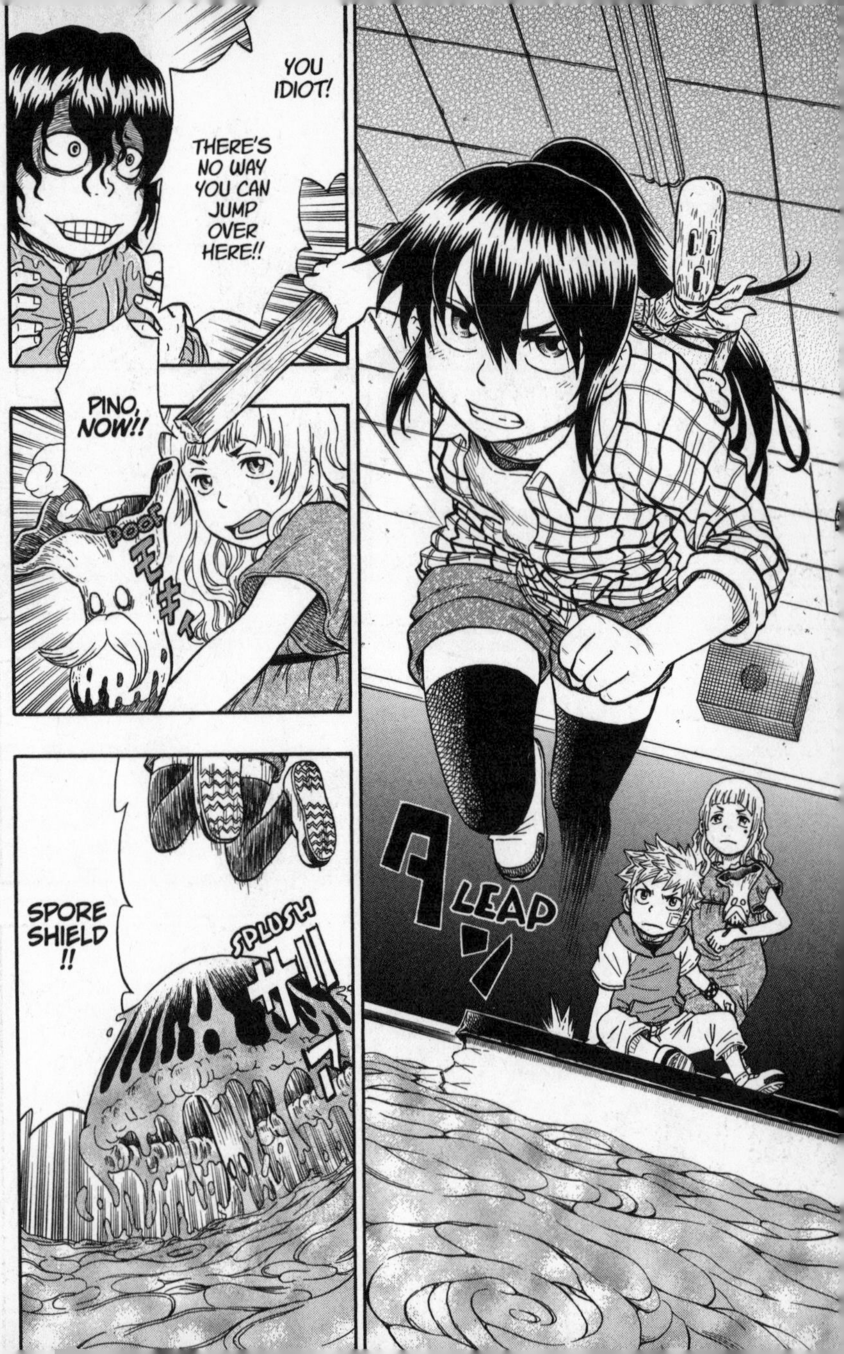
LEAP
YOU IDIOT!
THERE'S NO WAY YOU CAN JUMP OVER HERE!!
PINO, NOW!!
POOF
SPORE SHIELD!!
SPLOSH

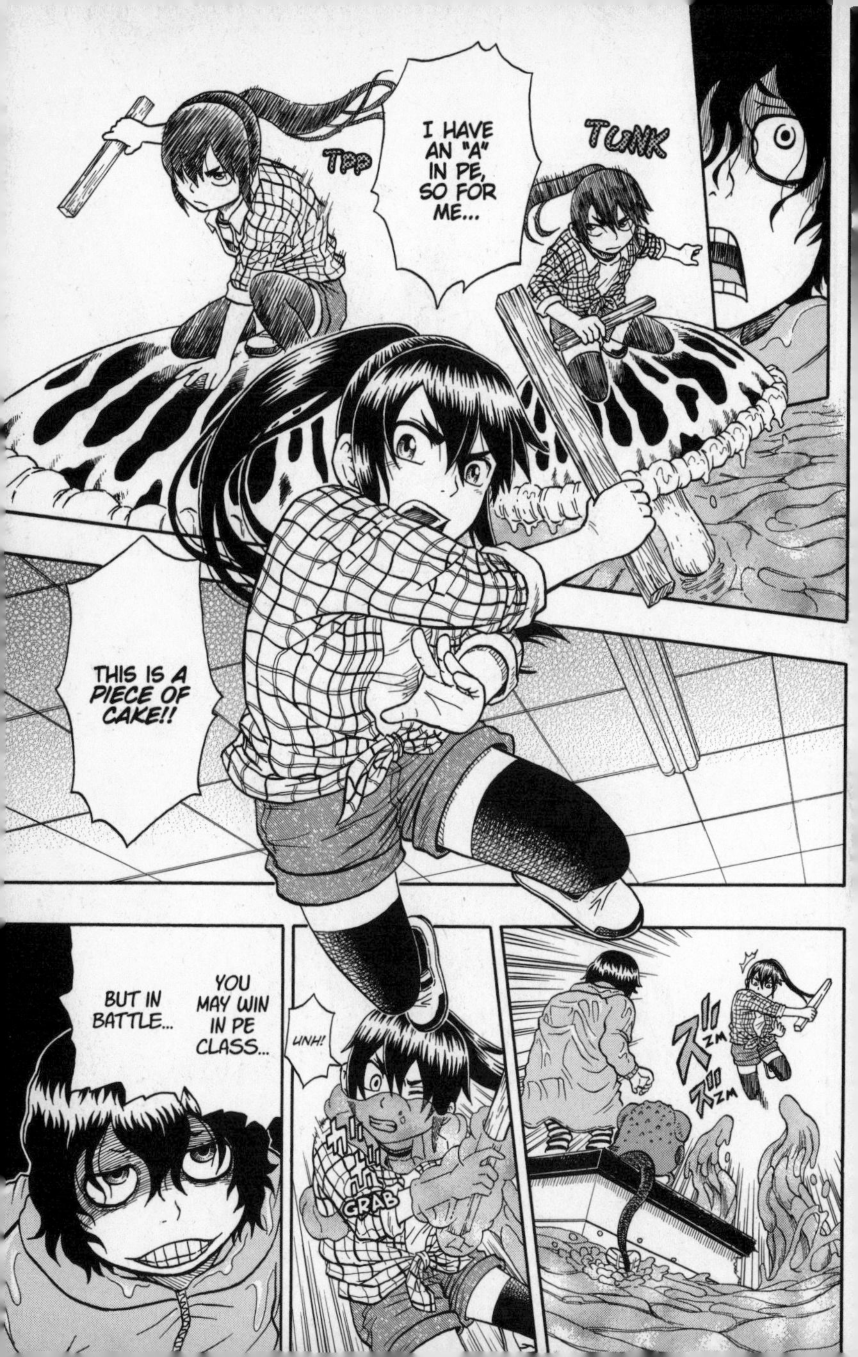
TUNK
I HAVE AN "A" IN PE, SO FOR ME...
TPP
THIS IS A PIECE OF CAKE!!
ZM
ZM
UNH!
GRAB
YOU MAY WIN IN PE CLASS...
BUT IN BATTLE...

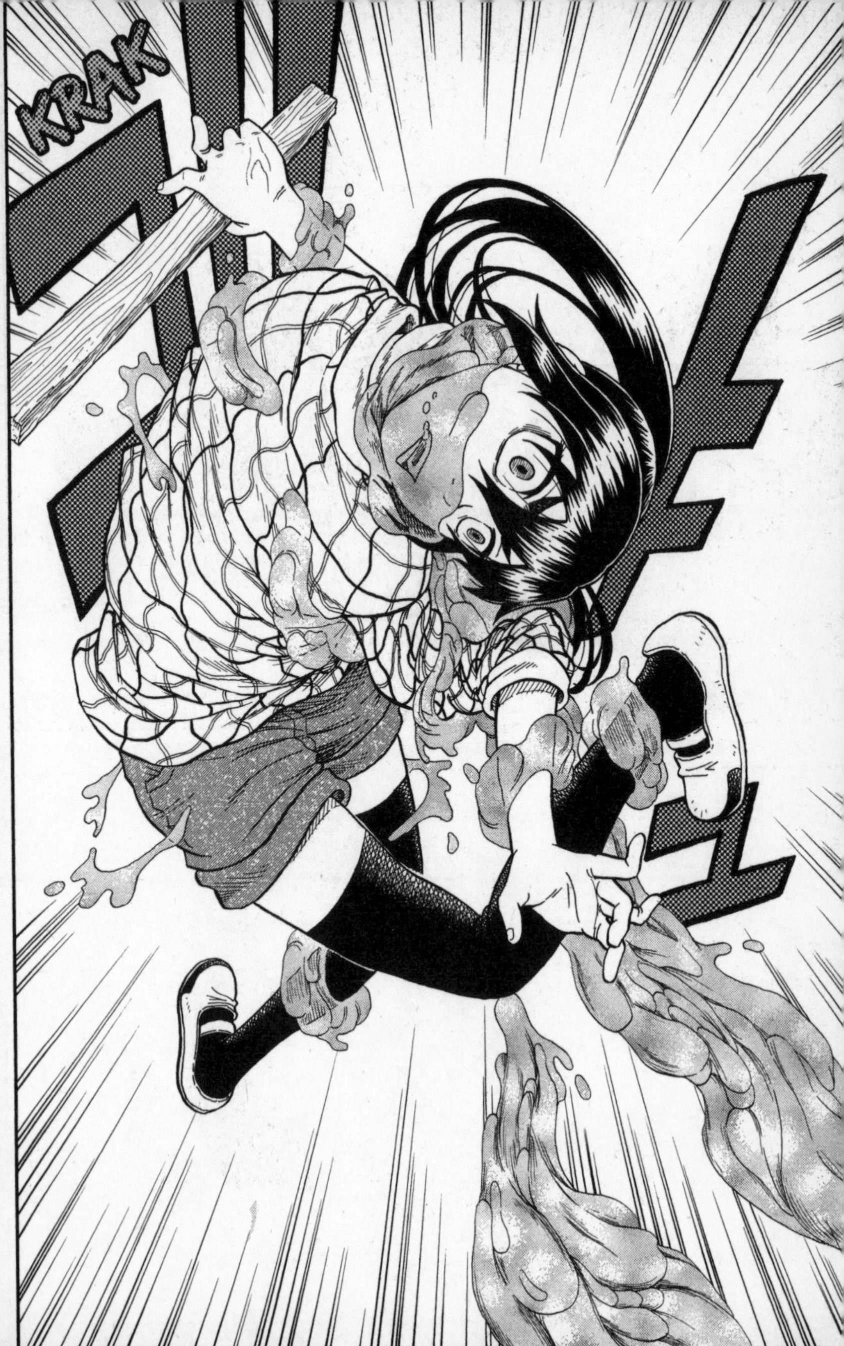
KRAK

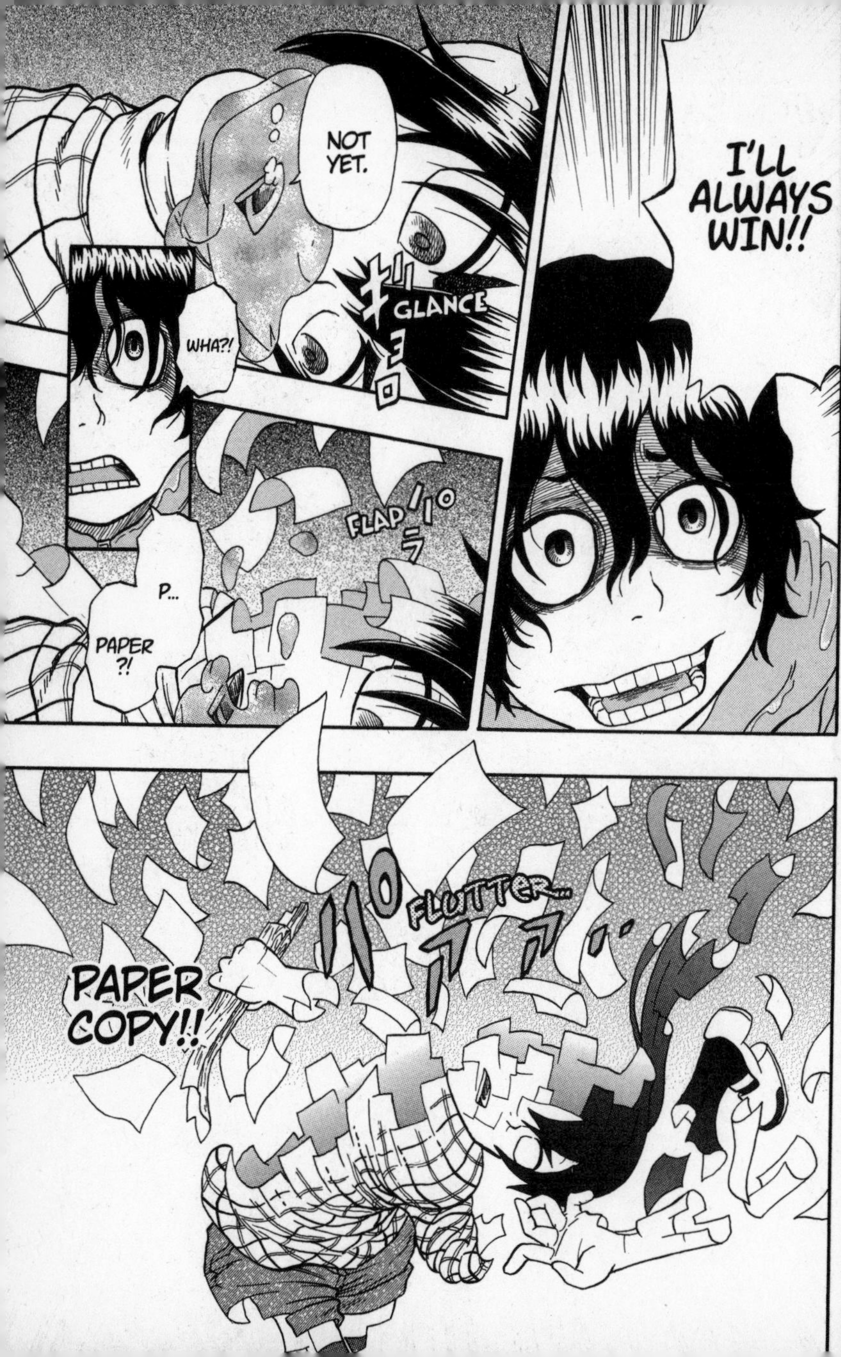
I'LL ALWAYS WIN!!
NOT YET.
GLANCE
WHA?!
FLAP
P...
PAPER?!
FLUTTER...
PAPER COPY!!

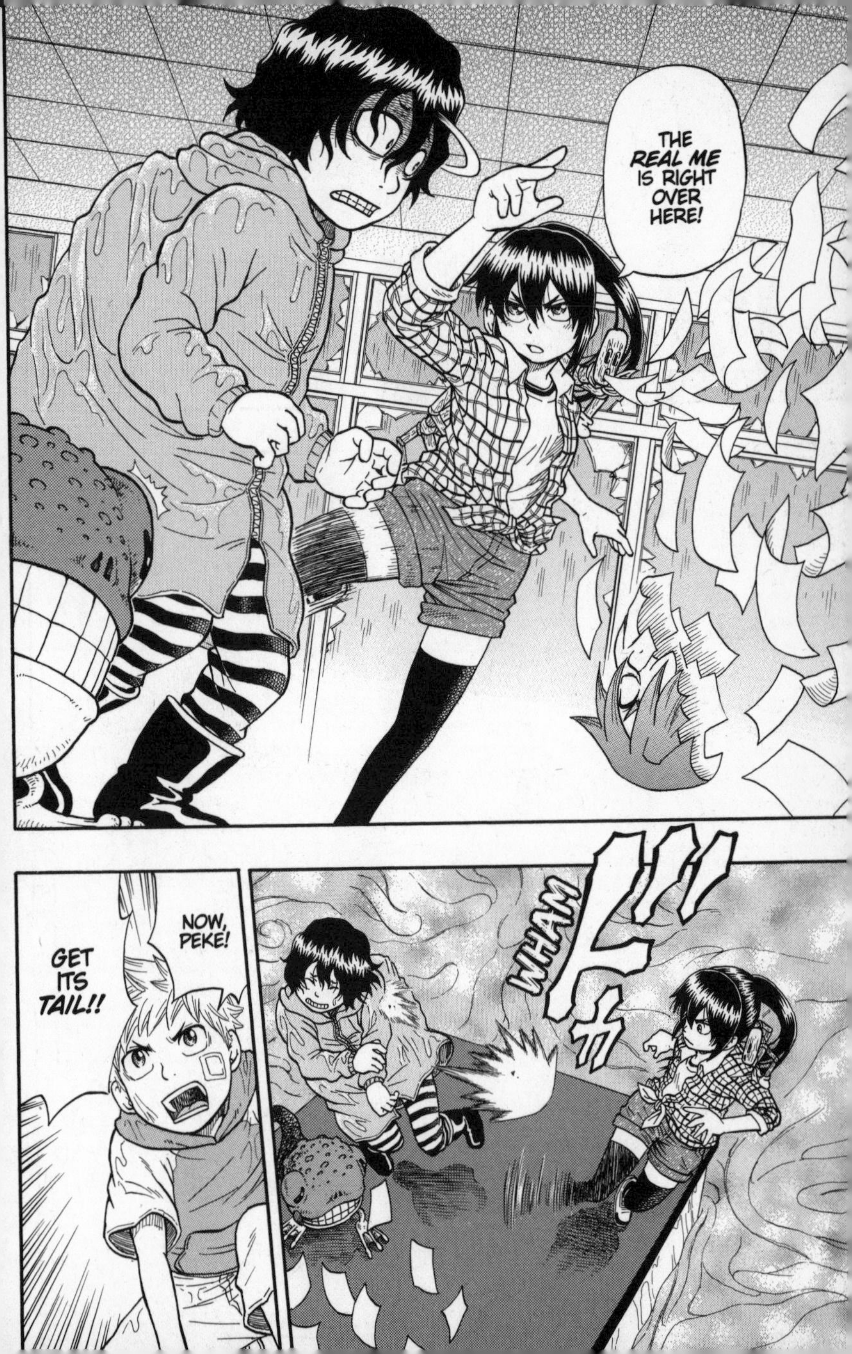
THE REAL ME IS RIGHT OVER HERE!
WHAM!!
NOW, PEKE!
GET ITS TAIL!!

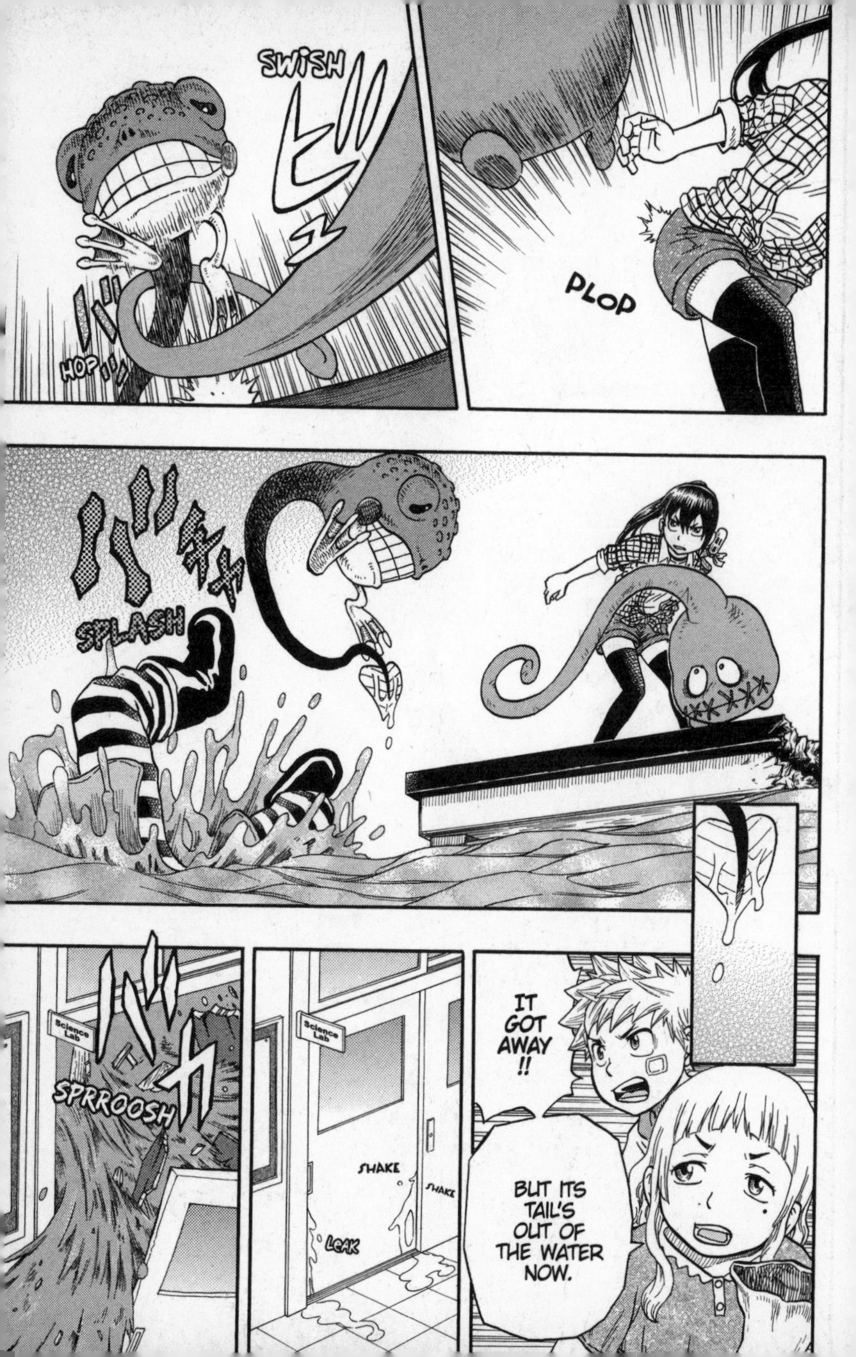
PLOP
SWISH
HOP!!
SPLASH
IT GOT AWAY!!
BUT ITS TAIL'S OUT OF THE WATER NOW.
Science Lab
SHAKE
SHAKE
LEAK
Science Lab
SPRROOSH

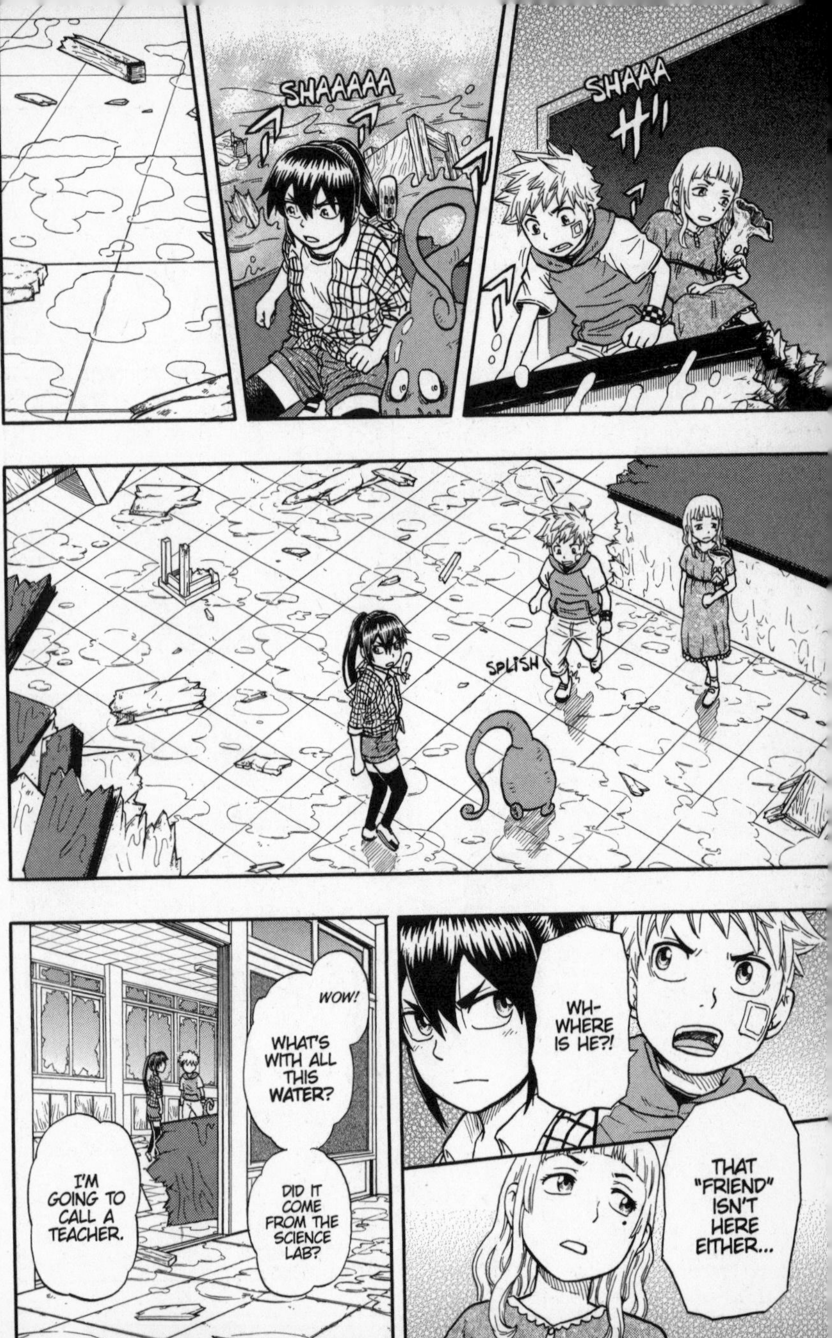
SHAAA
ザ
SHAAAAA
SPLISH
WH- WHERE IS HE?!
THAT "FRIEND" ISN'T HERE EITHER...
WOW!
WHAT'S WITH ALL THIS WATER?
DID IT COME FROM THE SCIENCE LAB?
I'M GOING TO CALL A TEACHER.

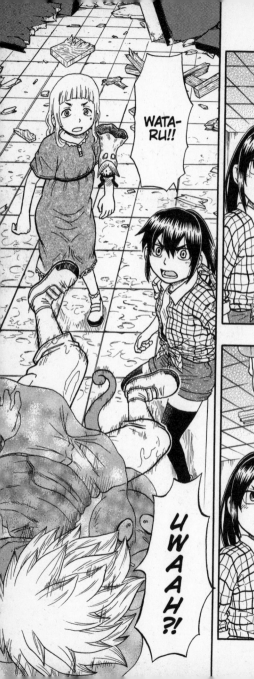

WATA-RU!!

UWAAH?!

IF PEOPLE SEE THIS...

THAT'S NOT GOOD.

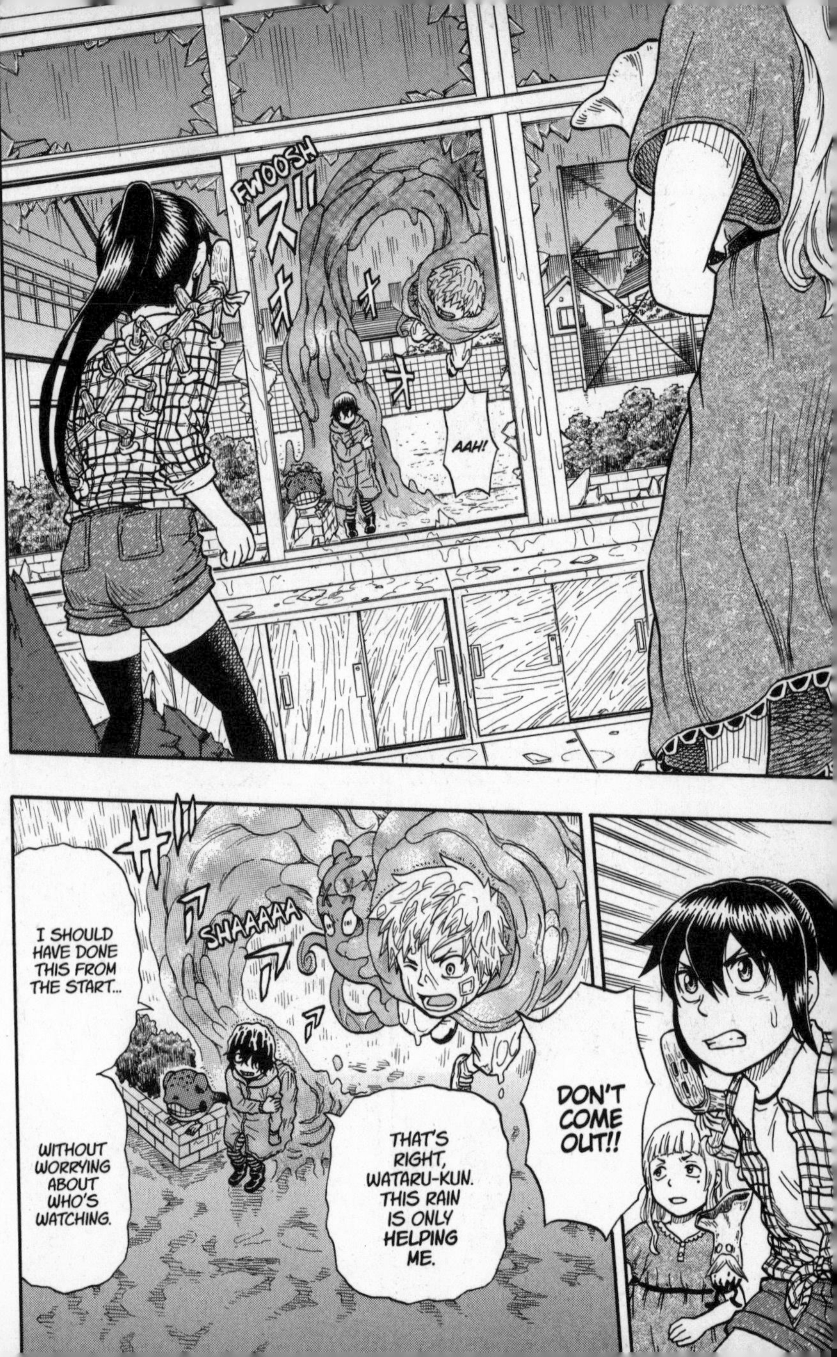
FWOOSH
スォォォ
AAH!
DON'T COME OUT!!
SHAAAAA
I SHOULD HAVE DONE THIS FROM THE START...
WITHOUT WORRYING ABOUT WHO'S WATCHING.
THAT'S RIGHT, WATARU-KUN. THIS RAIN IS ONLY HELPING ME.

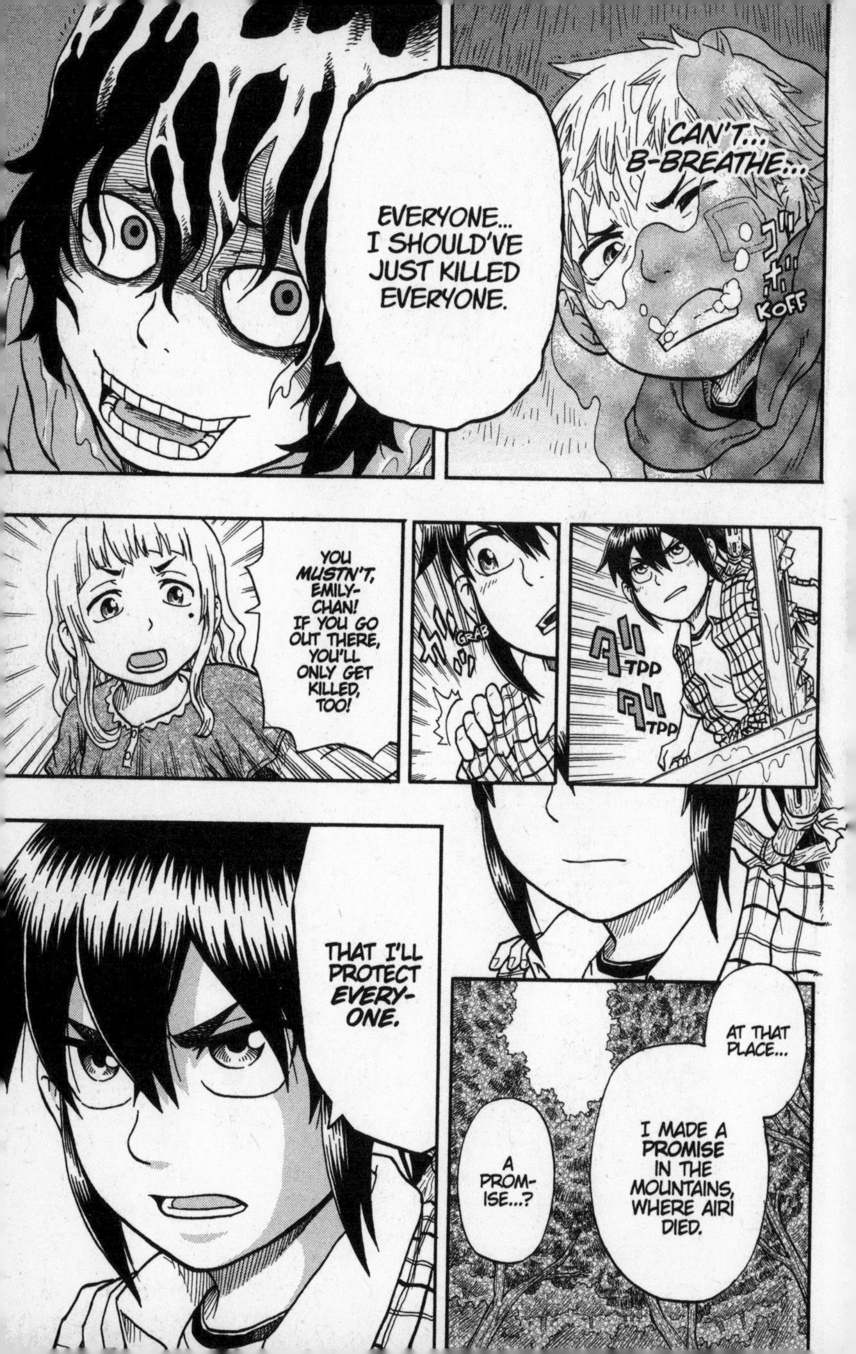
CAN'T... B-BREATHE...
KOFF
EVERYONE... I SHOULD'VE JUST KILLED EVERYONE.
TPP
TPP
GRAB
YOU MUSTN'T, EMILY-CHAN! IF YOU GO OUT THERE, YOU'LL ONLY GET KILLED, TOO!
AT THAT PLACE...
I MADE A PROMISE IN THE MOUNTAINS, WHERE AIRI DIED.
A PROMISE...?
THAT I'LL PROTECT EVERYONE.

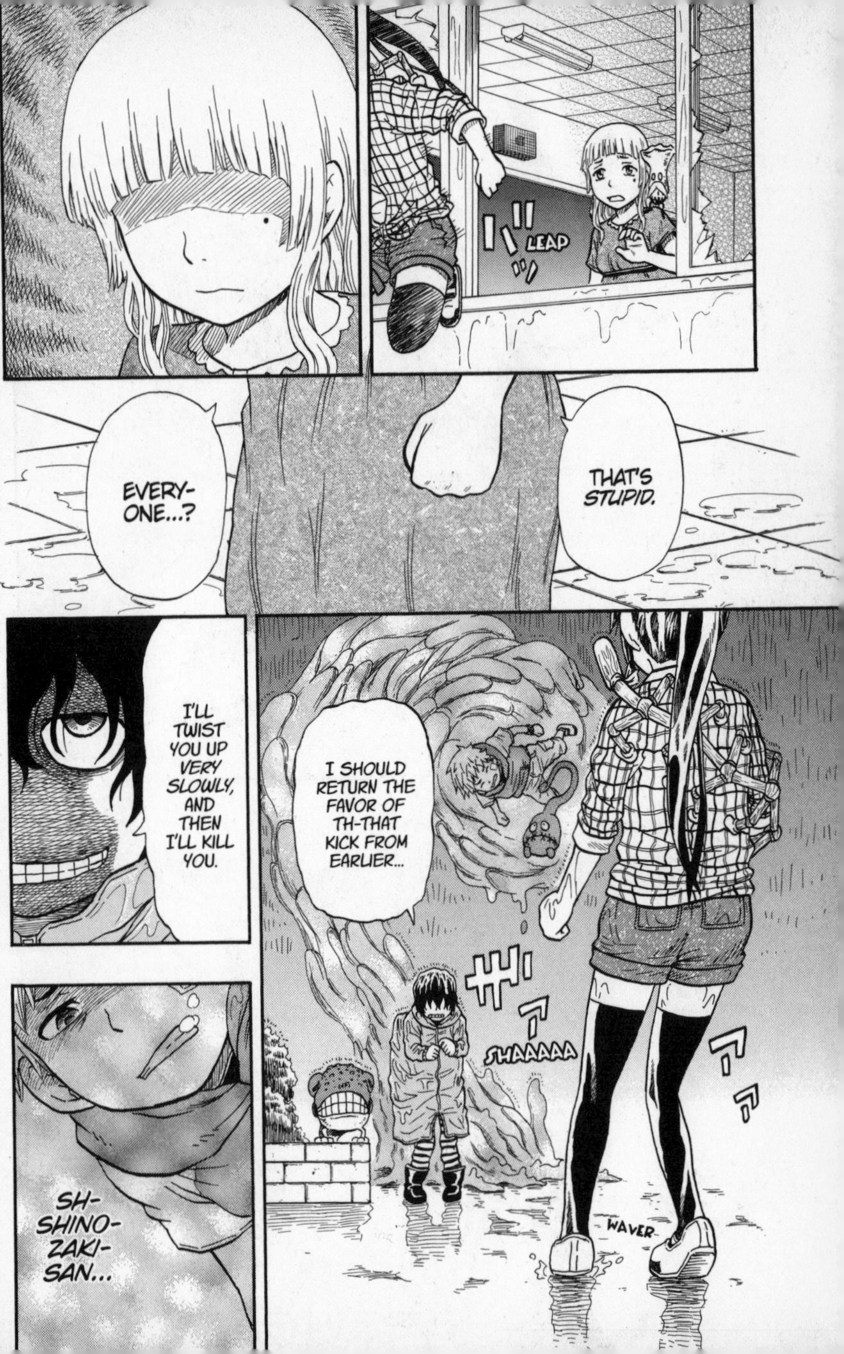
LEAP
THAT'S STUPID.
EVERY-ONE...?
I SHOULD RETURN THE FAVOR OF TH-THAT KICK FROM EARLIER...
SHAAAAA
WAVER
I'LL TWIST YOU UP VERY SLOWLY, AND THEN I'LL KILL YOU.
SH-SHINO-ZAKI-SAN...

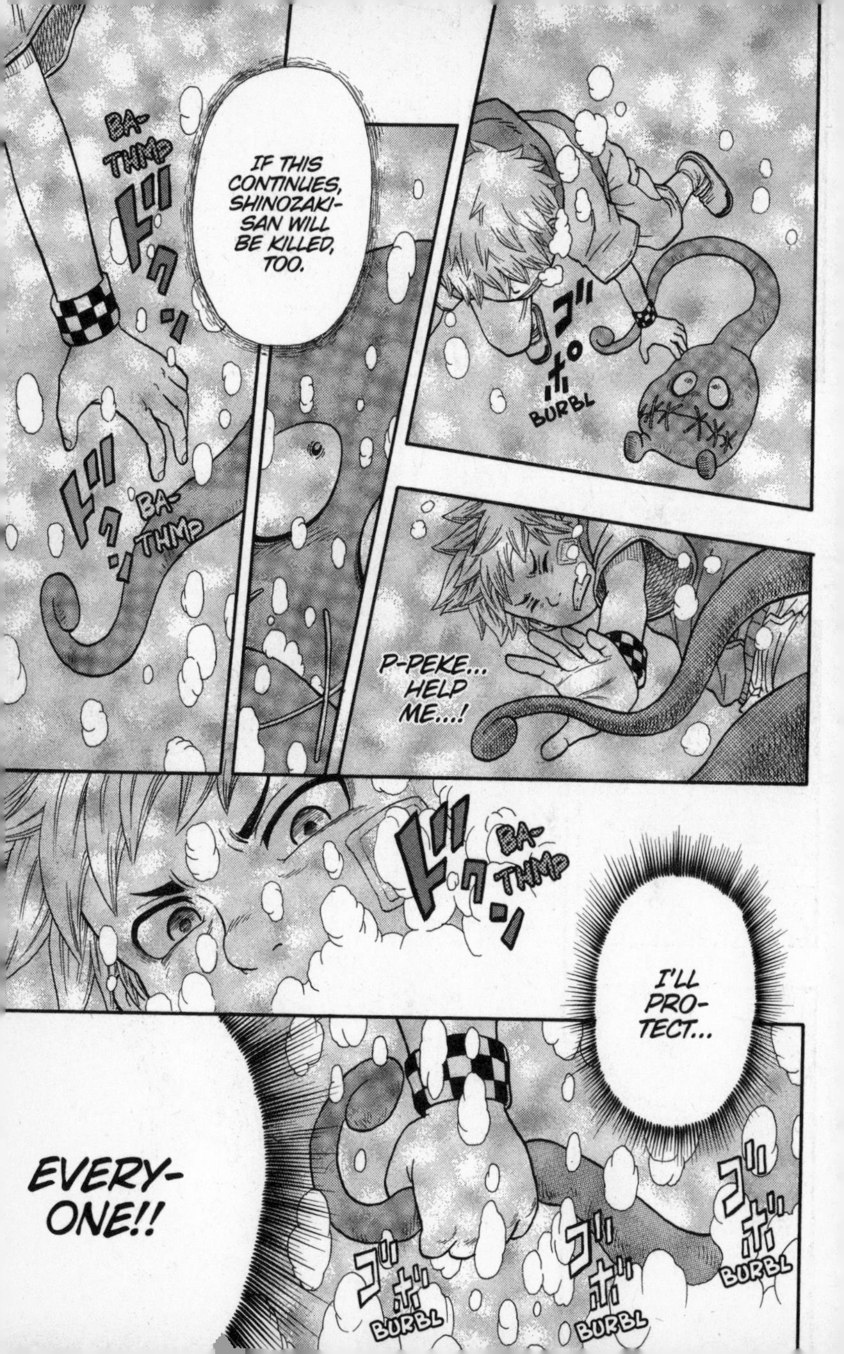
BURBL
P-PEKE... HELP ME...!
IF THIS CONTINUES, SHINOZAKI-SAN WILL BE KILLED, TOO.
BA-THMP
BA-THMP
BA-THMP
I'LL PROTECT...
EVERYONE!!
BURBL
BURBL
BURBL

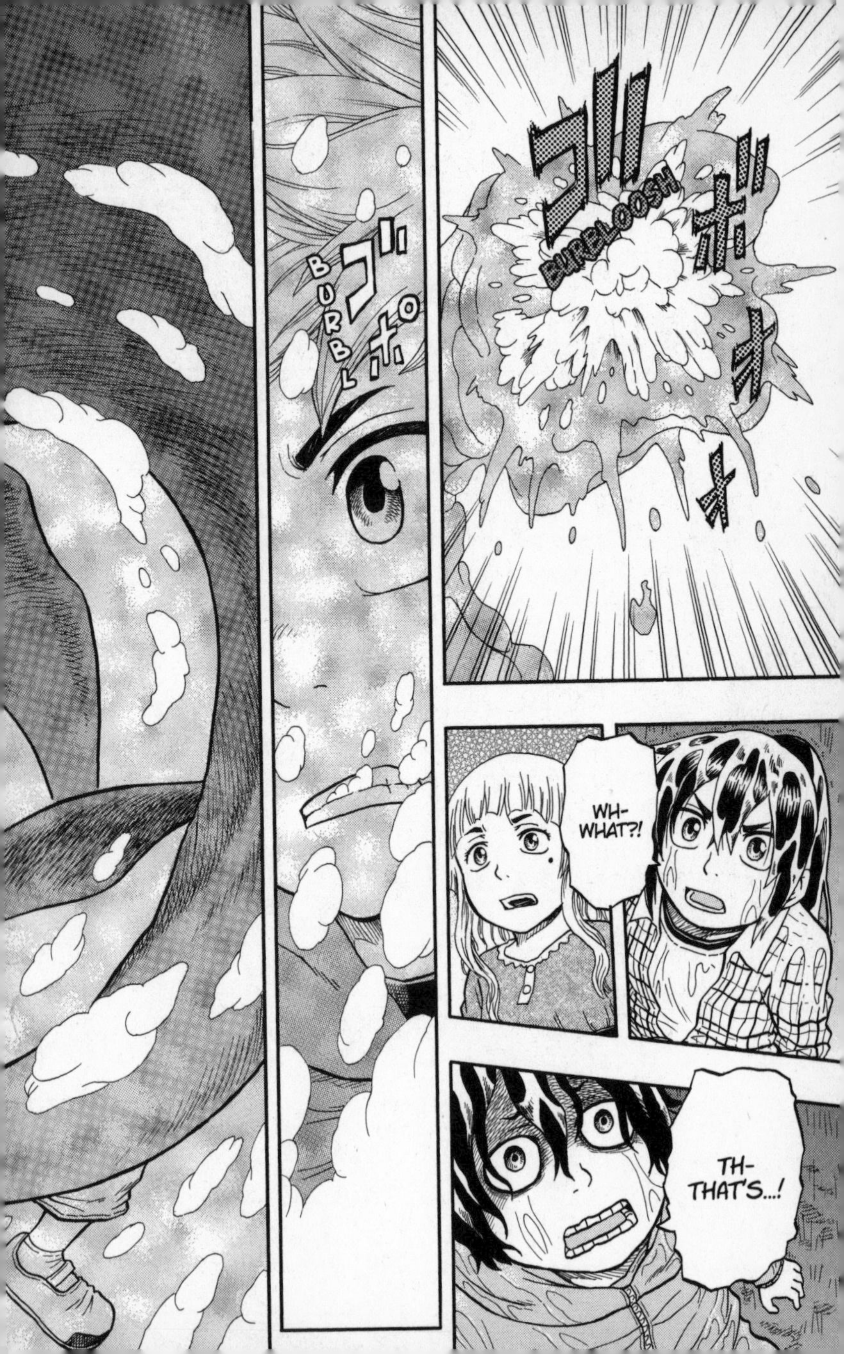

BUBBLOOSH
WH-WHAT?!
TH-THAT'S...!
BURBL

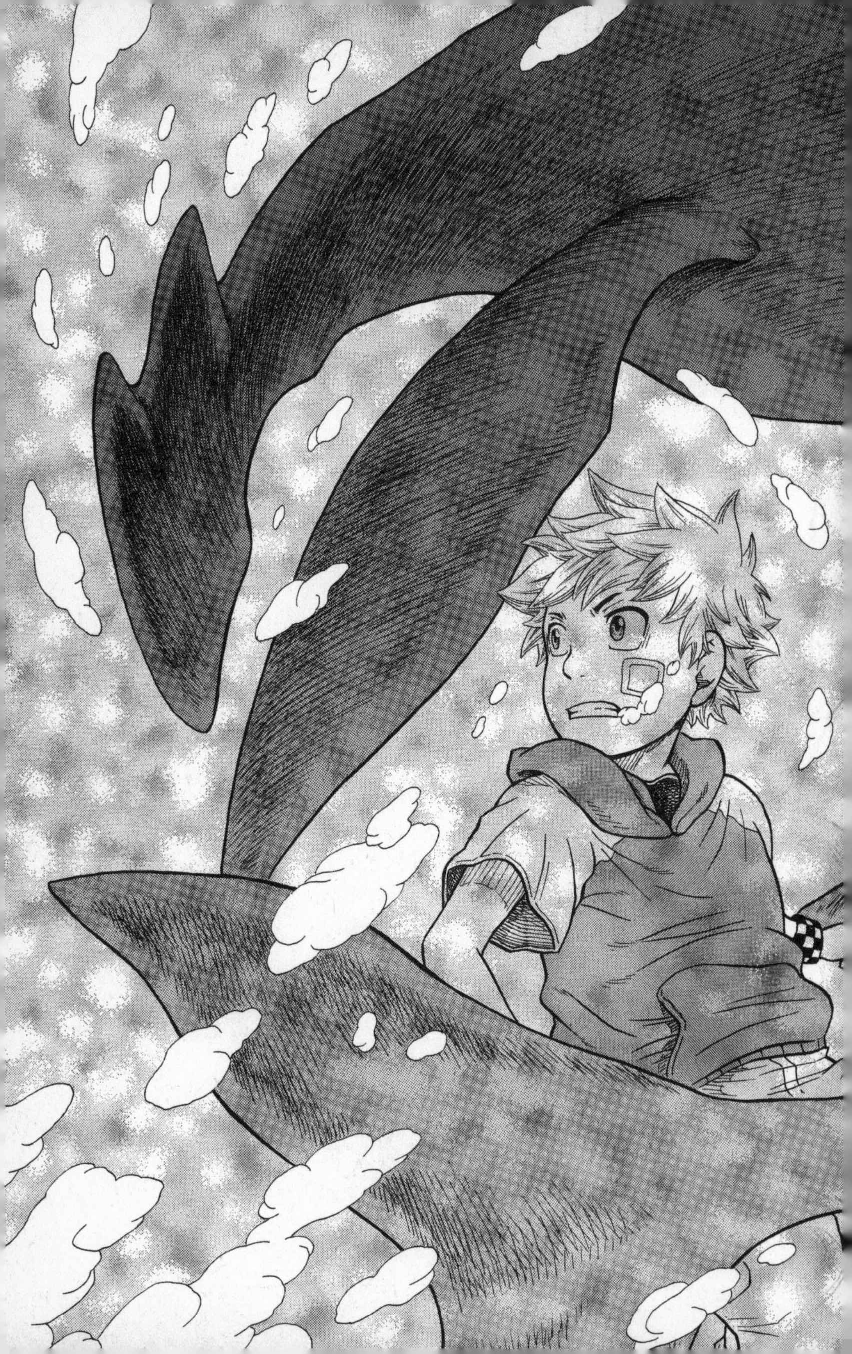

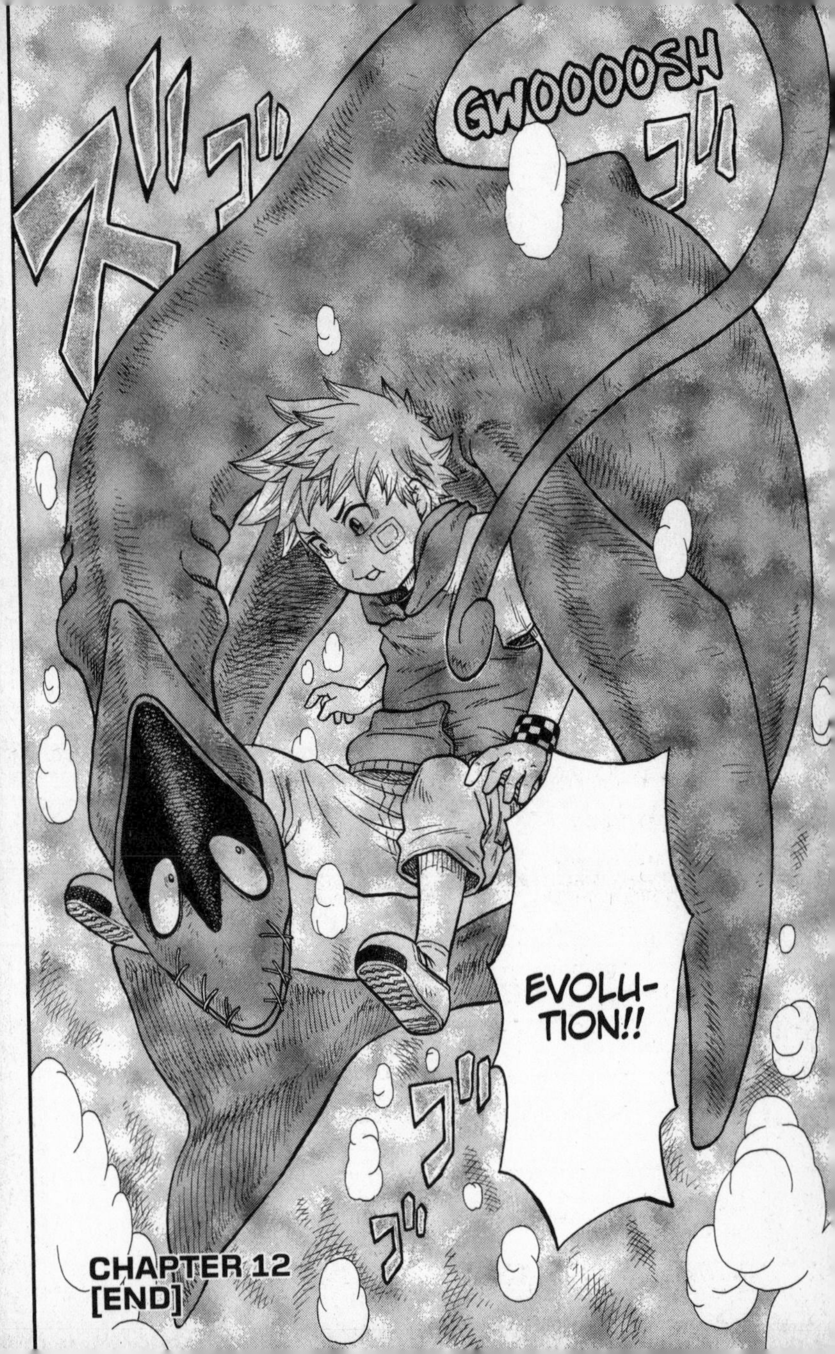
GWOOOOSH
EVOLU-
TION!!
CHAPTER 12
[END]

Friend Encyclopedia No.007

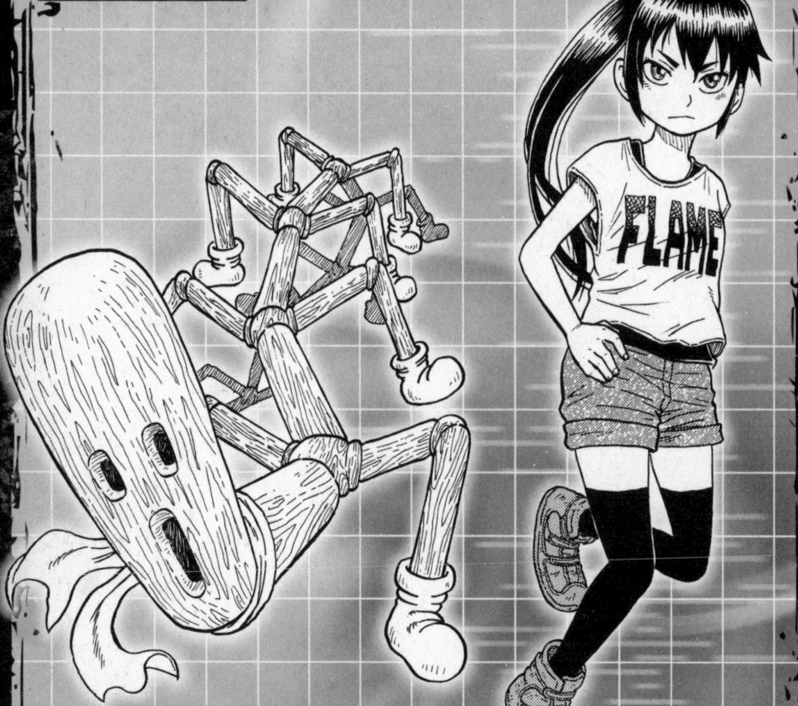
FLAME

Name: **Niru**

Partner:	Shinozaki Emily (6th grade)	**Speed:**	C
Attack:	D	**Dexterity:**	A
Defense:	C	**Special Abilities:**	A
Characteristics:	An insect-like Friend. It can spit out imitations identical to whatever its partner imagines.		
Special Abilities:	Paper Copy – Creates a double of its partner.		

Friend Encyclopedia No.008

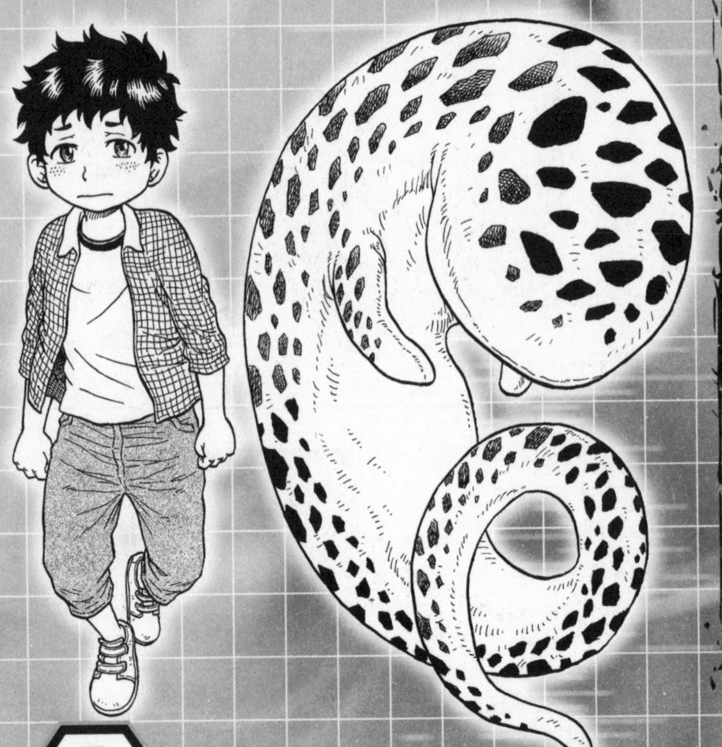

Name: ?

Partner:	Nakasato Fuku (3rd grade)	**Speed:**	?
Attack:	?	**Dexterity:**	?
Defense:	?	**Special Abilities:**	?
Characteristics:	A salamander-like Friend. Its abilities are unknown.		
Special Abilities:	Unknown.		

HELP ME...
BA-THMP
PEKE!!
BA-THMP
BA-THMP
Chapter 13
BLOP
BLOP
STRETCH...
BA-THMP
POP...
STRETCH...

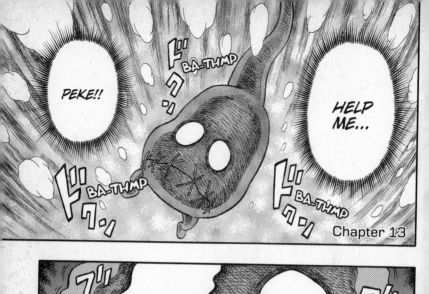

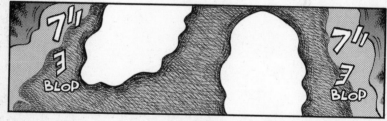

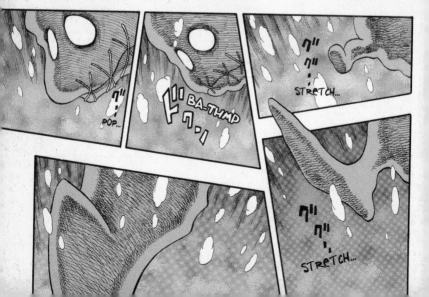

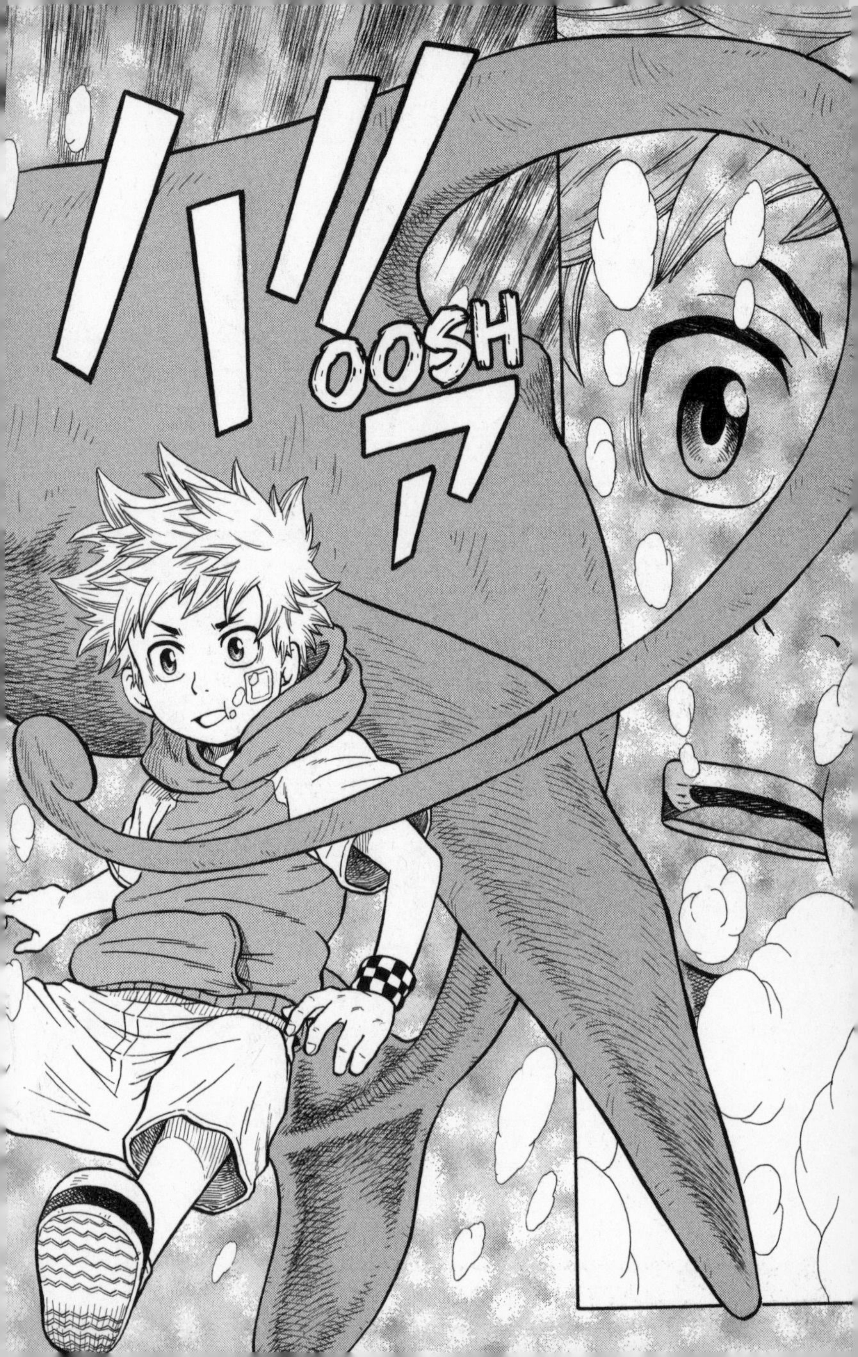
OOSH

CHAPTER 13 BATTLE IN THE WATER

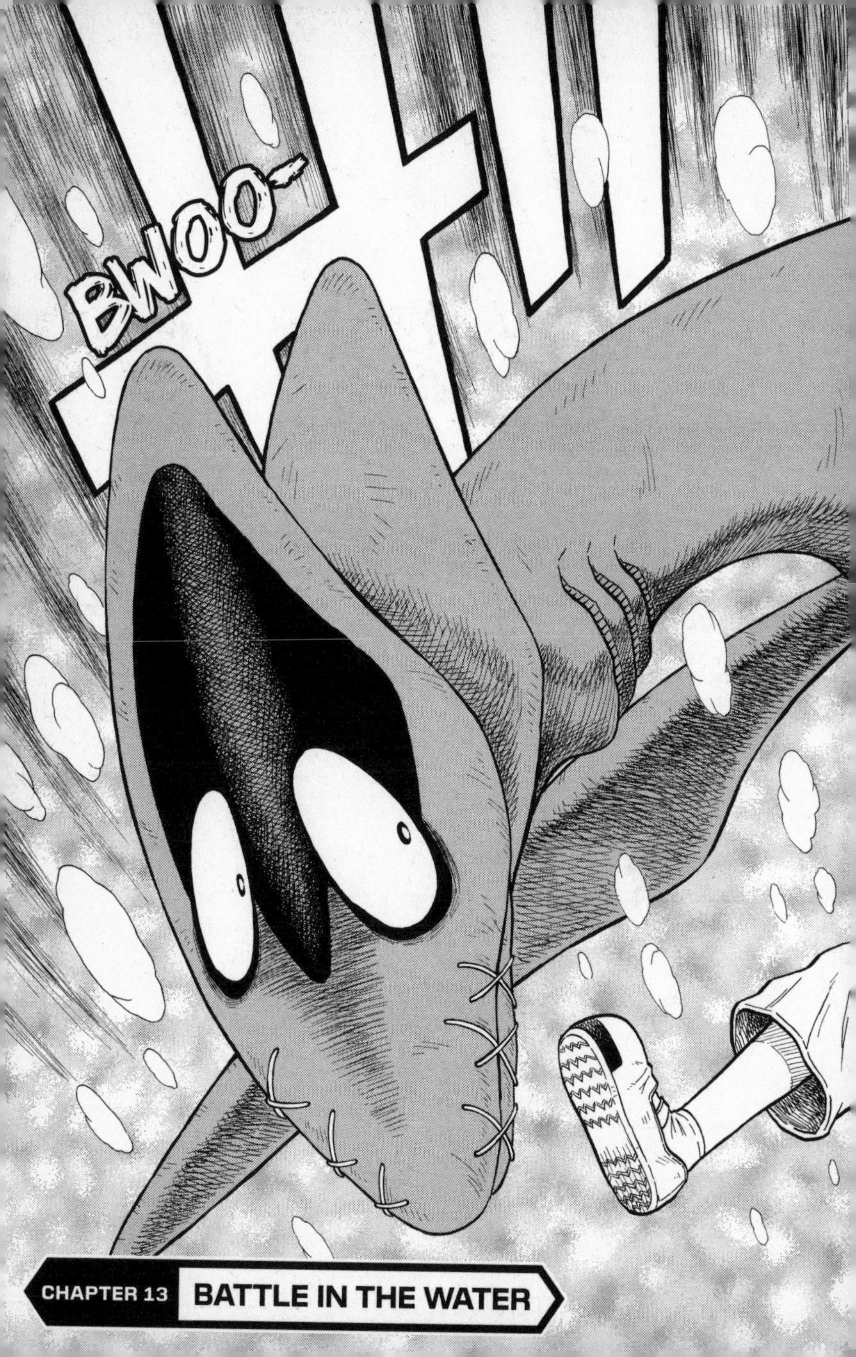
BWOO-

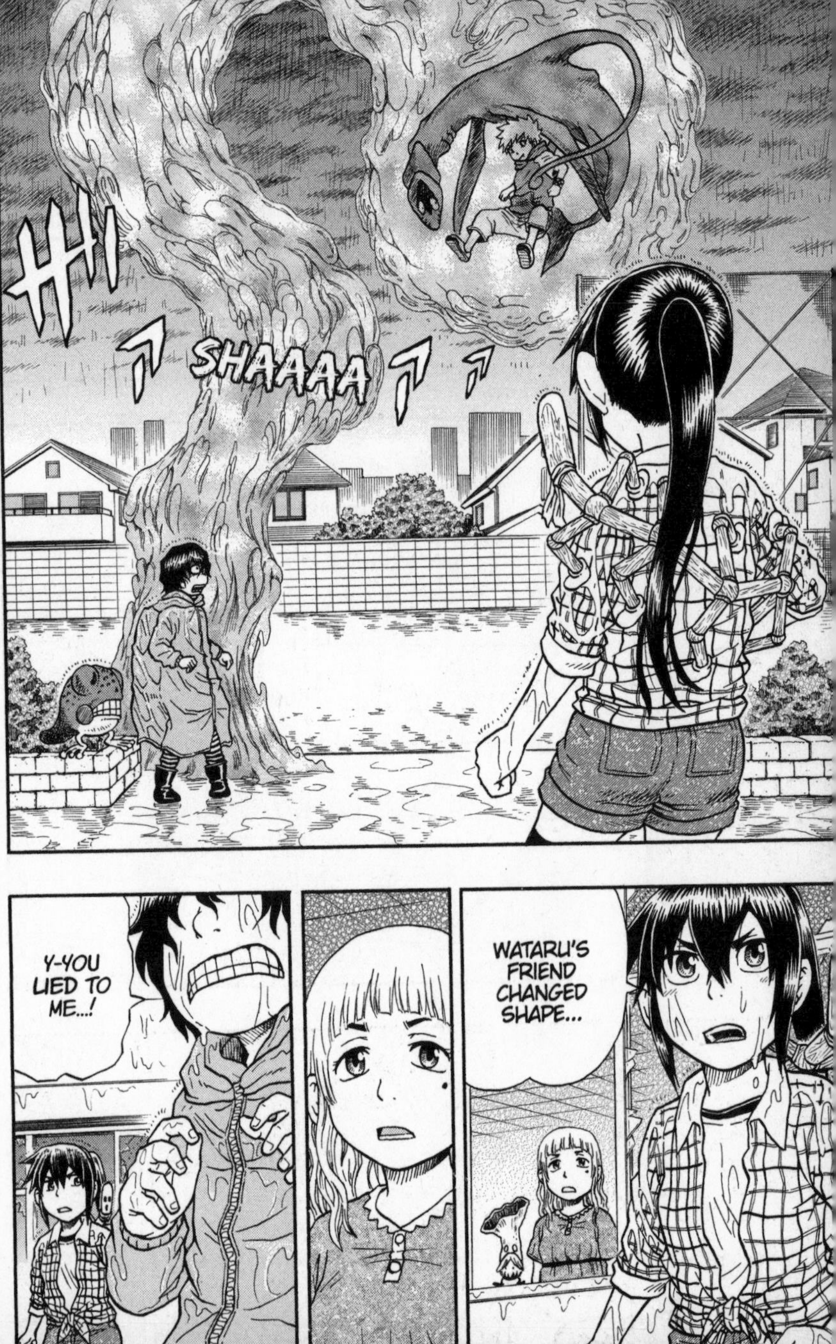
HI
SHAAAA
WATARU'S FRIEND CHANGED SHAPE...
Y-YOU LIED TO ME...!

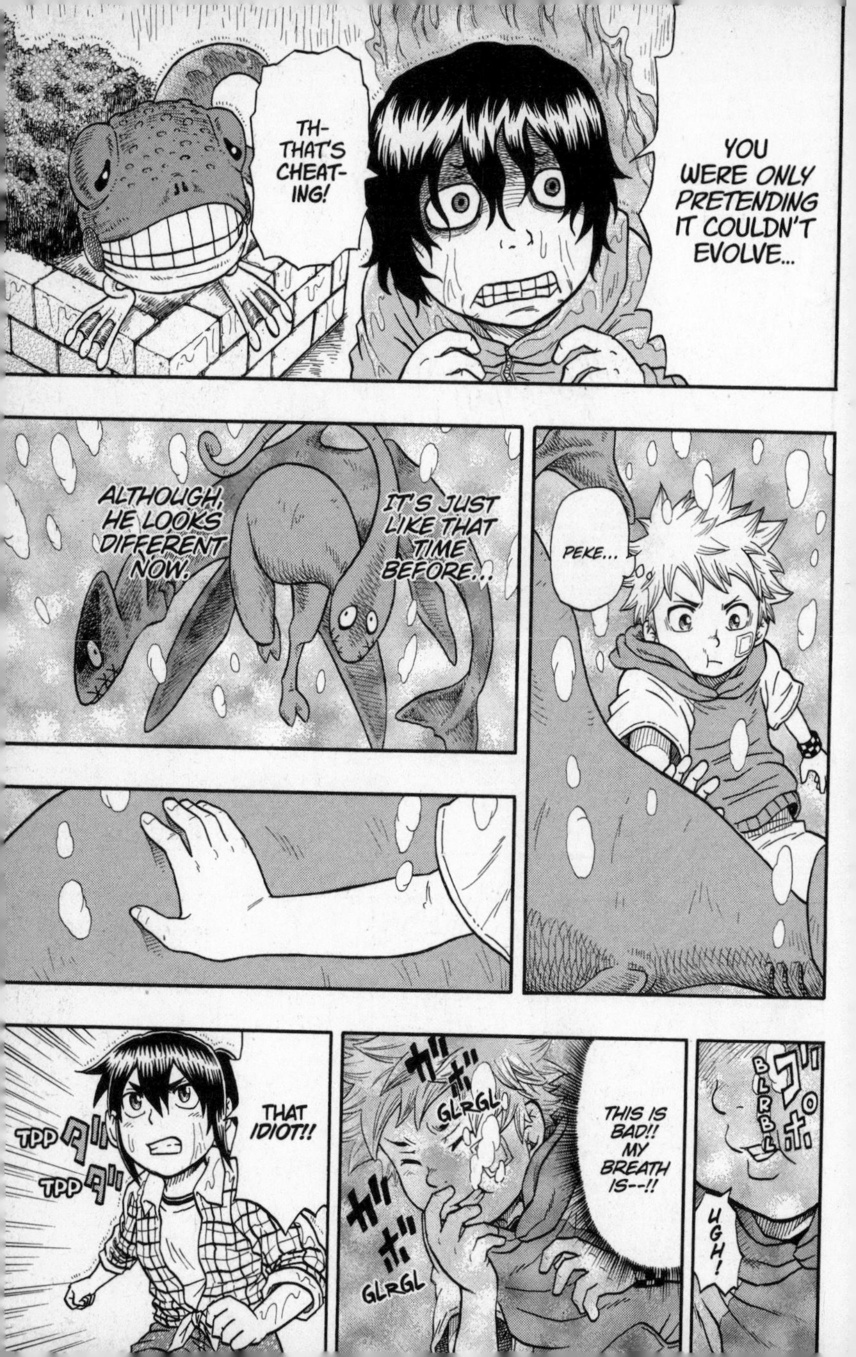
YOU WERE ONLY PRETENDING IT COULDN'T EVOLVE...
TH-THAT'S CHEATING!
PEKE...
IT'S JUST LIKE THAT TIME BEFORE...
ALTHOUGH, HE LOOKS DIFFERENT NOW.
BLRBL
UGH!
GLRGL
THIS IS BAD!! MY BREATH IS--!!
GLRGL
THAT IDIOT!!
TPP
TPP

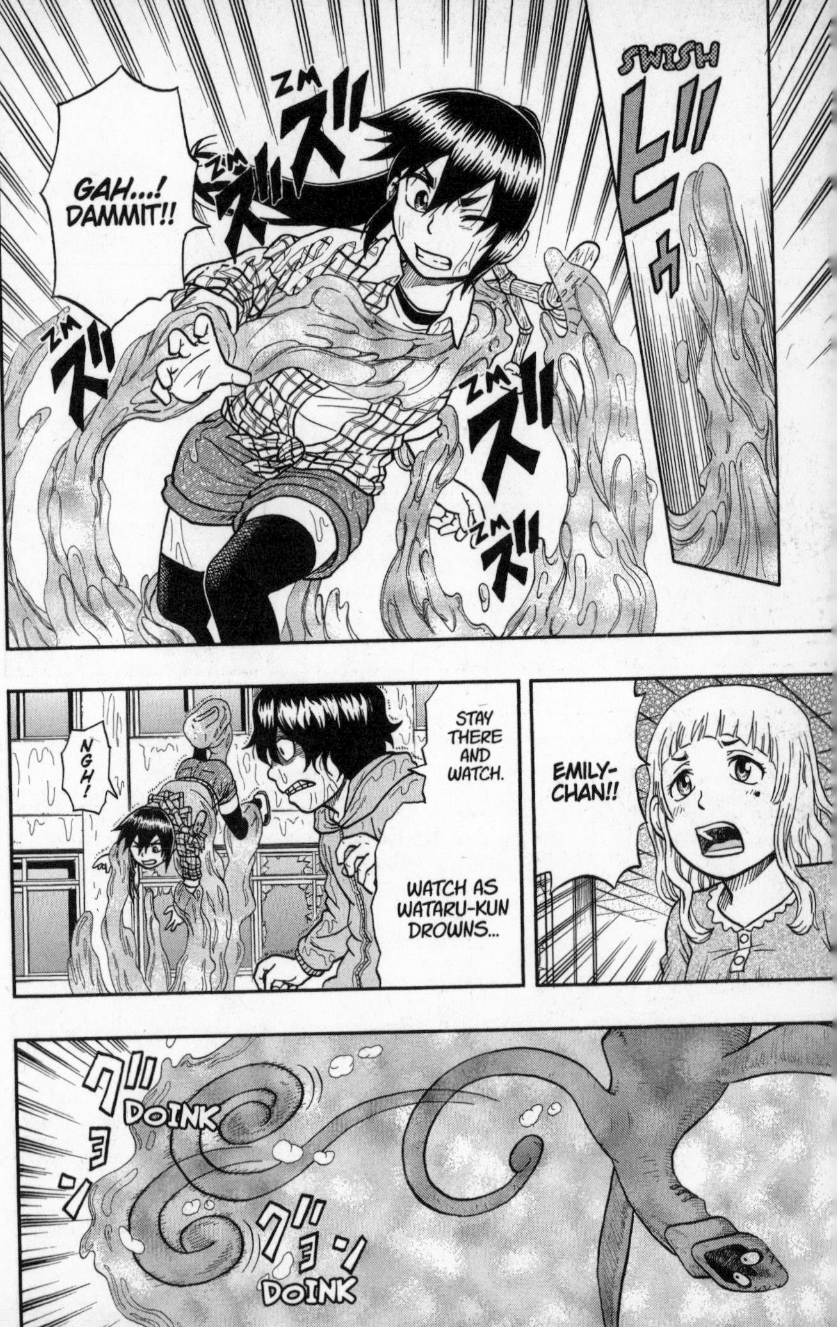
SWISH
ZM
ZM
GAH...! DAMMIT!!
ZM
ZM
ZM
EMILY-CHAN!!
STAY THERE AND WATCH.
WATCH AS WATARU-KUN DROWNS...
NGH!
DOINK
DOINK

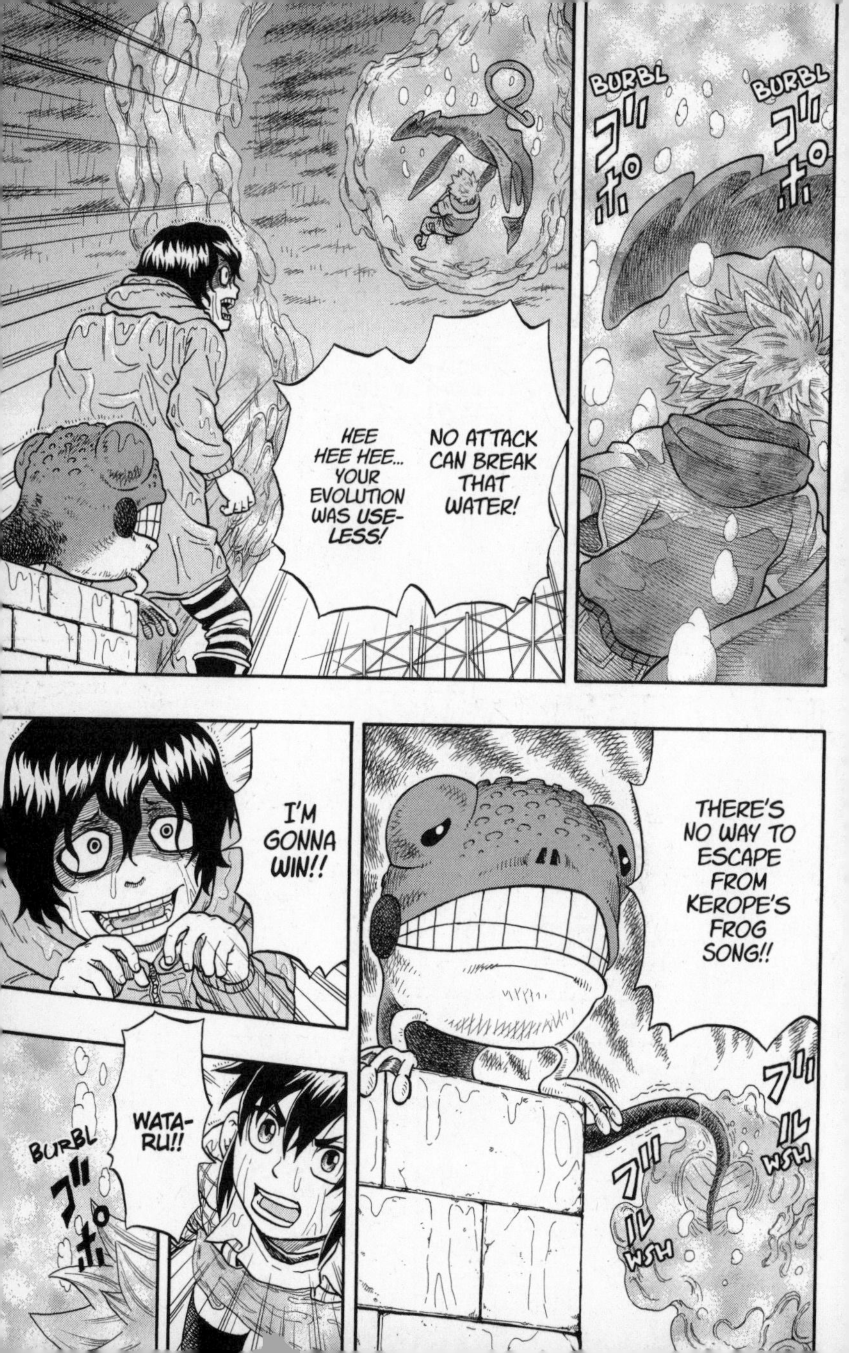
BURBL
BURBL
NO ATTACK CAN BREAK THAT WATER!
HEE HEE HEE... YOUR EVOLUTION WAS USE-LESS!
THERE'S NO WAY TO ESCAPE FROM KEROPE'S FROG SONG!!
WSH
WSH
I'M GONNA WIN!!
WATA-RU!!
BURBL

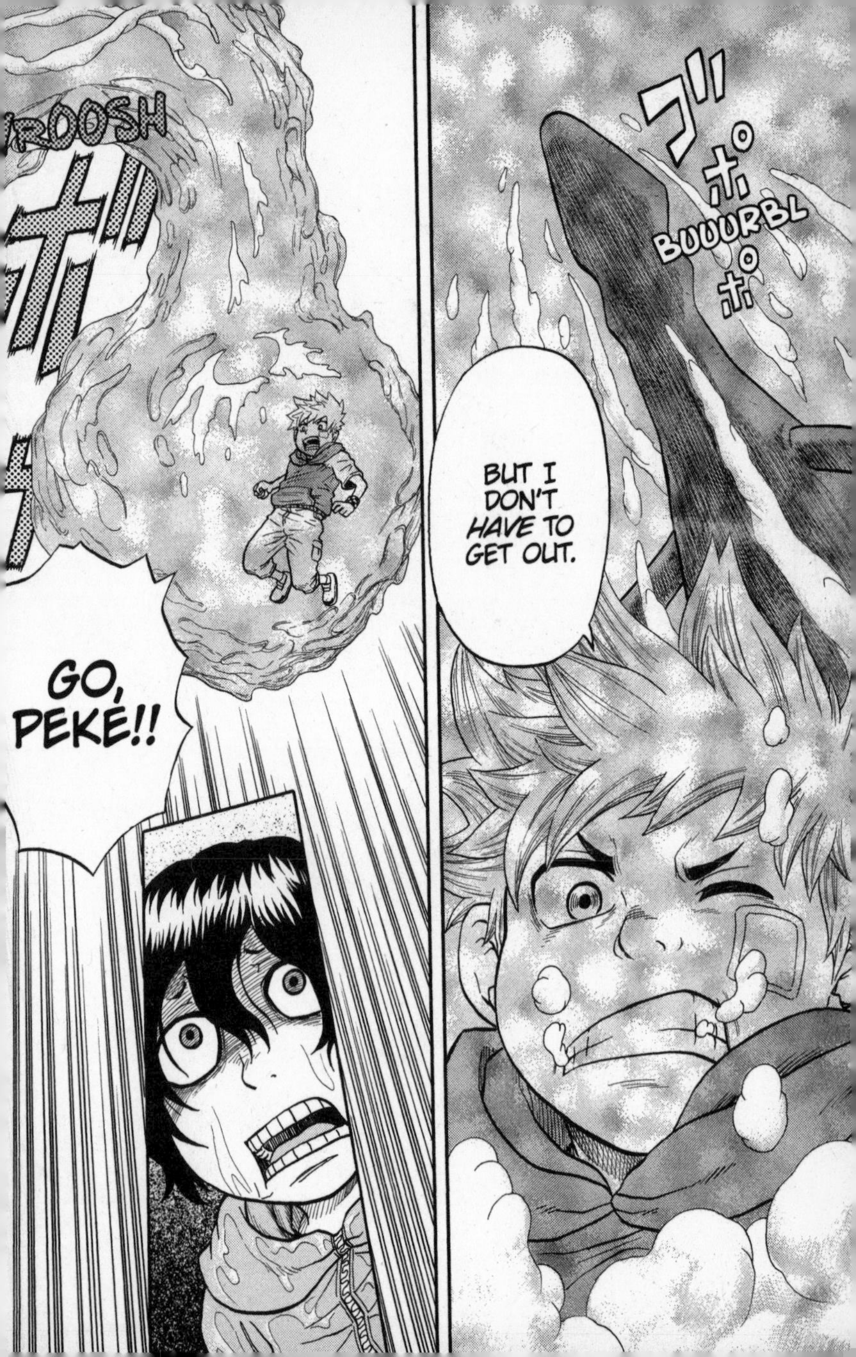
BUUURBL
BUT I DON'T HAVE TO GET OUT.
ROOSH
GO, PEKE!!

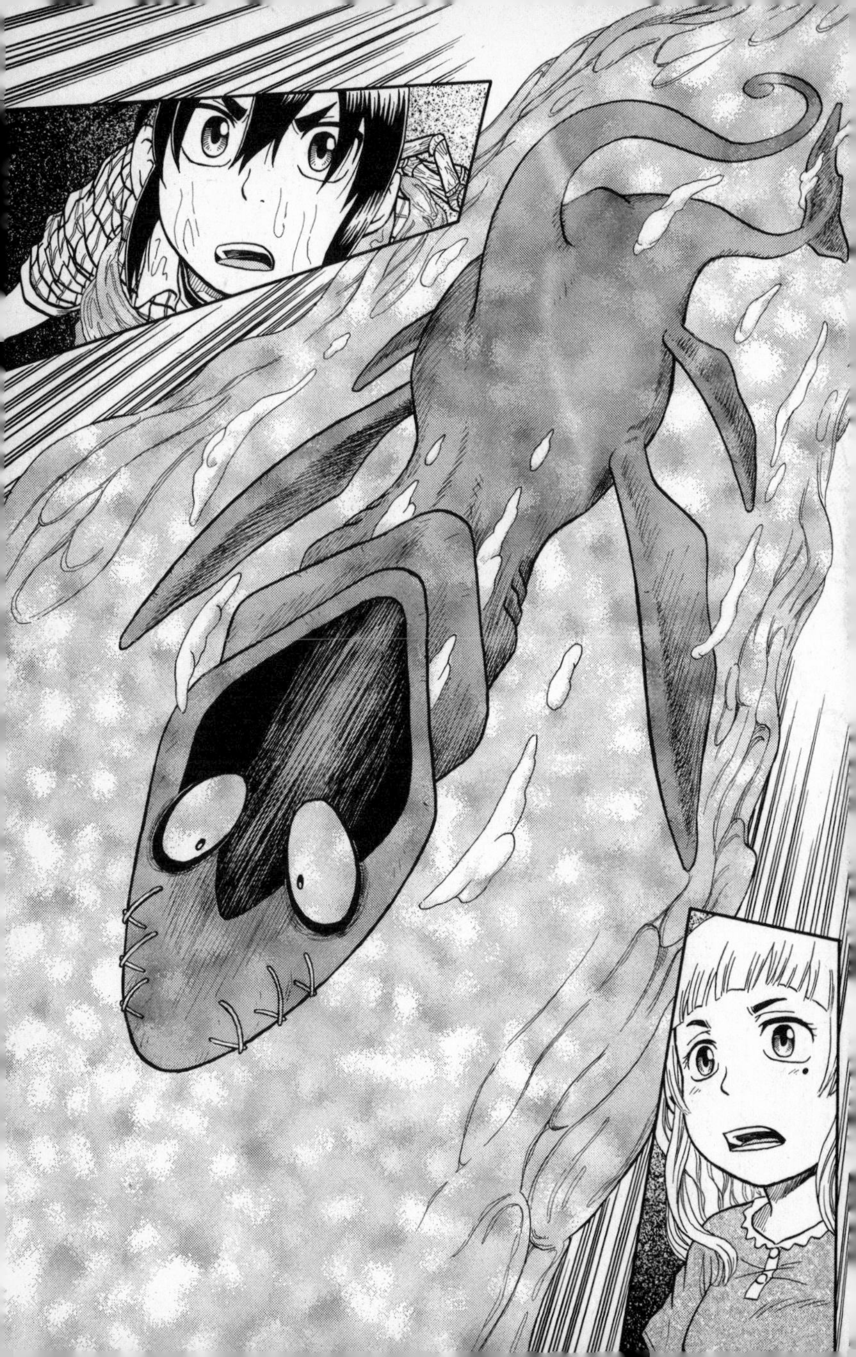

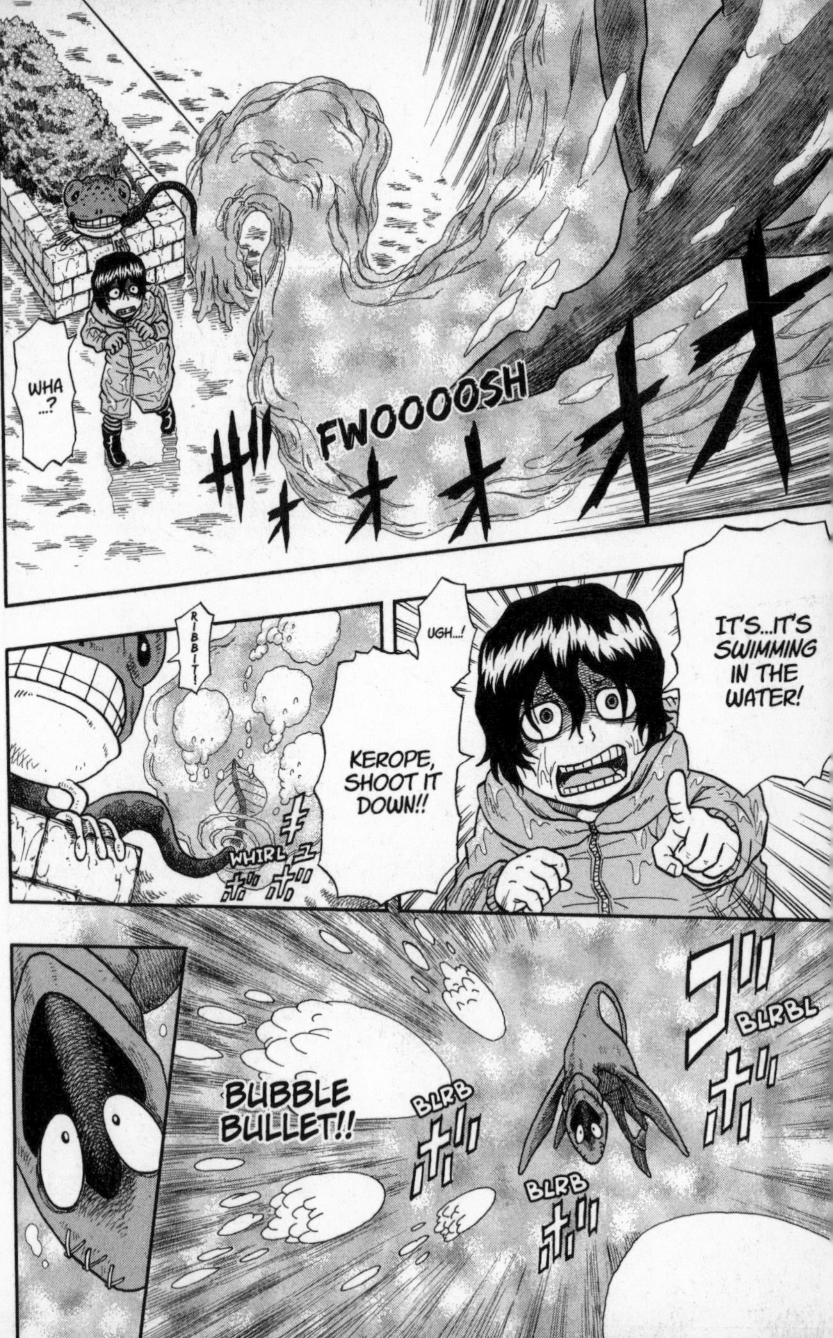
FWOOOOSH
WHA ...?
IT'S...IT'S SWIMMING IN THE WATER!
UGH...!
KEROPE, SHOOT IT DOWN!!
RIBBIT!
WHIRL
BLRBL
BLRB
BUBBLE BULLET!!
BLRB

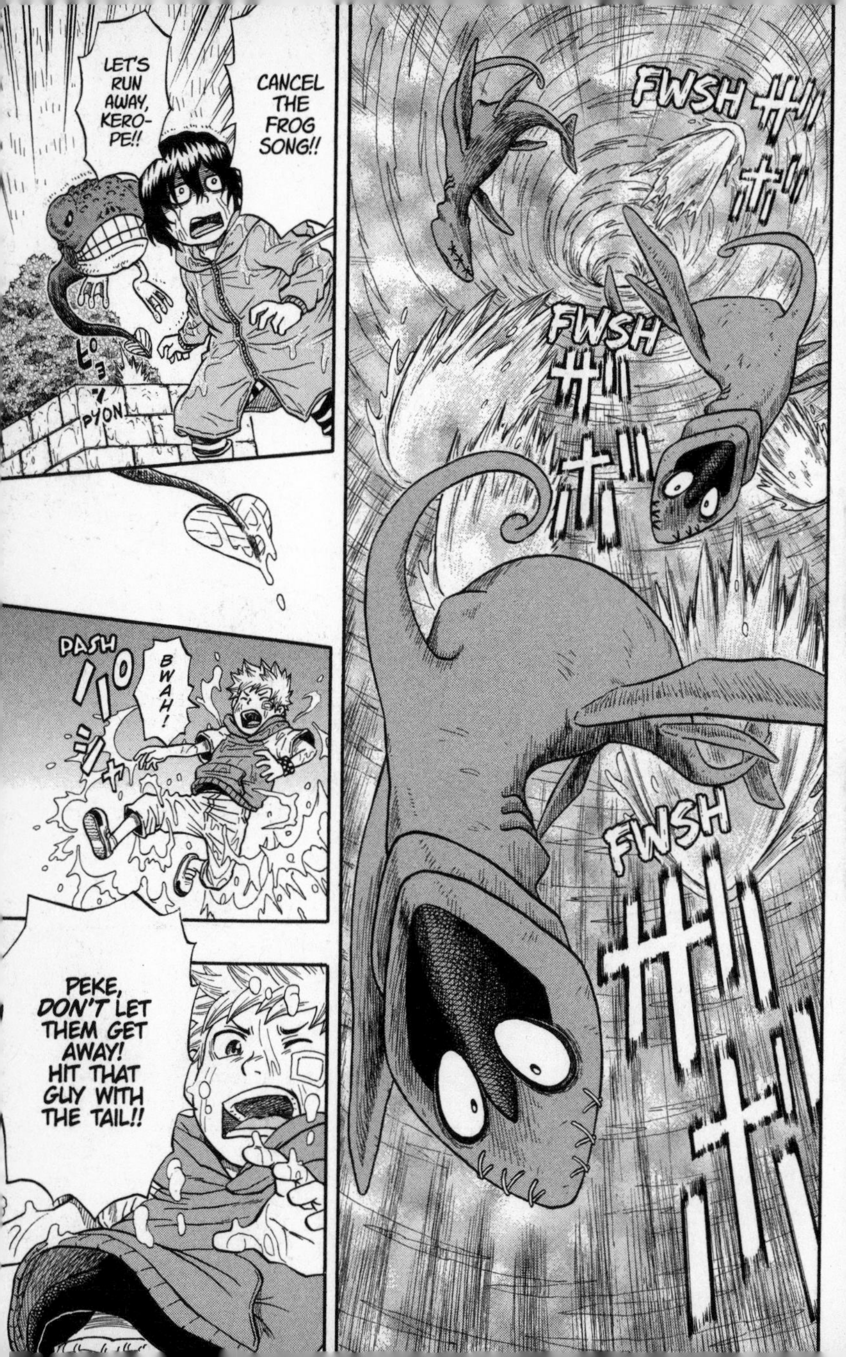
FWSH
FWSH
FWSH
CANCEL THE FROG SONG!!
LET'S RUN AWAY, KERO-PE!!
PYON
PASH
BWAH!
PEKE, DON'T LET THEM GET AWAY! HIT THAT GUY WITH THE TAIL!!

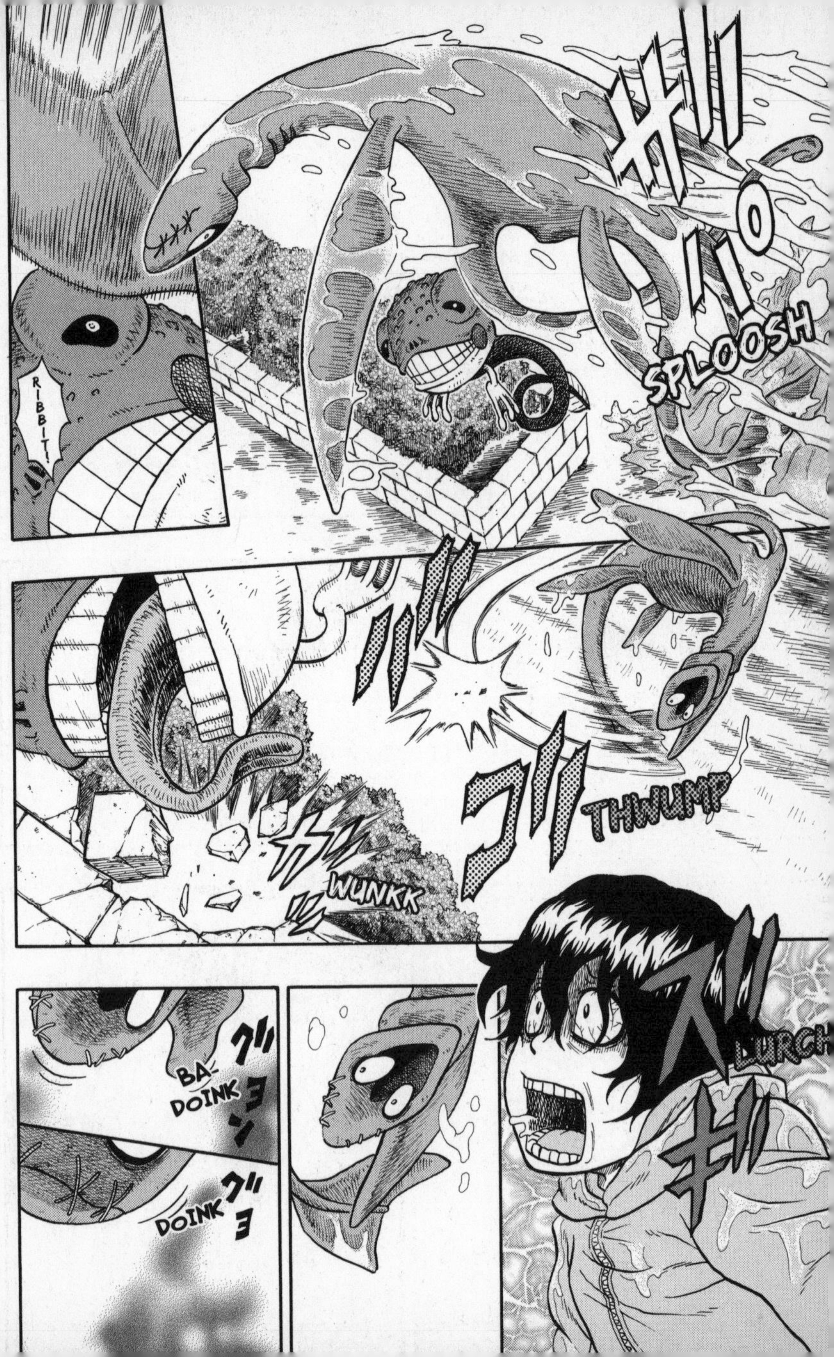
SPLOOSH
RIBBIT!
THWUMP
WUNKK
LURCH
BA DOINK
DOINK

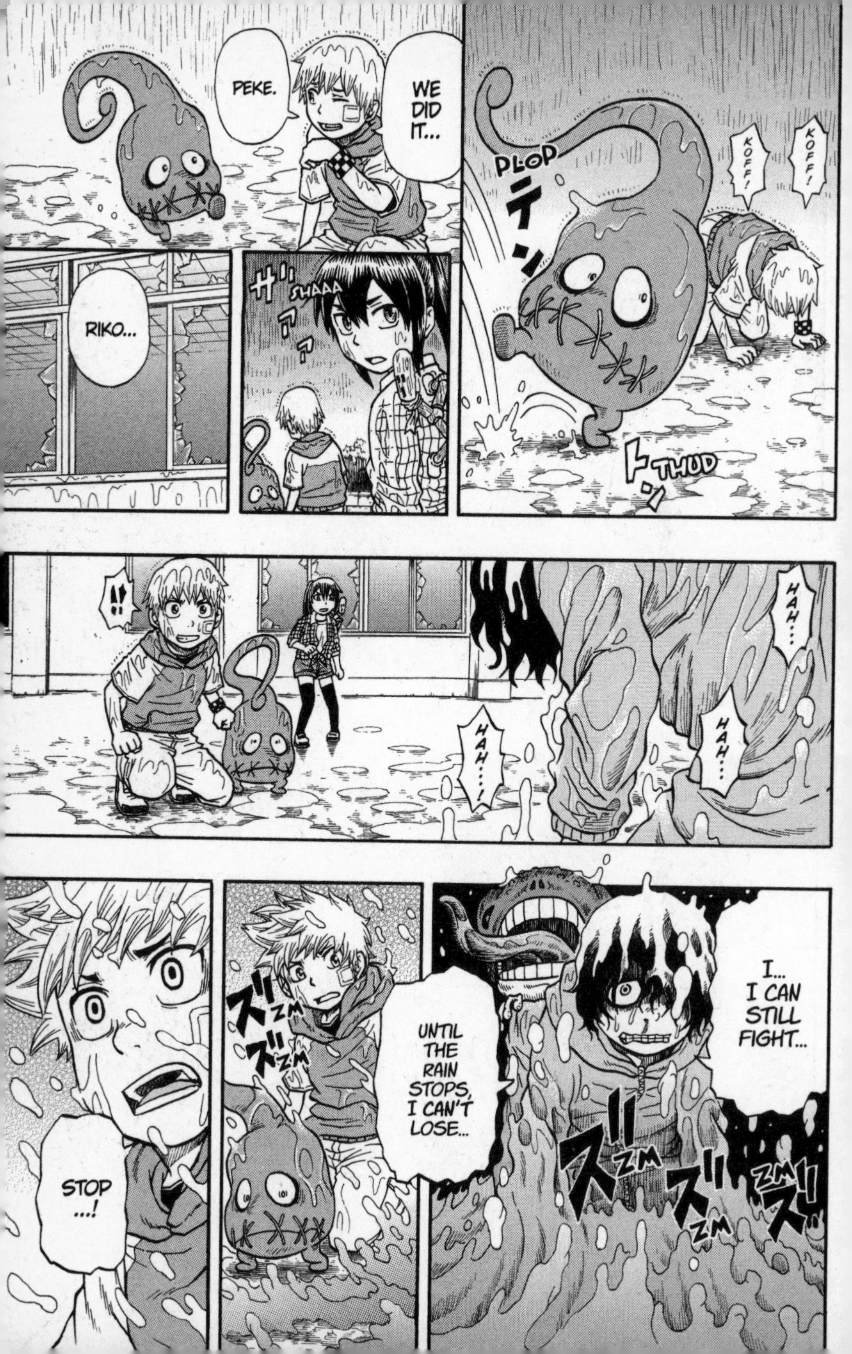
KOFF!
KOFF!
PLOP
THUD
WE DID IT...
PEKE.
SHAAA
RIKO...
HAH...
HAH...
HAH...!
!!
I... I CAN STILL FIGHT...
ZM
ZM
ZM
ZM
UNTIL THE RAIN STOPS, I CAN'T LOSE...
ZM
ZM
STOP ...!

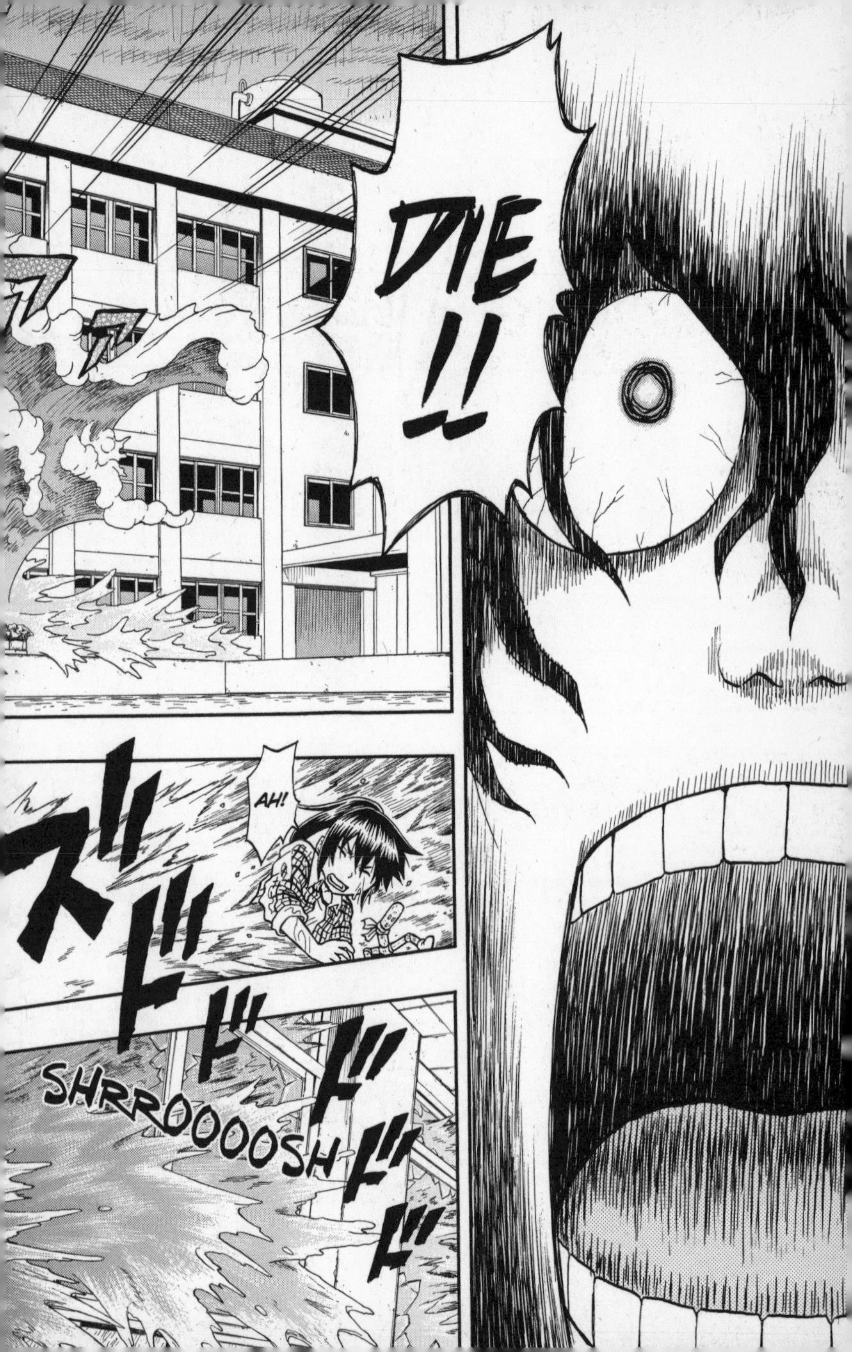
DIE!!
AH!
ズドドドドド
SHRROOOOSH

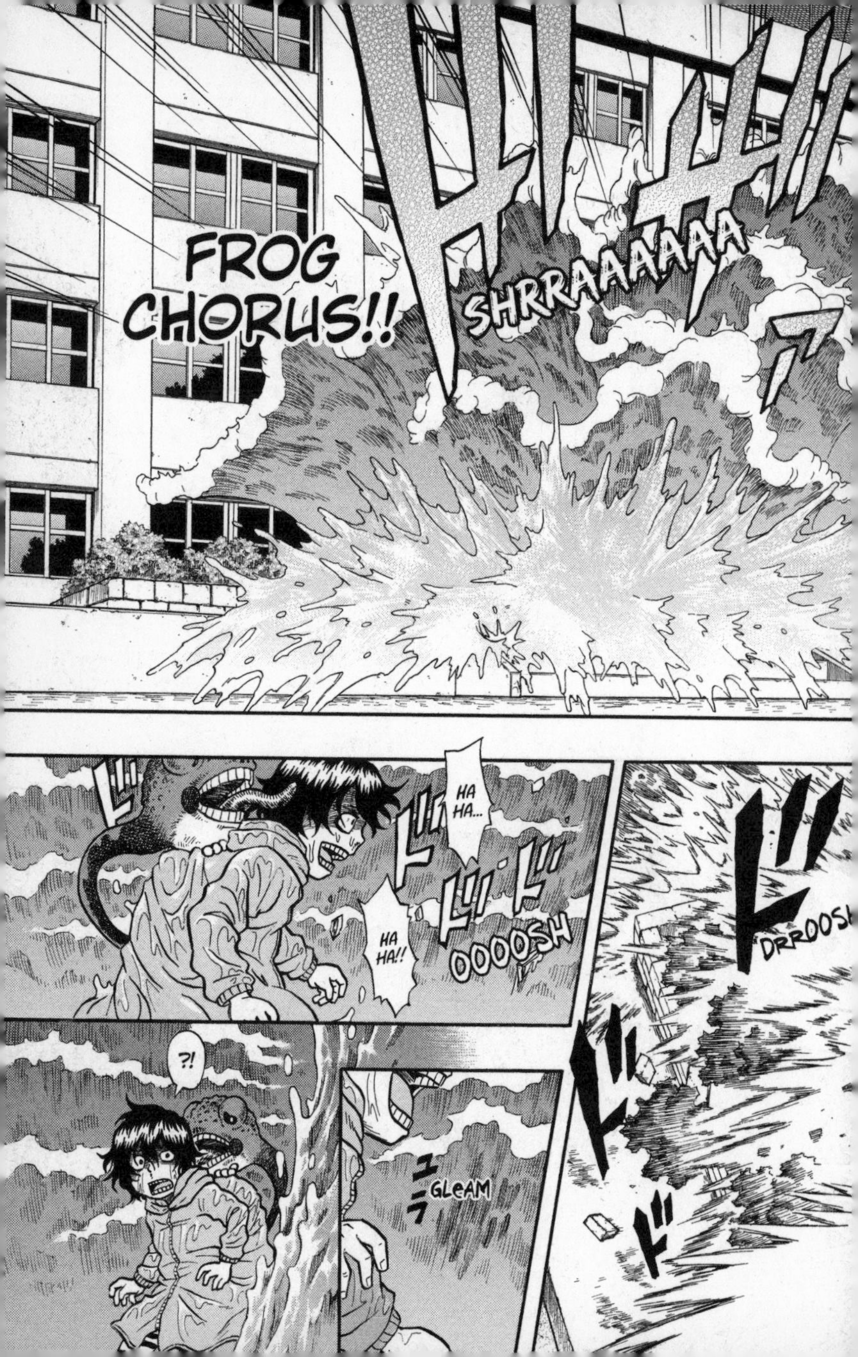
FROG CHORUS!!
SHRRAAAAAAA
DRROOS
HA HA...
HA HA!!
OOOOSH
GLEAM
?!

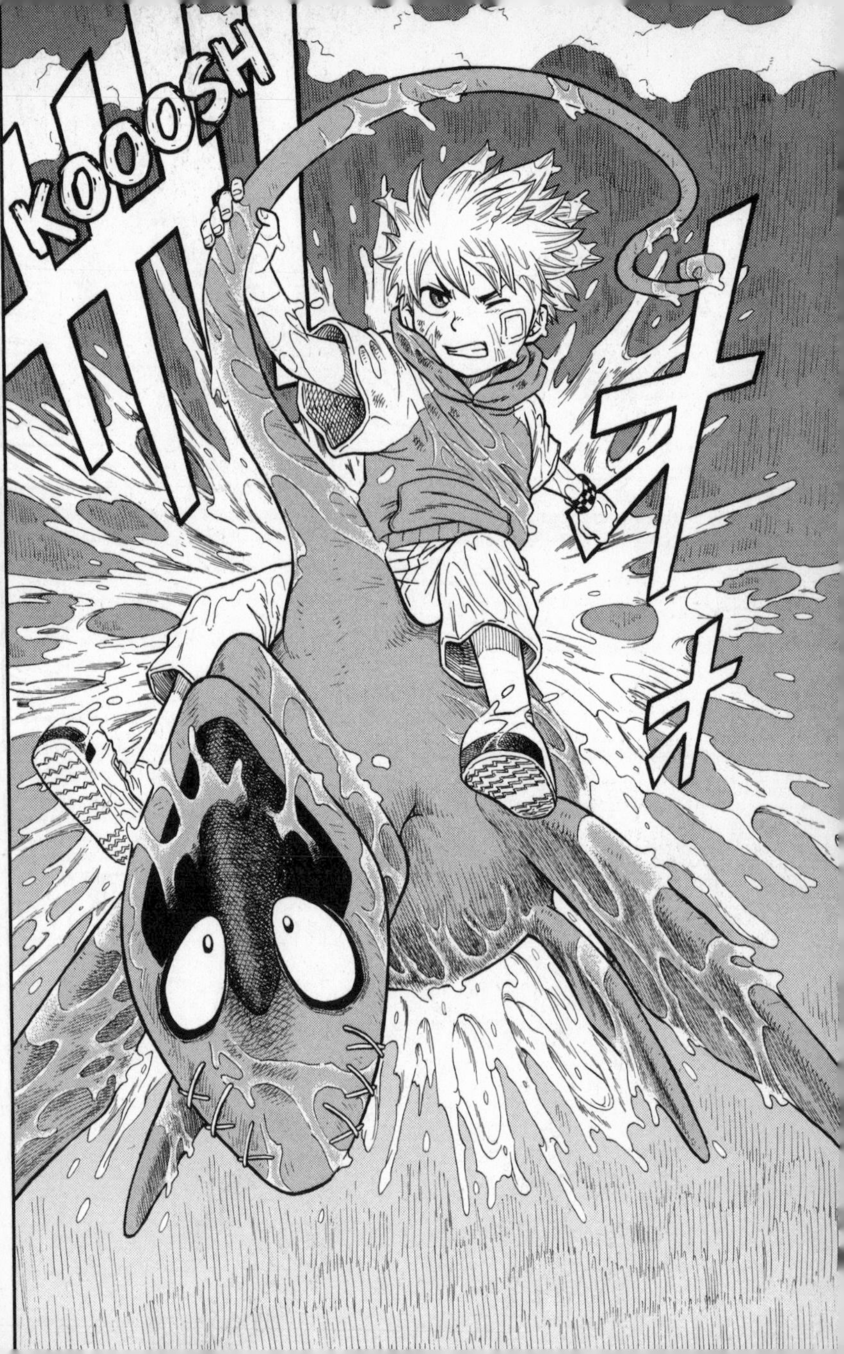
KOOSH

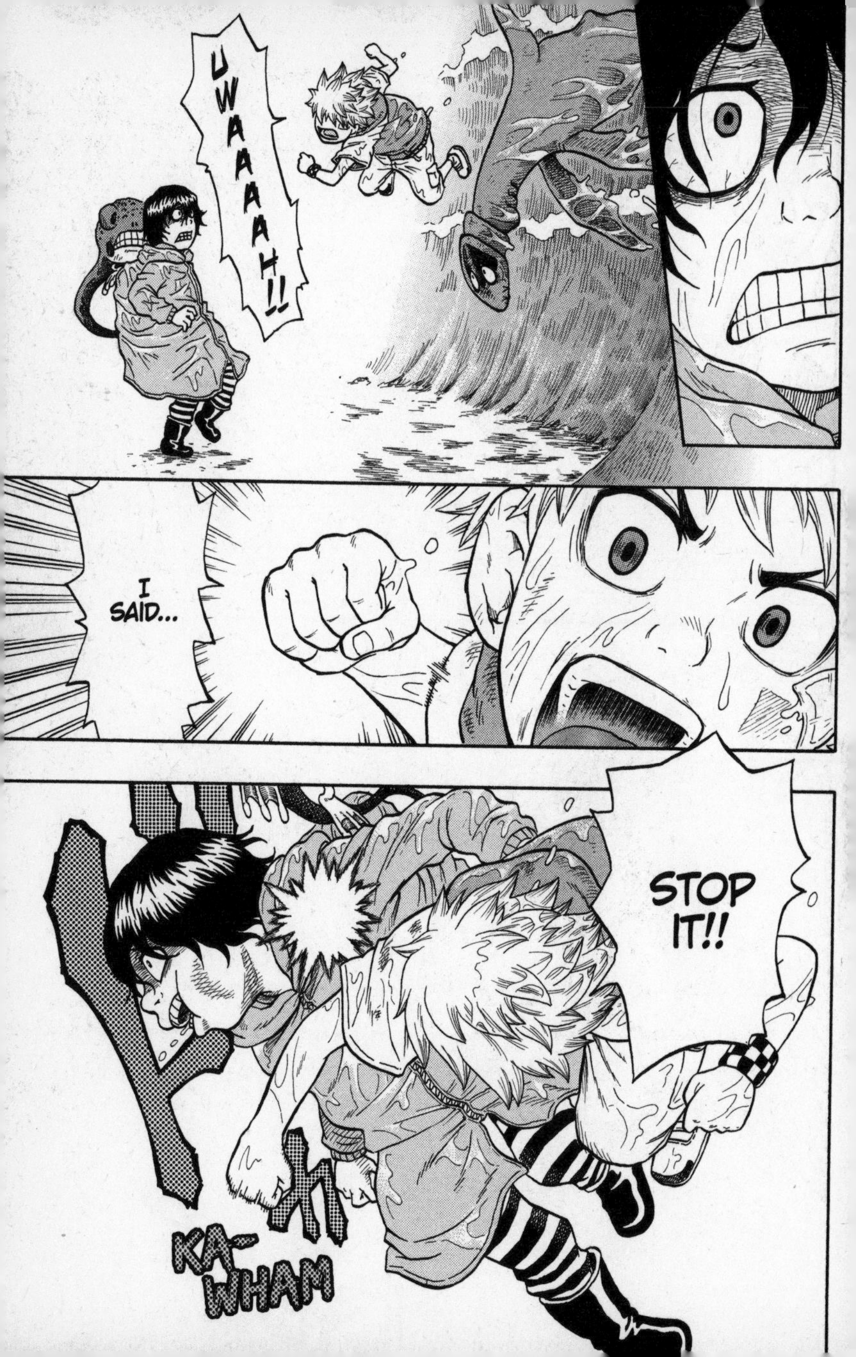
UWAAAAAAH!!
I SAID...
STOP IT!!
KA-WHAM

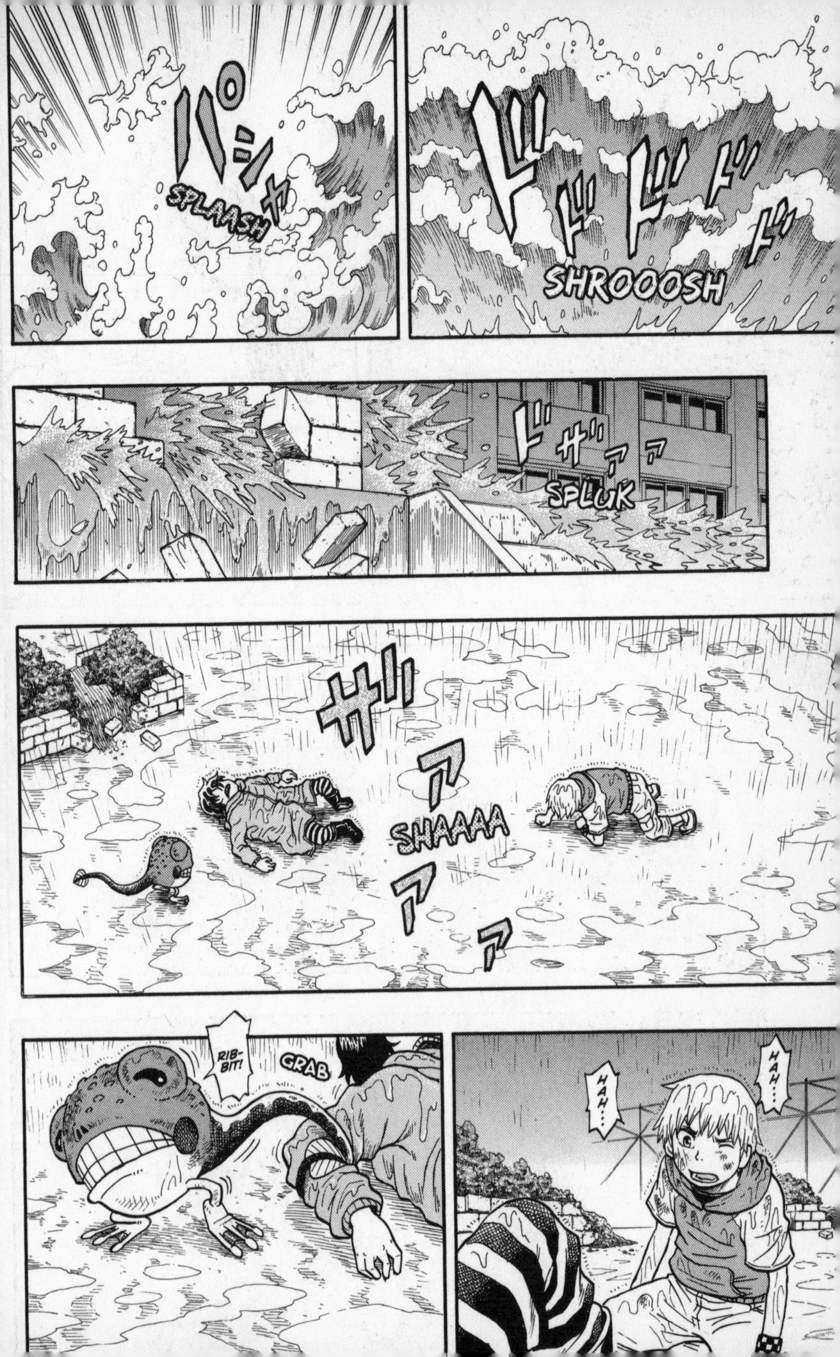
ドドドドドド
SHROOOSH
パシャ
SPLAASH
ドザァァ
SPLUK
ザァァァァ
SHAAAA
HAH...
HAH...
GRAB
RIB-BIT!

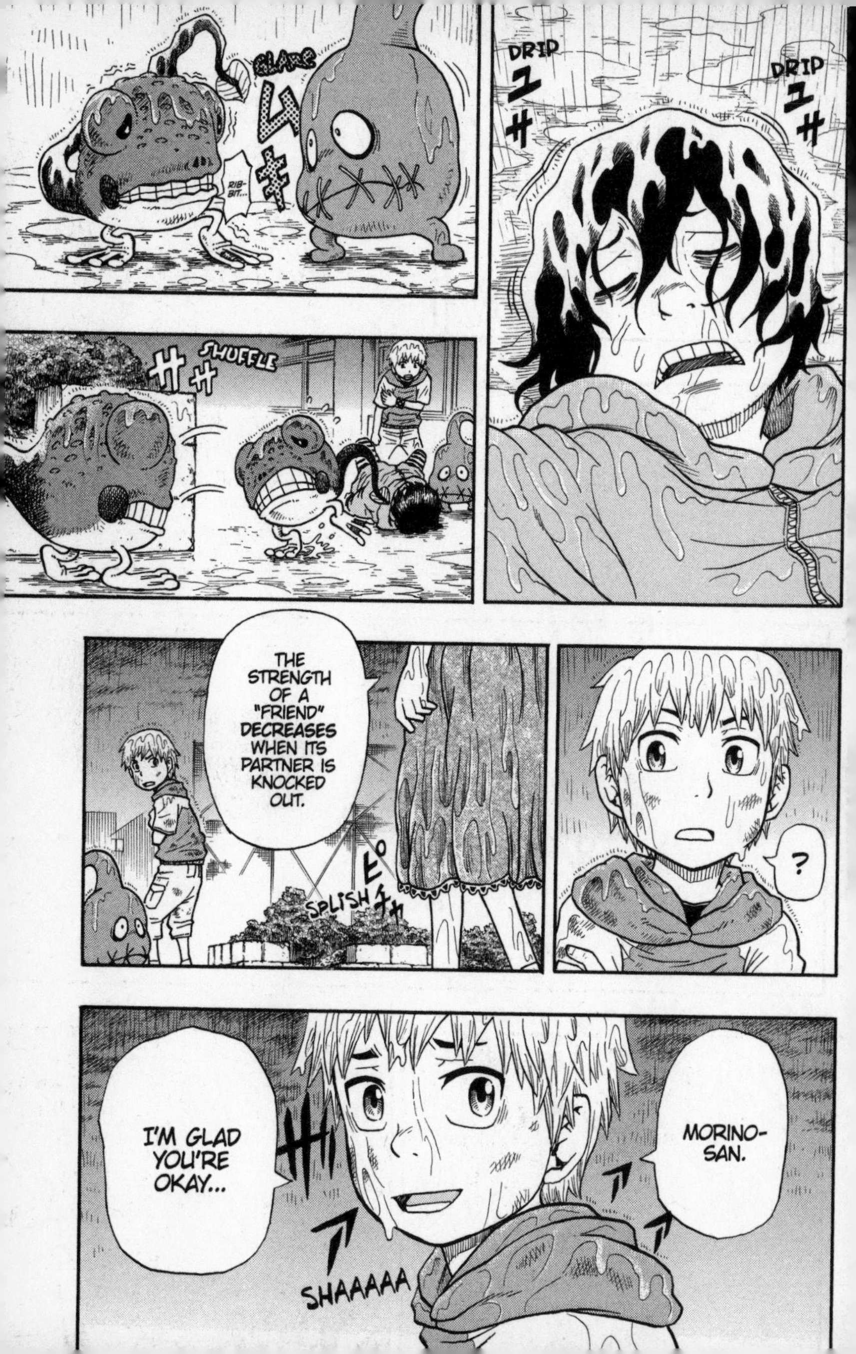
DRIP
DRIP
GLARE
RIB-BIT...
SHUFFLE
?
THE STRENGTH OF A "FRIEND" DECREASES WHEN ITS PARTNER IS KNOCKED OUT.
SPLISH
MORINO-SAN.
I'M GLAD YOU'RE OKAY...
SHAAAAA

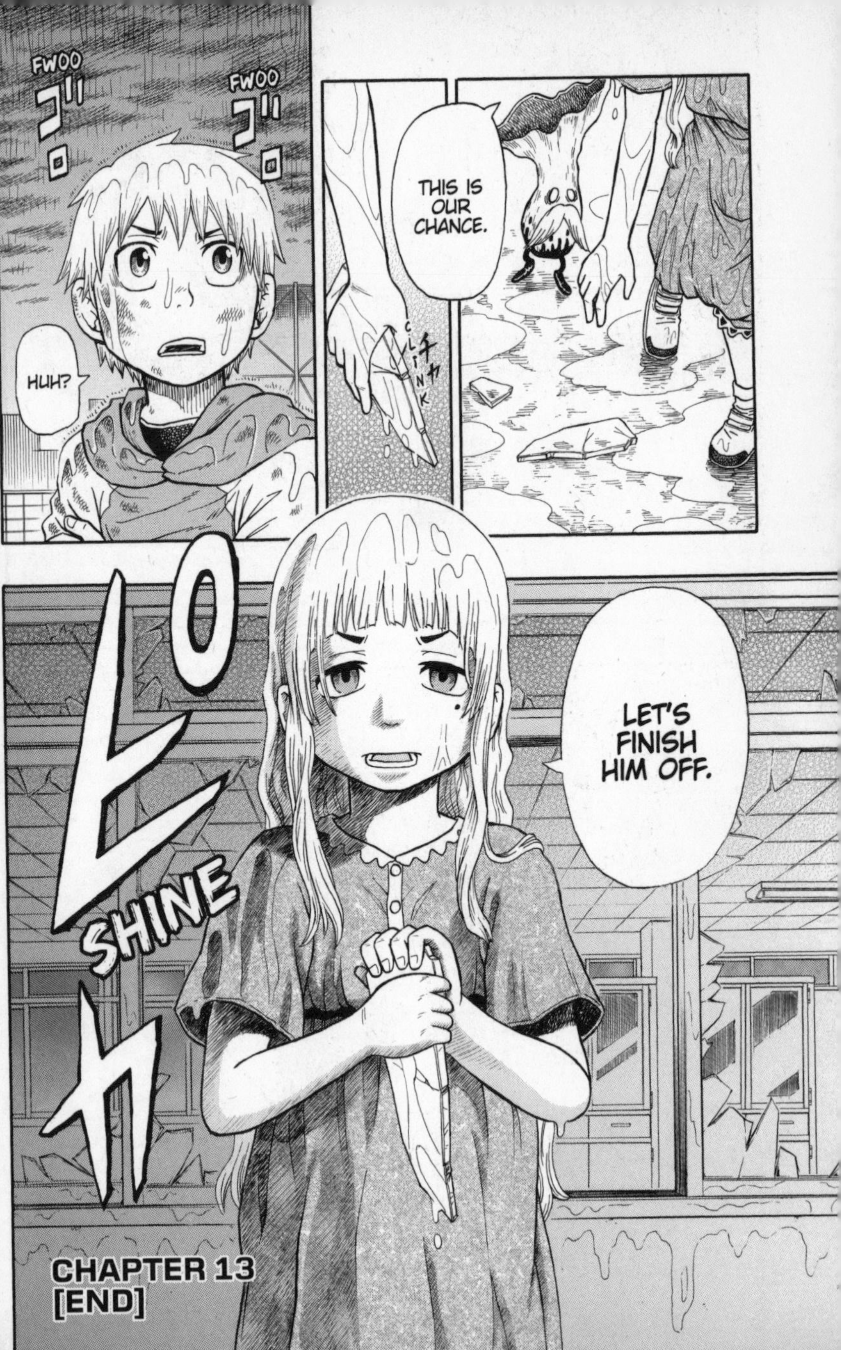
THIS IS OUR CHANCE.
CLINK
チカ
FWOO
ゴロ
FWOO
ゴロ
HUH?
LET'S FINISH HIM OFF.
ピカ
SHINE
CHAPTER 13 [END]

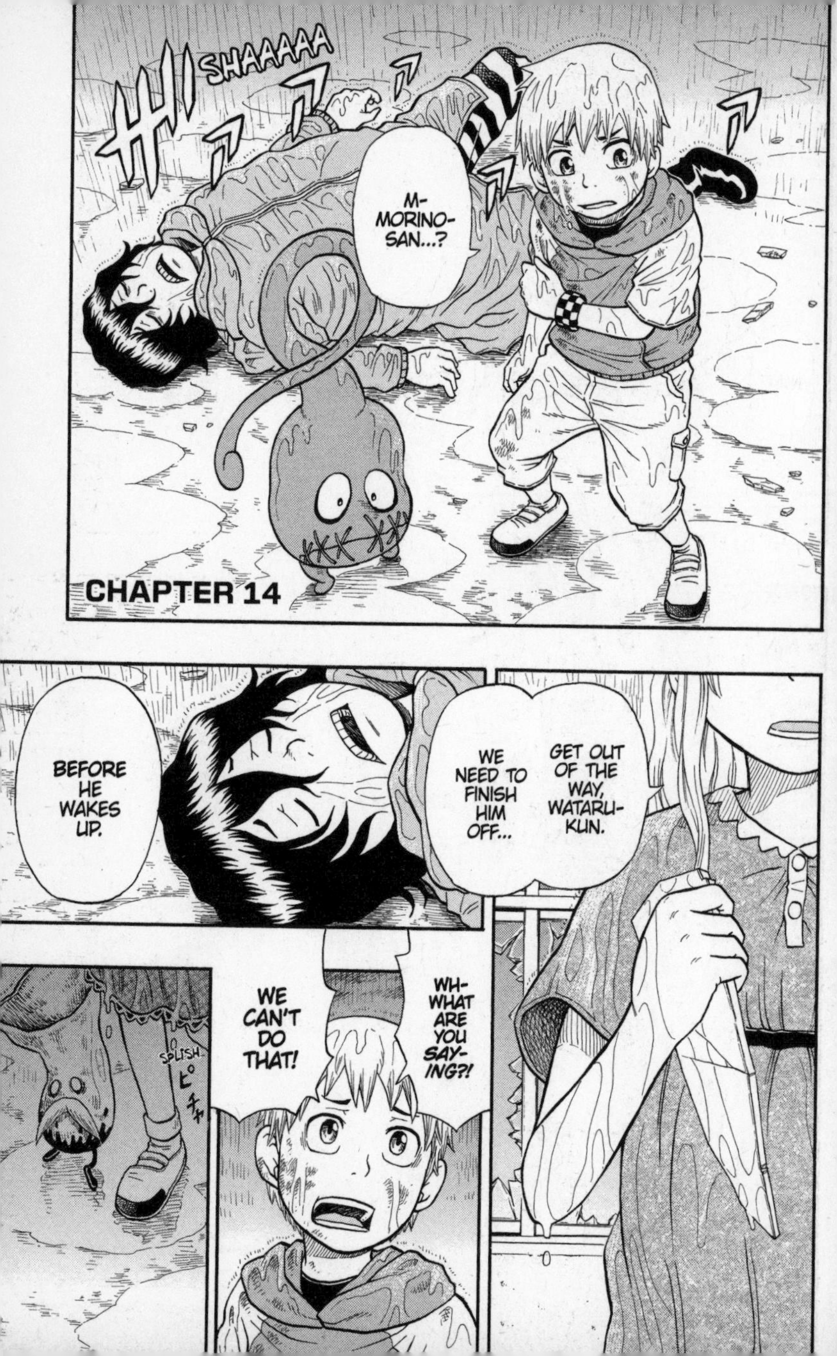
HISHAAAAA
M-MORINO-SAN...?
CHAPTER 14
GET OUT OF THE WAY, WATARU-KUN.
WE NEED TO FINISH HIM OFF...
BEFORE HE WAKES UP.
WH-WHAT ARE YOU SAYING?!
WE CAN'T DO THAT!
SPLISH
ピチャ

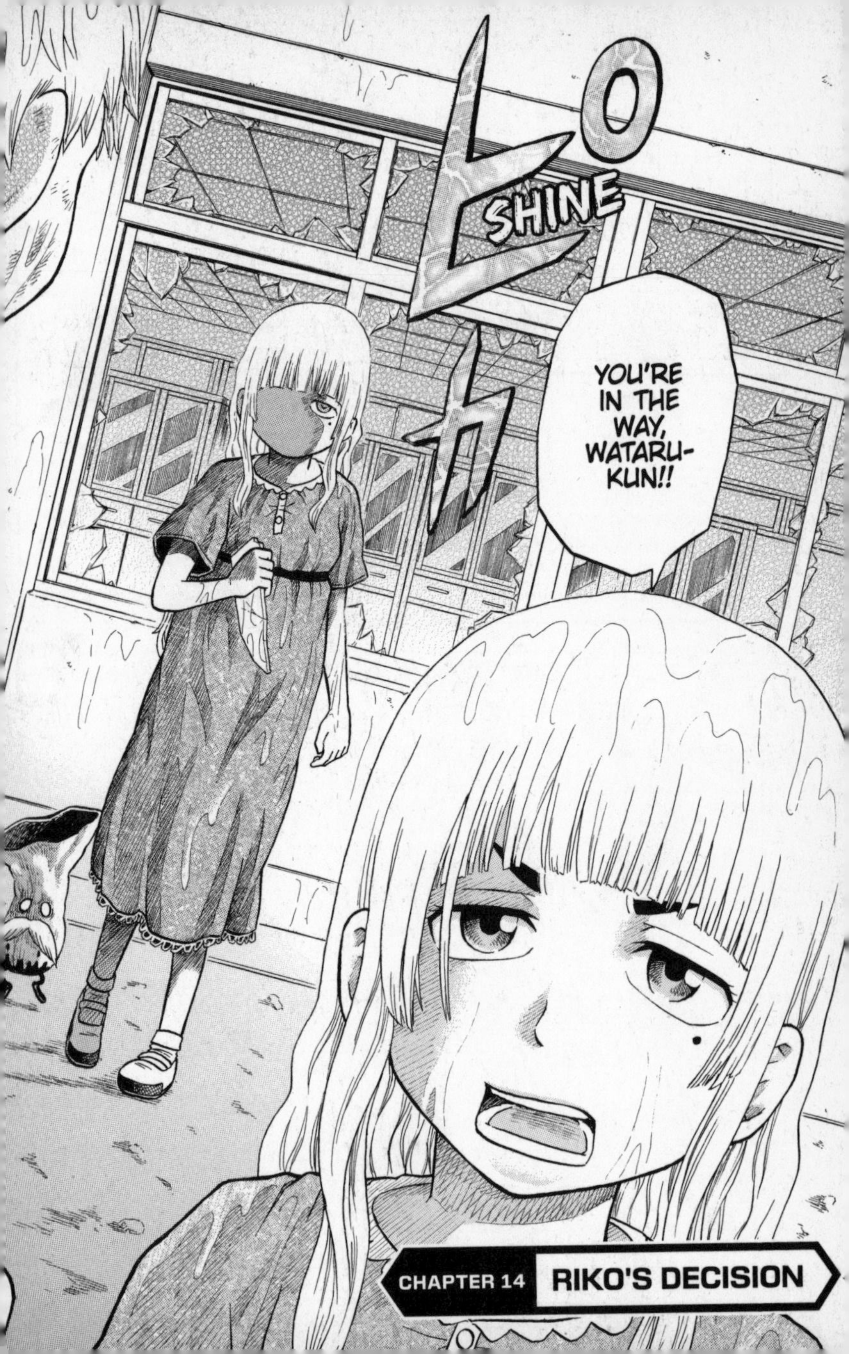
SHINE
YOU'RE IN THE WAY, WATARU-KUN!!
CHAPTER 14
RIKO'S DECISION

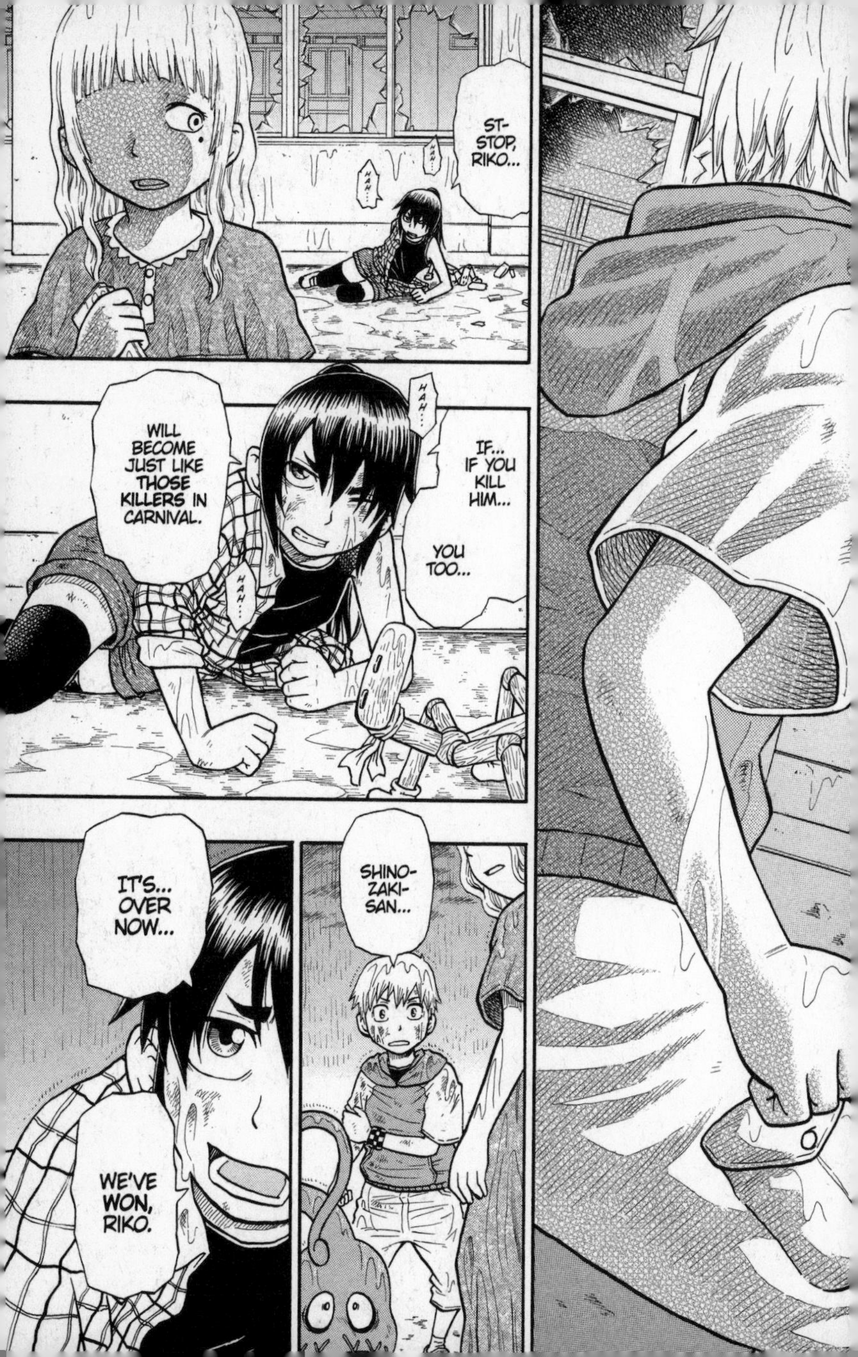
ST-STOP, RIKO...
HAH...
HAH...
HAH...
IF... IF YOU KILL HIM...
YOU TOO...
WILL BECOME JUST LIKE THOSE KILLERS IN CARNIVAL.
HAH...
SHINOZAKI-SAN...
IT'S... OVER NOW...
WE'VE WON, RIKO.

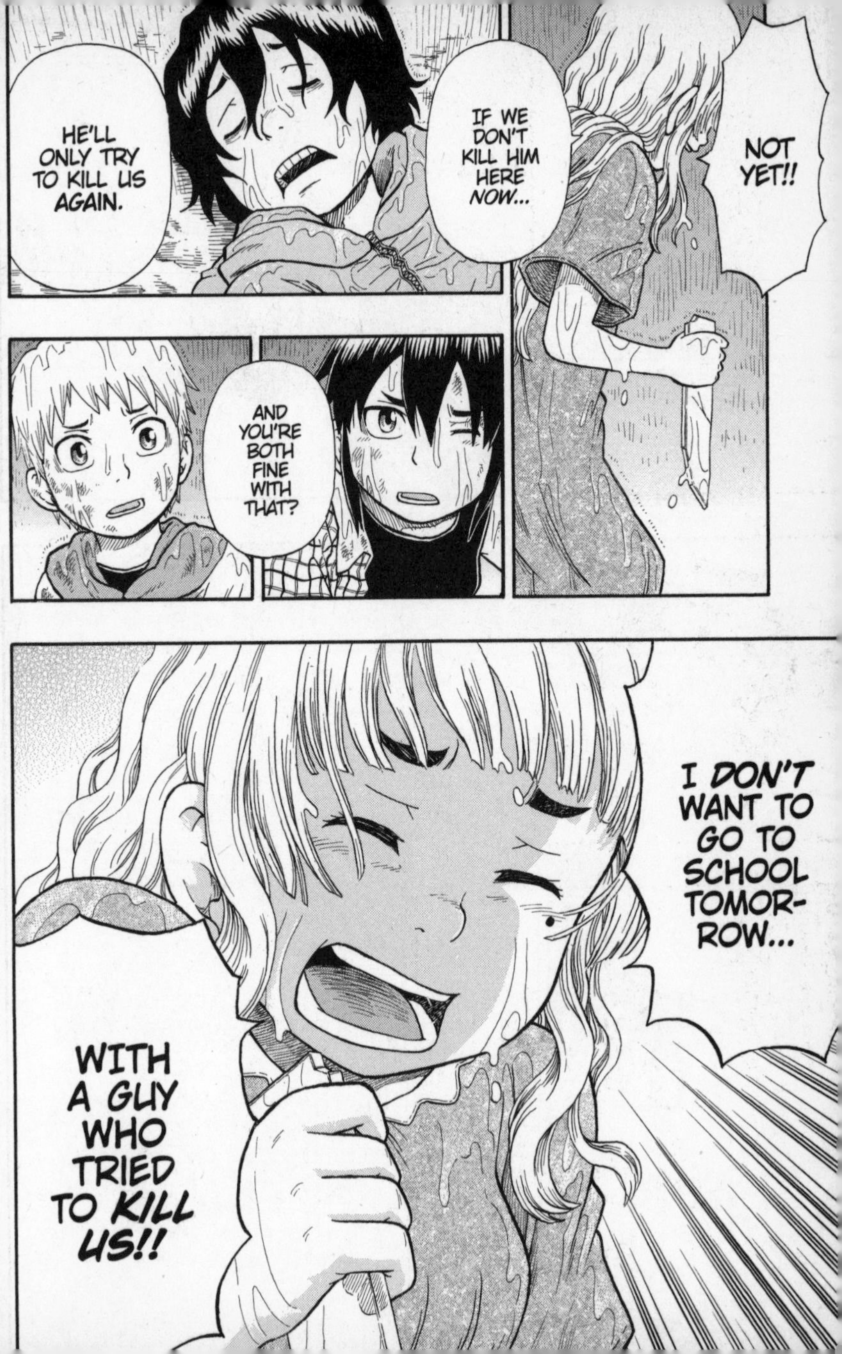
NOT YET!!
IF WE DON'T KILL HIM HERE NOW...
HE'LL ONLY TRY TO KILL US AGAIN.
AND YOU'RE BOTH FINE WITH THAT?
I DON'T WANT TO GO TO SCHOOL TOMOR-ROW...
WITH A GUY WHO TRIED TO KILL US!!

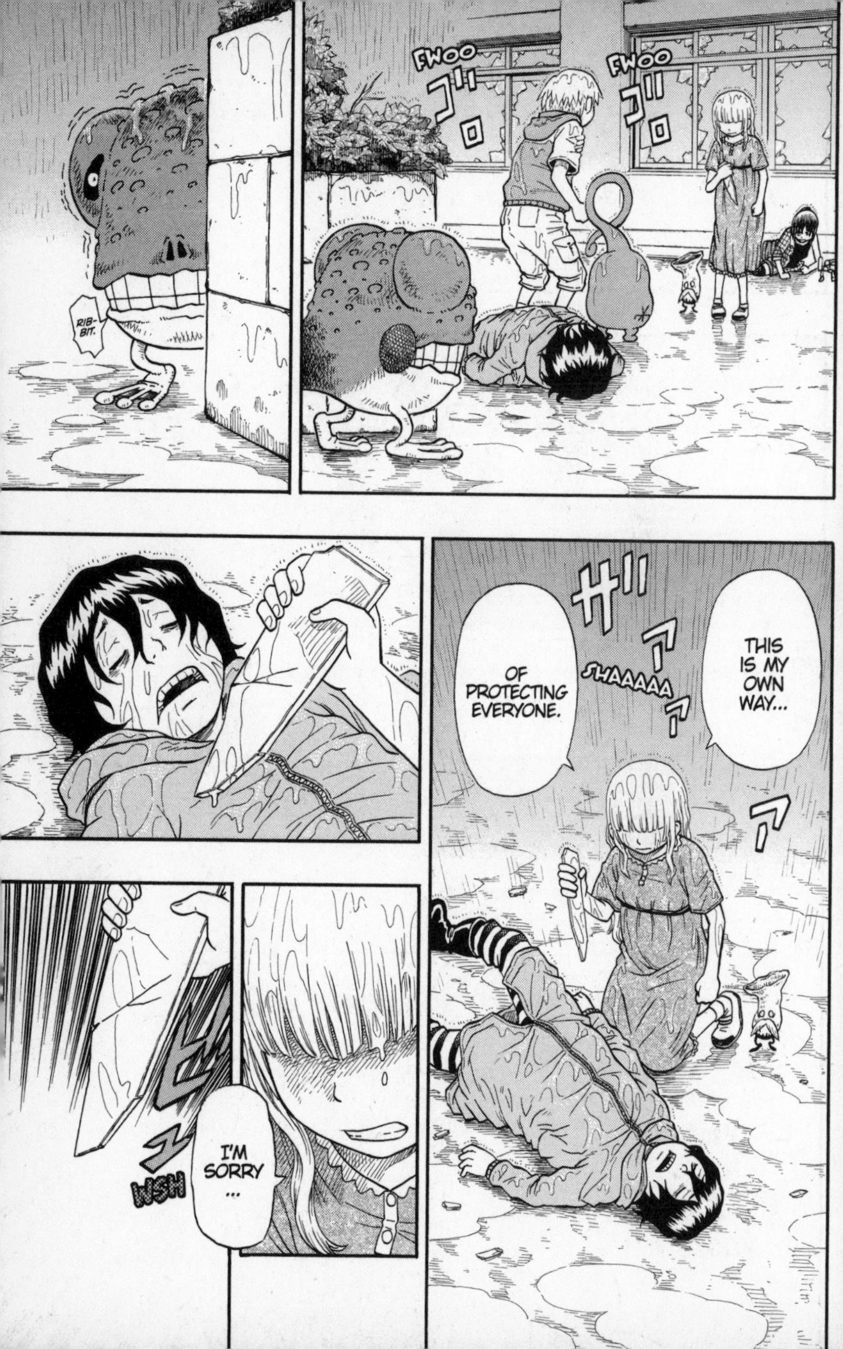
FWOO
FWOO
RIB-BIT.
SHAAAAA
THIS IS MY OWN WAY...
OF PROTECTING EVERYONE.
I'M SORRY ...
WSH

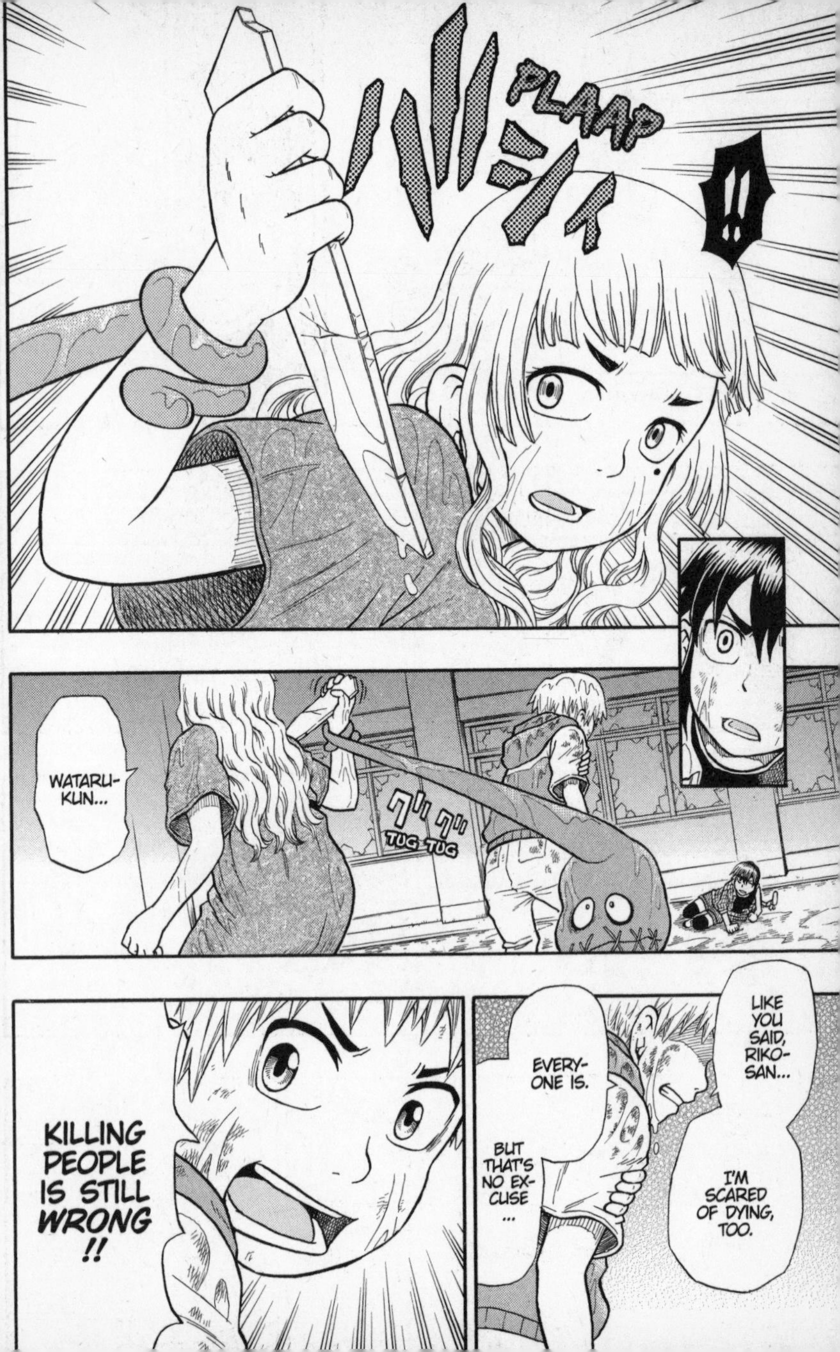
PLAAP
!!
WATARU-KUN...
TUG TUG
LIKE YOU SAID, RIKO-SAN...
I'M SCARED OF DYING, TOO.
EVERY-ONE IS.
BUT THAT'S NO EX-CUSE...
KILLING PEOPLE IS STILL WRONG!!

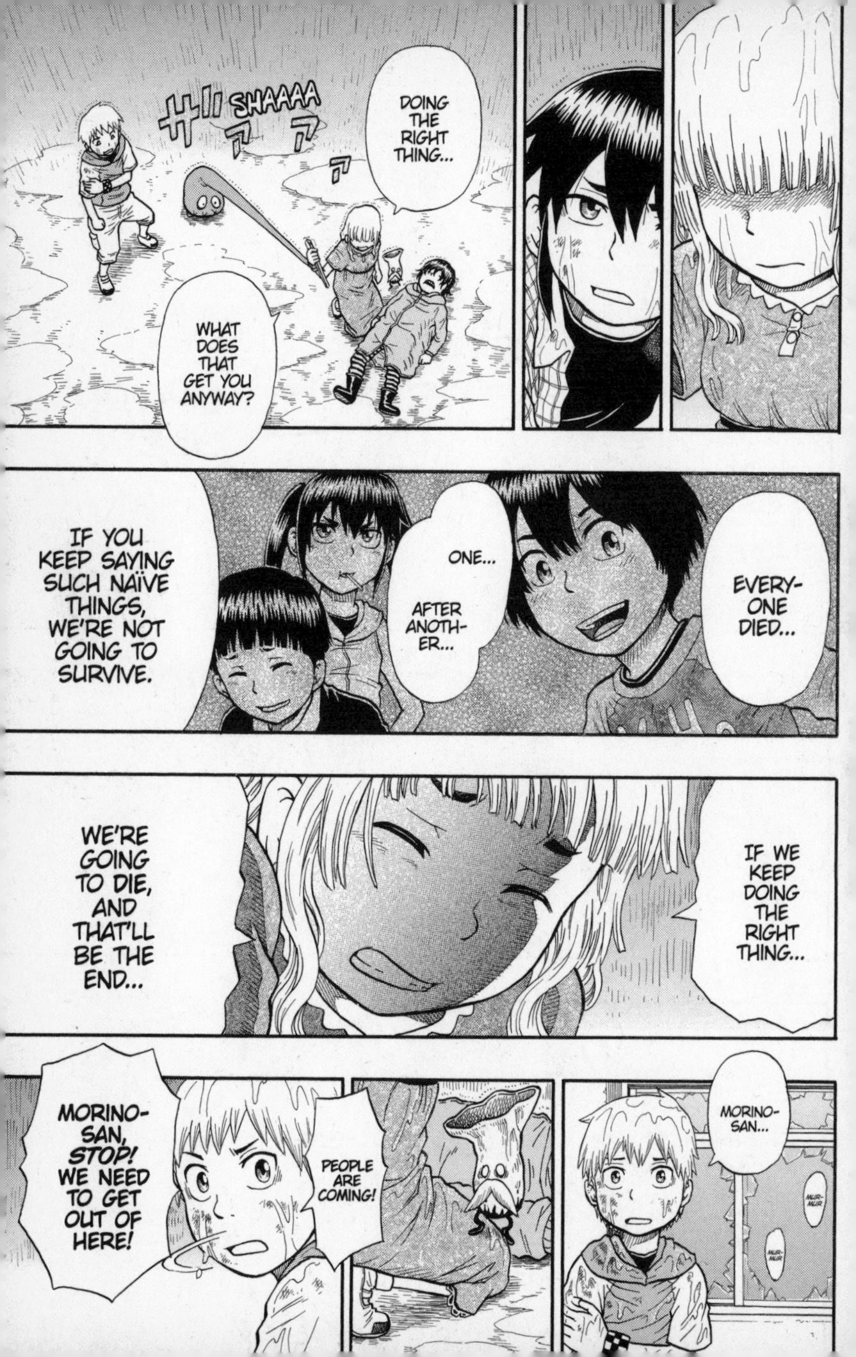
DOING THE RIGHT THING...
SHAAAA
WHAT DOES THAT GET YOU ANYWAY?
EVERY-ONE DIED...
ONE... AFTER ANOTHER-ER...
IF YOU KEEP SAYING SUCH NAÏVE THINGS, WE'RE NOT GOING TO SURVIVE.
IF WE KEEP DOING THE RIGHT THING...
WE'RE GOING TO DIE, AND THAT'LL BE THE END...
MORINO-SAN...
MUR-MUR
MUR-MUR
PEOPLE ARE COMING!
MORINO-SAN, *STOP!* WE NEED TO GET OUT OF HERE!

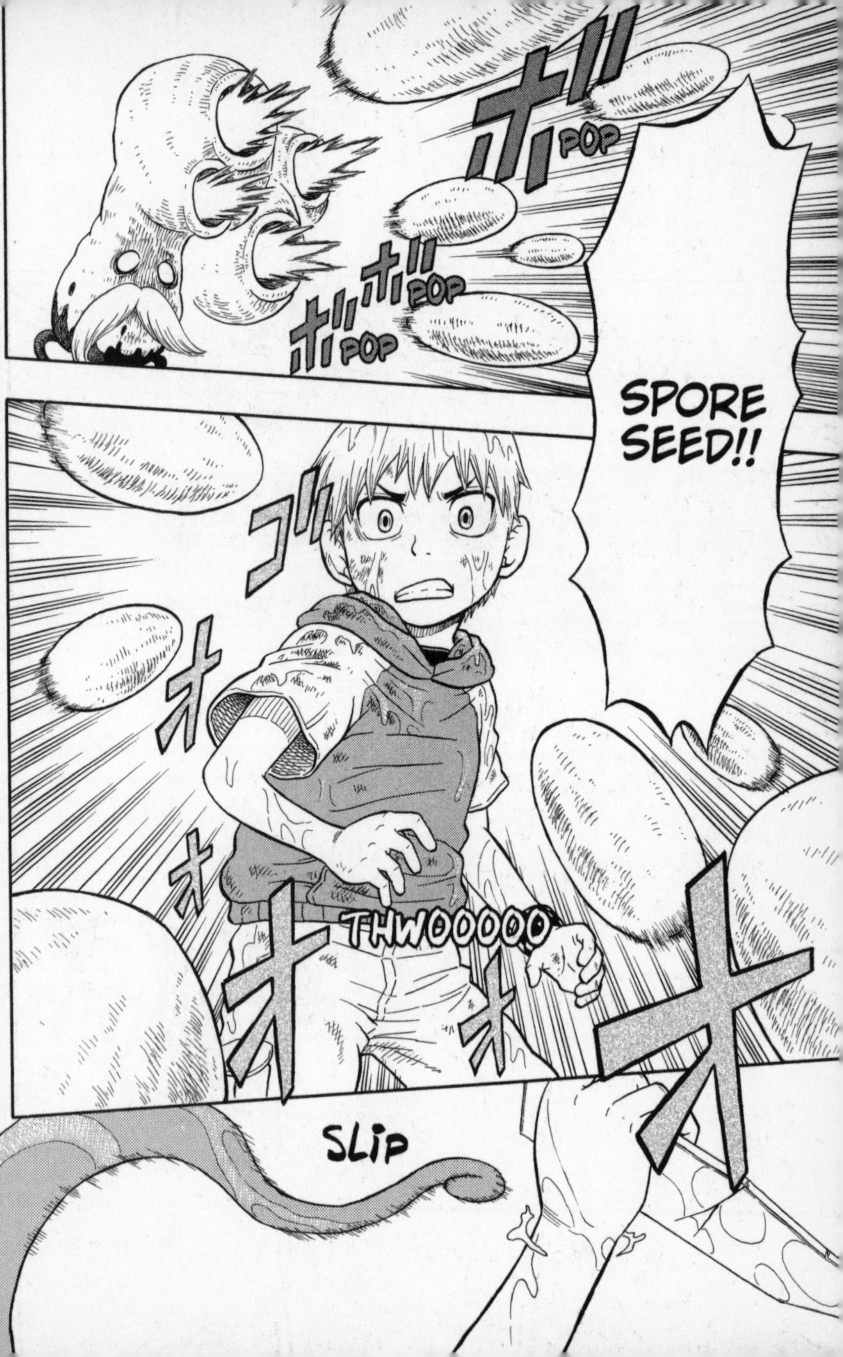
ボ
POP
SPORE SEED!!
ボボ
POP
POP
ゴオオオオ
THWOOOOO
SLIP

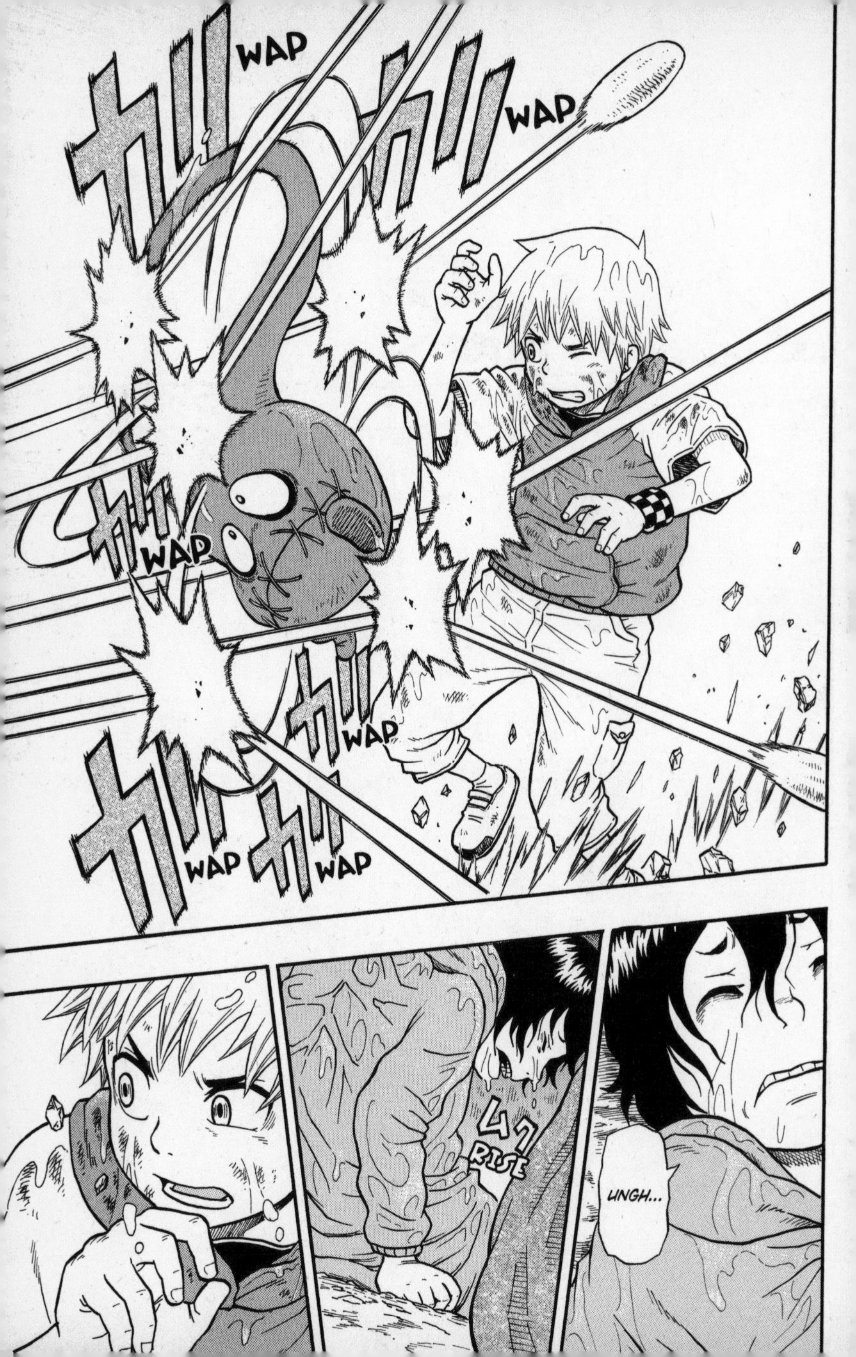
WAP
WAP
WAP
WAP
WAP
WAP
UNGH...
47
RISE

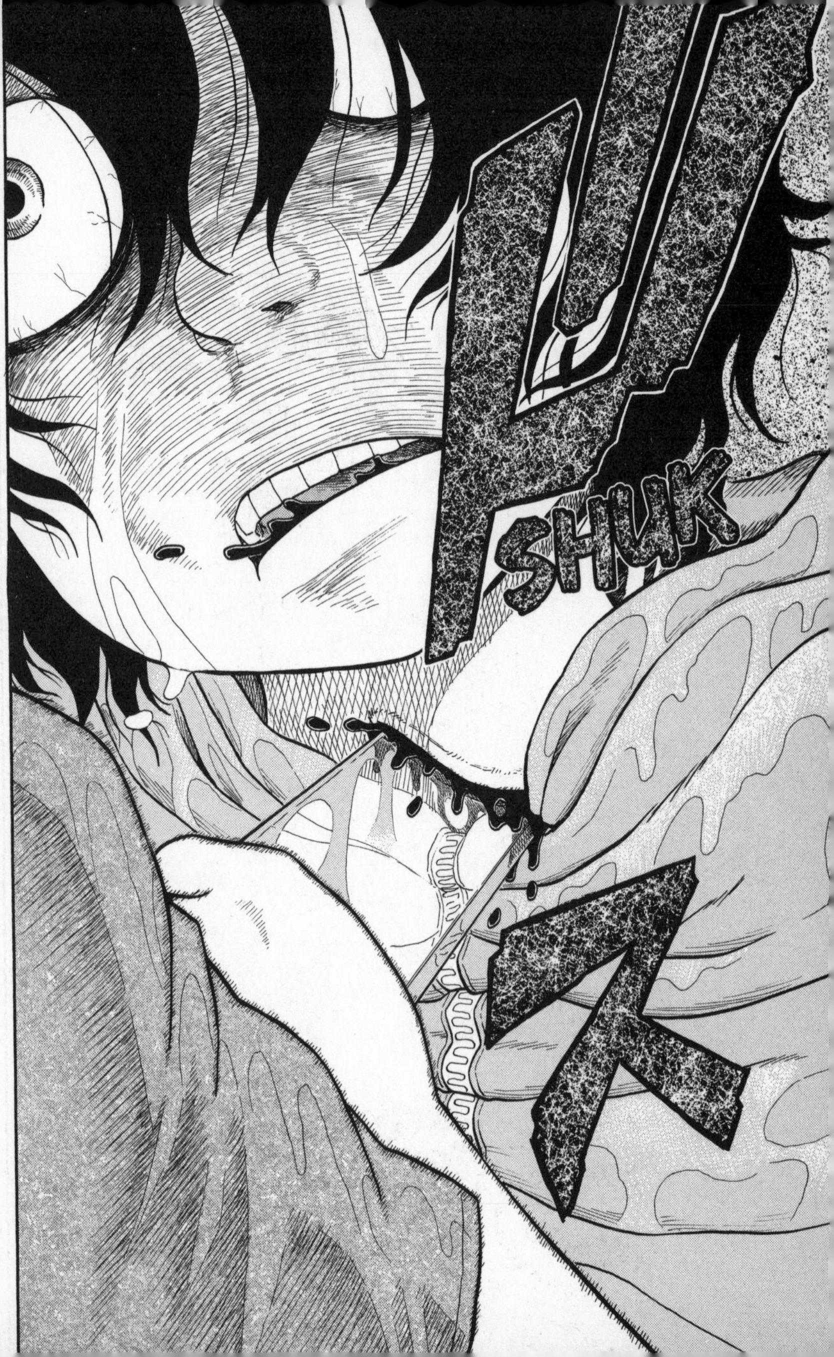
SHUK

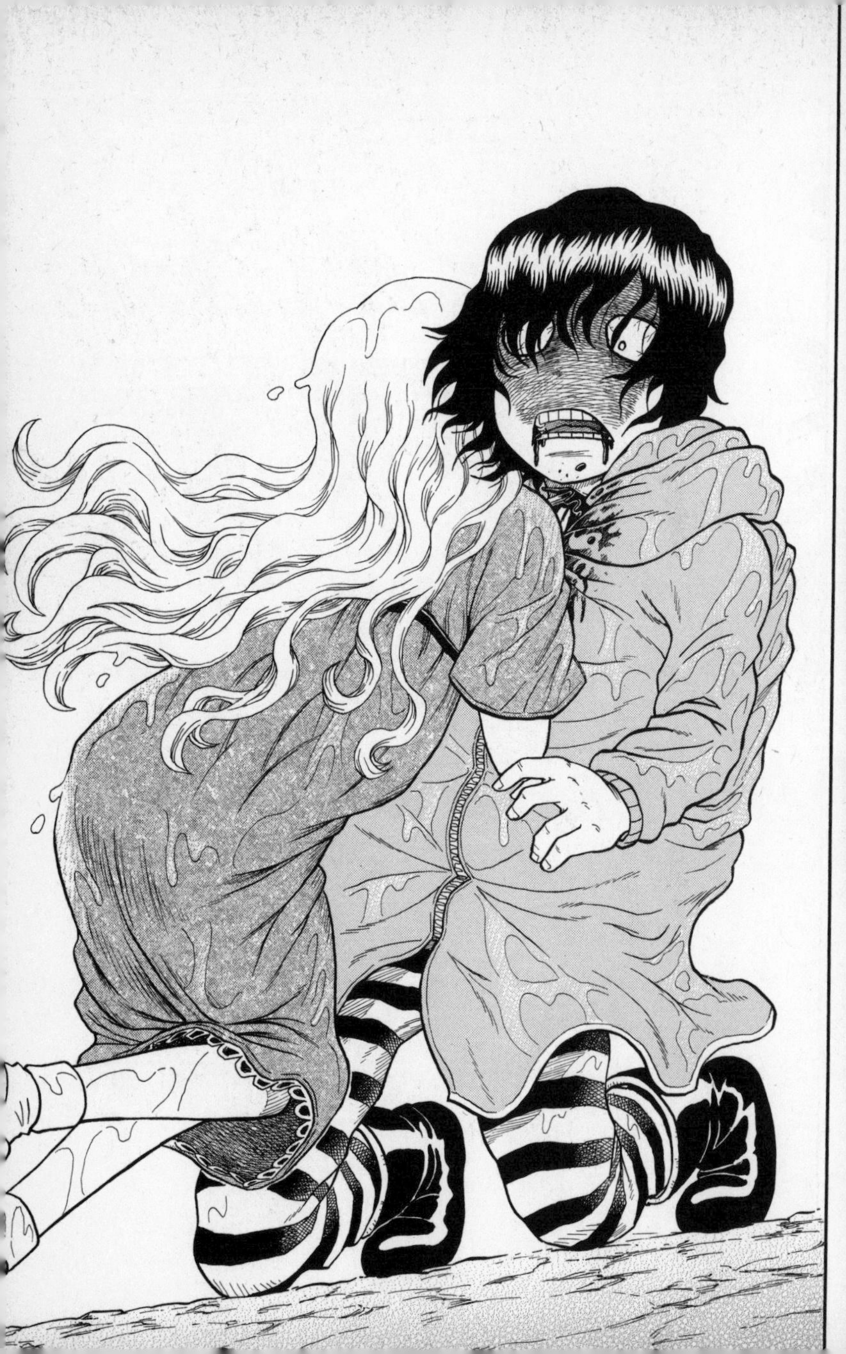

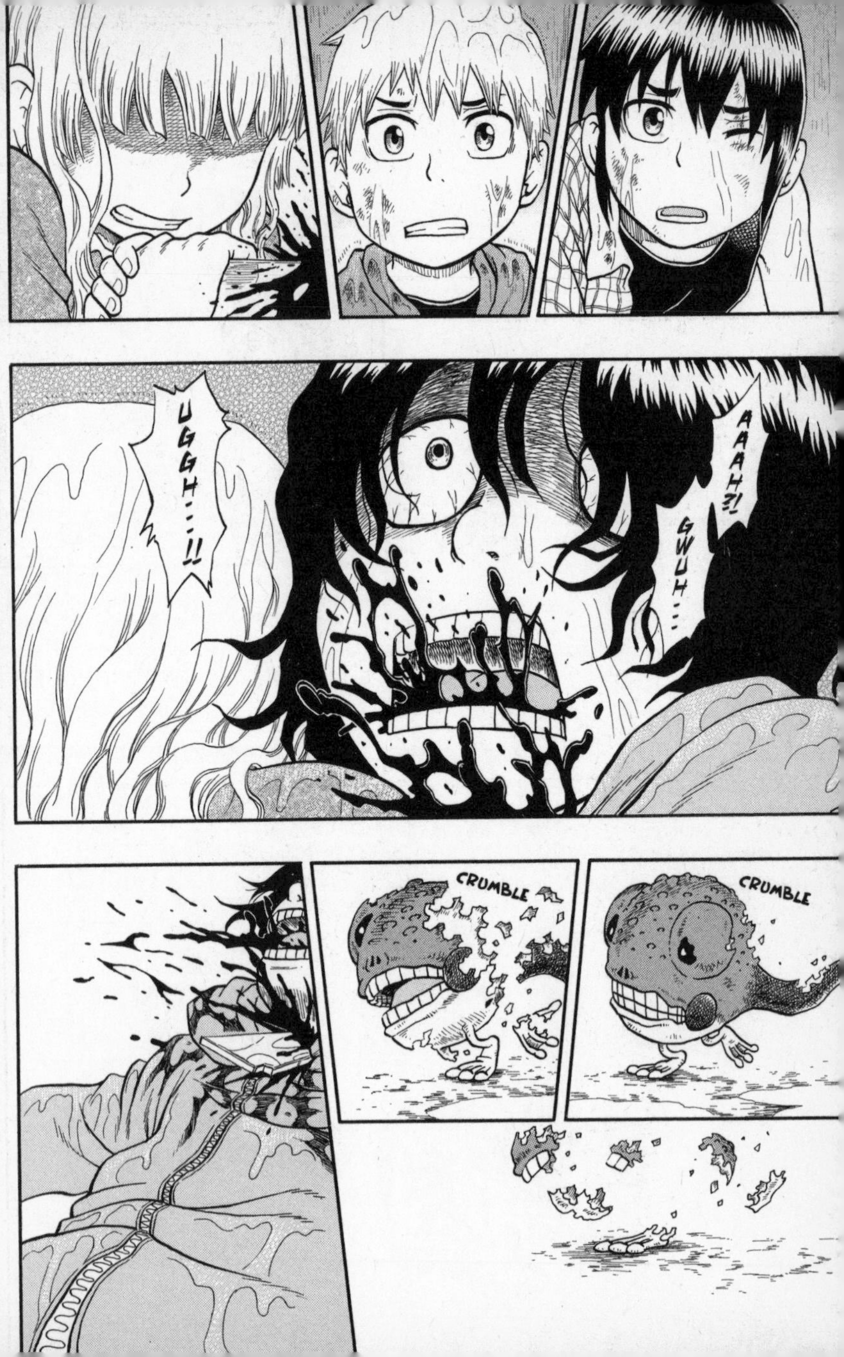
AAAAH?!
GWUH...
UGGH...!!
CRUMBLE
CRUMBLE

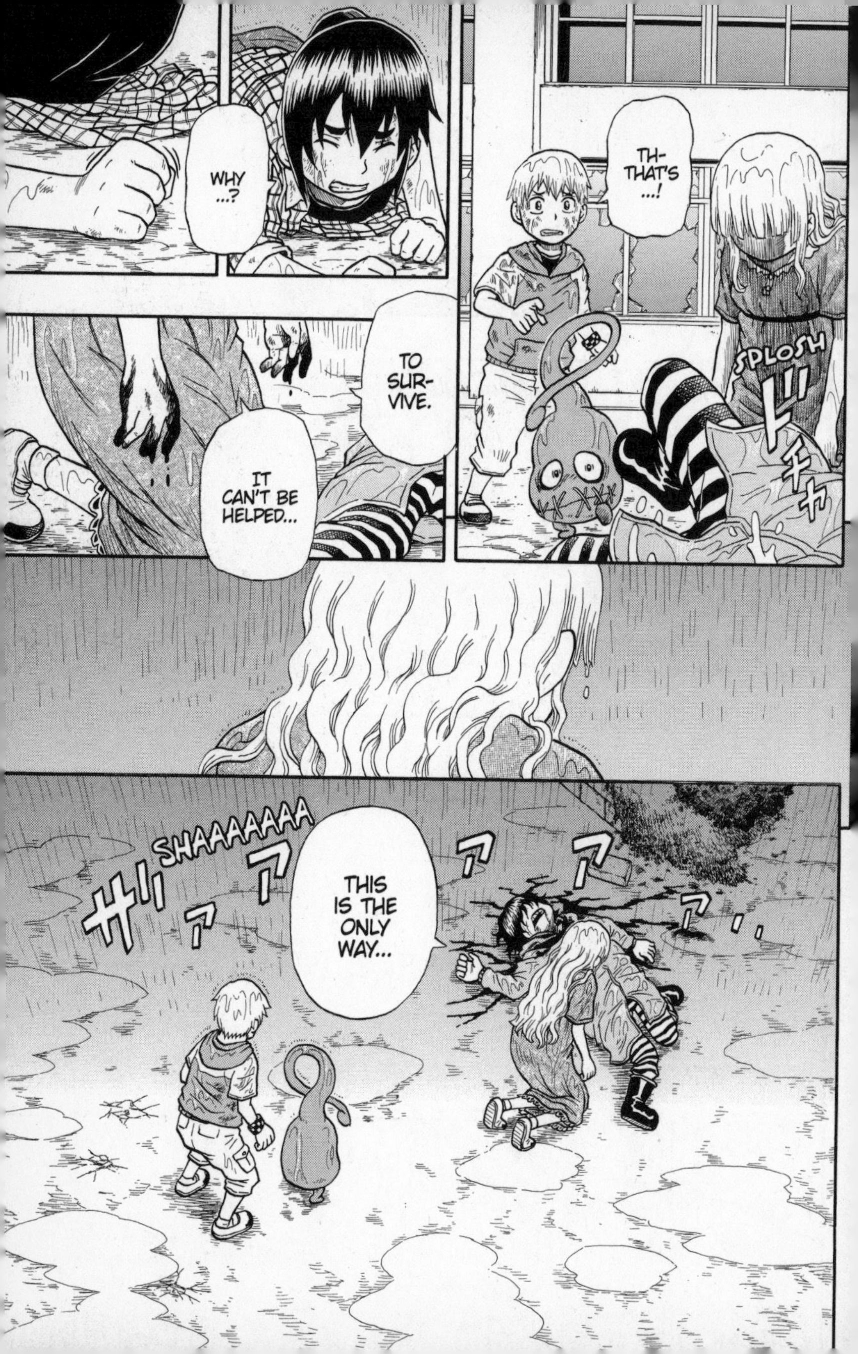

TH-THAT'S ...!
SPLOSH
WHY ...?
TO SUR-VIVE.
IT CAN'T BE HELPED...
SHAAAAAAA
THIS IS THE ONLY WAY...

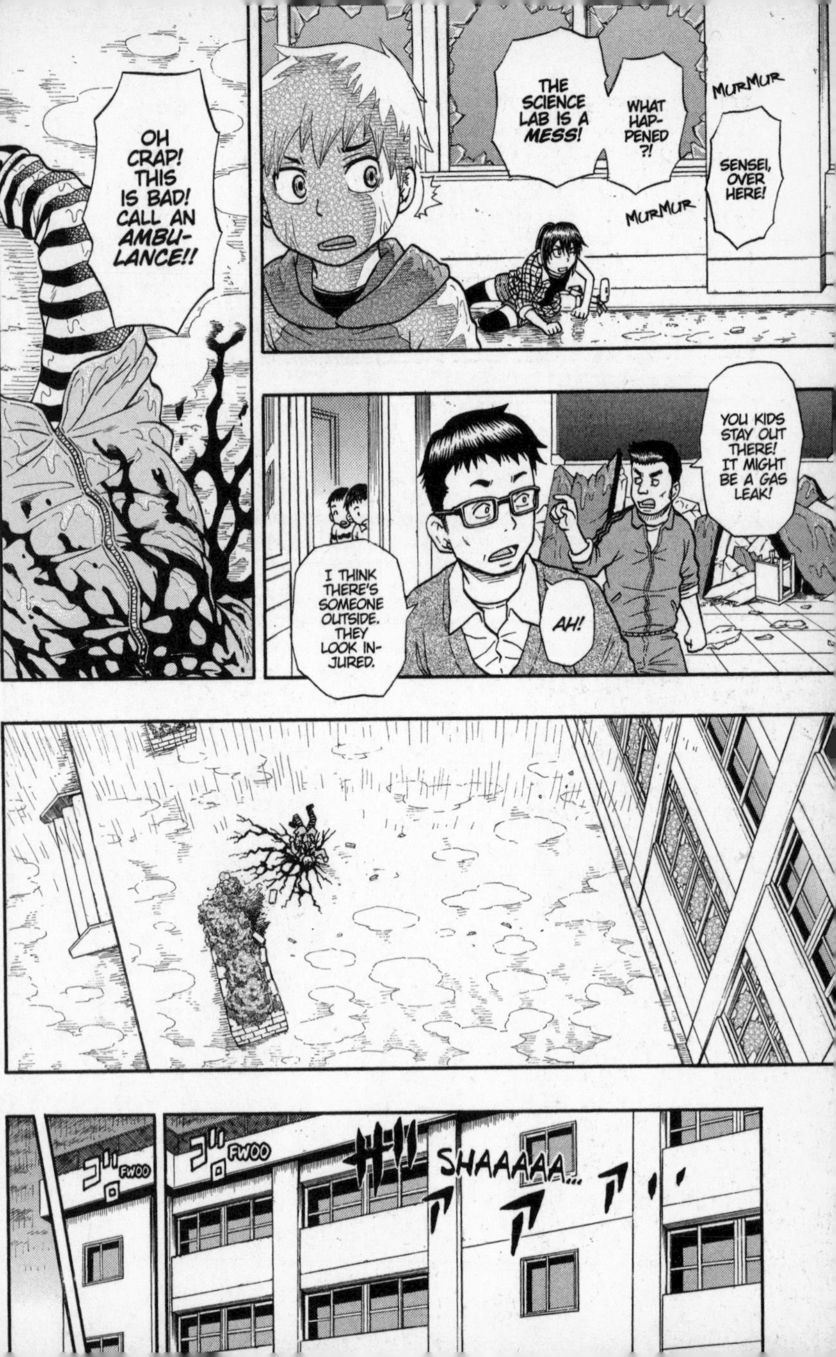

MURMUR
SENSEI, OVER HERE!
WHAT HAP-PENED?!
THE SCIENCE LAB IS A MESS!
MURMUR
YOU KIDS STAY OUT THERE! IT MIGHT BE A GAS LEAK!
AH!
I THINK THERE'S SOMEONE OUTSIDE. THEY LOOK IN-JURED.
OH CRAP! THIS IS BAD! CALL AN AMBU-LANCE!!
SHAAAAA...
FWOO
FWOO

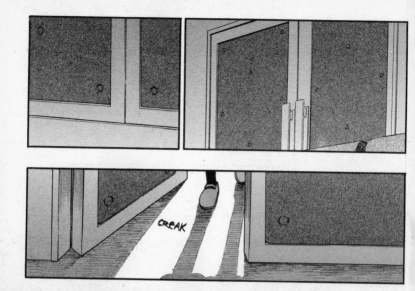

CREAK

GOOD JOB. IS IT STILL RAINING?

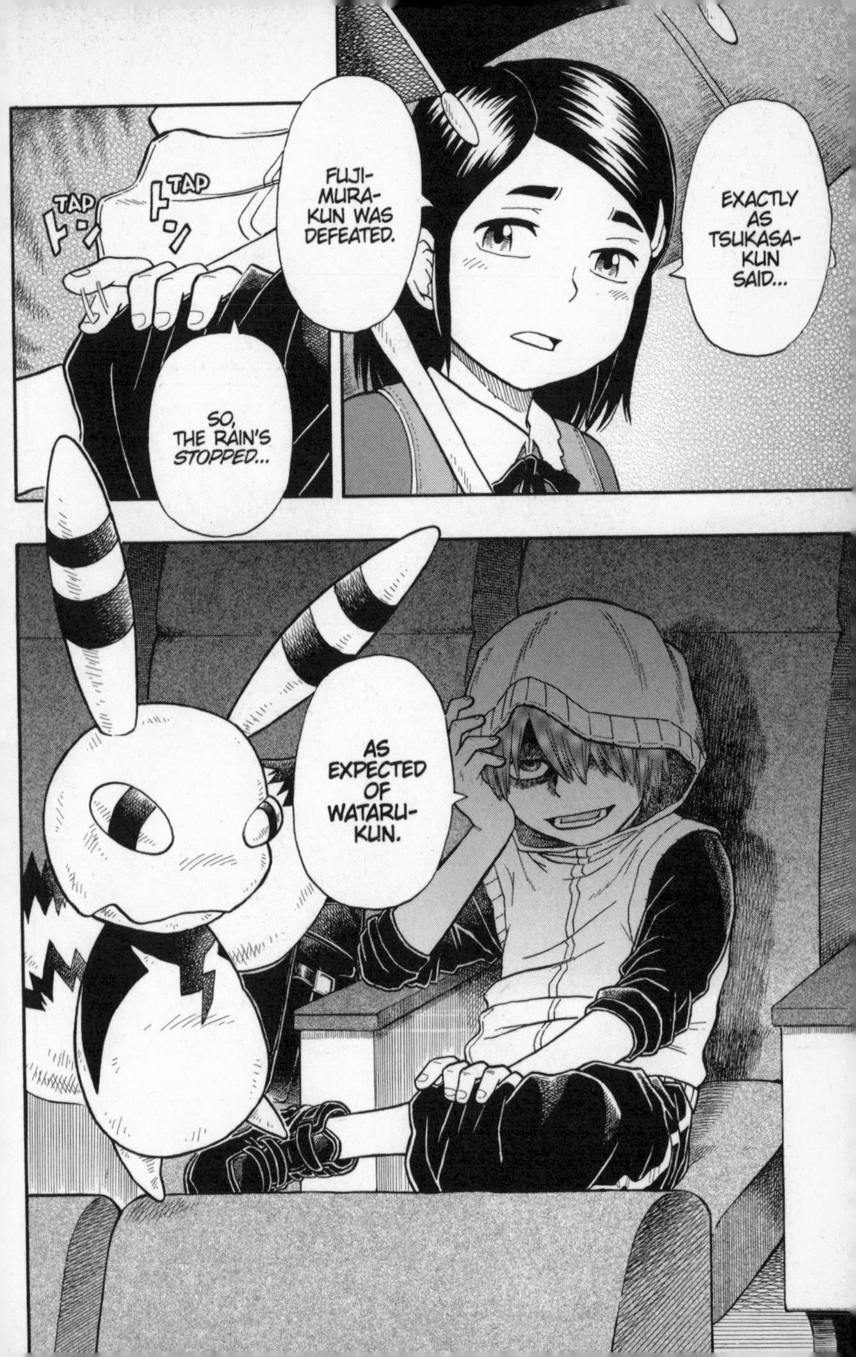
EXACTLY AS TSUKASA-KUN SAID...
FUJI-MURA-KUN WAS DEFEATED.
TAP
TAP
SO, THE RAIN'S STOPPED...
AS EXPECTED OF WATARU-KUN.

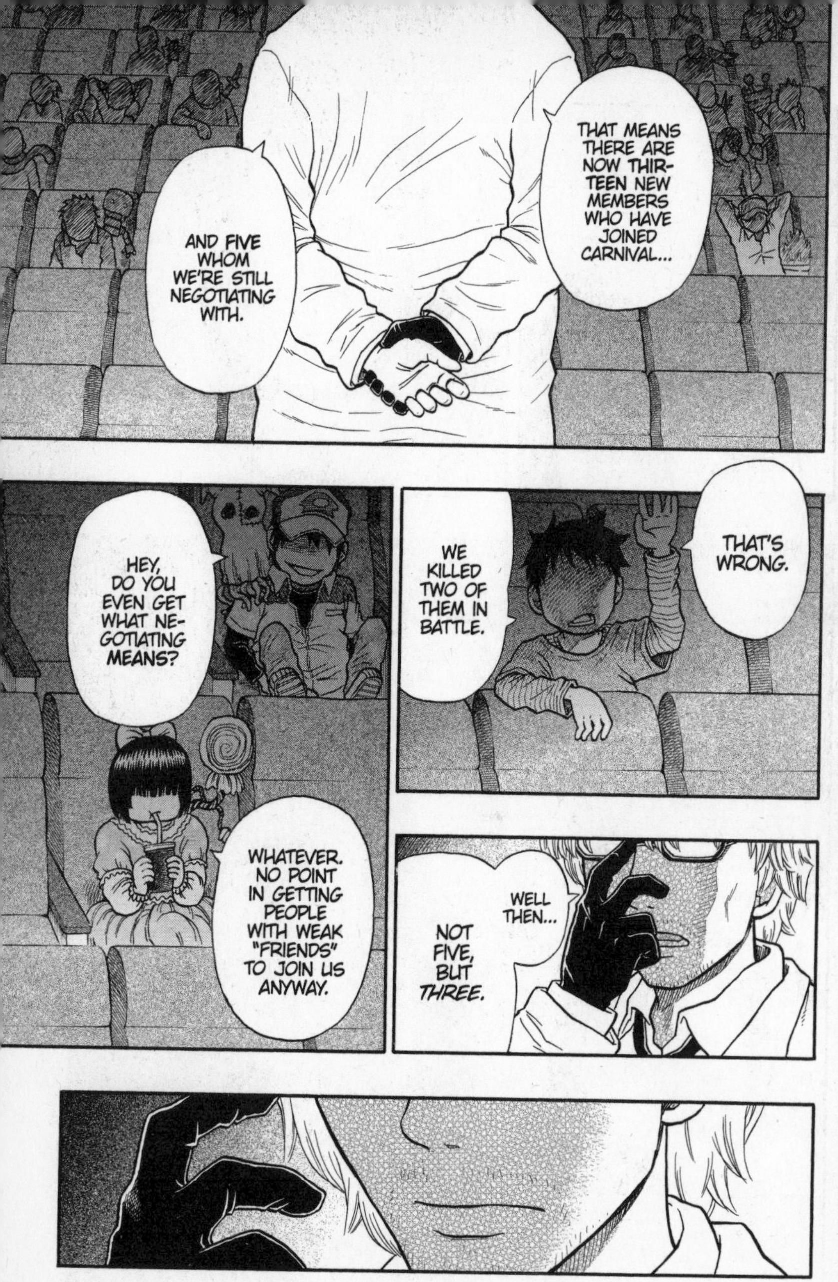
THAT MEANS THERE ARE NOW THIRTEEN NEW MEMBERS WHO HAVE JOINED CARNIVAL...
AND FIVE WHOM WE'RE STILL NEGOTIATING WITH.
THAT'S WRONG.
WE KILLED TWO OF THEM IN BATTLE.
WELL THEN...
NOT FIVE, BUT *THREE.*
HEY, DO YOU EVEN GET WHAT NEGOTIATING MEANS?
WHATEVER. NO POINT IN GETTING PEOPLE WITH WEAK "FRIENDS" TO JOIN US ANYWAY.

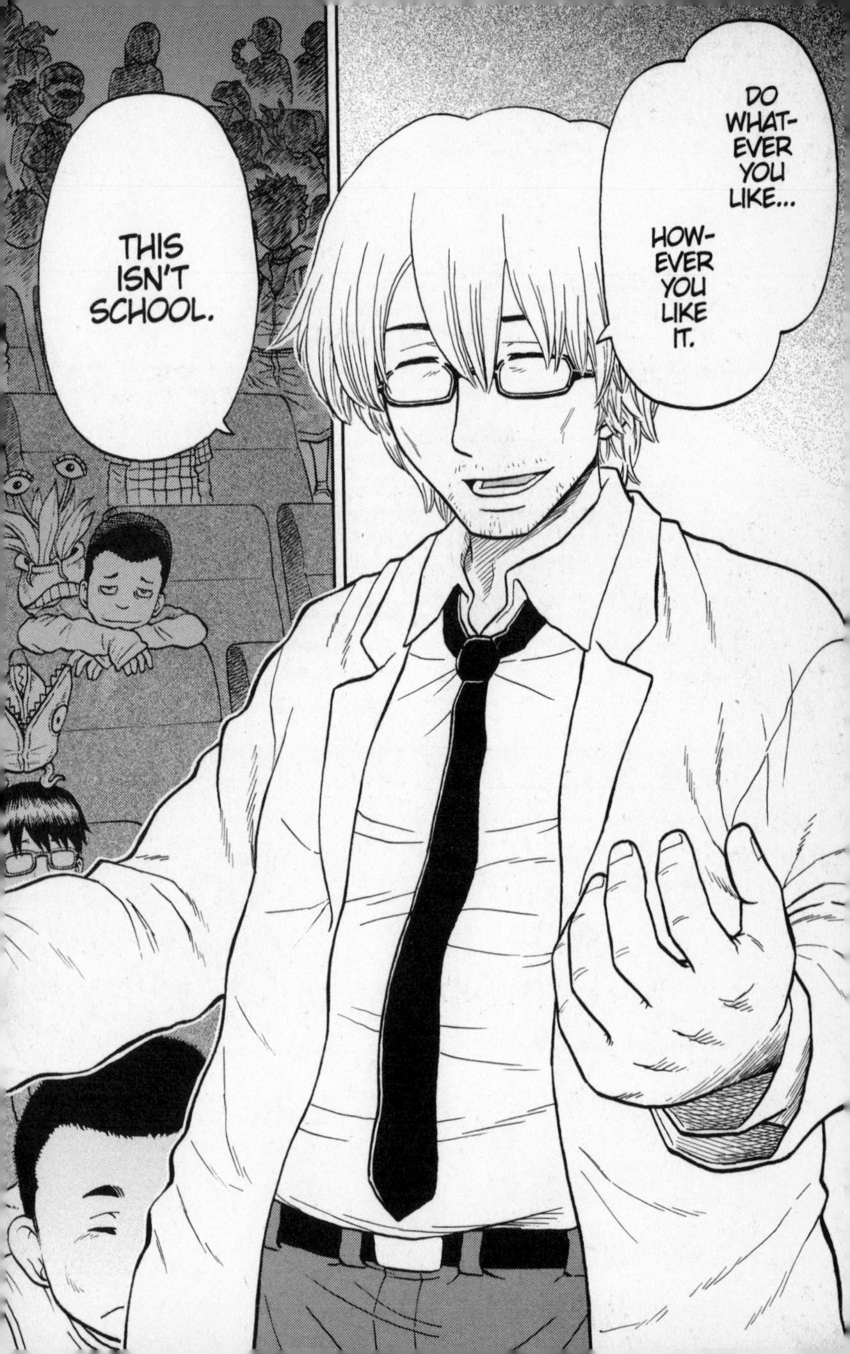
DO WHAT-EVER YOU LIKE...
HOW-EVER YOU LIKE IT.
THIS ISN'T SCHOOL.

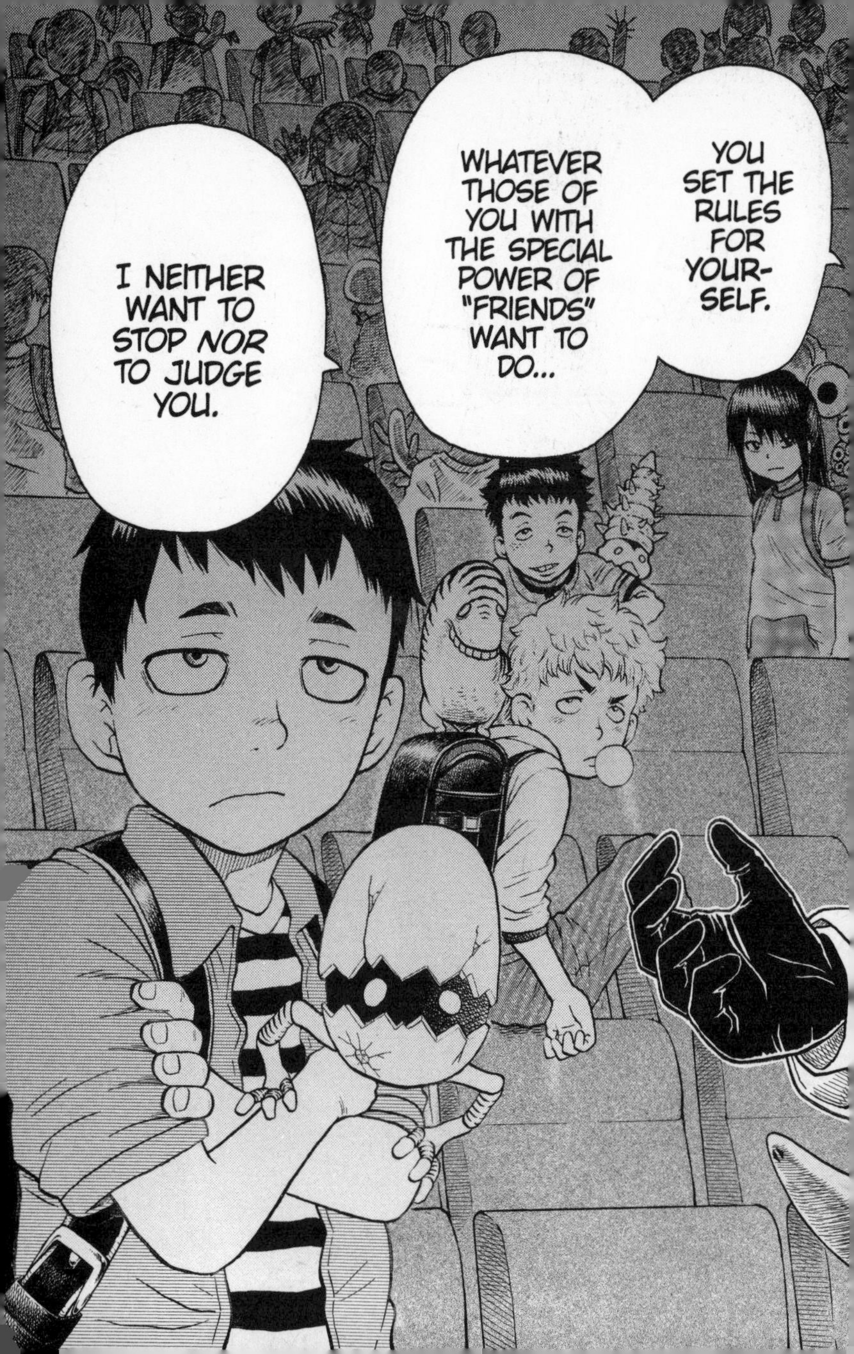
YOU SET THE RULES FOR YOURSELF.
WHATEVER THOSE OF YOU WITH THE SPECIAL POWER OF "FRIENDS" WANT TO DO...
I NEITHER WANT TO STOP *NOR* TO JUDGE YOU.

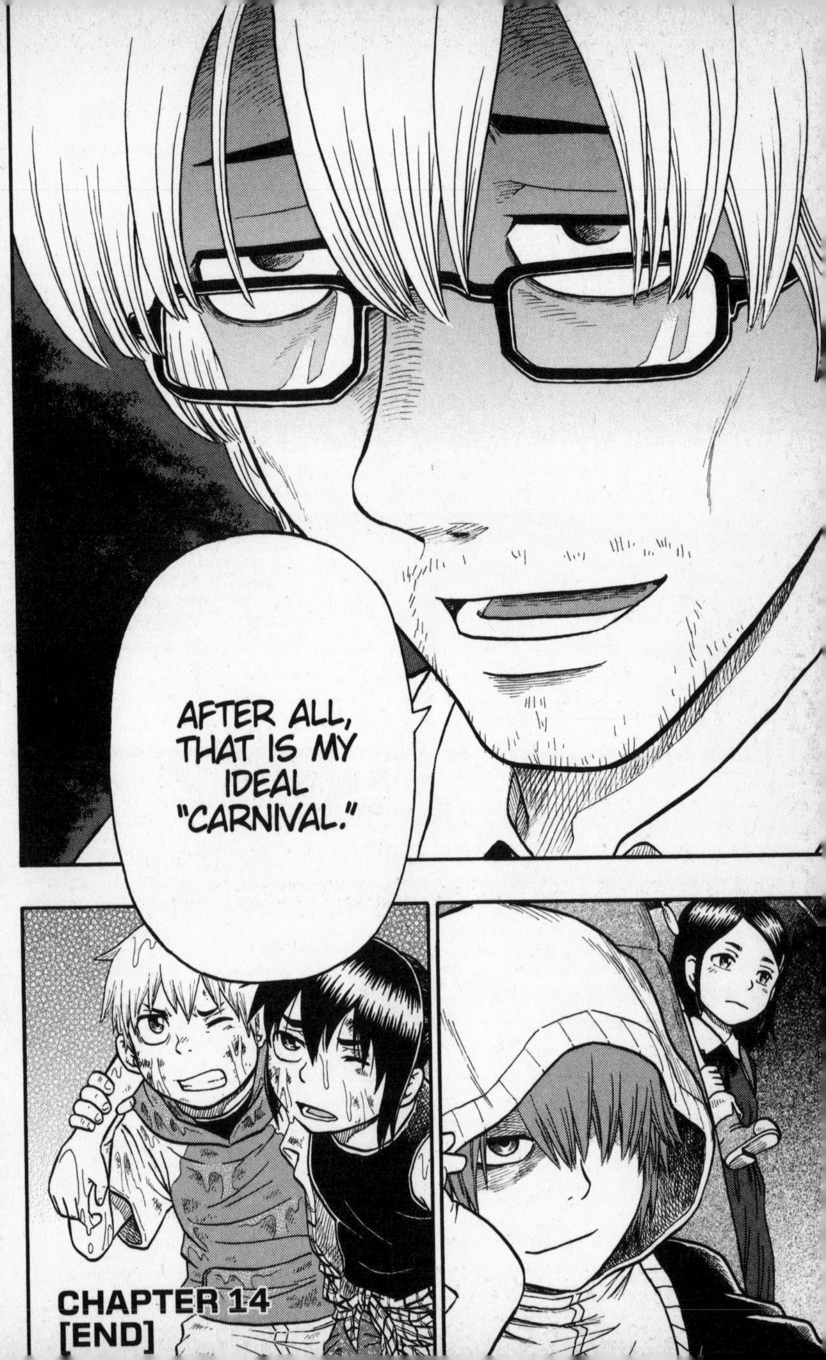
AFTER ALL, THAT IS MY IDEAL "CARNIVAL."
CHAPTER 14 [END]

Friend Encyclopedia No.009

Name: **Pino**

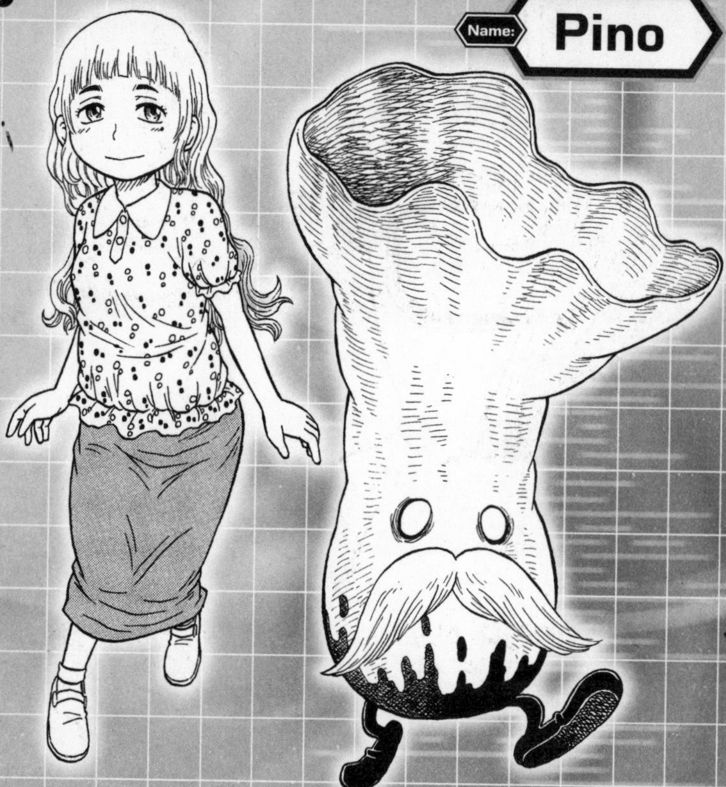

Partner:	Morino Riko (6th grade)	**Speed:**	C
Attack:	C	**Dexterity:**	C
Defense:	B	**Special Abilities:**	B
Chara-teristics:	A mushroom-like Friend. Aside from being good at scouting, it can also attack and defend.		
Special Abilities:	Spore Search – Releases spores that its partner can share her vision with to look for hidden things. Spore Shield – Creates a giant mushroom umbrella to guard against attacks. Spore Seed – Launches giant seeds from its head to attack.		

Name: **Kerope**

Partner:	Fujimura Taku (6th grade)	Speed:	C
Attack:	C (A when it's raining)	Dexterity:	C
Defense:	C (A when it's raining)	Special Abilities:	B
Characteristics:	A frog-like Friend. It can freely control water. It's very powerful during rainy days, but weak when there's no water.		
Special Abilities:	Frog Song – Freely controls the water it touches with its tail. Bubble Bullet – Shoots bullet-like bubbles of air in the water. Frog Chorus – Gathers a lot of water to start a tsunami.		

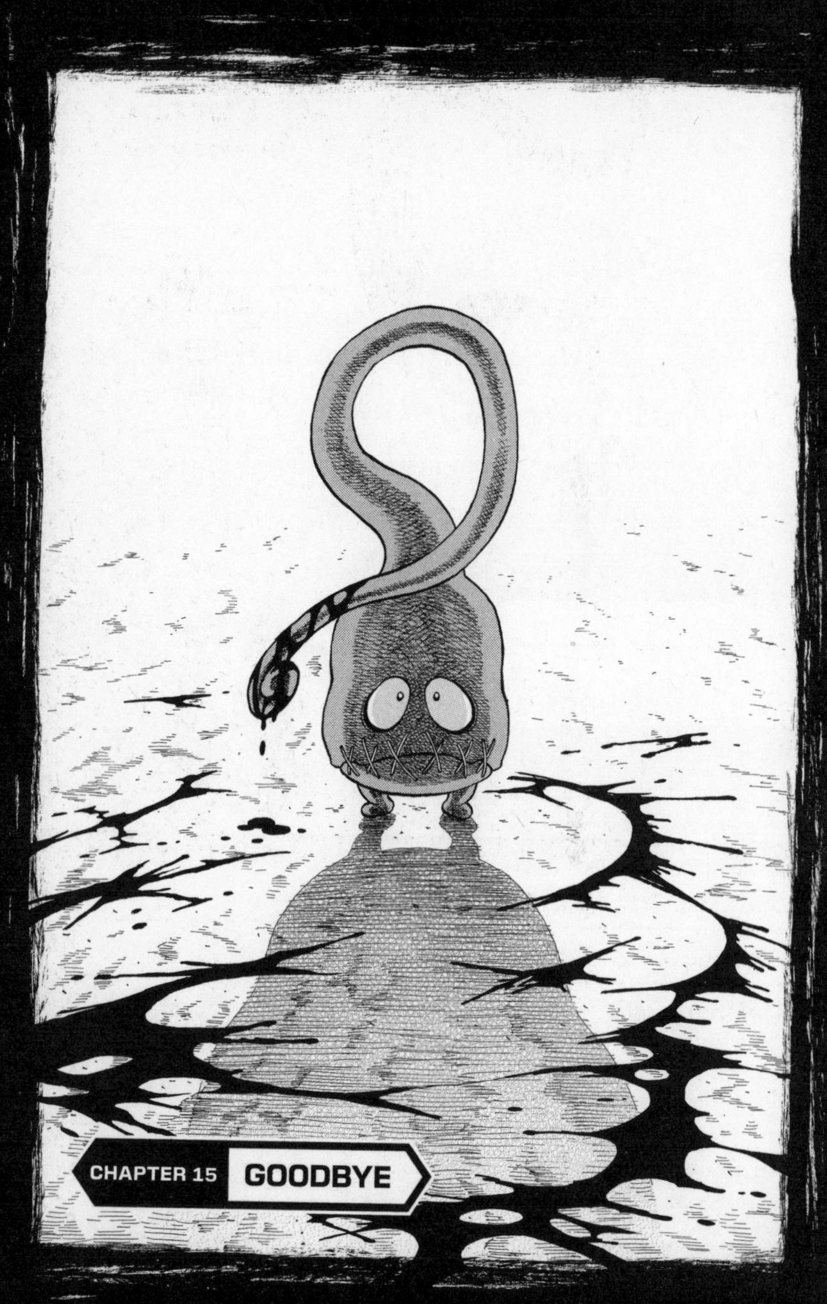
CHAPTER 15
GOODBYE

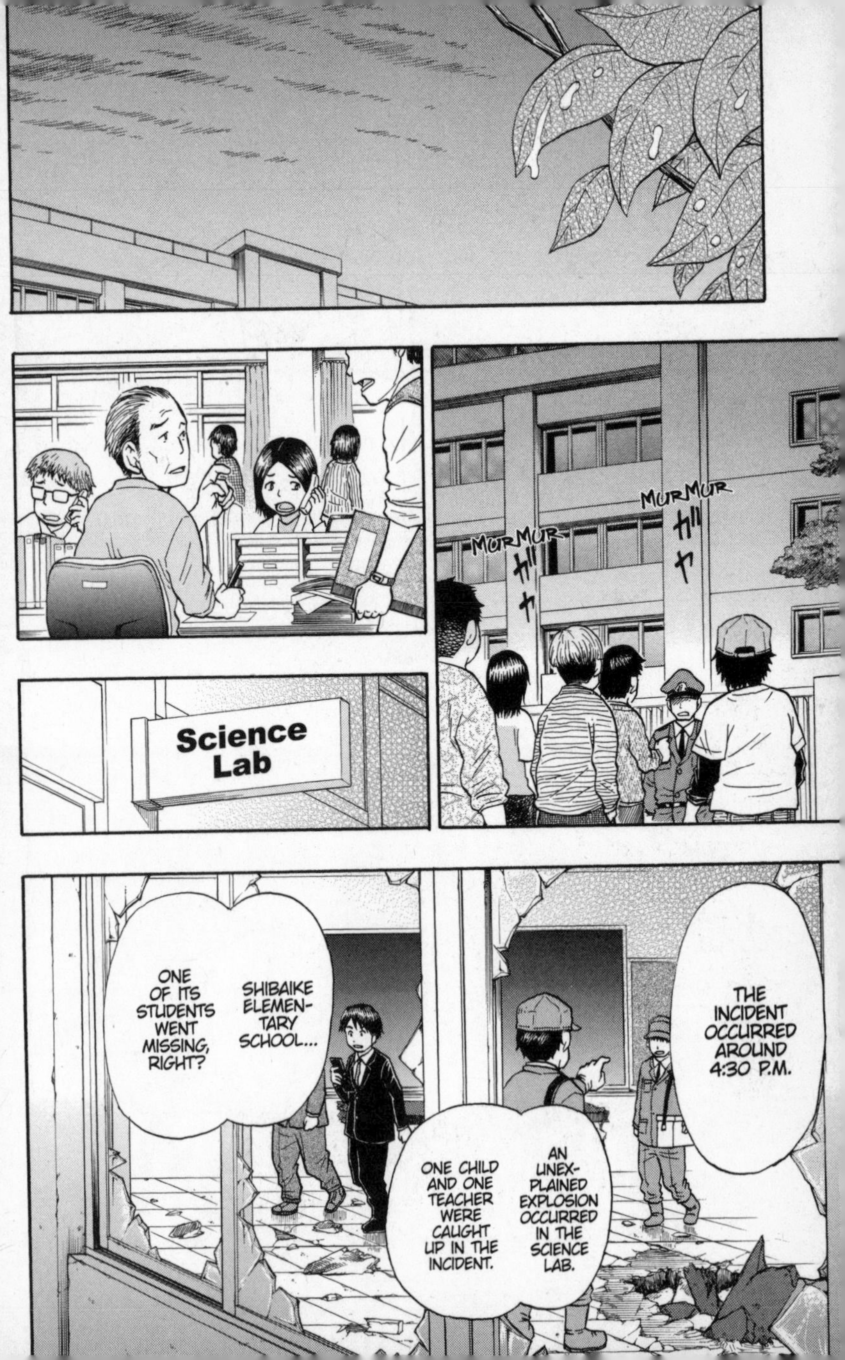
MURMUR
ガヤ
MURMUR
ガヤ
Science Lab
THE INCIDENT OCCURRED AROUND 4:30 P.M.
AN UNEXPLAINED EXPLOSION OCCURRED IN THE SCIENCE LAB.
ONE CHILD AND ONE TEACHER WERE CAUGHT UP IN THE INCIDENT.
SHIBAIKE ELEMENTARY SCHOOL...
ONE OF ITS STUDENTS WENT MISSING, RIGHT?

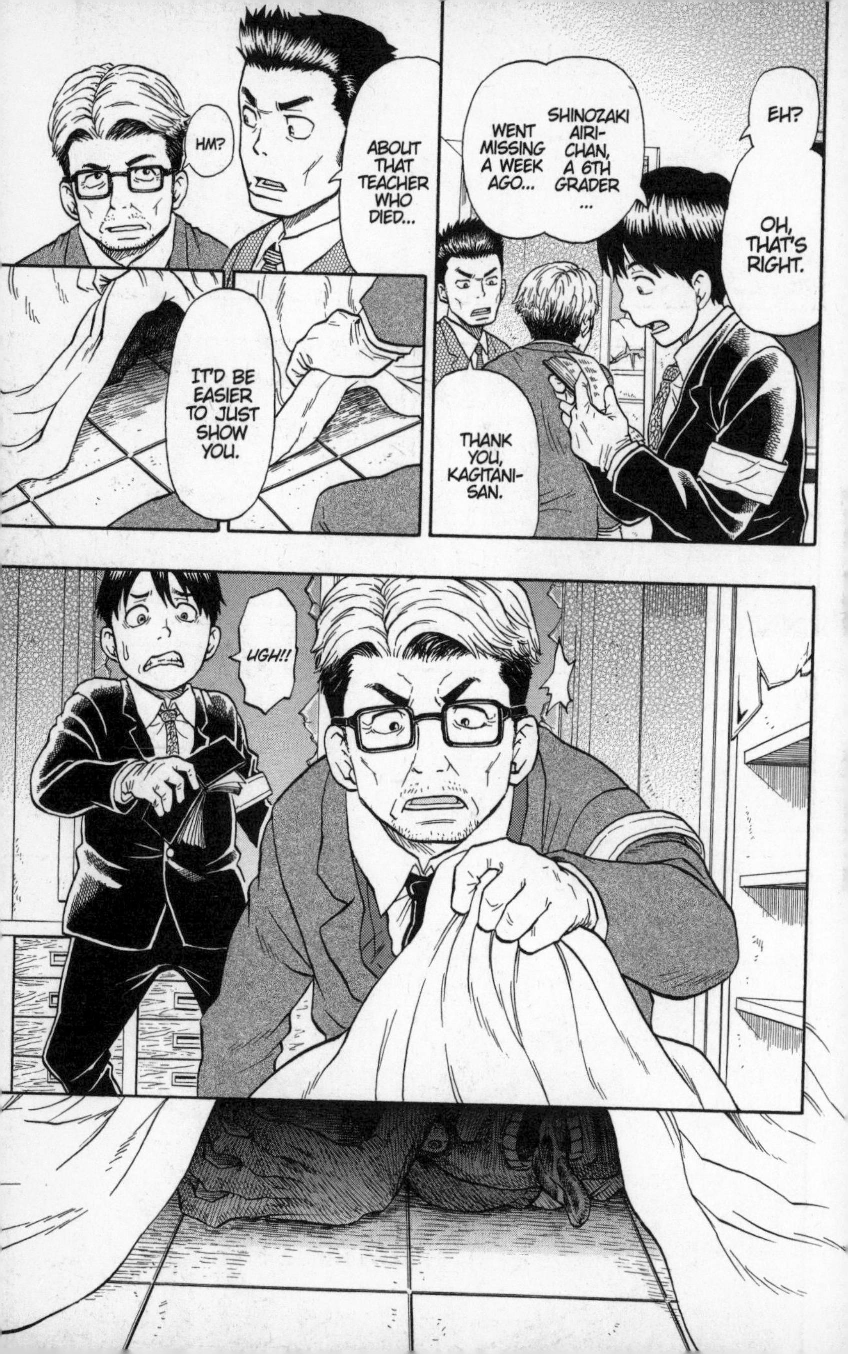
EH?
SHINOZAKI AIRI-CHAN, A 6TH GRADER ...
WENT MISSING A WEEK AGO...
OH, THAT'S RIGHT.
THANK YOU, KAGITANI-SAN.
ABOUT THAT TEACHER WHO DIED...
HM?
IT'D BE EASIER TO JUST SHOW YOU.
UGH!!

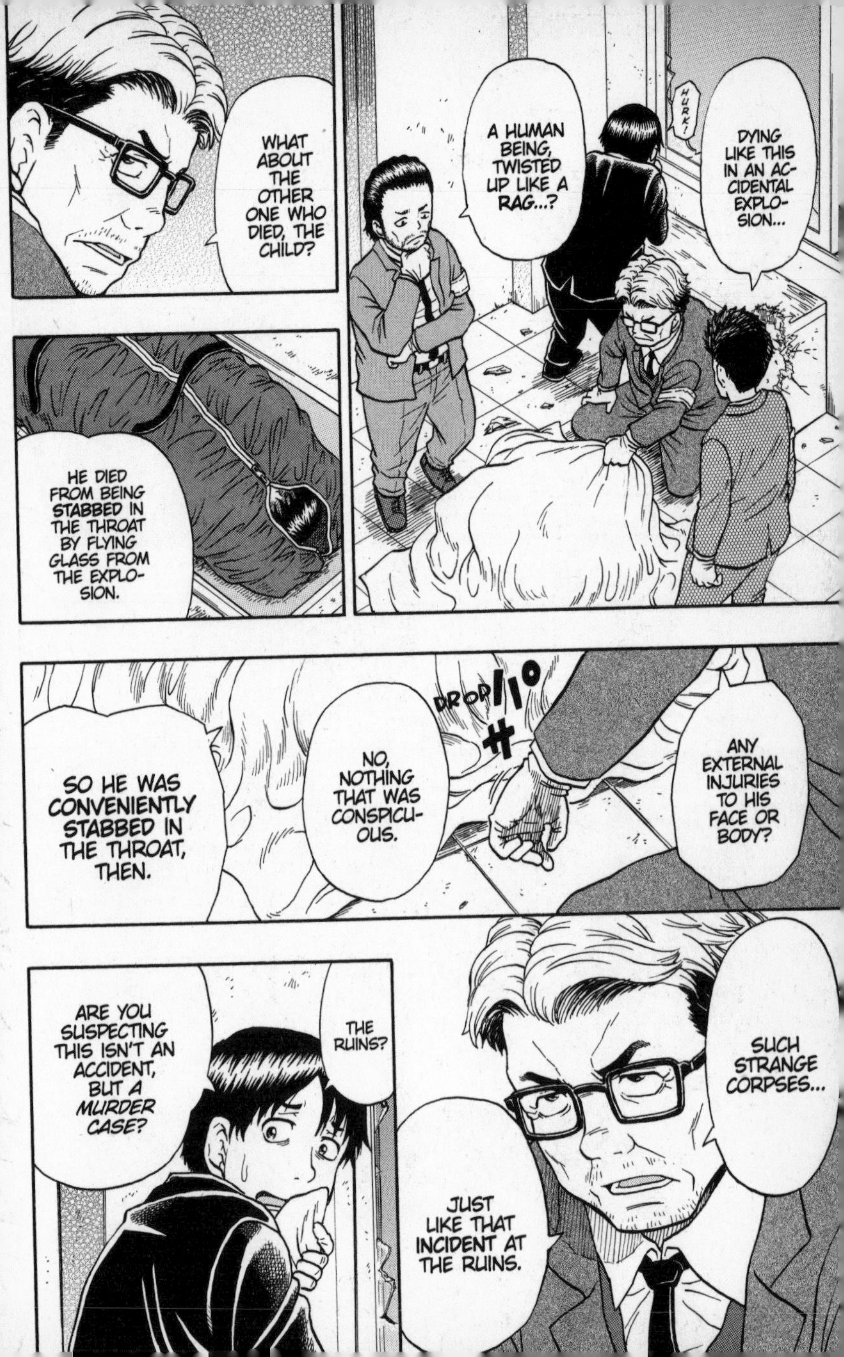
DYING LIKE THIS IN AN ACCIDENTAL EXPLOSION...
HURK!
A HUMAN BEING, TWISTED UP LIKE A RAG...?
WHAT ABOUT THE OTHER ONE WHO DIED, THE CHILD?
HE DIED FROM BEING STABBED IN THE THROAT BY FLYING GLASS FROM THE EXPLOSION.
ANY EXTERNAL INJURIES TO HIS FACE OR BODY?
DROP
NO, NOTHING THAT WAS CONSPICUOUS.
SO HE WAS CONVENIENTLY STABBED IN THE THROAT, THEN.
SUCH STRANGE CORPSES...
JUST LIKE THAT INCIDENT AT THE RUINS.
THE RUINS?
ARE YOU SUSPECTING THIS ISN'T AN ACCIDENT, BUT A *MURDER CASE*?

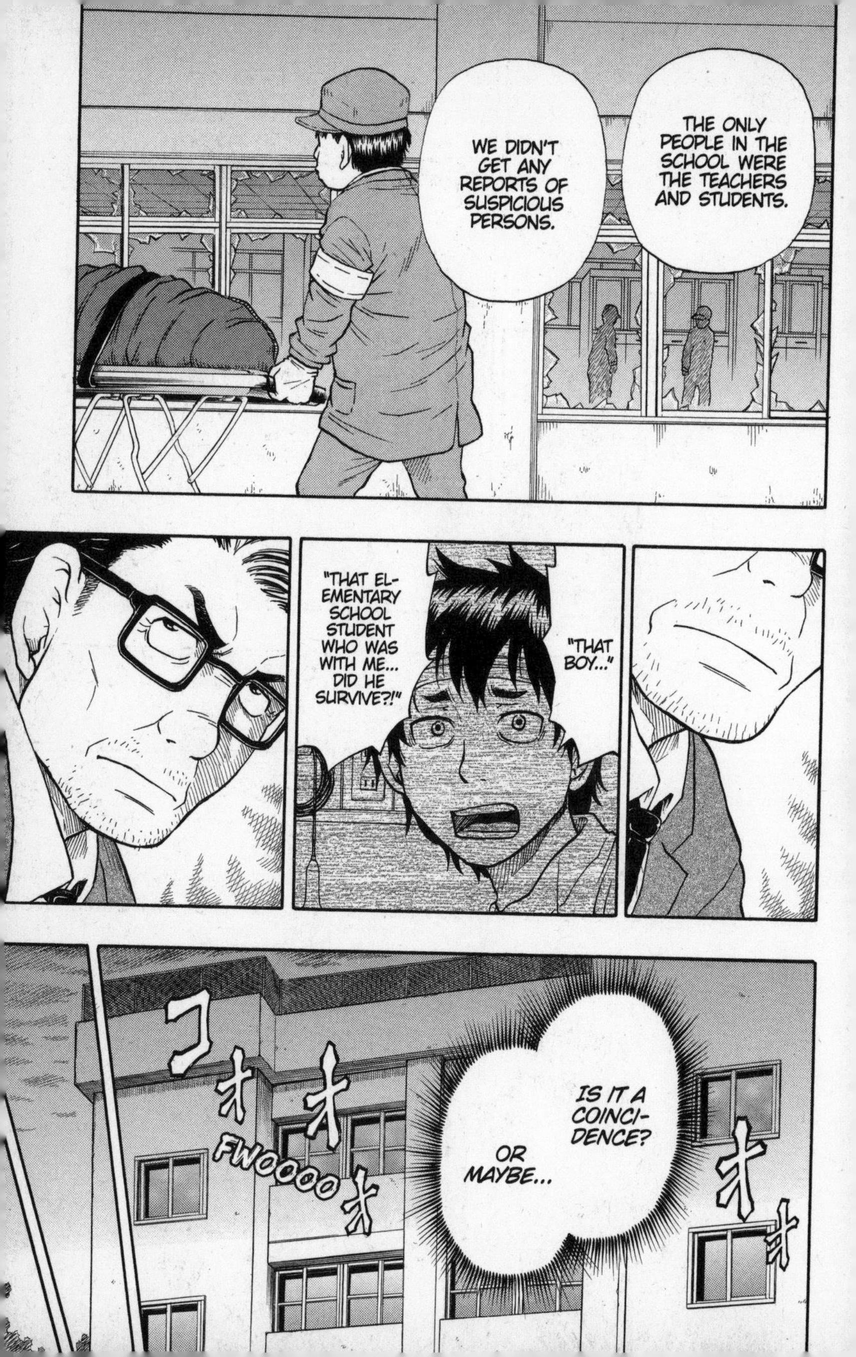
THE ONLY PEOPLE IN THE SCHOOL WERE THE TEACHERS AND STUDENTS.
WE DIDN'T GET ANY REPORTS OF SUSPICIOUS PERSONS.
"THAT BOY..."
"THAT EL-EMENTARY SCHOOL STUDENT WHO WAS WITH ME... DID HE SURVIVE?!"
コオオオオオ
FWOOOO
IS IT A COINCI-DENCE?
OR MAYBE...

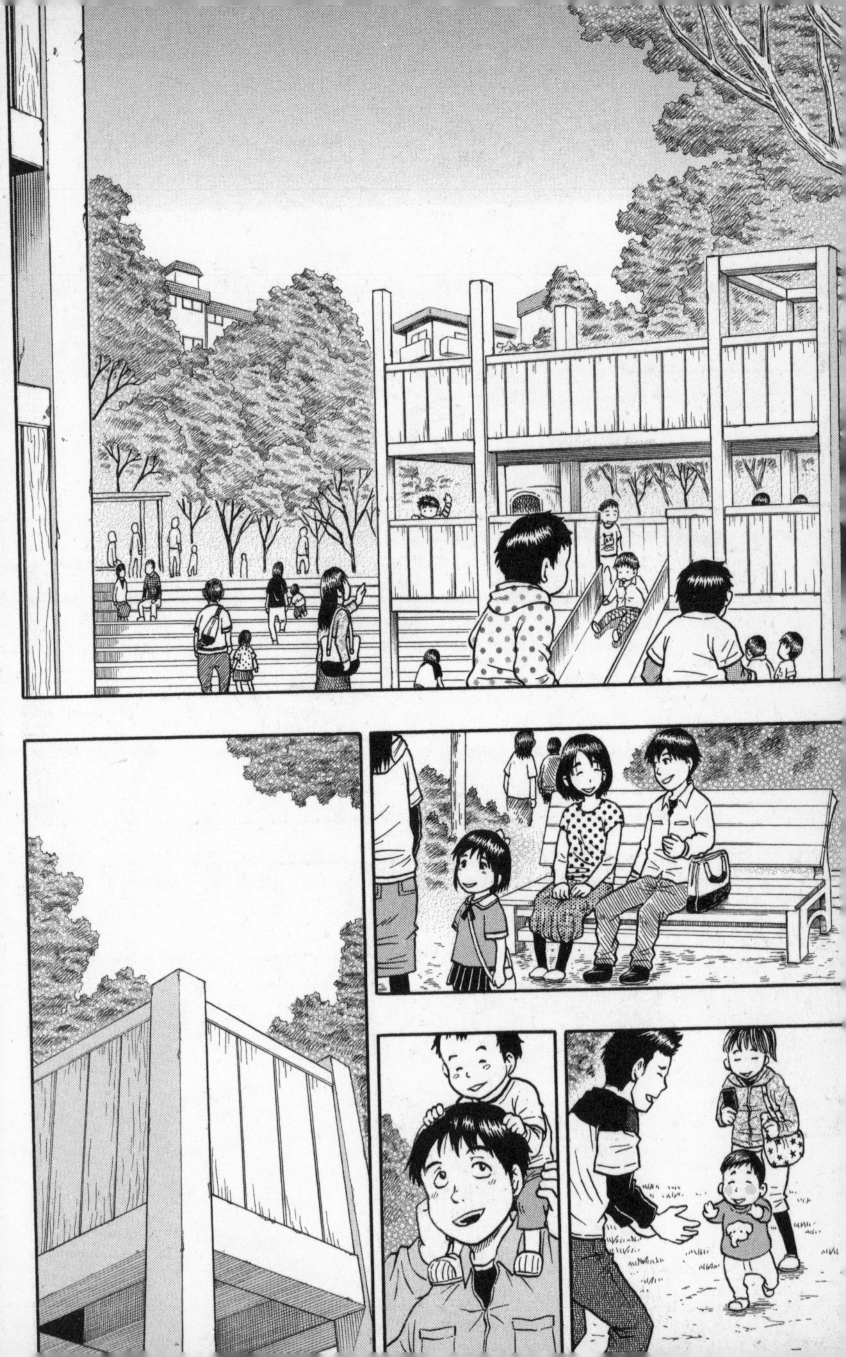

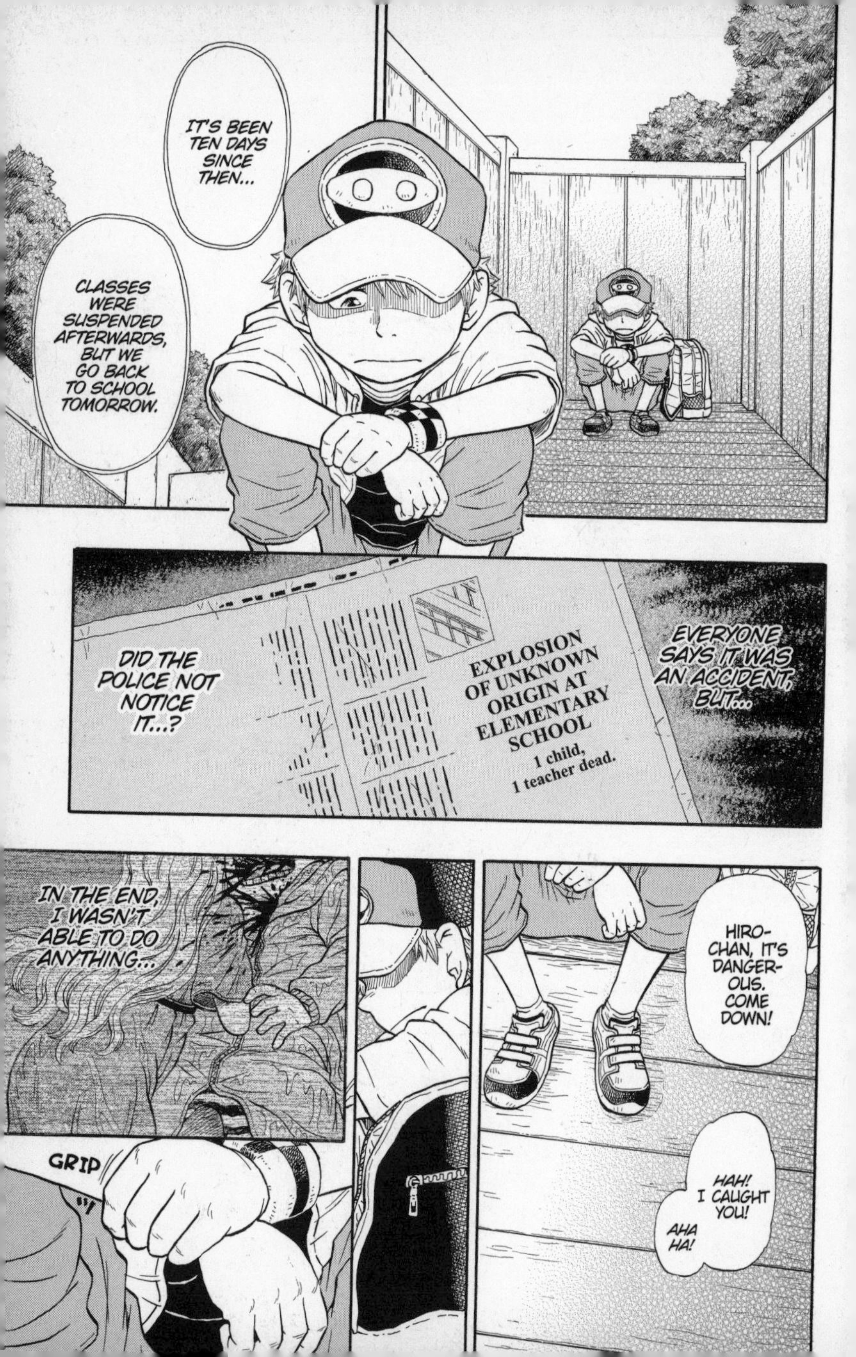
IT'S BEEN TEN DAYS SINCE THEN...
CLASSES WERE SUSPENDED AFTERWARDS, BUT WE GO BACK TO SCHOOL TOMORROW.
EVERYONE SAYS IT WAS AN ACCIDENT, BUT...
EXPLOSION OF UNKNOWN ORIGIN AT ELEMENTARY SCHOOL
1 child, 1 teacher dead.
DID THE POLICE NOT NOTICE IT...?
HIRO-CHAN, IT'S DANGER-OUS. COME DOWN!
HAH! I CAUGHT YOU!
AHA HA!
IN THE END, I WASN'T ABLE TO DO ANYTHING...
GRIP

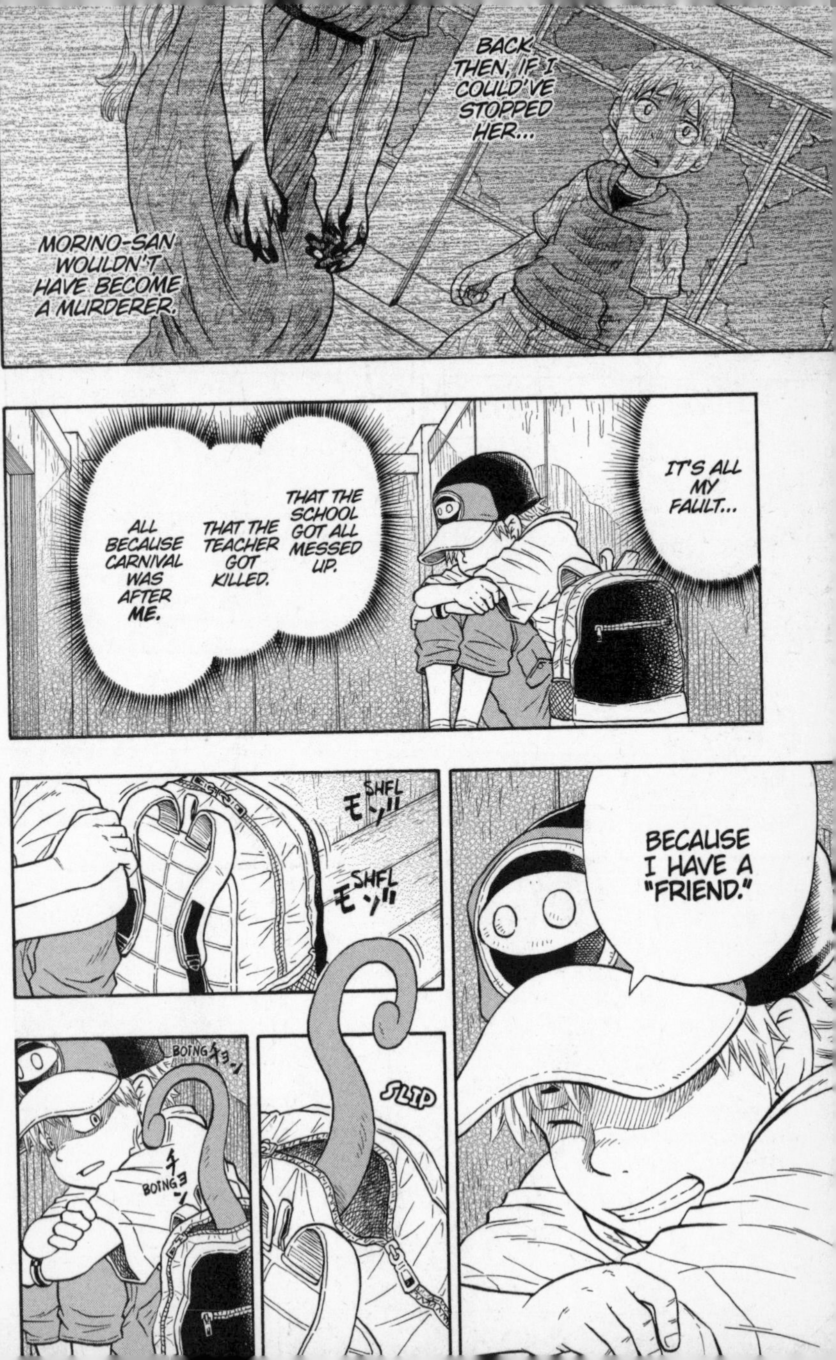
BACK THEN, IF I COULD'VE STOPPED HER...
MORINO-SAN WOULDN'T HAVE BECOME A MURDERER.
IT'S ALL MY FAULT...
THAT THE SCHOOL GOT ALL MESSED UP.
THAT THE TEACHER GOT KILLED.
ALL BECAUSE CARNIVAL WAS AFTER ME.
BECAUSE I HAVE A "FRIEND."
SHFL
SHFL
SLIP
BOING
BOING

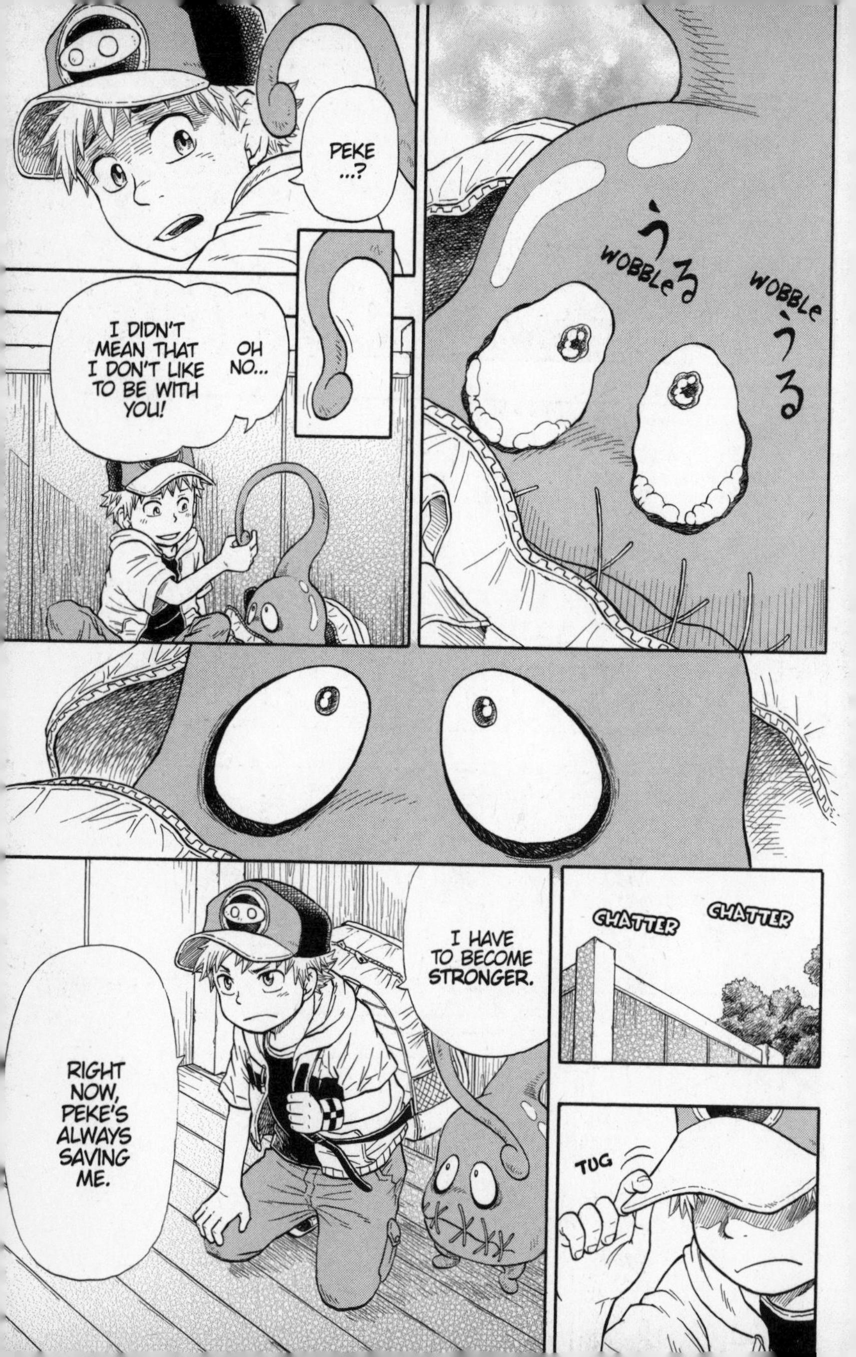
WOBBLE
うる
WOBBLE
うる
PEKE ...?
OH NO...
I DIDN'T MEAN THAT I DON'T LIKE TO BE WITH YOU!
CHATTER
CHATTER
TUG
I HAVE TO BECOME STRONGER.
RIGHT NOW, PEKE'S ALWAYS SAVING ME.

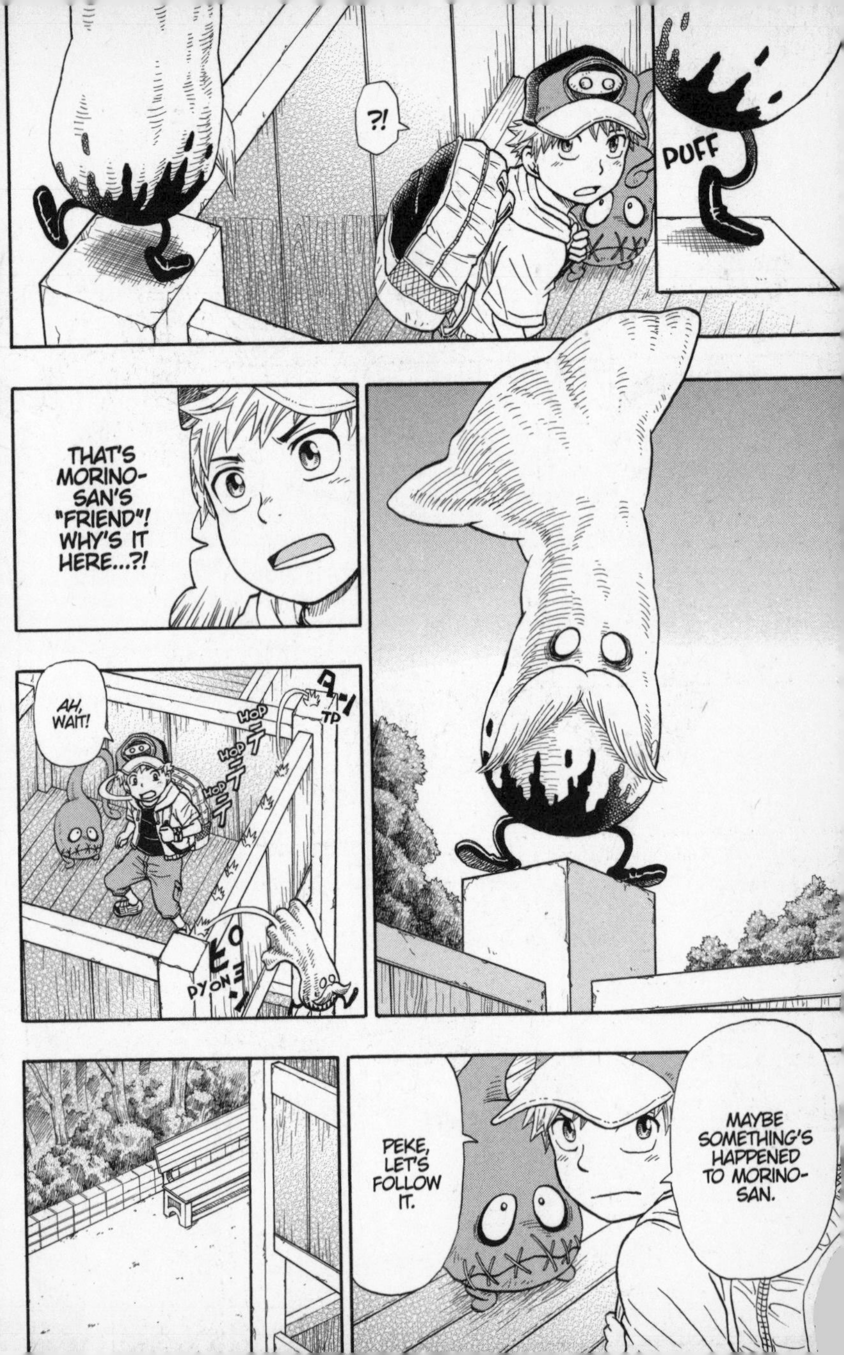
PUFF
?!
THAT'S MORINO-SAN'S "FRIEND"! WHY'S IT HERE...?!
TP
HOP
HOP
HOP
AH, WAIT!
PYON
MAYBE SOMETHING'S HAPPENED TO MORINO-SAN.
PEKE, LET'S FOLLOW IT.

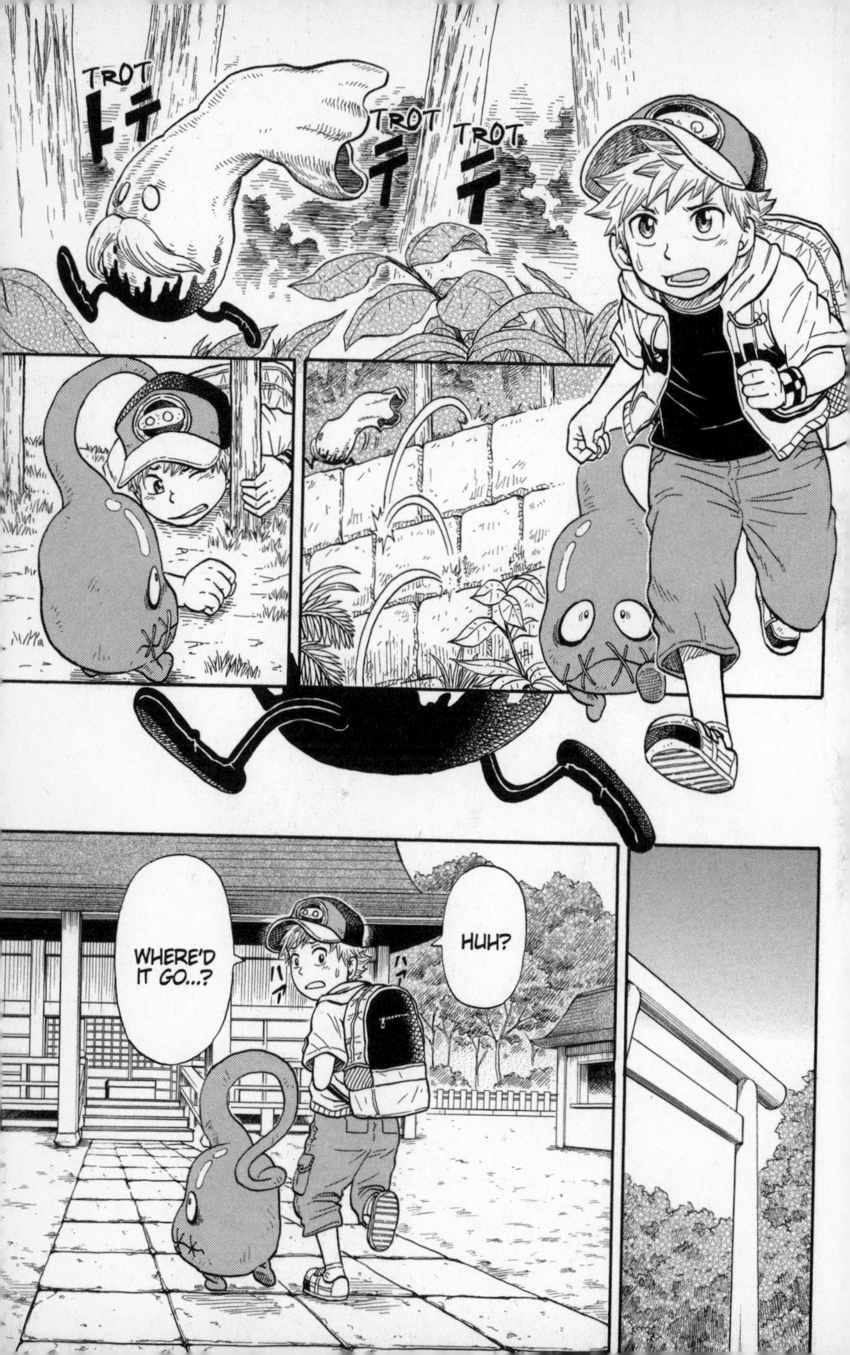
TROT
トテ
TROT
テ
TROT
テ
HUH?
WHERE'D IT GO...?

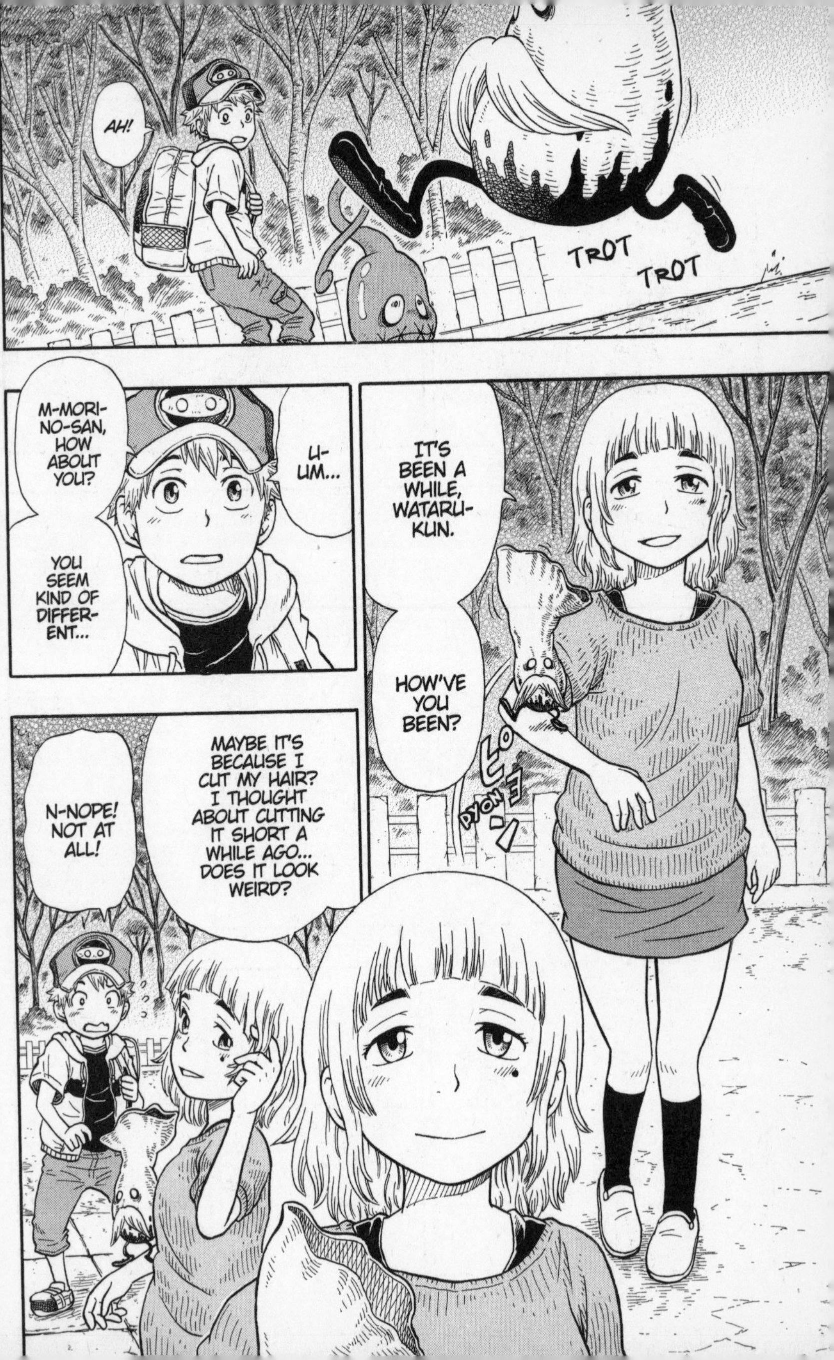
TROT
TROT
AH!
IT'S BEEN A WHILE, WATARU-KUN.
HOW'VE YOU BEEN?
DYON
U-UM...
M-MORI-NO-SAN, HOW ABOUT YOU?
YOU SEEM KIND OF DIFFER-ENT...
MAYBE IT'S BECAUSE I CUT MY HAIR? I THOUGHT ABOUT CUTTING IT SHORT A WHILE AGO... DOES IT LOOK WEIRD?
N-NOPE! NOT AT ALL!

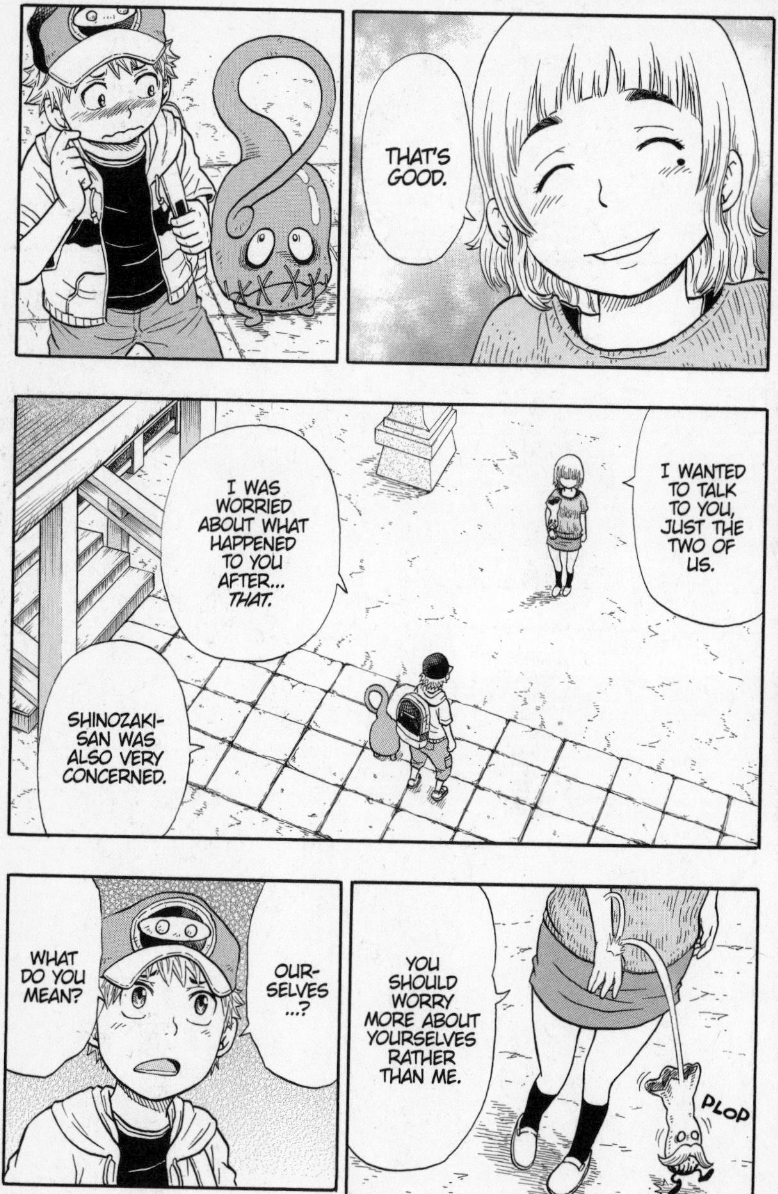
THAT'S GOOD.
I WANTED TO TALK TO YOU, JUST THE TWO OF US.
I WAS WORRIED ABOUT WHAT HAPPENED TO YOU AFTER... *THAT.*
SHINOZAKI-SAN WAS ALSO VERY CONCERNED.
YOU SHOULD WORRY MORE ABOUT YOURSELVES RATHER THAN ME.
PLOP
OUR-SELVES ...?
WHAT DO YOU MEAN?

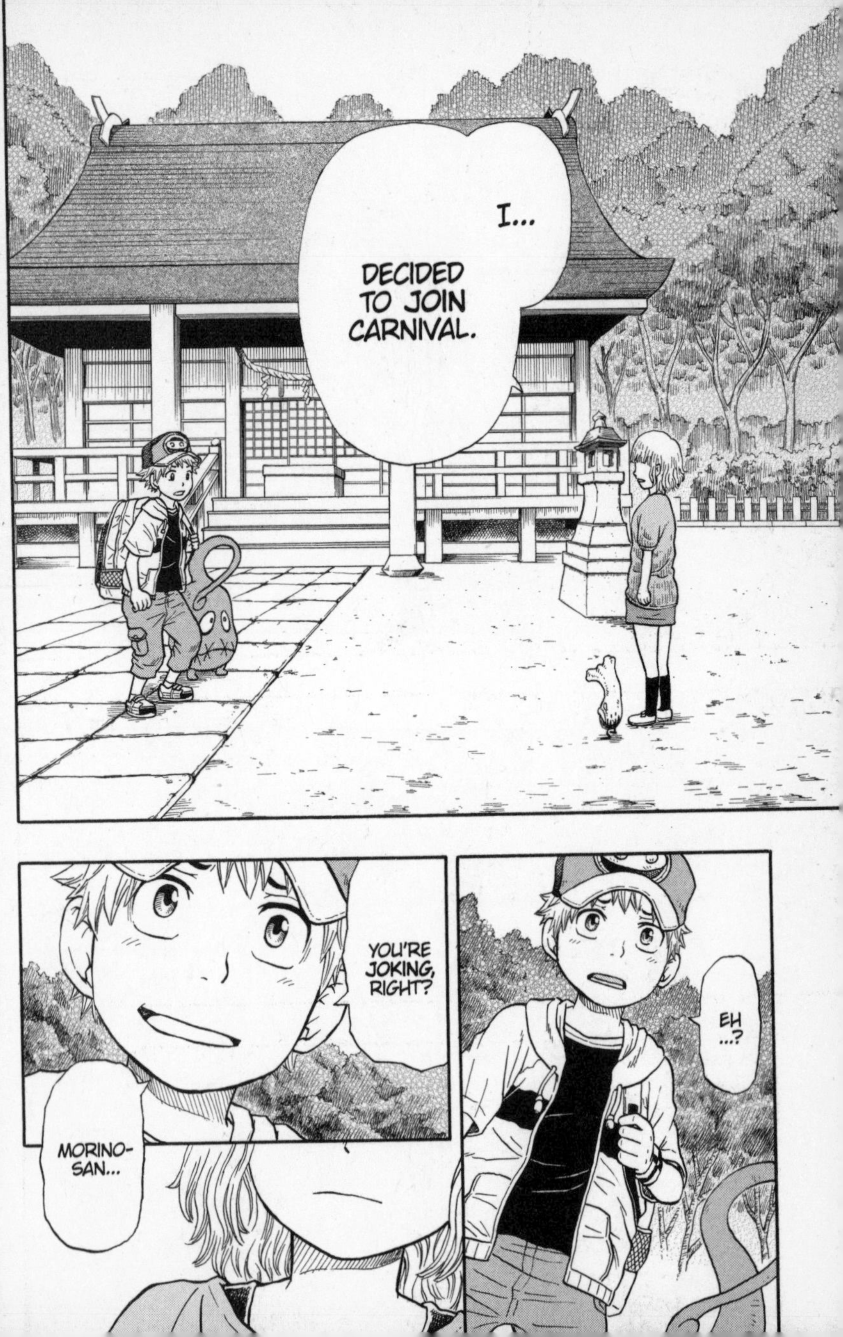
I...
DECIDED TO JOIN CARNIVAL.
EH ...?
YOU'RE JOKING, RIGHT?
MORINO-SAN...

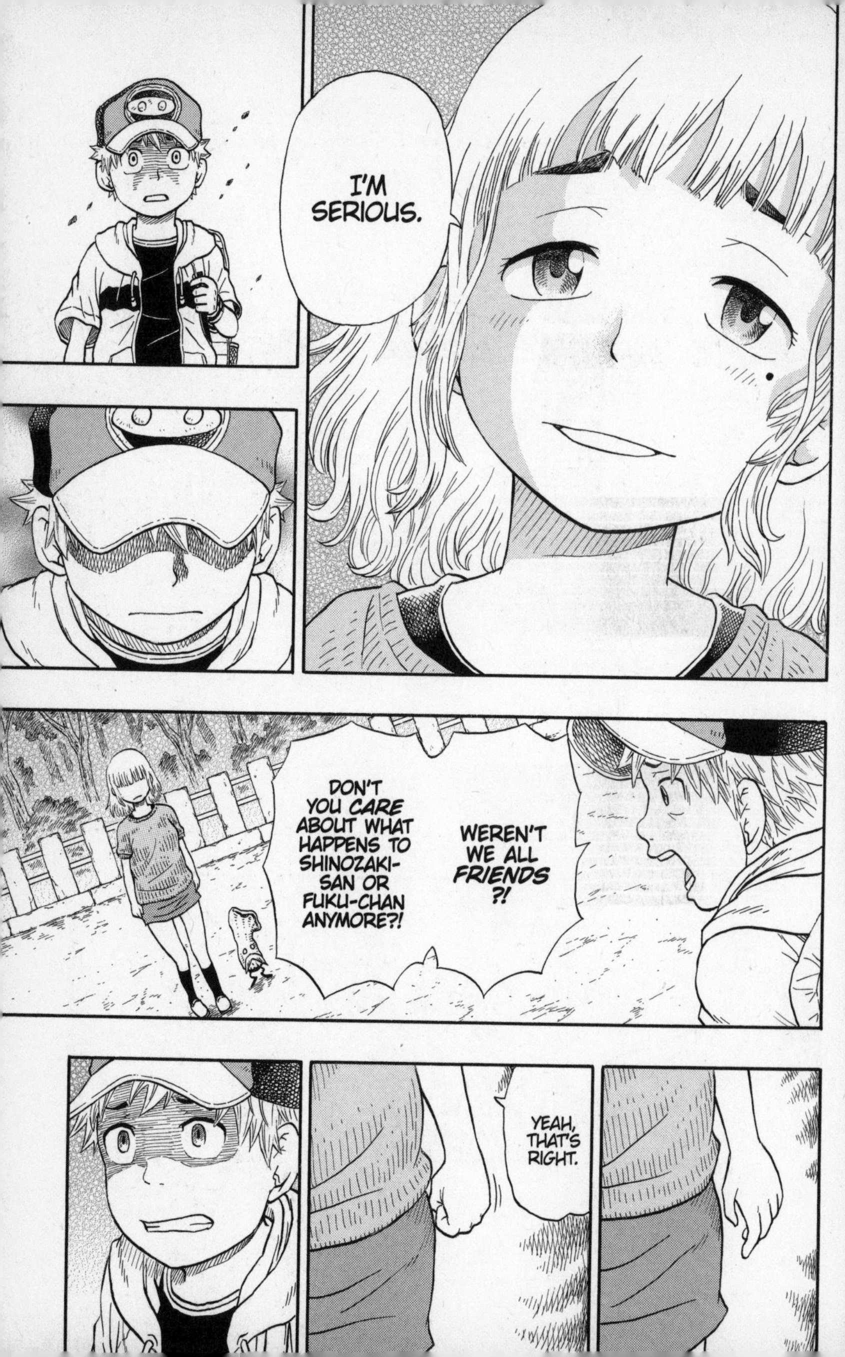
I'M SERIOUS.
WEREN'T WE ALL FRIENDS?!
DON'T YOU CARE ABOUT WHAT HAPPENS TO SHINOZAKI-SAN OR FUKU-CHAN ANYMORE?!
YEAH, THAT'S RIGHT.

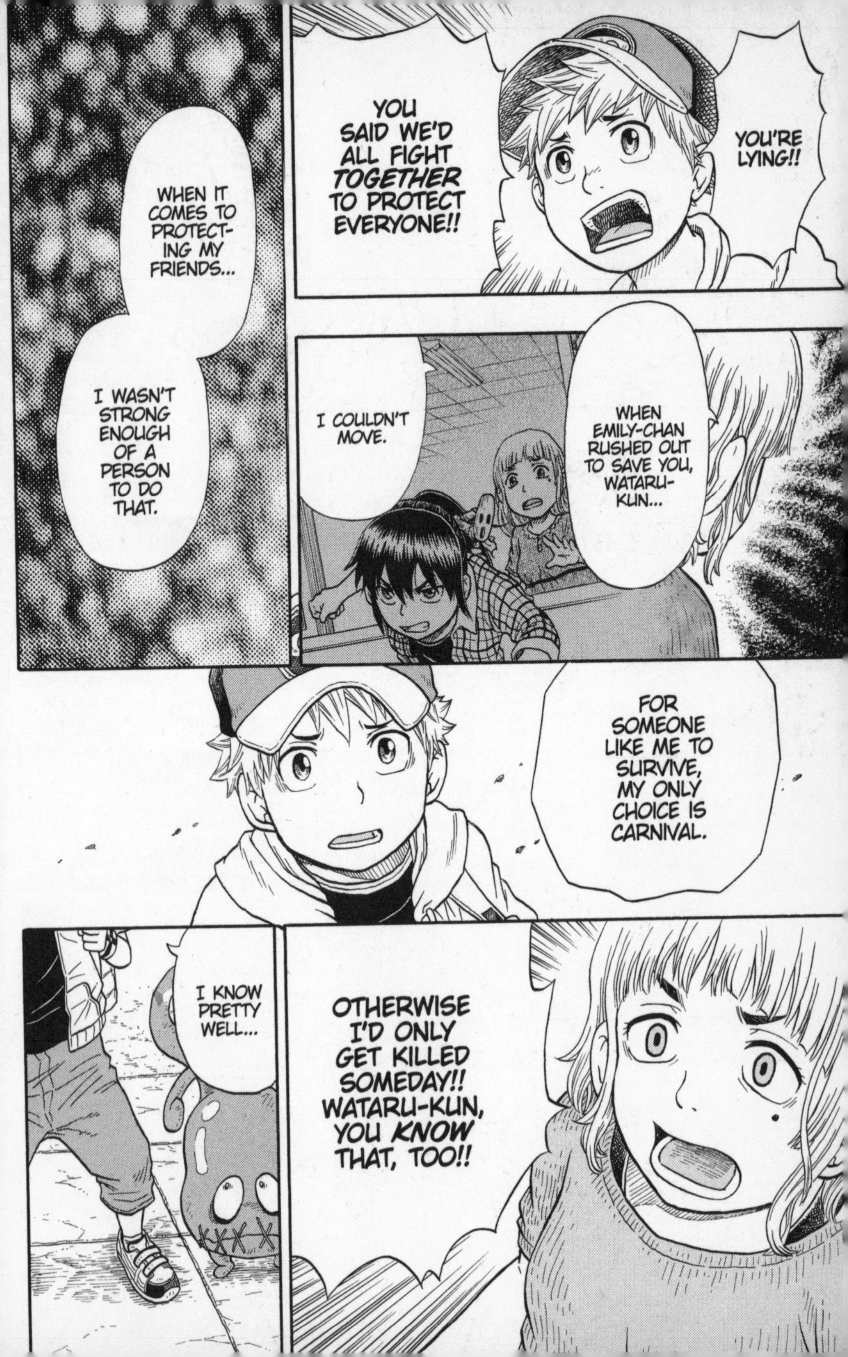
YOU'RE LYING!!
YOU SAID WE'D ALL FIGHT *TOGETHER* TO PROTECT EVERYONE!!
WHEN EMILY-CHAN RUSHED OUT TO SAVE YOU, WATARU-KUN...
I COULDN'T MOVE.
WHEN IT COMES TO PROTECTING MY FRIENDS...
I WASN'T STRONG ENOUGH OF A PERSON TO DO THAT.
FOR SOMEONE LIKE ME TO SURVIVE, MY ONLY CHOICE IS CARNIVAL.
OTHERWISE I'D ONLY GET KILLED SOMEDAY!! WATARU-KUN, YOU *KNOW* THAT, TOO!!
I KNOW PRETTY WELL...

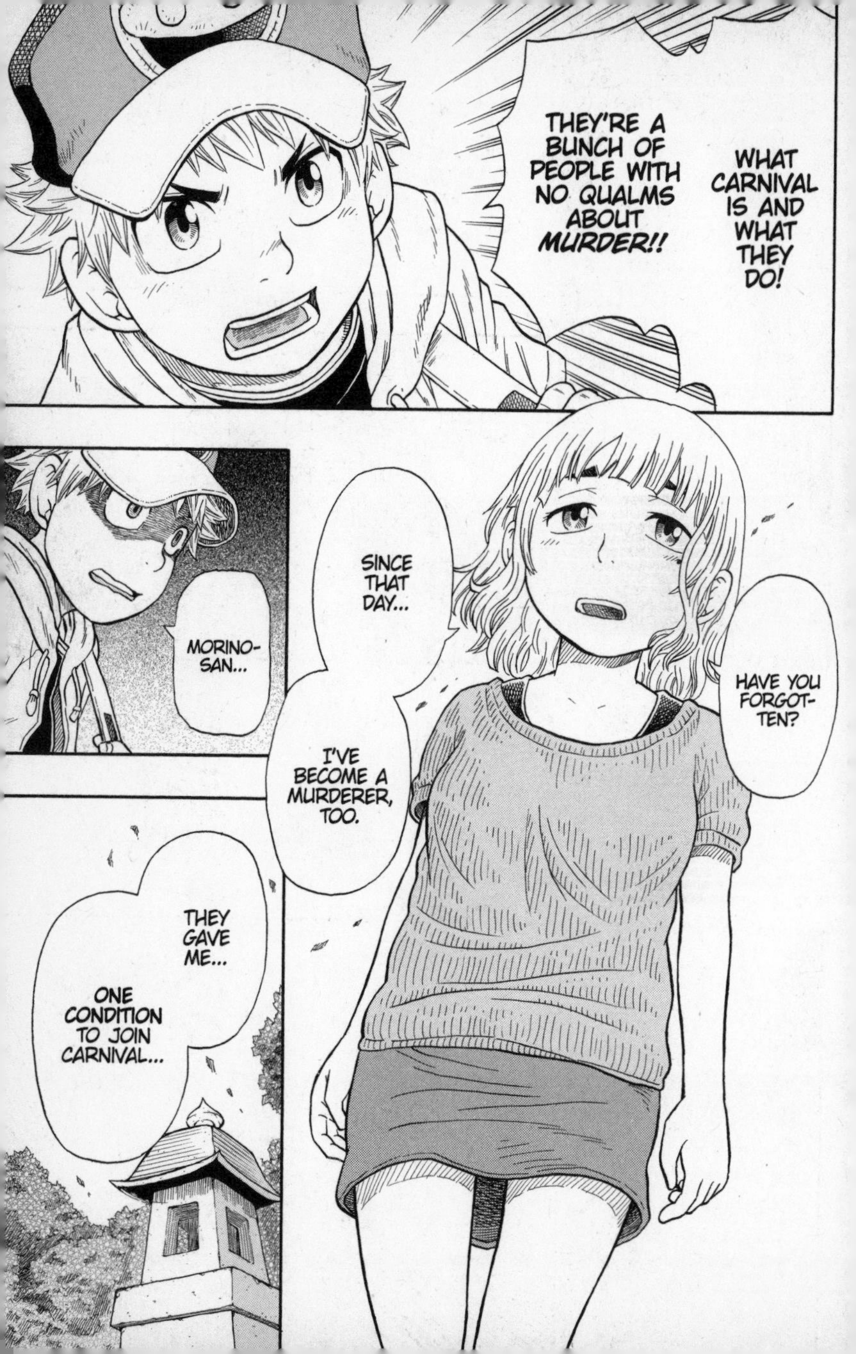
WHAT CARNIVAL IS AND WHAT THEY DO!
THEY'RE A BUNCH OF PEOPLE WITH NO QUALMS ABOUT *MURDER!!*
HAVE YOU FORGOT-TEN?
SINCE THAT DAY...
I'VE BECOME A MURDERER, TOO.
MORINO-SAN...
THEY GAVE ME...
ONE CONDITION TO JOIN CARNIVAL...

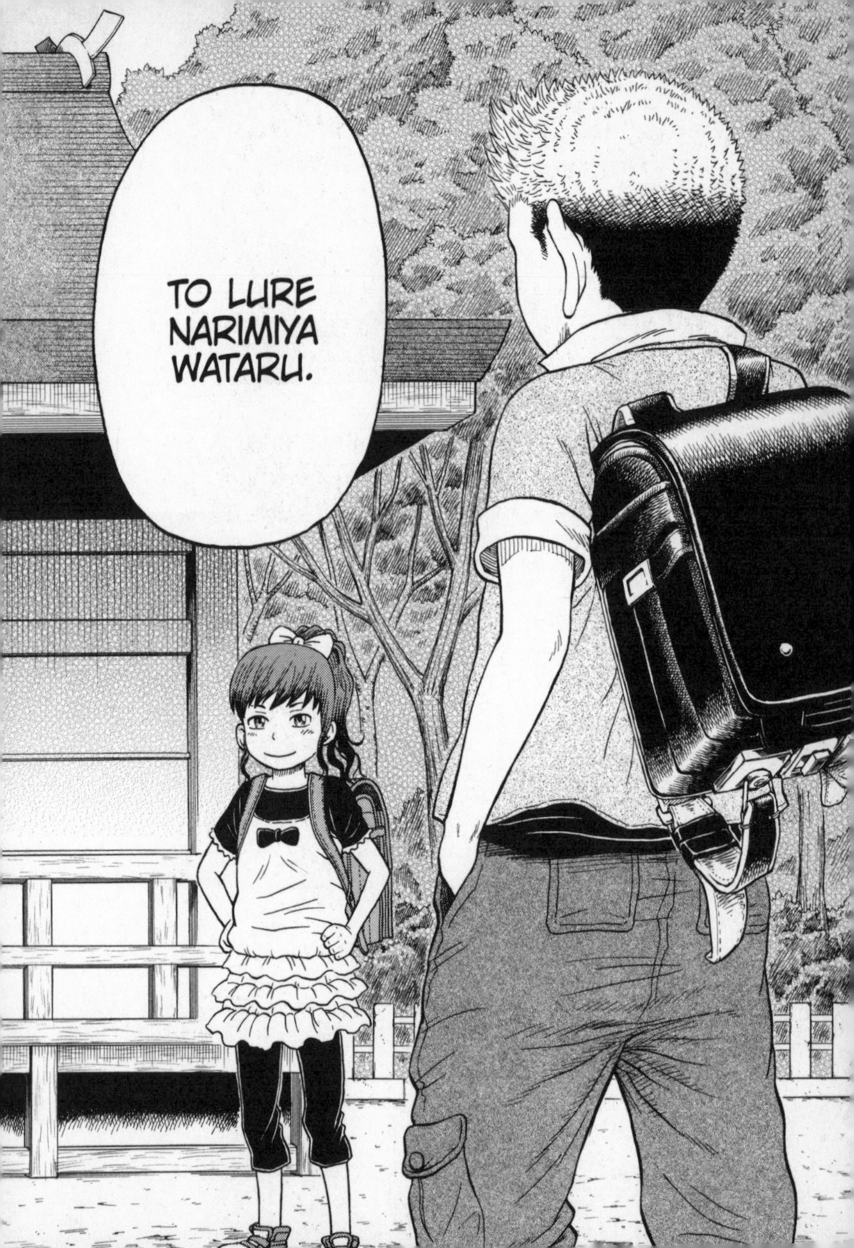
TO LURE NARIMIYA WATARU.

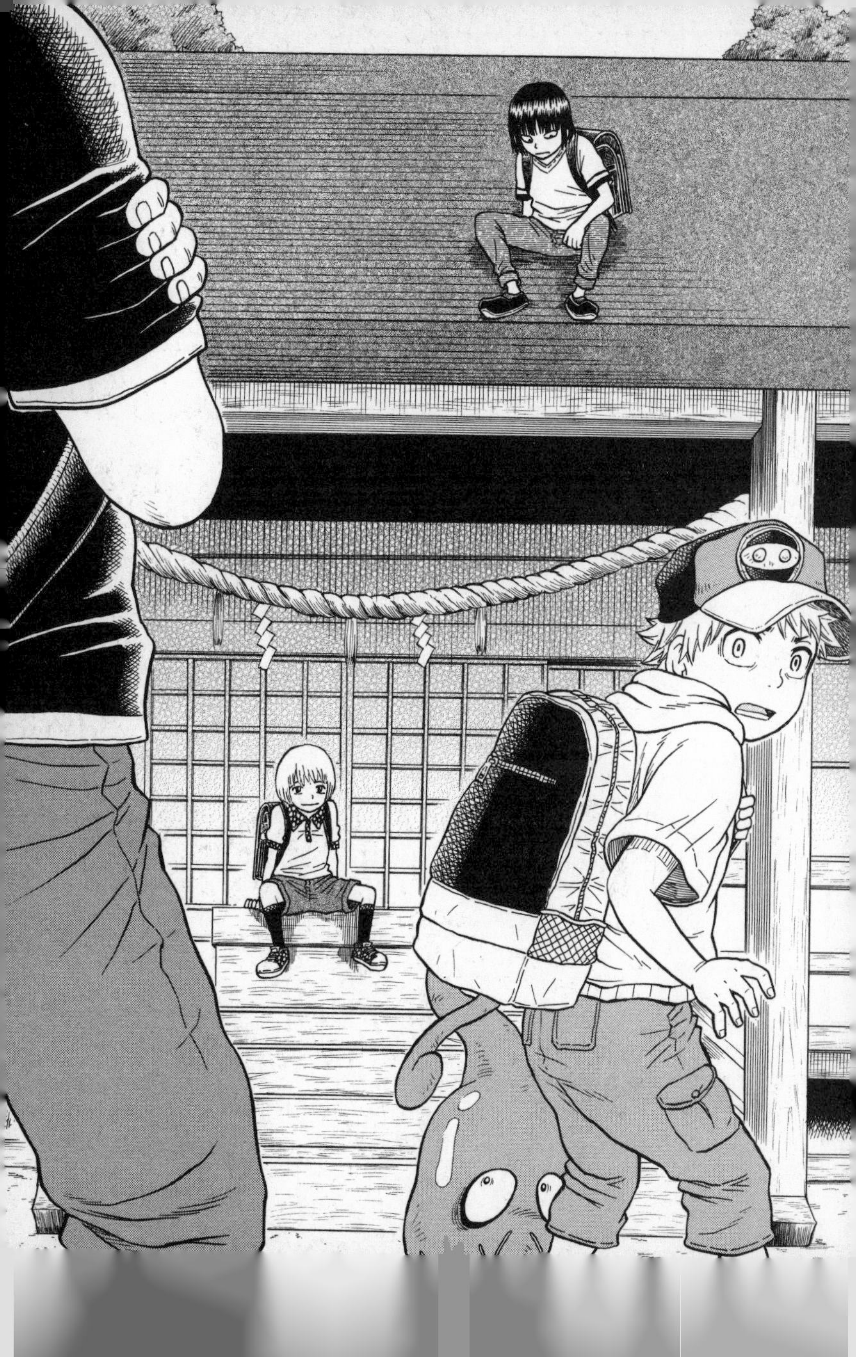

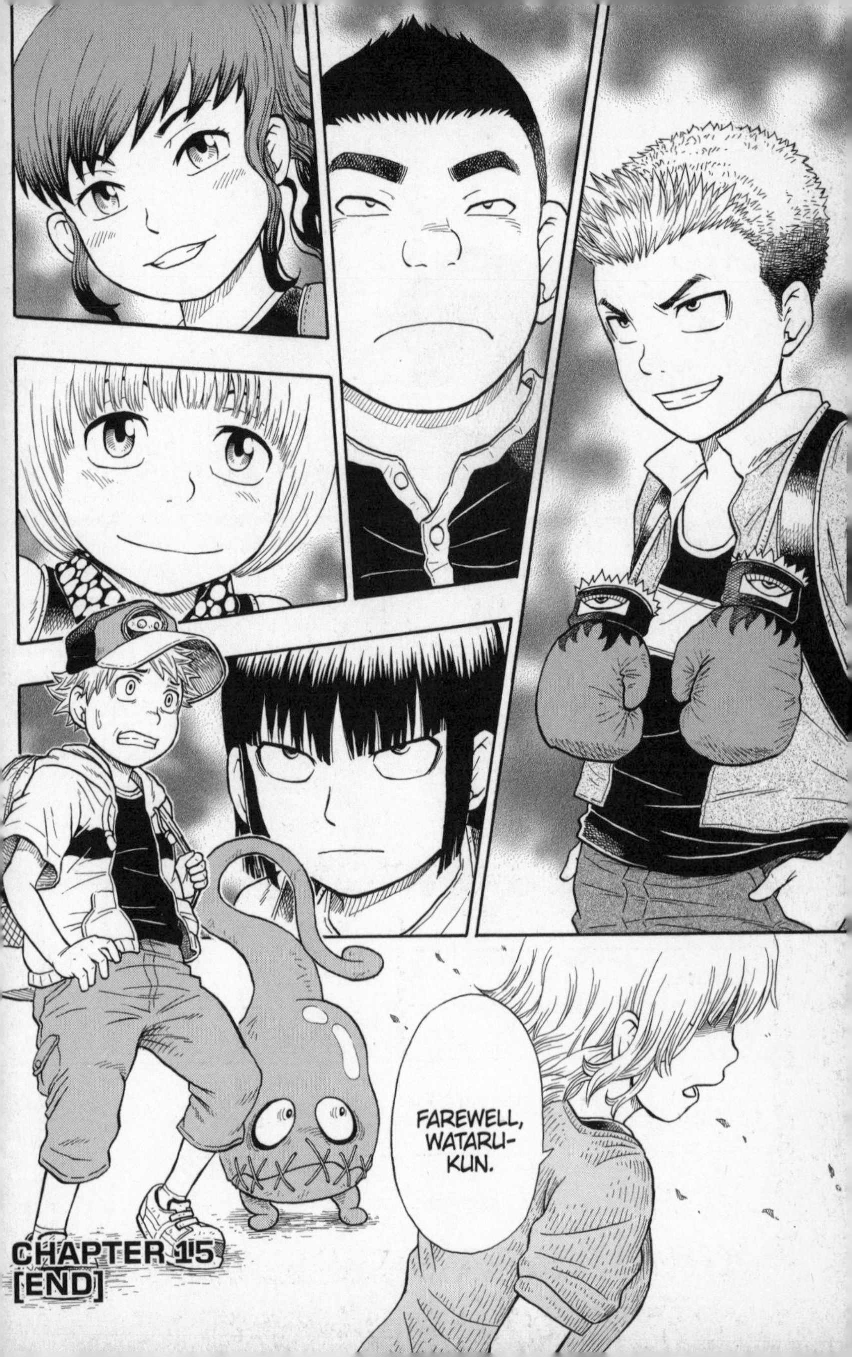
FAREWELL, WATARU-KUN.
CHAPTER 15 [END]

Friend Encyclopedia No.011

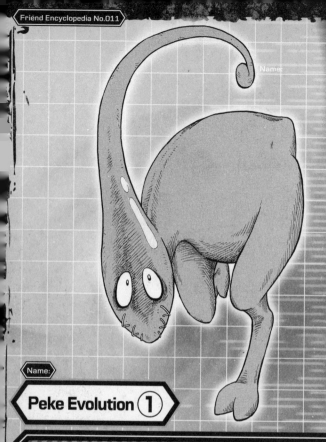

Name:

Peke Evolution ①

Partner:	Narimiya Wataru (6th grade)	**Speed:**	A
Attack:	B	**Dexterity:**	B
Defense:	C	**Special Abilities:**	D
Chara-teristics:	The evolved form of Peke. His speed and jumping abilities are greatly increased.		
Special Abilities:	High-speed movement.		

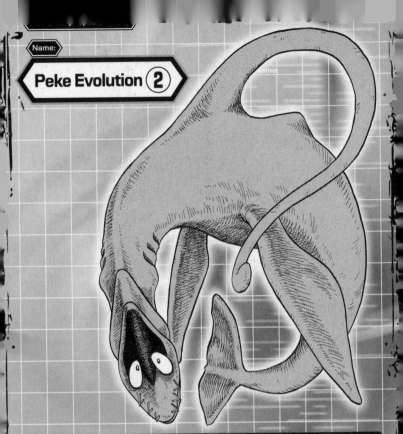

Name:

Peke Evolution ②

Partner:	Narimiya Wataru (6th grade)	Speed:	**D** (A when in water)
Attack:	**B**	**Dexterity:**	**B**
Defense:	**C**	**Special Abilities:**	**C**
Charateristics:	The second evolved form of Peke. It can now move through water quickly.		
Special Abilities:	Moving through water quickly.		

TOMODACHI X MONSTER

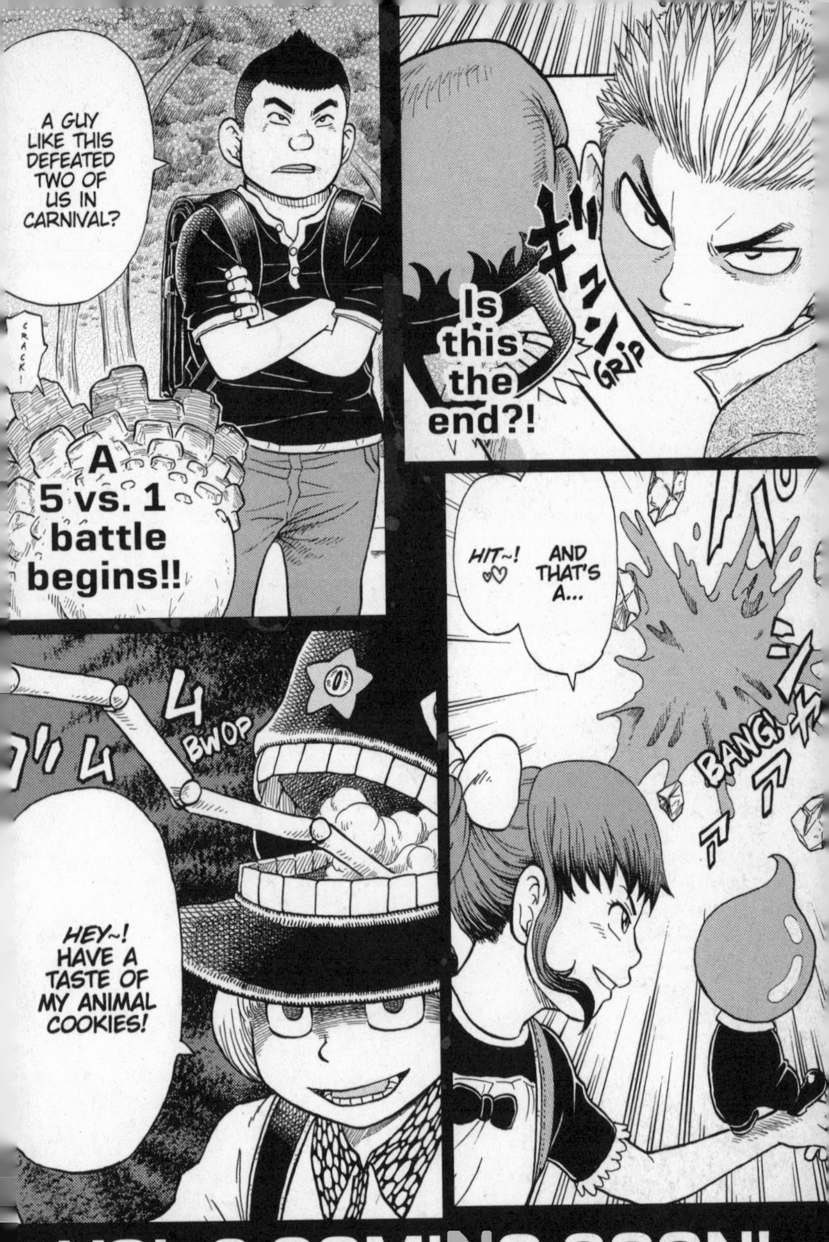
Is this the end?!
GRIP
A GUY LIKE THIS DEFEATED TWO OF US IN CARNIVAL?
CRACK!
A 5 vs. 1 battle begins!!
AND THAT'S A...
HIT~! ♡
BANG!
BWOP
HEY~! HAVE A TASTE OF MY ANIMAL COOKIES!

VOL 3 COMING SOON!

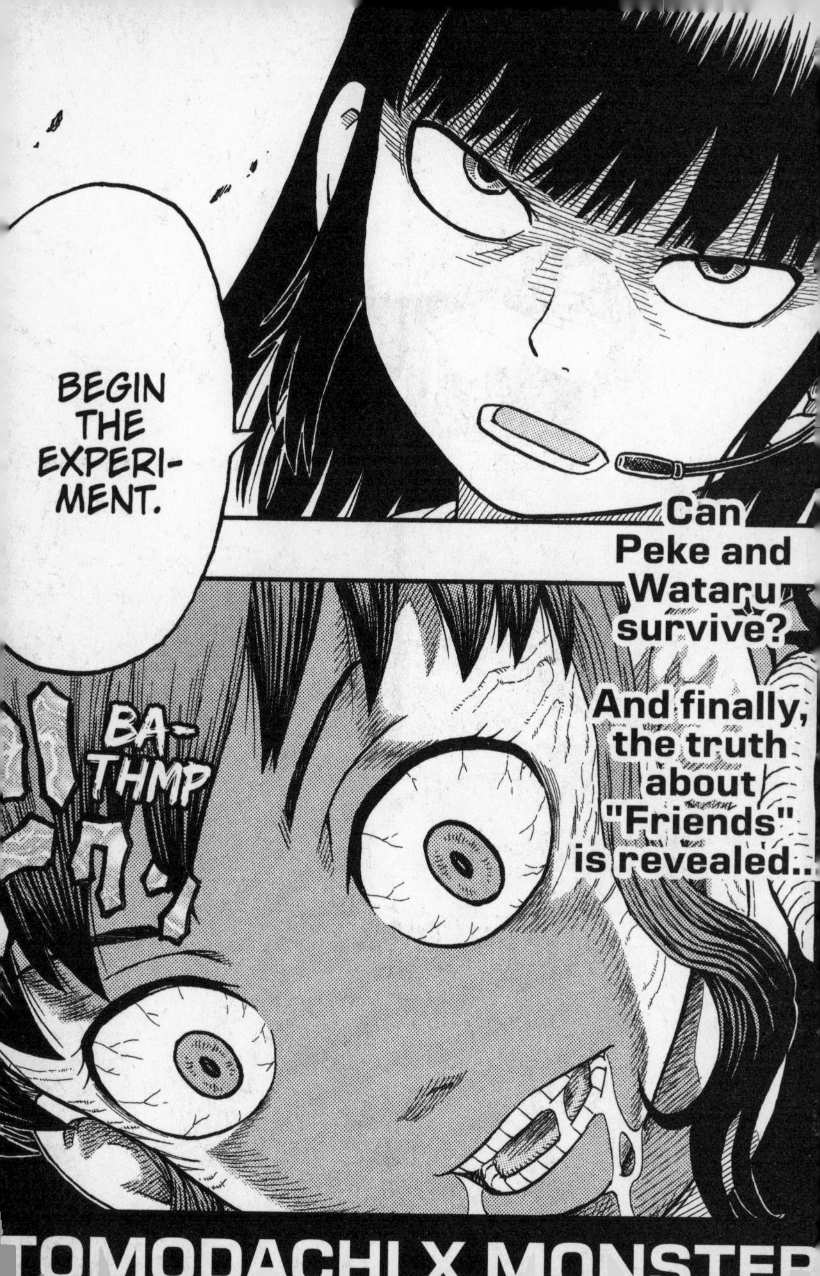
BEGIN THE EXPERI- MENT.
Can Peke and Wataru survive?
And finally, the truth about "Friends" is revealed...
BA-THMP

TOMODACHI X MONSTER

TOMODACHI
X
MONSTER

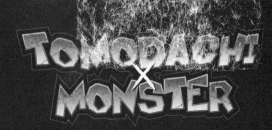

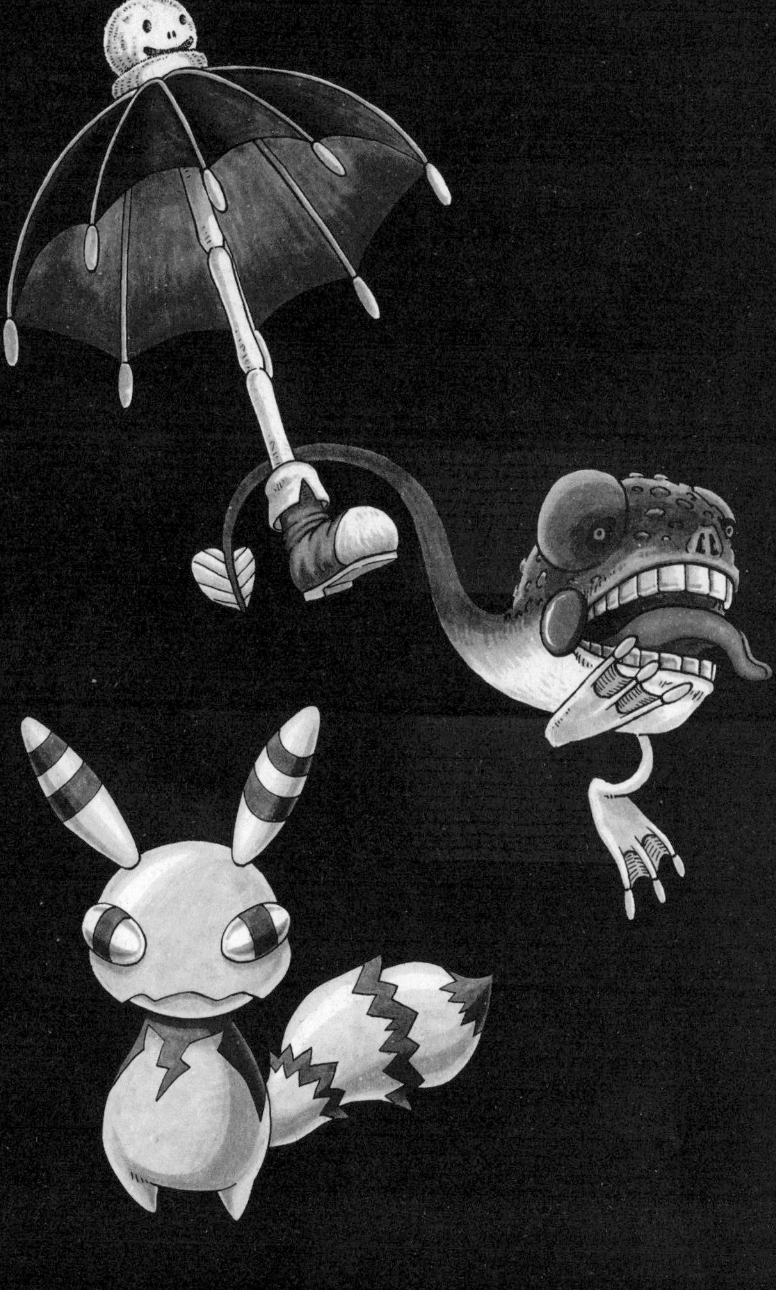